D0458588

WITHDRAWN
UTSA LIBRARIES

Algorithms in Ambient Intelligence

Philips Research

VOLUME 2

Editor-in-Chief
Dr. Frank Toolenaar
Philips Research Laboratories, Eindhoven, The Netherlands

SCOPE TO THE *'PHILIPS RESEARCH BOOK SERIES'*

As one of the largest private sector research establishments in the world, Philips Research is shaping the future with technology inventions that meet peoples' needs and desires in the digital age. While the ultimate user benefits of these inventions end up on the high-street shelves, the often pioneering scientific and technological basis usually remains less visible.

This 'Philips Research Book Series' has been set up as a way for Philips researchers to contribute to the scientific community by publishing their comprehensive results and theories in book form.

Dr. Ad Huijser
Chief Executive officer of Philips Research

Algorithms in Ambient Intelligence

Edited by

Wim Verhaegh
Emile Aarts
Jan Korst

Philips Research Laboratories,
Eindhoven, The Netherlands

KLUWER ACADEMIC PUBLISHERS
DORDRECHT / BOSTON / LONDON

A C.I.P. Catalogue record for this book is available from the Library of Congress.

ISBN 1-4020-1757-X

Published by Kluwer Academic Publishers,
P.O. Box 17, 3300 AA Dordrecht, The Netherlands.

Sold and distributed in North, Central and South America
by Kluwer Academic Publishers,
101 Philip Drive, Norwell, MA 02061, U.S.A.

In all other countries, sold and distributed
by Kluwer Academic Publishers, Distribution Center,
P.O. Box 322, 3300 AH Dordrecht, The Netherlands.

Printed on acid-free paper

Library
University of Texas
at San Antonio

All Rights Reserved
© 2004 Kluwer Academic Publishers
No part of this work may be reproduced, stored in a retrieval system, or transmitted
in any form or by any means, electronic, mechanical, photocopying, microfilming,
recording or otherwise, without written permission from the Publisher,
with the exception of any material supplied specifically for the purpose of
being entered and executed on a computer system, for exclusive use
by the purchaser of the work.

Printed in the Netherlands.

Contents

Contributing Authors

Emile Aarts
Philips Research Laboratories Eindhoven
Prof. Holstlaan 4, 5656 AA Eindhoven, The Netherlands
emile.aarts@philips.com

Lalitha Agnihotri
Philips Research Laboratories USA
345 Scarborough Rd., Briarcliff Manor, NY 10510, USA
lalitha.agnihotri@philips.com

Peter Beyerlein
Philips Research Laboratories Aachen
Weißhausstrasse 2, D-52066 Aachen, Germany
peter.beierlein@philips.com

Edgar den Boef
Philips Research Laboratories Eindhoven
Prof. Holstlaan 4, 5656 AA Eindhoven, The Netherlands
denboef@natlab.research.philips.com

Jeroen Breebaart
Philips Research Laboratories Eindhoven
Prof. Holstlaan 4, 5656 AA Eindhoven, The Netherlands
jeroen.breebaart@philips.com

Nevenka Dimitrova
Philips Research Laboratories USA
345 Scarborough Rd., Briarcliff Manor, NY 10510, USA
nevenka.dimitrova@philips.com

Joep van Gassel
Philips Research Laboratories Eindhoven
Prof. Holstlaan 4, 5656 AA Eindhoven, The Netherlands
joep.van.gassel@philips.com

Sandeep Kumar Goel
Philips Research Laboratories Eindhoven
Prof. Holstlaan 4, 5656 AA Eindhoven, The Netherlands
sandeepkumar.goel@philips.com

Srinivas Gutta
Philips Research Laboratories USA
345 Scarborough Rd., Briarcliff Manor, NY 10510, USA
srinivas.gutta@philips.com

Jaap Haitsma
Philips Research Laboratories Eindhoven
Prof. Holstlaan 4, 5656 AA Eindhoven, The Netherlands
jaap.haitsma@philips.com

Matthew Harris
Philips Research Laboratories Aachen
Weißhausstrasse 2, D-52066 Aachen, Germany
matthew.harris@philips.com

Ton Kalker
Philips Research Laboratories Eindhoven
Prof. Holstlaan 4, 5656 AA Eindhoven, The Netherlands
ton.kalker@ieee.org

Jan Kneissler
Philips Research Laboratories Aachen
Weißhausstrasse 2, D-52066 Aachen, Germany
jan.kneissler@philips.com

Jan Korst
Philips Research Laboratories Eindhoven
Prof. Holstlaan 4, 5656 AA Eindhoven, The Netherlands
jan.korst@philips.com

Kaushal Kurapati
IBM Software Group
17 Skyline Dr., Hawthorne, NY 10532, USA
kaushal@us.ibm.com

Jan van Leeuwen
Utrecht University – Information and Computing Sciences
Padualaan 14, 3584 CH Utrecht, The Netherlands
j.vanleeuwen@cs.uu.nl

Erik Jan Marinissen
Philips Research Laboratories Eindhoven
Prof. Holstlaan 4, 5656 AA Eindhoven, The Netherlands
erik.jan.marinissen@philips.com

Sven C. Martin
Philips Research Laboratories Aachen
Weißhausstrasse 2, D-52066 Aachen, Germany
sven.c.martin@philips.com

Martin F. McKinney
Philips Research Laboratories Eindhoven
Prof. Holstlaan 4, 5656 AA Eindhoven, The Netherlands
martin.mckinney@philips.com

Carsten Meyer
Philips Research Laboratories Aachen
Weißhausstrasse 2, D-52066 Aachen, Germany
carsten.meyer@philips.com

Anton Nijholt
University of Twente – Centre of Telematics and Information Technology
P.O. Box 217, 7500 AE Enschede, The Netherlands
anijholt@cs.utwente.nl

Job Oostveen
Philips Research Laboratories Eindhoven
Prof. Holstlaan 4, 5656 AA Eindhoven, The Netherlands
job.oostveen@philips.com

Steffen Pauws
Philips Research Laboratories Eindhoven
Prof. Holstlaan 4, 5656 AA Eindhoven, The Netherlands
steffen.pauws@philips.com

Verus Pronk
Philips Research Laboratories Eindhoven
Prof. Holstlaan 4, 5656 AA Eindhoven, The Netherlands
verus.pronk@philips.com

Ronald Rietman
Philips Research Laboratories Eindhoven
Prof. Holstlaan 4, 5656 AA Eindhoven, The Netherlands
ronald.rietman@philips.com

David Schaffer
Philips Research Laboratories USA
345 Scarborough Rd., Briarcliff Manor, NY 10510, USA
dave.schaffer@philips.com

Frank Thiele
Philips Research Laboratories Aachen
Weißhausstrasse 2, D-52066 Aachen, Germany
frank.o.thiele@philips.com

Wim F.J. Verhaegh
Philips Research Laboratories Eindhoven
Prof. Holstlaan 4, 5656 AA Eindhoven, The Netherlands
wim.verhaegh@philips.com

Ruud Wijnands
Philips Research Laboratories Eindhoven
Prof. Holstlaan 4, 5656 AA Eindhoven, The Netherlands
ruud.wijnands@philips.com

Clemens C. Wüst
Philips Research Laboratories Eindhoven
Prof. Holstlaan 4, 5656 AA Eindhoven, The Netherlands
clemens.wust@philips.com

Preface

The advent of the digital era, the Internet, and the development of fast computing devices that can access mass storage servers at high communication bandwidths have brought within our reach the world of ambient intelligent systems. These systems provide users with information, communication, and entertainment at any desired place and time. Since its introduction in 1998, the vision of Ambient Intelligence has attracted much attention within the research community. Especially, the need for intelligence generated by smart algorithms, which run on digital platforms that are integrated into consumer electronics devices, has strengthened the interest in Computational Intelligence. This newly developing research field, which can be positioned at the intersection of computer science, discrete mathematics, and artificial intelligence, contains a large variety of interesting topics including machine learning, content management, vision, speech, data mining, content augmentation, profiling, contextual awareness, feature extraction, resource management, security, and privacy.

Over the past years major progress has been made in the development and analysis of intelligent algorithms for ambient intelligent systems. This has led to the build-up of a new community of practice within Philips Research, and hence we organized the Symposium on Intelligent Algorithms (SOIA) to provide all those who are actively involved in the design and analysis of intelligent algorithms within Philips with the opportunity to gather and exchange information about the progress achieved in this new field of research. As we considered the presented material to be of interest to a much larger audience, we invited the authors to submit their papers to this book.

The book consists of an introductory chapter and 16 selected submissions. The introductory chapter gives an overview of the field of computational intelligence, and discusses its position in the view of ambient intelligence. The 16 selected submissions are split over two parts: user interaction and system interaction.

The chapters in the user interaction part focus on computational intelligence that is used to support the interaction between a user and a system. This type of computational intelligence directly involves the user. In Chapter 2, Anton Nijholt discusses multimodality in interface technology and the resulting problems and opportunities. He also gives a roadmap for multimodal interaction. In Chapter 3, Srinivas Gutta discusses personalization, which is a key aspect of ambient intelligent systems, in the TV domain. He addresses the initialization problem of personalization systems. Chapters 4–7 discuss aspects of content retrieval. Steffen Pauws presents a technique to retrieve songs by humming them, making the interaction style a very natural one. Lalitha Agnihotri & Nevenka Dimitrova discuss the support of the retrieval task by generating summarizations of videos, and the content analysis required for that. Content analysis in the audio domain is the subject of the chapter by Jeroen Breebaart & Martin McKinney, which they use to classify audio, e.g. to distinguish speech from music. Matthew Harris, Jan Kneissler & Frank Thiele next consider the retrieval of spoken text documents, in Chapter 7. In Chapter 8, Jan van Leeuwen discusses approaches in machine learning, and meta-learning techniques such as bagging and boosting. The latter technique is used in the following chapter, by Carsten Meyer & Peter Beyerlein, to increase the accuracy of a speech recognizer. In the final chapter of the user interaction part, Sven Martin discusses the problem of phrase classification, which is used in telephony applications, for the support of natural dialogues.

The second part, system interaction, focuses on computational intelligence that does not involve smart user interaction, but is used in order to make systems behave more intelligently in their execution. In Chapter 11, Job Oostveen, Jaap Haitsma & Ton Kalker discuss how robust fingerprints can be derived from audio and video content, in order to have a unique content identifier, and how one can efficiently search a database for such a fingerprint. Next, Chapters 12–16 discuss resource management aspects in ambient intelligent systems, in order to make best use of the available hardware. The three basic types of resources are communication resources, processing resources, and storage resources. The first one is discussed by Wim Verhaegh, Ronald Rietman & Jan Korst, who consider the scheduling of packets in the transmission network of a near-video-on-demand system, and by Edgar den Boef, Emile Aarts, Jan Korst & Wim Verhaegh, who discuss the sharing of the resources in an in-home network, in order to allow as many data streams to be transported in parallel as possible. Next, Clemens Wüst & Wim Verhaegh discuss in Chapter 14 the problem of how to control scalable media processing applications, making full use of the available processing power while still meeting real-time requirements. Storage resources are considered by Jan Korst, Joep van Gassel & Ruud Wijnands in Chapter 15, where they want to switch a disk as long as possible to an idle mode in order to save energy, and by Verus Pronk in Chapter 16, who discusses the placement of multimedia data on a multi-zone disk such that the fastest zones are used as much as possible. Finally, as ambient intelligent systems require many and complex integrated circuits to implement all functionality, Sandeep Kumar Goel & Erik Jan Marinissen discuss in Chapter 17 intelligent algorithms that are needed to make these circuits testable for manufacturing defects.

As the reader can see, the chapters presented in this book compile an interesting collection of applications of computational intelligence techniques in ambient intelligence. We hope that this book may contribute to the conviction that this indeed is an interesting new research field, and that it provides new challenges to the scientific community.

WIM F.J. VERHAEGH, EMILE AARTS, AND JAN KORST
Philips Research Laboratories Eindhoven

Acknowledgments

We would like to thank Dee Denteneer, Hans van Gageldonk, Wim Jonker, Ton Kalker, Dietrich Klakow, Jan van Leeuwen, Jan Nesvadba, and Peter van der Stok for the time and effort they spent on reviewing the contributed chapters.

Chapter 1

ALGORITHMS IN AMBIENT INTELLIGENCE

Emile Aarts, Jan Korst, and Wim F.J. Verhaegh

Abstract   In this chapter, we discuss the new paradigm for user-centered computing known as ambient intelligence and its relation with methods and techniques from the field of computational intelligence, including problem solving, machine learning, and expert systems.

Keywords   Algorithms, ambient intelligence, computational intelligence, problem solving, machine learning, expert systems, computational complexity.

1.1   Introduction

Ambient intelligence opens a world of unprecedented experiences: the interaction of people with electronic devices will change as context awareness, natural interfaces, and ubiquitous availability of information are realized. The concept of ambient intelligence imposes major challenges on algorithm design, simply because of the fact that the intelligence that ambient intelligent environments exhibit will be achieved to a large extent by algorithms whose functionality is perceived as intelligent by people who live in these environments. This opens a new and challenging field of research with strong relations to the field of computational intelligence. In this introductory chapter we briefly review the concept of ambient intelligence and elaborate on the relation with computational intelligence. The emphasis of the chapter is on qualitative aspects bringing together those elements in the field of computational intelligence that serve as a basis for ambient intelligence. We first review some the most profound developments in computing. As distributed computing and new interaction technologies are growing mature, new ways of computing can be pursued thus enabling more natural interaction styles between computing devices and their user. In this way electronics can be moved into people's background allowing users to move to the foreground. Next, we define and clarify the concept of ambient intelligence. We formulate some of its key features and discuss their relation with existing research domains such as embedded sys-

W. Verhaegh et al. (eds.), Algorithms in Ambient Intelligence, 1-19.
© 2004 *Kluwer Academic Publishers. Printed in the Netherlands.*

tems and computational intelligence. The field of computational intelligence is further deepened to indicate the relevant relationships with ambient intelligence. The chapter ends with some conclusions.

1.2   Advances in computing

At the occasion of the fiftieth anniversary of the *Association of Computing Machinery* in 1997, computer scientists from all over the world were asked for their opinion about the next fifty years of computing [Denning & Metcalfe, 1997]. Their reaction was strikingly consistent in the sense that they all envisioned a world consisting of distributed computing devices that were surrounding people in a non-obtrusive way. *Ubiquitous computing* is one of the early paradigms based on this vision. It was introduced by Weiser [1991] who proposes a computer infrastructure that succeeds the mobile computing infrastructure and situates a world in which it is possible to have access to any source of information at any place at any point in time by any person. Such a world can be conceived as a huge distributed network consisting of thousands of interconnected embedded systems that surround the user and satisfy his needs for information, communication, navigation, and entertainment.

1.2.1   New technologies

Ubiquitous computing can be viewed as a first approach to the development of third-generation computing systems; the first two generations being determined by the main frame and the personal computer, respectively. Currently, a tremendous effort is being unrolled in the world to develop concepts for this third generation of computing systems. MIT's Oxygen project [Dertouzos, 1999] is probably one of the most ambitious and promising approaches. Most of these approaches are aimed at increasing professional productivity of humans, and Dertouzos claims that the Oxygen technology might provide a gain of as much as a factor of three. Considering the effort to install, start up, and maintain presently available software systems and the considerable time spent to search for the right information, this might be well achievable. But at the very same time it opens an opportunity to divert from productivity and enter personal entertainment. Another challenging vision results from the observation of the developments in semiconductor industry. It is generally known and accepted that developments in this domain follow the generalized Moore's law [Noyce, 1977], which states that the integration density of systems on silicon doubles every eighteen months. This law seems to hold a self-fulfilling prophecy because the computer industry follows this trend for already four decades. Moreover, other characteristic quantities of information processing systems, such as communication bandwidth, storage capacity, and cost per bit seem to follow similar rules. These developments have a great impact on interaction technology. The advances in digital recording technology make it possible to develop consumer devices that can record several hundreds of hours video material, thus enabling personalized television recording and time-shifted watching. Poly-LED technology made it possible to construct the world's first matrix addressable display on a foil of a few micron thickness, thus enabling the development of flexible ultra thin displays of arbitrary size. Developments in materials science have enabled the construction of electronic foils that exhibit paper-like properties. These so-called electronic paper devices introduce a new dimension in the use of electronic books or calendars. LCD projection allows very large high-definition images being displayed on white walls from a small invisibly built-in unit. Advances in semiconductor process technology have made it possible to separate the active silicon area from its substrate, and to put it onto other carriers, for instance glass, thus enabling the integration of active circuitry into any conceivable material, for instance, wearables. Advances in digital signal processing have made it possible to apply audio and video watermarking and fingerprinting that enable conditional access, retrieval, and copy protection of audio and video material. Compression schemes such as MPEG4 and MPEG7 enable effective transmission and compositionality of video material. Recent developments in speech processing and vision introduce interaction technology for the development of conversational user interfaces, which are a first step towards the development of natural interfaces. And this is just a list of recent technology examples. For a more detailed treatment of of the technologies relevant for ambient intelligence the reader is referred to Aarts & Marzano [2003]. The exponential growth implied by Moore's law enables new applications rather suddenly and sometimes even unexpectedly. What is completely infeasible at one time can rather suddenly become a reality. More concrete, it implies that technology is entering a stage where it has become feasible to think of integrating electronics into any conceivable physical object, that is into clothing, furniture, carpets, walls, floors, ceilings, etc. This opens up new opportunities for electronic devices, because it implies that we can leave the age of the box and enter a new age in which functionalities such as audio, video, communication, and gaming, which were confined to boxes up to now, may become freely available from the environment, supporting people to have free access to their functionality and enabling natural interaction with them.

1.2.2 Moving electronics into the background

The notion ubiquitous computing as introduced by Weiser [1991] calls for large-scale distributed processing and communication architectures. Ubiquitous computing expands on distribution of storage and computing until a huge collective network of intelligently cooperating nodes is formed. A pronounced advantage of the increased distribution of storage and processing is the fact that such networks may exhibit emerging features, similar to those in biological and neural systems, which are generally believed to facilitate true intelligence. Communication and interaction nodes in a ubiquitous computing system may be external or internal. External nodes, which are often called *terminals*, account for input and output and will interact directly with the environment and the user. Examples are sensors and actuators, interactive displays, and input devices for speech, handwriting, and tactile information. The terminals often will be small, handy, and portable, which introduces the need for low-power electronics, as people start to carry the devices with them. In this respect one speaks of *wearables*, indicating that electronics will be integrated into clothing [Mann, 1997]. Internal nodes predominantly refer to computing elements that carry out certain network functions such as data processing, storage, and routing. Here, also low-power issues will play an important role in addition to storage capacity and speed. The internal nodes are servers, routers, processing units, storage devices, and all kinds of other embedded units. Most of the information handling will take place in the internal nodes and they have to provide the service quality that is needed to operate the network smoothly. The communication in a ubiquitous home system should meet certain requirements. In the first place it should support *interoperability*, which refers to a situation in which terminals are easy to add, replace, or remove. Furthermore, it must support multiple media, including graphics, video, audio, and speech. There is also the issue of *wireless communication*. Most appliances should connect wirelessly to the network without mediation. This introduces the need for network protocols that can handle authentication, partial information, and multiple media in a secure way. Clearly, the Internet, in its capacity of the only existing true ubiquitous computing system in the world, may play an important role in the pursuit to let electronics disappear. By facilitating wireless Web access of handheld devices users can access information on the Web at any time and any place. The development of the *Semantic Web* in combination with all kinds of high-level applications such as *content-aware media browsers* will further enhance the Internet as an interactive large-scale distributed computing environment [Berners-Lee, Hendler & Lassila, 2001].

1.2.3   Moving the user into the foreground

If we are capable of moving the technology into the background, we must face the challenge of developing concepts that provide ubiquitous computing environments with functions that support easy, intelligent, and meaningful interaction. After fifty years of technology development for designing computers that require users to adapt to them, we now must enter the era of designing equipment that adapts to users. This requires the design and implementation of application scenarios that place the user in the center of his digital environment. This concept is often referred to as *human-centric computing* and in his last book Dertouzos [1999] gives a compelling vision on the developments in this field, both from a technological and a societal viewpoint. Winograd [1996] edited a collection of essays by leading software designers that focus on this issue. Ambient intelligence wants to achieve human-centric computing by making people's environments intelligent. Belief in ambient intelligent environments is determined by two major aspects: the social nature of the user interface that is used, and the extent to which the system can adapt itself to the user and its environment. The social character of the user interface will be determined by the extent to which the system complies with the intuition and habits of its users. The self-adaptability is determined by the capability of the system to learn through interaction with the user. The combination of human-specific communication modalities such as speech, handwriting, and gesture, as well as the possibility to personalize to user needs, play a major role in the design of novel applications and services. Finally, ubiquitous computing environments should exhibit some form of emotion to make them truly ambient intelligent. To this end, the self-adaptive capabilities of the system should be used to detect user moods and react accordingly. This issue has led to the development of a novel research area that is called *affective computing*, and which again is characterized by a multidisciplinary approach, combining approaches from psychology and computer science [Picard, 1997]. The design of functions and services in ambient intelligence is often based on the concept of *user-centered design* [Beyer & Holtzblatt, 2002; Norman, 1993]. Within this design concept the user is placed in the center of the design activity, and through a number of design cycles in which the designer iterates over concept design, realization, and user evaluation, the final interaction design is created. Many interaction designers follow the *media equation* introduced by Reeves & Nass [1996] who argued that the interaction between man and machine should be based on the very same concepts as the interaction between humans is based, i.e., it should be intuitive, multi-modal, and based on emotion. Clearly, this conjecture is simple in its nature but at the same time it turns out to be very hard to realize. It requires novel approaches to interaction technologies and computational intelligence.

1.3   Ambient intelligence

Ambient intelligence aims at taking the integration results provided by ubiquitous computing one step further by realizing environments that are sensitive and responsive to the presence of people [Aarts, Harwig & Schuurmans, 2001]. The focus is on the user and his experience from a consumer electronics perspective, which introduces several new basic problems related to natural user interaction and context-aware architectures supporting human-centered information, communication, service, and entertainment. For a detailed treatment of ambient intelligence we refer the reader to Aarts & Marzano [2003] who cover in their book many different related aspects ranging from materials science up to business models and issues in interaction design.

1.3.1   A new paradigm

As already mentioned, ambient intelligence is a new paradigm that is based on the belief that future electronic devices will disappear into the background of people's environment, thus introducing the challenging need to enhance user environments with virtual devices that support a natural interaction of the user with the dissolved electronics. The new paradigm is aimed at improving the quality of life of people by creating the desired atmosphere and functionality via intelligent, personalized, interconnected systems and services. The notion *ambience* refers to the environment and reflects the need for typical requirements such as distribution, ubiquity, and transparency. *Distribution* refers to non-central systems control and computation; *Ubiquity* means that the embedding is overly present, and *transparency* indicates that the surrounding systems are invisible and non-obtrusive. The notion *intelligence* reflects that the digital surroundings exhibit specific forms of social interaction, i.e., the environments should be able to recognize the people that live in it, adapt themselves to them, learn from their behavior, and possibly show emotion. In an ambient intelligent world people will be surrounded by electronic systems that consist of networked intelligent devices that are integrated into their surrounding and that provide them with information, communication, services, and entertainment wherever they are and whenever they want. Furthermore, the devices will adapt and even anticipate people's needs. Ambient intelligent environments will present themselves in a very different way than our contemporary handheld or stationary electronic boxes, as they will merge in a natural way into the environment around us and as they will allow much more natural and human interaction styles. The major new thing in ambient intelligence is the involvement of the user. Most of the earlier developments are aimed at facilitating and improving productivity in business environments, and it goes beyond saying that these developments have played a major role in the development of ambient intelligence. The next step, however, is to bring ubiquity and ambient intelligence to people and to people's homes. This is not simply a matter of introducing the productivity concepts to consumer environments. It is far more than that, because a totally new interaction paradigm is needed to make ambient intelligence work. The productivity concept is to a large extent still based on the graphical user interface known as the *desktop metaphor* that was developed at Xerox PARC in the 1970s, and which has become a

world standard ever since [Tesler, 1991]. What we need is a new metaphor
with the same impact as the desktop metaphor that enables natural and social
interaction within ambient intelligent environments, and this is a tremendous
challenge. Philips' HomeLab [Aarts & Eggen, 2002] is an example of such
an experience prototyping environment in which this challenge is addressed.
It is a laboratory consisting of a house with a living, a kitchen, a hall, a den,
two bedrooms, and a bathroom. The house contains a rapid prototyping environment with integrated speech control, wireless audio-video streaming, and
context-awareness technology, which enables the realization of new applications within short development times. Furthermore, the house is equipped with
a sophisticated observation system that allows behavioral scientists to observe
users in an unobtrusive way for possibly long periods of times. In this way it
has been shown that it is possible to investigate the true merits of novel ambient
intelligence applications [De Ruyter, 2003].

1.3.2   Key features of ambient intelligence

To refine the notion of ambient intelligence the following five key technology features have been formulated [Aarts & Marzano, 2003].

- Embedded: Many networked devices that are integrated into the environment;

- Context Aware: that can recognize you and your situational context;

- Personalized: that can be tailored towards your needs;

- Adaptive: that can change in response to you, and

- Anticipatory: that anticipate your desires without conscious mediation.

The first two elements relate to the integration of hardware devices into the
environment, and refer to embedded systems in general. Embedded systems
play an important role in the realization of ambient intelligence because they
account for the embedding of electronic devices into people's surroundings.
An extensive overview of recent developments and challenges in embedded
systems is given by the research agenda compiled by the National Research
Council [2001]. MIT's Oxygen project [Dertouzos, 2001] and IBM's effort on
pervasive computing [Satyanarayanan, 2001] are other networked embedded
systems approaches addressing the issue of integrating networked devices into
people's backgrounds. A first approach to the full integration of embedded systems in people's homes is given by the device tri-partition of Aarts & Roovers
[2003], who distinguish between three different types of devices, i.e., disposables, mobiles, and statics. *Disposables* are small environmental circuits that
empower themselves by making use of physical changes in the environment

such as pressure and temperature. They communicate wirelessly at very low bit rates, a few bit per second, and have ultra small processing capabilities, a few instructions per second. *Mobiles* are devices that people can carry around. They are empowered by batteries and communicate wirelessly at medium bit rates, up to some 10 Mbit/sec. They have moderate computational power up to 1 Gops. *Statics* are big stationary devices like large storage and display equipment that are empowered by wired power networks and can communicate and compute at high speeds. The combination of these three device types constitutes a hybrid network that supports sensory input-output communication, such as audio, video, speech, and gesture as well as context awareness. The three other key elements of ambient intelligence are concerned with the adjustment of electronic systems in response to the user. They all can be viewed as systems adjustments, but done at different time scales. Personalization refers to adjustments at a short time scale, for instance to install personalized settings. Adaptation involves adjustments resulting from changing user behavior detected by monitoring the user over a longer period of time. Ultimately, when the system gets to know the user so well that it can detect behavioral patterns, adjustments can be made ranging over a very long time scale. For the latter we often refer to the classical Victorian butler, a person whom the family members did not know very well, but who knew the family members often better that they did themselves with respect to certain rituals or stereotypical behavioral patterns. So anticipation could help them just at the point where they concluded that they needed some support. Finally, we mention that the key elements of ambient intelligence introduced above not only apply to home environments; they also apply to other environments such as *mobile spaces*, e.g., car, bus, plane, and train, *public spaces*, e.g., office, shop, and hospital, and *private spaces*, e.g., clothing. They support a variety of human activities including work, security, healthcare, entertainment, and personal communications and open an entirely new world of interaction between humans and their electronic environments [Aarts & Marzano, 2003].

1.3.3   Design for intelligence

The design of ambient intelligent environments imposes several challenging research questions with respect to the way intelligence is embedded and configured in such systems. Below, we discuss three elements that are related to system aspects, user aspects, and integration aspects, respectively. For more detailed treatments of related aspects we refer to the other chapters of this volume. Firstly, we distinguish the class of algorithms that exhibit some form of intelligent user-perceived behavior upon execution. This predominantly refers to algorithms that enable natural interaction between users and electronic systems. Classical examples are algorithms for speech processing tasks such as speech recognition, speech dialogue, and speech synthesis. Other examples are algorithms for vision such as tracking, object recognition, and image segmentation techniques. More recently, algorithms have gained attraction that enable users to have a personalized access to content, e.g., through collaborative filtering and recommender techniques. Also sophisticated data browsing techniques that allow search based on intentions rather than on formal queries are attracting attention recently. Secondly, we distinguish the class of algorithms that can be applied to control systems. As ambient intelligent environments will consist of many distributed devices, there is a need for intelligent algorithms that can manage data and computations within a networked system. This field is called *resource management* if the emphasis is on the distribution of activities over the available resources and *quality of service* if the emphasis is on the perceived quality of the tasks that are carried out. Both fields are concerned with the design and analysis of adaptive algorithms that can control and change system functionalities. Especially, requirements that are related to real-time and on-line execution of tasks are of prime interest. Also adaptation through learning is considered as an important issue in this domain. Thirdly we mention the challenge of determining where the intelligence should reside within ambient intelligent systems. As pointed out ambient intelligent systems are not standalone devices; they will appear as integrated environments consisting of networked embedded devices. Ambient intelligent environments can be seen as clusters of computing, storage, and input-output devices that are connected through ubiquitous broadband communication networks allowing data rates up to a few Gigabytes per second. The ubiquitous communication network contains servers that act as routers and have internal storage devices. This implies that one can trade off the location of the software that provides the system intelligence. Roughly speaking there are two extremes, which are referred to as 'ambient intelligence inside' versus 'ambient intelligence outside'. In the inside case the system intelligence resides as embedded software in the terminals. They are big-footprint devices that can efficiently process large software stacks that implement sophisticated computational intelligence algorithms. The network that connects the devices is rather straightforward from a functional viewpoint just allowing data communication, possibly at high bit rates. In the opposed view of ambient intelligence outside the terminals may be small-footprint devices just allowing for the data communication that is required to generate output or to take new input. The system intelligence is residing at the powerful servers of the ubiquitous communication network where it can be accesses by the terminals. Clearly the trade-off between ambient intelligence inside and outside relates to complex design decisions that need to be evaluated at a system level. The resulting design problem is referred to as *inside-outside co-design*, and imposes several new challenges for system and algorithm design.

1.4   Computational intelligence

The algorithmic techniques and methods that apply to design for intelligence in ambient intelligent systems are rooted in the field of computational intelligence, which is the scientific and technological pursuit that aims at designing and analyzing algorithms that upon execution give electronic systems intelligent behavior. Engelbrecht [2002] presents a scholarly introduction into the field. Sinčák & Vaščák [2000] present an overview of recent advances in the field. For the purpose of our presentation we distinguish the following features to characterize intelligent behavior in electronic systems, i.e., the ability to solve problems, to predict and adapt, and to reason. Below we discuss a number of algorithmic approaches in computational intelligence that can be structured along the lines of these three characteristic features. The domain of problem solving contains a collection of well-known search methods. Prediction and adaptation is covered by machine learning techniques. Finally, the domain of reasoning is treated by expert systems. For all three domains we present some applications in ambient intelligence. We also briefly address the topic of computational complexity, which plays a major role in computational intelligence, because many problems in this field are intrinsically hard to solve. Computational intelligence can be viewed as a subfield of *artificial intelligence* and for that reason we start with a short exposition of this quite interesting field in computer science.

1.4.1   Artificial intelligence

Early visionairs working at the crossroad of artificial intelligence and multimedia proposed ideas on intelligent man-machine interaction that fit well into the ambient intelligence paradigm. For a clear and lucid overview we refer the reader to Negroponte [1995] and Winograd & Flores [1987]. According to Minsky [1986], artificial intelligence is the science of making machines do things that require intelligence if done by men. The origin of the subject dates back to the early days of computing science, which was marked by the introduction of the first models for electronic computing introduced by Turing [1950]. The main topics of investigation are vision, natural language and speech processing, robotics, knowledge representation, problem solving, machine learning, expert systems, man- machine interaction, and artificial life; see Rich & Knight [1991] and Nilsson [1998]. Artificial intelligence has produced a number of interesting results over its half a century of existence. McCorduck [1979] gives an excellent popular account of the achievements made in the first two decades. Boden [1996] covers the more recent developments.

We mention a few of the great achievements. *Expert systems* have been developed that use speech and dialogue technology to support hotel reservation booking and travel planning. Two other well-known examples are MYCIN

[Shortliffe, 1976], the first computer program to assist physicians in making diagnosis, and PROSPECTOR [Duda & Shortliffe, 1983], a program that could aid geologists to explore oil fields. *Robots* have been constructed that can play baseball or climb stairs, and IBM's Deep Blue was the first chess computer that could compete at world masters level. For an overview of the developments in robots and *animats* we refer to Brooks [2002] and Meyer & Wilson [1991]. *Neural networks* were introduced as artificial computing models based on an analogy with the human brain. NETtalk [Sejnowski & Rosenberg, 1987] was the first operational neural network that could produce speech from written text. In all these cases it can be argued that the major achievements were realized through the use of sophisticated algorithmic methods that make excellent use of the vast growth in computational power. More recently, the field has given birth to several new exciting developments. One example is the development resulting from the strong involvement of elements from cognitive science. For instance, the general belief that human intelligence does not follow a specific predetermined path to accomplish a task, but merely responds to a current situation, has given rise to a novel concept that is referred to as *situated action*. This concept has been applied with great success in robotics by replacing classical path planning by approaches that are governed by environmental response mechanisms. Another new development is the use of *case-based reasoning*, which follows the idea of solving problems by making use of common sense understanding of the world based on the use of ontologies. These ontologies are embedded by agents that carry information about the meaning of fundamental everyday life concepts such as time, objects, spaces, materials, events and processes [Liang & Turban, 1993].

1.4.2 Problem solving

Problem solving concerns finding a solution from a large set of alternatives that minimizes or maximizes a certain objective function [Papadimitriou & Stieglitz, 1982]. Usually, the set of possible solutions is not given explicitly, but implicitly by a number of variables that have to be assigned numerical values and a number of constraints that have to be obeyed by this assignment. Often, this results in a compact description of an exponentially large solution set. One classical method to search such a solution space for an optimum is called *branch and bound*. This method recursively splits the solution space into sub-spaces by e.g. fixing the value of a variable. This is called the branching part, and it results in a tree-like search. The bounding part is used to prune as many parts from the search tree as possible, by comparing bounds on what can be achieved in a sub-space corresponding to a sub-tree, with an existing solution, e.g., a feasible solution that has already been found. A second classical method is called *dynamic programming*. This method, which is generally more efficient, is applicable if the problem contains a certain structure, based on solution states. Basically, if one has to assign values to a number of variables, one considers one variable at a time, and checks for each solution state what happens if one chooses any of the possible values of this variable, in the sense of its direct (cost) effect, and the state in which one ends up. Consequently, the number of variables is decreased by one, and this can be repeated until all variables have been assigned a value. A third classical method, called *linear programming*, is applicable if all constraints and the objective function can be expressed linearly in the variables, which are continuous. In this situation, an optimal solution can be found in a running time that is polynomial in the size of the problem instance. For an overview of the theory of combinatorial optimization we refer the reader to [Korte & Vygen, 2000] and Wolsey [1998]. Many problems cannot be solved to optimality in a reasonable time. In this situation one may resort to the use of heuristics, which drop the requirement of finding an optimal solution at the benefit of substantially shorter running times [Osman & Kelly, 1996]. *Local search* is an example of such an approach [Aarts & Lenstra, 1997]. Its working is based on making small alterations to a solution, i.e., one has a solution, and iteratively this solution is changed a bit, and the effect of this change on the objective function is evaluated. If the effect is favorable, the new solution is accepted, and used for the next iteration. If the solution deteriorates, the new solution may be rejected unconditionally (iterative improvement), or a mechanism may be used to accept it with a certain probability, which decreases with the amount of deterioration and the elapsed time of the algorithm (simulated annealing). Local search is easily applicable in the sense that it requires hardly any specific problem knowledge, and it has given good results for various well-known problems. An alternative approach is not to iterate with one solution, but a population of solutions at the same time, as is done in *genetic algorithms* [Goldberg, 1989]. Then, one can define crossover schemes between different solutions, to generate offspring from two parent solutions. Survival of the fittest reduces the increased population to only keep the best ones, which are the parents in the next iteration. In this way, good solutions are found by a kind of evolution process. Genetic algorithms play a major role in computational intelligence because of their flexibility and power to find good solutions in complex problem solving situations. Search problems do not always come with an objective function, but sometimes only a feasible solution is required. A common method that can be used in this situation is called *constraint satisfaction* [Tsang, 1993]. In this method, the domains of the values that variables can assume are reduced by combining several constraints, which is called constraint propagation. When domains cannot further be reduced, a variable is chosen, and it is assigned a value from its remaining domain. Then again constraint propagation is applied and a new variable is assigned a value, etc. The strength of this method depends on the possibility to delete infeasible values by combining constraints, and quite some research has been spent on the types of constraints that are best suited for constraint propagation. The field of constraint satisfaction can be positioned at the intersection of mathematical programming and artificial intelligence, and the fact that it contributed to the merger of these two fields is probably one of its major contributions in addition to the fact that it is quite a powerful method that can be applied to a large range of problems.

1.4.3 Machine learning

Machine learning is a key element to predict and adapt in ambient intelligent systems. It concerns learning a certain input-output behavior from training examples, which makes it adaptive, and generalizing this behavior beyond the observed situations, to make predictions [Mitchell, 1997]. The best-known approach in machine learning is probably given by *neural networks*, which follow an analogy with the human brain [Hertz, Krogh & Palmer, 1991]. In these networks, we have neurons with inputs and outputs, where outputs of neurons are connected to inputs of other neurons. Each neuron takes a weighted sum of its inputs and sends a signal to its output depending on the result. For the communication with the outside world there are also input neurons and output neurons. In the training phase, the input pattern of a training example is fed to the input neurons, and the weights are adjusted such that the required output pattern is achieved. In the application phase, the input pattern of a new situation is fed to the input neurons, and the output neurons are read for the predicted response. When the output function is binary, we speak about classification. Apart from neural networks, *support vector machines* have recently been introduced for this task [Christianini & Shawe-Taylor, 2000]. They perform classification by generating a separating hyper-plane in a multidimensional space. This space is usually not the space determined by the input variables, but a higher-dimensional space that is able to obtain classifications that are non-linear in the input variables. A strong element of support vector machines is that they perform structural risk minimization, i.e., they make a trade-off between the error in the training examples and the generalization error. *Bayesian classifiers* use a probabilistic approach [Pearl, 1988]. Here, the assumption is that classification rules are based on probability theory, and the classifier uses probabilistic reasoning to produce the most probable classification on a new example. To this end, Bayes' rule of conditional probabilities is used to come from a priori probabilities to a posteriori probabilities. An advantage of Bayesian classifiers is that prior knowledge can be taken into account. The combination of analytic knowledge about a problem area and inferred knowledge is an important subject in current research in machine learning in general.

1.4.4   Expert systems

An expert system is a computer program that provides solutions to search problems or gives advice on intricate matters making use of reasoning mechanisms within specific knowledge domains [Lenat, 1990]. The characteristic features of such systems can be summarized as follows. It can emulate human reasoning using appropriate knowledge representations. It also can learn from past experiences by adjusting the reasoning process to follow promising tracks that were discovered on earlier occasions. Furthermore, it applies rules of thumb often called *heuristics* to exhibit guessing behavior. The behavior of expert systems should be transparent in the sense that they can explain the way in which solutions are obtained. The execution of expert systems often enables the use in on-line decision situations, which requires real-time behavior. The criteria used to evaluate the performance of expert systems are typically deduced from human task-performance measures, such as consistency, regularity, typicality, and adaptability, which all relate to the basic requirement that repetition and small input changes should produce results that make sense. Early expert systems used reasoning mechanisms based on logical rules. More recent approaches apply probabilistic reasoning and reasoning mechanisms that can handle uncertainty. Most recently, the concept of semantic engineering has been applied based on important aspects such as belief, goals, intentions, events, and situations, which are often expanded to the use of ontologies. Especially the use of the *Semantic Web* is a new intriguing development that can further stimulate the development of expert systems with a truly convincing performance within a broad application domain [Berners-Lee & Hendler & Lassila, 2001; Davies, Fessel & Van Harmelen, 2003]. Recently, much attention has been devoted to *agent systems*, which are collections of small intelligent software programs that handle certain tasks in a collective way [Maes, 1990]. Their salient features can be described as follows. Agents execute continuously and they exhibit intelligent behavior such as adaptability and automated search. In addition they exhibit anthropomorphic properties in their interaction with users through expression of belief and obligation, and even through their appearance. They act autonomously, i.e., independent of human control or supervision. They are also context aware in the sense that they are sensitive and responsive to environmental changes. The can interact with other agents and migrate through a network. Agents have the ability to develop themselves to become reactive, intentional, and eventually social. The development of agent technology is a quickly growing field of computational intelligence. Since their introduction about a decade ago, intelligent agents have been widely recognized as a promising approach to embed intelligence in interactive networked devices and for that reason it is of special interest to ambient intelligence.

1.5 Computational complexity

Theoretical computer science has provided a foundation for the analysis of the complexity of computational intelligence algorithms based on the original computational model of the Turing machine [Turing, 1950]. This has led to a distinction between *easy problems*, i.e., those that can be solved within polynomial running times, and *hard problems*, i.e., those for which it is generally believed that no algorithm can exist that solves the problem within a time that can be bounded by a polynomial in the instance size. Consequently, instances of hard problems may require running times that grow exponentially in the problem size which implies that eventually certain tasks cannot be accomplished successfully within reasonable time. For some problems running times can easily extend beyond a man's lifetime if the instance size is sufficiently large. Garey & Johnson [1979] provided an extensive list of intractable problems in their landmark book. The so-called *intractability* calls for workarounds. One frequently resorts to methods that do not carry out the task optimally but rather approximate the final result. These so-called approximation algorithms indeed can reduce computational effort, but if one imposes the requirement that the quality of the final result is within certain limits then again for many well-known problems exponential running times are inevitable. Therefore, one often resorts to the use of heuristics without performance guarantees, which improve running times considerably but at the cost of final solutions that may be arbitrarily bad in theory. The computational complexity theory of learning studies a number of problems that are all related to the question how closely a learning hypothesis that is built by a learning system resembles the target function if this function is not known. *Identification in the limit* refers to the capability of a learning system to converge to the target function for a given problem representation. Early work in computer science, building on Popper's principle of falsification, implies that this may not be possible, which implies that there are certain learning tasks that cannot be achieved. A general principle in computational learning is *Ockham's razor*, which states that the most likely hypothesis is the simplest one that is consistent with all training examples. The *Kolmogorov complexity* [Li & Vitanyi, 1993] provides a quantitative measure for this, given by the length of the shortest program accepted by a universal Turing machine, implementing the hypothesis. It thus provides a theoretical basis for the intuitive simplicity expressed by Ockham's razor. The theory of *Probably Approximately Correct* (PAC) learning addresses the question how many training examples must be applied before a learning hypothesis is correct within certain limits with a high probability [Kearns & Vazirani, 1994]. The theory reveals that for certain non-trivial learning tasks this number may be exponentially large in the size of the input of the learning system, thus requiring exponentially many training examples and exponential running times.

1.6   Conclusion

Computational intelligence can claim an important role in the development of ambient intelligence. Much of the intelligence that is exposed by ambient systems is generated by techniques originating from the field of computational intelligence. We mention a few examples. In *personal recommender systems* machine learning techniques, such as Bayesian classifiers, neural networks and support vector machines are used to capture the viewing or listening behavior of users into personal profiles. Playlists are generated using sophisticated search methods that select titles that have an optimal match with respect to the profile. In *collaborative recommender systems* one often uses expert systems techniques to compile a collective profile that reflects the preferences of a set of users followed by sophisticated search techniques to compile a playlist that matches the collective profile. First applications of collaborative recommenders exist that make use of the Semantic Web, thus making use of collective-knowledge representations built by communities of Web users. Intentional search applications such as *query by humming* [Pauws, 2003] allow users to browse through music databases by simply humming the songs. It applies sophisticated string matching techniques such as dynamic programming to find approximate matches between the melodies extracted from the humming, and the melodies in the music database. These techniques are extremely efficient in their search for matches and allow on-line data mining. The domain of intentional search applications for media browsing is quickly developing techniques that can effectively analyze audio and video material and generate so-called meta-data that provide information about the content at higher abstraction levels, such as object types and genres. These information items can be the nodes in a data network, and the arcs in the network can be used to represent semantic relations between the items. Search techniques can then be used to reason in the network aiming at the support of certain queries. Neural networks can be used to generate meta-data from media files by analyzing patterns and deducing spatial and temporal relations. They can be used to analyze audio and video streams in order to extract specific features from it. Examples are music genre classification, speaker identification, scene detection, and image recognition. Neural networks can also be used to select characteristic pieces of speech or images as a content-addressable memory. Within ambient environments the use of computational intelligence techniques are abundant. A broad field of interest is given by systems that are context aware. Analogue neural networks can be used as adaptive sensing devices that detect and adjust low-level signals within a domestic or mobile environment to control, regulate, and personalize environmental conditions such as temperature, humidity, draft, loudness, and lighting. A next step is to reason about these environmental conditions in order to determine more global environmental states that can be attributed to events or states such as a thunderstorm, day or nighttime, or an empty room. A third step then could be to reason about these events and states to deduce pre-responsive actions or suggestions to a user. For instance, if it is nighttime, the room is empty and the light is on, it will suggest to turn off the light. It goes without saying that we have great expectations about ambient intelligence. Technology will not be the limiting factor in its realization. The ingredients to let the computer disappear are available, but the true success of the paradigm clearly depends on the ability to come up with concepts that make it possible to interact in a natural way with the digital environments that can be built with the invisible technology of the forthcoming century. The role of intelligent algorithms in this respect is apparent since it is the key-enabling factor in realizing natural interaction.

References

Aarts, E., and B. Eggen (eds.) [2002]. *Ambient Intelligence Research in HomeLab*. Philips Research, Eindhoven.

Aarts, E., H. Harwig, and M. Schuurmans [2001]. Ambient intelligence. In: J. Denning (ed.), *The Invisible Future*, McGraw Hill, New York, pages 235–250.

Aarts, E., and J.K. Lenstra (eds.) [1997]. *Local Search in Combinatorial Optimization*. Wiley, Chichester.

Aarts, E., and S. Marzano (eds.) [2003]. *The New Everyday: Visions of Ambient Intelligence*. 010 Publishing, Rotterdam, The Netherlands.

Aarts, E., and R. Roovers [2003]. Ambient intelligence challenges in embedded systems design. In *Proc. Design Automation and Test in Europe*, Munich, pages 2–7.

Berners-Lee, T., J. Hendler, and O. Lassila [2001]. The semantic web. *Scientific American*, 284(5):28–37.

Beyer, H., and K. Holtzblatt [2002]. *Contextual Design: A Customer-centered Approach to Systems Design*. Morgan Kaufmann, New York.

Boden, M.A. (ed.) [1996]. *Artificial Intelligence*. Academic Press, San Diego, CA.

Brooks, R.A. [2002]. *Flesh and Machines*. Pantheon Books, New York.

Christianini, N., and J. Shawe-Taylor [2000]. *An Introduction to Support Vector Machines*. Cambridge University Press, Cambridge, UK.

Davies, J., D. Fessel, and F. van Harmelen [2003]. *Towards the Semantic Web: Onthology-Driven Knowledge Management*. Wiley, Chichester.

Denning, P., and R.M. Metcalfe [1997]. *Beyond Calculation: The Next Fifty Years of Computing*. Copernicus, New York.

Dertouzos, M. [1999]. The Future of Computing. *Scientific American*, 281(2):52–55.

Dertouzos, M. [2001], *The Unfinished Revolution*. HarperCollins Publishers Inc., New York.

De Ruyter, B. [2003]. *365 Days of Ambient Intelligence Research in HomeLab*. Philips Research, Eindhoven.

Duda, R.O., and E.H. Shortliffe [1983]. Expert systems research. Science 220:261–268.

Engelbrecht, A.P. [2002]. *Computational Intelligence: An Introduction*. Wiley, Chichester.

Garey, M.R., and D.S. Johnson [1979]. *Computers and Intractability: A Guide to the Theory of NP-Completeness*. W.H. Freeman and Co., San Francisco, CA.

Goldberg, D.E. [1989]. *Genetic Algorithms in Search Optimization and Machine Learning*. Addison Wesley, Reading, MA.

Hertz, J., A. Krogh, and R. Palmer [1991]. *Introduction to the Theory of Neural Computation.* Addison Wesley, Reading, MA.

Kearns, M., and U. Vazirani [1994]. *An Introduction to Computational Learning Theory.* MIT Press, Cambridge, MA.

Korte, B., and J. Vygen [2000]. *Combinatorial Optimization, Theory and Algorithms.* Springer-Verlag, Berlin.

Lenat, D.B. [1990]. *Building Large Knowledge Based Systems.* Addison-Wesley, Reading, MA.

Li, M., and V. Vitanyi [1993]. *An Introduction to Kolmogorov Complexity and its Applications.* Springer-Verlag, New York.

Liang, T.-P., and E. Turban (eds.) [1993]. *Expert Systems with Applications,* 6(1), Special issue on case-based reasoning and its applications.

Maes, P. [1990]. *Designing Autonomous Agents.* MIT Press, Cambridge, MA.

Mann, S. [1997]. Wearable computing: a first step toward personal imaging, *IEEE Computer,* February 1997, 25–32.

McCorduck, P. [1979]. *Machines Who Think.* McGraw Hill, New York.

Meyer, J.A., and S.W. Wilson, (eds.) [1991]. *From Animals to Animats.* MIT Press, Cambridge, MA.

Minsky, M. [1986], *The Society of Mind.* Simon and Schuster, New York.

Mitchell, T.M. [1997]. *Machine Learning.* McGraw-Hill, New York.

National Research Council [2001]. *Embedded Everywhere.* National Academy Press, Washington DC.

Negroponte, N.P. [1995]. *Being Digital.* Alfred A. Knopf Inc., New York.

Nilsson, N.J. [1998]. *Artificial Intelligence: A New Synthesis.* Morgan Kaufmann, San Francisco, CA.

Norman, A.M. [1993], *Things That Make Us Smart.* Perseus Books, Cambridge, MA.

Noyce, R.N. [1977]. Microelectronics, *Scientific American,* 237(3):63–69.

Osman, I.H., and J.P. Kelly (eds.) [1996]. *Meta-Heuristics: Theory and Applications.* Kluwer Academic Publishers, Boston, MA.

Papadimitriou, C.H., and K. Steiglitz [1982]. *Combinatorial Optimization: Algorithms and Complexity.* Prentice-Hall, Englewood Cliffs, NJ.

Pauws, S. [2003]. QubyHum: Algorithms for query by humming. In: W.F.J. Verhaegh, E. Aarts, and J. Korst (eds.), *Algorithms in Ambient Intelligence,* Kluwer Academic Publishers, New York, pages 71–88.

Pearl, J. [1988]. *Probabilistic Reasoning in Intelligent Systems: Networks of Plausible Inference.* Morgan Kaufmann, Dan Mateo, CA.

Picard, R. [1997]. *Affective Computing.* MIT Press, Cambridge, MA.

Reeves, B., and C. Nass [1996]. *The Media Equation.* Cambridge University Press, Cambridge, MA.

Rich, E., and K. Knight [1991]. *Artificial Intelligence* (2nd edition). McGraw-Hill, New York.

Satyanarayanan, M. [2001]. Pervasive computing, vision and challenges. *IEEE Personal Communications,* August 2001, 10–17.

Sejnowski, T., and C. Rosenberg [1987]. Parallel networks that learn to pronounce English text, *Complex Systems,* 1:145–168.

Shortliffe, E.H. [1976]. *Computer Based Medical Consultations: MYCIN.* Elsevier, New York.

Sinčák, P., and J. Vaščák (eds.) [2000]. *Quo Vadis Computational Intelligence? New Trends and Approaches in Computational Intelligence.* Physica Verlag, Heidelberg.

Tesler, L.G. [1991]. Networked computing in the 1990s. *Scientific American,* 265(3):54–61.

Tsang, E.P.K. [1993]. *Foundations of Constraint Satisfaction.* Academic Press, London.

Turing, A. [1950]. Computing machinery and intelligence. In: E.A. Feigenbaum and J. Feldman (eds.), *Computers and Thought,* McGraw-Hill, New York, 1963.

Weiser, M. [1991], The computer for the twenty-first century, *Scientific American*, 265(3):94–
    104.
Winograd, T. (ed.) [1996]. *Bringing Design to Software*. Addison-Wesley, Reading, MA.
Winograd, T., and F. Flores [1987]. *Understanding Computers and Cognition: A New Founda-
    tion for Design*. Addison-Wesley, Reading, MA.
Wolsey, L.A. [1998]. *Integer Programming*. Wiley, Chichester.

Part I

USER INTERACTION

Chapter 2

MULTIMODALITY
AND AMBIENT INTELLIGENCE

Anton Nijholt

Abstract   In this chapter we discuss multimodal interface technology. We present examples of multimodal interfaces and show problems and opportunities. Fusion
of modalities is discussed and some roadmap discussions on research in multimodality are summarized. This chapter also discusses future developments
where, rather than communicating with a single computer, users communicate
with their environment using multimodal interactions and where the environmental interface has perceptual competence that includes being able to interpret
what is going on in the environment. We contribute roles to virtual humans in
order to allow daily users of future computing environments to establish relationships with the environments, or more in particular, these virtual humans.

Keywords   Multimodal interactions, language and speech technology, ambient intelligence,
environmental interfaces, virtual reality, embodied conversational agents.

2.1   Introduction

It is tempting to assume that language and speech are the most natural
modalities for human-human communication. There are good reasons to attack this assumption. In communication between humans non-verbal aspects
are important as well. When trying to establish efficient communication we
may concentrate on the literal meaning of what is being said. However, even
when efficiency is an aim, it is often useful to take other communication aspects into account. Whom are we attracted to and do we want to speak? What
roles are played by facial expression and body posture? Gaze, eye contact or
a smile may mean more for human-human communication than a right choice
of words. A blink of the eye may give a completely different meaning to what
was just said or it may even replace a long sequence of words. The same
holds for avoiding eye contact. As observed by the linguist Robin Lakoff, in
the majority of cases people don't say what they mean, but what they want to

W. Verhaegh et al. (eds.), Algorithms in Ambient Intelligence, 23-53.
© 2004 *Kluwer Academic Publishers. Printed in the Netherlands.*

say. Nevertheless they can communicate with each other. Speech and language need to be interpreted in a context where other communication modalities are available (seeing, touching, smelling, tasting).

When looking at human-computer interaction we can certainly try to model speech and language in their context. Attempts are being made to model dialogues between humans and computers using natural speech in the context of a particular domain, a particular task and even taking into account knowledge of a particular user. However, there is a second reason to consider a different view on the importance of speech and language. When looking at computer technology that aims at assisting humans in their daily work and recreation we want non-intrusive technology. The computer should interpret what is going on in an environment where there is one or more occupants, assist when asked or take the initiative when useful, either for the occupants or for future use. This situation differs from traditional human-computer interaction where there is explicit addressing of *the* computer.

In documents of the European Community we see the mentioning of 'the real world being the interface'. In particular the 'Ambient Intelligence' theme of the European Framework 6 Research Programme demands systems, which are capable of functioning within natural, unconstrained environments - within scenes. Hence notions of space, time and physical laws play a role and they are maybe more important than the immediate and conscious communication between a human and a computer screen. In a multi-sensory environment, maybe supported with embedded computer technology, the environment can capture and interpret what the user is doing, maybe anticipating what the user is doing or wanting, and therefore can be pro-active and re-active, just capturing what is going on for later use, or acting as an environment that assists the user in real-time or collaborates with the user in real-time. Hence, speech and language, or whatever modalities we want to consider, are part of a context where temporal and spatial issues play important roles.

All this certainly does not mean that traditional ways of interacting with computers will disappear, at least not in the next ten years. There are tasks that can be done efficiently with keyboard and mouse. Constructing a text, for example. Other tasks can profit from speech input, a head nod or shake detector, a touch screen, a data glove allowing manipulation of virtual objects, translation of body movements to interpretations, e.g., a choreography, force-feedback to help in the design of a gear-lever and, obviously, there will be tasks where combinations of these modalities can help to obtain efficient or entertaining communication with the computer. However, as just mentioned, this is about communication with a computer and about using the computer to perform a certain task. Ubiquitous computing technology will spread computing and communication power all around us. That is, in our daily work and home environment and we need computers with perceptual competence in order to profit from this technology.

Embedded computers will appear everywhere but at the same time they will become less visible as computers. Nevertheless, we need interfaces. For some applications these can be big, for example the walls of room or the surface of a tabletop. In other situations the interface may consist of invisible attentive sensors. Current interface technology works well in controlled and constrained conditions. Extending the existing technology to obtain multisensorial interfaces capable of functioning within natural environments is an important challenge.

In this chapter we look at and discuss examples of multimodal and environmental interfaces. In our research we have introduced multimodal interfaces for several applications. Some of them will be discussed here, showing problems and opportunities. Although most of the work has been done in the context of extensions of traditional interfaces, we think that designing these extensions as integrations of different interaction modalities, will allow us to extend the research to environmental interfaces and to build on the results that have been obtained. One reason to think so is the emphasis in our research on actions and interactions in the context of visualized worlds, either the graphical user interface to which references may be made using different modalities, or virtual worlds that have been used as a laboratory where real-world actions and interactions can be visualized.

In Section 2.2 we discuss some of our multimodal interaction environments. In Section 2.3 we look at multimodal interaction modeling in general. We shortly introduce the results of a roadmap discussion on multimodal research held a few years ago and explain that the views developed there were rather conservative. Nevertheless, the research advocated there is more than useful. In Section 2.4 we discuss the role of computers as social actors. Should we continue to see computers as social actors or does new technology for ubiquitous computing invite us to consider other paradigms? Section 2.5 is about embodied conversational agents or virtual humans. In our view they can play the role of social actors, being able to build relationships with humans working and recreating in computer-supported environments. Finally, in Section 2.6 we repeat the main findings of this chapter.

2.2 Multimodality: Background and examples

In this section we show examples of multimodal systems we have been working on. Generally our approach has been bottom-up. That is, we started with a specific practical problem rather than with a theoretical problem. The assumption was, and still is, that theory on syntactic, semantic and pragmatic aspects of multimodality is rather underdeveloped. On the other hand, interface technology allows the building of multimodal interfaces, the use of many non-traditional interaction devices (6-DOF navigation devices, haptic devices, eye trackers, camera's for tracking gestures and body movement, facial expression recognition, etc.) and that rather than waiting for a more mature theory the development of theory can profit from experiences and experiments with multimodal interfaces and environments. Below we introduce four environments. The virtual music center, a 3D environment inhabited by several agents, where, among others, the user or visitor can interact in a multimodal way with an agent called Karin that knows about performances and performers in this theater. The second system we discuss is a multimodal tutoring environment. In this environment an agent called Jacob is able to monitor the actions of a student that tries to solve the problem of the Towers of Hanoi. The third research environment is meant to experiment with multimodal tools that support the visitor to navigate in a virtual environment. How does a visitor make clear where she wants to go? How does the system explain where a visitor can go or what can be found in the environment? Finally, our last example is on a system that tries to recognize and interpret events in a room and interactions between occupants of this room.

What do these examples have in common? In research on multimodality speech and language often take primateship. This certainly shows in these examples. As a consequence, multimodal interaction modeling often starts with attainments from speech and language research and other modalities are considered as add-ons. Our view on what is important in human-computer communication is determined by our view on the role of speech and language in human-human interaction. However, but this will not be discussed in this section, we would prefer to have an emphasis on human behavior 'modalities' (or characteristics) rather than on human communication modalities when considering the future role of computing and communication technology. The environments we discuss show the importance of information fusion, taking into account synchronization issues, they show the importance of cross-modal reference resolution and the importance of being able to reason beyond modality borders, and they show the importance of coordination in multimodal information presentation. In the examples there is no explicit discussion about syntactic, semantic and pragmatic level representation of information obtained from different media sources. In Section 2.3 we will shortly address this question.

2.2.1   Multimodal information presentation and transaction

The first environment we discuss is the Virtual Music Center. This is a virtual reality environment modeled on the real Music Hall in Enschede and is built using VRML (Virtual Reality Modeling Language). It is inhabited by a number of agents that can provide the user with information. Each agent has its specific task and domain knowledge. One of the agents, Karin, provides information about the agenda of performances and is able to sell tickets to visitors. Embedding the dialogue system in a visual context made it possible to present information through other modalities. Because the agent became embodied, this made us look into aspects of non-verbal communication that could now be modeled as well.

Figure 2.1. View from the entrance to the inside.

In Figure 2.1 we see a screenshot taken from the entrance of the virtual theater. With a virtual reality browser plugged into one of the usual web browsers, visitors can explore this virtual environment, walking from one location to another, looking at posters and other information sources and clicking on smart objects that set music and video tracks in motion. Behind the desk, the agent Karin is waiting to inform the visitor about performances, artists and available tickets. Karin can engage in a natural language dialogue with the visitor. She has access to an up-to-date database about all the performances in the various theaters. Karin has a cartoon-like 3D face that allows facial expressions and lip movements that are synchronized with a text-to-speech system to mouth the dialogue system's utterances to the user. Synchronization of sound and lip movements is currently implemented robustly because of the current limitations of web technology. Further design considerations that allow an embodied agent like Karin to display combinations of verbal and non-verbal behavior can be found in [Nijholt & Hulstijn, 2000].

All of this means that we have conversations and other forms of interaction between agents, between visitors, and between visitors and agents. Because communication is situated in a shared visible or otherwise observable virtual environment, communication partners are allowed to support their linguistic communicative acts by other means of interaction, referencing objects by gazing or pointing toward them, for instance. Using embodied conversation agents as information sources in a virtual environment has allowed us to investigate a number of issues in natural and multimodal human-computer interactions.

Figure 2.2 shows a snapshot of a typical conversation between Karin and the user. The 3D environment with the typical buttons to navigate in 3D space

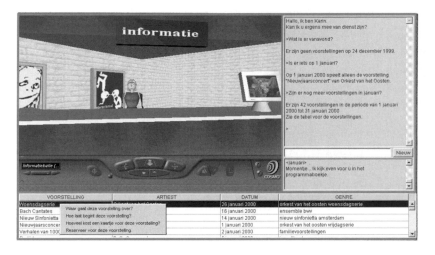

Figure 2.2.   The dialogue windows for Karin.

shows Karin behind the information desk. It is just one frame in the window that also contains a dialogue frame in which the user types in questions and in which Karin's replies are shown. Note that Karin's answer does not just appear in the dialogue frame but that it is also read out loud using speech with proper lip-synchronization. The Dutch text-to-speech system Fluency was used for this.

A table containing information about performances takes up another part of the window. When the reply to an information request is a long list of performances, the system decides to present the reply in the table. Having Karin read out all the information would take too long. Therefore, Karin's reply will merely consist in directing the user to the information presented in the table. The user can click on the individual cells and menus will pop up with further information or with a suggestion of some frequently asked questions about performances (What is this performance about? What time does it start? Etc.). Karin can interpret and generate references to items in the table. A question like "Please give me more information about the third performance." will be understood correctly as making a reference to the third performance in the table.

The conversational agent Karin is essentially an embodied version of a spoken dialogue manager allowing natural language interactions with the user. The dialogue management system behind Karin is not very sophisticated from a linguistic point of view but reasonably intelligent from a practical and pragmatic point of view. The dialogues are assumed to be task-oriented dialogues about information and transaction. Karin knows information about performances only and expects the user to ask questions about these or to make a reservation for them. This assumption guides Karin's dialogues moves. The system prompts are designed in such a way that the users are gently adapted to Karin's way of thinking.

Linguistic analysis is performed by a rewriting system. Input sentences are processed by a series of transducers that rewrite the input form to a canonical form that can be interpreted and acted upon by the dialogue manager. Although the linguistic analysis is crude, the restrictions on the kind of information that can be queried and on the types of dialogues that are normally undertaken allow the system to produce adequate responses in the majority of cases assuming reasonable user behavior. The original specification for the dialogue system was based on a corpus of dialogues obtained by a Wizard of Oz experiment. This corpus provided insight in the kind of utterances and dialogues visitors would engage in.

The rewriting system that implements the natural language analysis robustly had important benefits in the initial development of the virtual environment in that it allowed us to build a reliable and fast tailor-made system without having to spend much time developing it. However, its simplicity also has its drawbacks. In the rewriting step, information is lost that is needed for the naturalness of the dialogues. For instance, the system may forget the exact phrases uttered by the visitor and use its own wording instead. This may give the impression that the system is correcting the user; an effect that was obviously not intended.

2.2.2 Multimodal tutoring with Jacob

Our second environment concerns a virtual teacher (Jacob) that guides a student in solving the problem of the Towers of Hanoi [Evers & Nijholt, 2000] (see also Figure 2.3), a classic toy problem from the field of programming language teaching. In this game, the student has to move a stack of blocks from one peg to another using an auxiliary peg. The student can only move single blocks from peg to peg; it is not allowed to place a larger block on top of a smaller one. During the moving of blocks Jacobs monitors the student, he can correct the student and when asked demonstrate a few next steps. Obviously, a more generic way to look at this application is to consider it as an environment where tasks have to be performed that involve moving objects, pressing buttons, pulling levers, etcetera, and where an intelligent agent provides assistance.

Before looking at the interaction with Jacob we shortly discuss the (generic) architecture of the system. The software architecture is layered in order to separate the concerns of the 3D visualization from the basic functionality of the system. The abstract 3D world contains objects representing e.g. blocks, pegs, and Jacob's physical manifestation. An avatar object represents a user.

Figure 2.3.   Jacob demonstrates the Towers of Hanoi.

We have defined an interface layer between the abstract and concrete 3D world layers to make the system more robust to changes. The concrete 3D world layer consists of a hierarchical structure of VRML nodes, like transformation nodes, geometry nodes, and sensor nodes. The interface layer exposes only the essential properties of the nodes in the concrete 3D world, like the position of an object. All other details are hidden. The abstract 3D world layer provides simulation of physical properties. For the Towers of Hanoi, we have implemented basic collision avoidance so that objects cannot be moved through each other. Furthermore, we have implemented a simple gravity variant that makes objects fall at a constant speed. A task model and an instruction model together form Jacob's mind. They act as controllers that observe the abstract world and try to reach specific instruction objectives by manipulating Jacob's body.

The interaction between the user and Jacob is multimodal. An important issue in this project was how natural language dialogue and nonverbal actions are to be integrated and what knowledge of the virtual environment is needed for that purpose. The Jacob agent behaves in an intelligent way, helping the user proactively and learning from the interaction. Moreover, visualization of Jacob plays an important role, including natural animation of the body, generation of facial expressions, and synchronization of lip movement and speech. Unfortunately, apart from some simple eyebrow movements, this has not been implemented. Both the user and Jacob are however able to manipulate objects in the virtual environment. The student can use mouse and keyboard to manipulate objects. A data glove could have been used as well, without making changes to the architecture.

The interaction between Jacob and student uses keyboard natural language and animations by Jacob. A sample dialogue between Student (S) and Jacob (J) is:

S: "What should I do?"

J: "The green block should be moved from the left to the right peg. Do you want me to demonstrate?"

S: "Yes, please."

Jacob moves the green block

S: "Which block should I move now?"

J: "I will show you."

Jacob picks up the red block

The student accepts the red block and puts it on the right peg

J: "That was good. Please continue!"

As becomes clear from this sample dialogue, Jacob knows about the current situation, making it possible to react in an appropriate way on user utterances that deal with the current situation. In this system no attention has been paid to references made by the user to events or parts of the dialogue history that go back a few steps in time. The system has very limited intelligence and only observes the current situation. The system displays information by giving verbal responses to the student and by animating the Jacob agent and having him perform movements from blocks from one peg to the other, shaking his head to show his disagreement or, when the user is really stupid, walking away. The user can use speech input to communicate with Jacob (see Figure 2.4), but he cannot make detailed references to the objects in the virtual world or about the actions that are being performed, either by the student or by Jacob. Blocks can be moved using the mouse or the keyboard, not by using speech input.

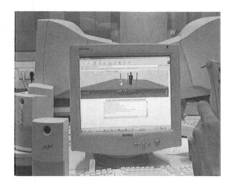

Figure 2.4. Student interacting with Jacob.

2.2.3 Multimodal navigation in 2D and 3D intelligent environments

In Section 2.2.1 we met Karin. She knows how to access the theater database and to generate answers concerning performers and performances. Our world has been made accessible to the audience. More generally, as visitors of an unknown world, be it a physical space, a public space on the web, a smart room or home environment, or a 3D virtual world, we often need other types of information as well. To whom do we address our questions about the environment and its functions? To whom do we address our questions about how to continue when performing a certain task, where to find other visitors or where to find domain or task related information?

At this moment we are following different approaches to solve this problem. These approaches are related and can be integrated since all of them are agent-oriented and based on a common framework of communicating agents. In addition, we have built this framework in such a way that different agents with different abilities can become part of it: Karin who knows about theater performances, tutors that monitor the student's actions (a virtual piano teacher [Broersen & Nijholt, 2002], Jacob that follows the student's progress while solving the Towers of Hanoi [Evers & Nijholt, 2000], a teacher that presents modules in nurse education [Hospers et al., 2003] and navigation agents that have knowledge about a particular environment and that allows users to make references to a visualized environment while interacting with the agent.

Developing a navigation agent poses a number of questions. How can we build navigation intelligence into an agent? What does navigation intelligence mean? How can we connect this intelligence to language and vision intelligence? We know at least that visitors of an environment are language users and recognize and interpret what they see. There is a continuous interaction between verbal and nonverbal information when interpreting a situation in our virtual environment. Modeling this interaction and the representation and interpretation of these sources, together with generating multimedia information from these sources is a main issue in navigation research. For observations on the preferences that users have for navigation support, the reader is referred to [Darken & Silbert, 1996; Höök et al., 1998].

As a case study we introduced a 2D map and a multimodal dialogue agent to our VMC laboratory environment. A first version appeared in [van Luin et al., 2001]. The work is in progress, meaning that the system is there, but no effort has been made to add 'graphic sugar' to the layout and the integration of the different windows that are used.

In Figure 2.5 we display a floor map of the VMC. In Figure 2.6 a view on part of the virtual world is presented. In this view the user has been brought to the stairs leading to the next floor of the building. The visitor can ask questions, give commands and provide information when prompted by the agent. This is done by typing natural language utterances (in a more recent version we have added speech recognition [Hofs et al., 2003]) and by moving the mouse pointer over the map to locations and objects the user is interested in.

On the map the user can find the performance halls, the lounges and bars, selling points, information desks and other interesting locations and objects.

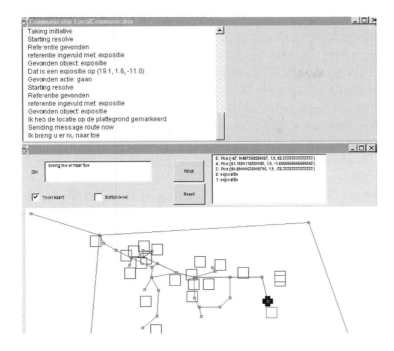

Figure 2.5. 2D Floor map (ground floor) of the VMC.

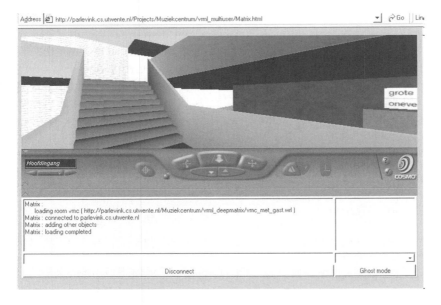

Figure 2.6. The visitor has been brought to the stairs.

The current position of the visitor in the virtual environment is marked on the map. While moving in virtual reality the visitor can check her position on this floor map. When using the mouse to point at a position on the map, references can be made by both user (in natural language) and system to the object or location pointed at [van Luin et al., 2001].

As we mentioned, the navigation agent can be accessed using natural language. We have annotated a small corpus of user utterances that appear in navigation dialogues. On the one hand we find complete questions and commands. On the other hand we also have short phrases that are given by the user in reply to a clarifying question of the navigation agent. An example of a question is: "What is this?" while pointing at an object on the map, or "Is there an entrance for wheel chairs?" Examples of commands are "Bring me there." or "Bring me to the information desk." Examples of short phrases are "No, that one." or "Karin." From the annotated corpus a grammar was induced and a unification-type parser for Dutch was used to parse these utterances into feature structures.

Three agents communicate to fill in missing information in the feature structure (when the information given by the user in her question, answer or command is not yet complete) and to determine the action that has to be undertaken (answering the question, prompting for clarification or missing information, displaying a route on the map or guiding the user in virtual reality to a certain position). The navigation agent, the dialogue manager agent and the browser agent do this in co-operation. The latter can communicate with the virtual reality browser (embedded in a standard web browser) to retrieve the current position of the visitor and to have a smooth transition from the user's viewpoint along a route that has been computed. Not yet implemented is the possibility that not only the position but also what is in the eyesight of the visitor can be retrieved. This will allow better resolution of references in the dialogue to objects that are visible for the visitor in the virtual environment.

An illustrative example of a navigation dialogue is given below:

Visitor:	[Clicks on an object on the map] What is this?
Agent:	That is an exposition.
Visitor:	Where is it?
Agent:	You can find it in the lounge.
Visitor:	Let's go there.
Agent:	I bring you there.

The prototype navigation agent that we discussed here is certainly not our final solution to assisting visitors of our smart environment. There are several issues we are working on right now. The first issue concerns speech recognition. A web-based speech architecture has been introduced [Hofs et al., 2003]. The second issue concerns the modeling of speech dialogues. We introduced an approach to multimodal dialogue modeling for navigation that emphasized

Figure 2.7. You go UP the STAIRS.

— and tried to find solutions — for cross-modal reference resolution and for sub dialogue modeling. In a next phase, we need to concentrate on the communication with other agents that are available in the environment. How can we ensure that a question reaches the appropriate agent? How can we model the history of interaction in such a way that different agents do not only know about their own role in this interaction but also about others? Unlike others, our environment allows the investigation of communication between active and passive agents that inform the visitor about the possibilities and the properties of an information-rich virtual environment (see also [Nijholt et al., 2003]). Embodiment of the navigation agent, as illustrated in Figure 2.7, adds an other dimension to navigation in a virtual, visualized, environment.

2.2.4 Multimodal actions and interactions in smart environments

While in the previous examples we discussed interactions between users and visitors of environments, where the environment was represented on the screen of a PC as a menu-based graphical user interface, a 2D or 3D world or a virtual reality environment, we can also look at the interaction with or taking place in physical environments, where these environments are equipped with sensors that capture audio- and visual information. For example, in the 5th framework IST project Multi-Modal Meeting Manager (M4) we are involved with research on the semantics of the interactions and the events during a meeting. Obviously, these events and interactions are of multimodal nature. Apart from the verbal and nonverbal interaction between participants, many events take place that are relevant for the interaction between participants and that therefore have impact on their communication content and form. For example, someone enters the meeting room, someone distributes a paper, the chairman opens or closes the meeting, ends a discussion or asks for a vote, a participants asks or is invited to present ideas on the whiteboard, a PowerPoint presentation is given with the help of laser pointing and later discussed, someone has to leave early and the order of the agenda is changed, etc. Participants make references in their utterances to what is happening, to presentations that have been shown, to behavior of other participants, etc. They look at each other, to the person they address, to the others, to the chairman, to their notes and to the presentation on the screen, etc. Participants have and use facial expressions, gestures and body posture that display or emphasize their opinion, etc.

The aim of the M4 project is to design a meeting manager that is able to translate the information that is captured from microphones and cameras into annotated meeting minutes. In fact, but this is certainly too ambitious for the current project, it should be possible to generate everything that has been going on during a particular meeting from these annotated meeting minutes, for example, in a virtual meeting room, with virtual representations of the participants. The more modest goals of the M4 project include the summarization of a meeting and the retrieval of multimedia information from these annotated meeting minutes. In future projects it is expected to tackle the more ambitious goals that deal with virtual reality generation.

Figure 2.8.   Three camera's capturing a M4 meeting.

Clearly, we can look at the project as research on smart environments or on ambient intelligence. While in the previous sections we looked at multimodality in the context of one particular user that communicates with a computer screen, here we have a situation where there is no explicit or active communication between user and environment. The environment registers and interprets what's going on, but is not actively involved. The environment is attentive, but does not give feedback or is pro-active with respect of the users of the environment or the participants of a collaborative event. Real-time participation of the environment requires not only attention and interpretation, but also intelligent feedback and pro-active behavior of the environment. It requires also presentation by the environment of multimedia information to the occupants of the environment.

In order to collect multimodal meeting information scripted meetings have been organized in which participants act according to prescribed rules that define periods of monologue, discussion, note taking, or a whiteboard presentation. The corpus thus obtained allows study of meeting participants' behavior. In Figure 2.8 we show a three-camera view of a meeting between four persons. In addition to the cameras there are lapel microphones and circular microphone arrays available for the meeting manager to capture audio. In the near future it is expected that white board pen capture can be added.

On a more detailed level the objectives of the project are the collection and annotation of a multimodal meetings database, the analysis and processing of the audio and video streams, robust conversational speech recognition, to produce a word-level description, recognition of gestures and actions, multimodal identification of intent and emotion, multimodal person identification and source localization and tracking. Models are needed for the integration of the multimodal streams in order to be able to interpret events and interactions. These models include statistical models to integrate asynchronous multiple streams and semantic representation formalisms that allow reasoning and cross-modal reference resolution. These models form the basis of browsing, retrieval, extraction and summarization methods. Textual 'side information' (the agenda, discussion papers, slides) enables the application of useful constraints. It may be used to adapt the language model of the speech recognizer or as query expansion information for retrieval.

A straightforward meeting browser can follow the structure of an agenda. Each agenda item can be associated with different views on that topic. For example, a textual summary, a diagrammatic discussion flow indicating which participants were involved (speaker turn patterns), and audio and video key frames that give the essence of the discussion. Obviously, in order to track the discussion and find the interesting parts features need to be distinguished that can be recognized by the meeting manager.

Presently there are two approaches that are followed. The first one is the recognition of joint behavior, that is, the recognition of group actions during the meeting. Examples of group actions are presentations, discussions, consen-

Figure 2.9.   Pointing, rising and voting.

sus and note taking. Probabilistic methods based on Hidden Markov Models
(HMMs) are used for this purpose [McCowan et al., 2003]. The second approach is the recognition of the actions of the individuals independently, and
fuse them at a higher level for further recognition and interpretation of the interactions. When looking at the actions of the individuals during a meeting
several useful pieces of information can be collected. First of all, there can be
person identification using face recognition. Current speaker recognition using
multimodal information (e.g., speech and gestures) and speaker tracking (e.g.,
while the speaker rises from his chair and walks to the whiteboard) are similar issues. Other, more detailed but nevertheless relevant meeting acts can be
distinguished. In [Zobl et al., 2003] recognition of individual meeting actions
by video sequence processing in the context of the M4 project is discussed.
Examples of actions that are distinguished are entering, leaving, rising, sitting,
shaking head, nodding, voting (raising hand) and pointing (see Figure 2.9).
These are rather simple actions and clearly they need to be given an interpretation in the context of the meeting. Or rather, these actions need to be interpreted
as part of other actions and verbal and nonverbal interactions between participants. Presently models, annotation tools and mark-up languages are being
developed in the project that allow the description of the relevant issues during
a meeting, including temporal aspects and including some low-level fusion of
media streams. Higher-level fusion, where also semantic modeling of verbal
and nonverbal utterances is taken into account has not been done yet. In some
cases it turns out to be more convenient to make shortcuts to a pragmatic level
of fusion using knowledge from the application.

   The M4 meeting manager captures the events and interactions in the meeting
room. After capturing the gathered information becomes available for both
participants and non-participants. A next step is to allow remote participants
to take part in the meeting and integrate their interactions as well. Making
the meeting room intelligent and providing real-time support for efficient and
effective interactions is an other objective. Clearly, as mentioned above, in

this way we enter the research area of smart multi-party environments and intelligent collaborative workspaces [Mikic et al., 2000; Potter, 2003]. In all these environments we need to model the fusion of multi-sensory information in such a way that spatial and temporal aspects have to be taken into account.

2.3   Multimodality: Issues and roadmaps

There is no uniformity in terminology on modes and media, on multimodality and multimedia. In [Maybury & Wahlster, 1988] media, modes and codes are distinguished. Examples of media are text, audio and video. Modes refer to the human perceptual system. For example, visual, auditory or tactile modalities. Formalization is done in syntactical, semantical and pragmatic languages. These are called the codes, allowing us to speak of multimodal codes. Others prefer to speak of multimodal input where every separate information stream or channel is an input modality for the system and where every information stream can have a syntactic, semantic and pragmatic representation. However, in order to obtain multimodal interpretation these input modalities have to be fused. This can be done, again, one a syntactic, semantic and pragmatic level, but it seems to be more appropriate to have partial fusion at these levels in order to allow mutual disambiguation and cross modal reference resolution.

At a low level we encounter the 'wait' problem. Input on multiple channels is not always strictly synchronized. How long does the system have to wait for input in other channels before it triggers an action? For example, if gestural input is available, it may be a gesture-only utterance, or part of a multimodal utterance. In the first case action should be immediately taken, in the latter the system should wait for the following natural language utterance. This is related to the distinction between early and late integration.

Early integration takes part at the data-level, late integration at the semantic level. In an early fusion architecture, the recognition process in one mode influences the course of recognition in the other. The advantage is an intensive cooperation between the various modalities, which may result in a more accurate interpretation. An example where this can be useful is with synchronized modalities such as speech and lip movements.

Late integration enables the reuse of recognition modules for individual modalities [Oviat et al., 2000]. Moreover, at the pragmatic level it may be decided how detailed the fusion at lower levels need to be for a particular multimodal domain and application.

Methods for integration include unification-based integration [Johnston et al., 1997], the melting pot approach [Nigay & Coutaz, 1995] HMM and finite state methods (e.g., [Johnston & Bangalore, 2000]), constructive type theory [Bunt & Beun, 2001] and extensions of discourse representation theory [Bunt et al., 2003]. Finally, multimodal output generation requires content selection, media allocation and rendering of output on presentation mechanisms and display devices.

2.3.1   Roadmaps

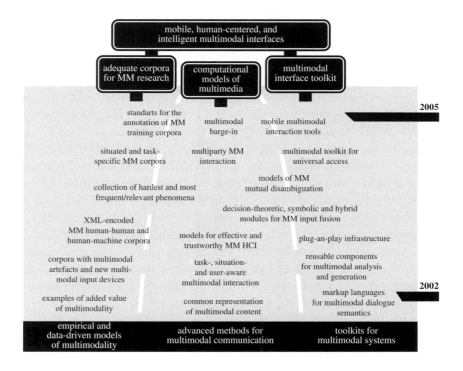

Figure 2.10.   Near-term roadmap for multimodal communication.

The aim of this section is to introduce the reader to some recent roadmaps that have been designed for multimodal communication [Bunt et al., 2003]. The three lanes in Figure 2.10 distinguish the collecting of multimodal corpora, including coding schemes and annotation tools, the computational modeling of multimodality, including modeling of multimodal syntax, semantics and pragmatics, and, as a third lane, the development of toolkits for input fusion and output coordination. Figure 2.10 is the roadmap in the near-term. In Figure 2.11 the long-term roadmap is illustrated. Here we have more attention paid to multimodal environments, collaboration, multi-users, usability and user modeling and affective computing. As may become clear from the figures the staring point of the foreseen research is again the individual user that interacts in a multimodal way with a computer system. This is reflected in the choice of theories: from speech act to dialogue act to multimodal dialogue act, rather than starting with multimodal acts. This can be contrasted with the current M4 project (see Section 2.2.4) where domain specific multimodal acts (meeting acts) are defined and where syntactic modeling, using for example HMMs, and semantic modeling is done to integrate modes into multimodal, domain-specific, meeting acts.

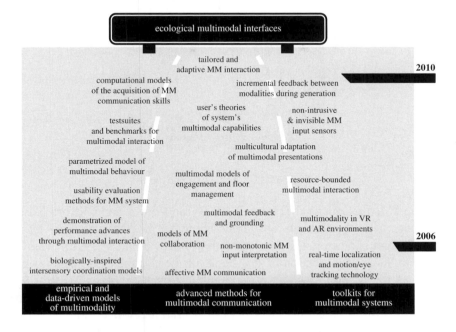

Figure 2.11. Long-term roadmap for multimodal communication.

2.4 Disappearing computers, social actors and embodied agents

In the previous sections we discussed examples of systems that allow multi-modal interactions. Many existing research and prototype systems introduced embodied agents, assuming that they allow a more natural conversation or dialogue between user and computer. In this section we will first take a look at how in general people react to computers. We will look at some of the theories, in particular the CASA ("Computers Are Social Actors") paradigm, and then discuss how new technology, for example ambient intelligence technology, needs to anticipate the need of humans to build up social relationships. One way to anticipate is to do research in the area of social psychology, to translate findings there to the human-computer situation and to investigate technological possibilities to include human-human communication characteristics in the interface. For that reason we will discuss embodied conversational agents, the role they can play in human-computer interaction (in face-to-face conversation), in ambient intelligence environments and in virtual communities.

2.4.1   Computers are social actors

Figure 2.12.   The media equation.

In the "Media Equation" (Figure 2.12) Byron Reeves and Clifford Nass report about their experiments on human-computer interaction where humans assign human characteristics to computers [Reeves & Nass, 1996]. Many experiments have been done after this book has been published. They became known as the "social reactions to communication technology" (SRCT) perspective in which "computers are social actors". An example of an experiment is the following. A student is asked to sit behind a computer and to perform a particular task. When finished, the student needs to answer questions: how helpful was the computer, was it friendly, was it polite, etc. Two computers were available for answering these questions: the computer that was used for performing the task and another computer just for presenting the questionnaire and having the student answer it. It turned out that when the questionnaire had to be answered on the computer that had been used to communicate the task with the student and to help the student when performing this task, students answered much more positive and politely than when answering similar questions posed by the second computer. Clearly, people don't like to offend a computer that has tried to be helpful to them.

Many similar experiments have been performed. Computer users turned out to be sensitive for flattery and humor; moreover, they were very much influenced, when assigning personality characteristics to a computer, by the properties of the synthesized voice in text-to-speech synthesis. And, as became clear from the experiments, it is not just a matter of contributing personality characteristics to computer, it is also a matter of being influenced by these properties while communicating with the computer. Hence, the book's conclusion was as follows:

*"Our strategy for learning about media was to go to the social science section of the library, find theories and experiments about human-**human** interaction — and then borrow. We did the same for information about how people respond to the natural environment, borrowing freely. Take out a pen, cross out "human" or "environment," and substitute **media**. When we did this, all of the predictions and experiments led to the media equation: People's responses to media are fundamental social and natural."*

For a future situation where a house, a sitting room, a working room, an office and in fact every environment and its objects allow perception of what is going on in the environment and allow interaction by its occupants and visitors to exchange information (including emotions), it is certainly useful to investigate how we can design social interfaces, emphasizing human-to-human communication properties, rather than concentrating purely on designing intelligence. One important aspect in the design is the appearance of the interface. When offering intelligence and emotion, shouldn't we offer virtual humans (or embodied conversational agents) in the interface? They offer communication properties that make us feel being appreciated and that make us feel being understood. It makes it possible for us to act in a smart, but also in a social environment.

2.4.2 Social actors, interpersonal relationships and the disappearing computer

In the previous section we introduced the computer as a social actor. In human-computer interaction we recognize characteristics of human-human interaction. There is human-like behavior when interacting with the computer and human-like behavior of the computer is expected. Can we expect similar behavior when the user is interacting with an environment rather than with a desktop screen? In future environments computers will be embedded in walls, furniture, cloths, and in objects that are natural in the environment. Moreover, there is communication between these embedded computational devices allowing a much more comprehensive overview of environment and events taking place than is possible with a single computing device. How will humans interact with such environments? Are they able to build some kind of relationship with these environments like they are able to build relationships with a computer that is perceived as a social actor? Or do we need to introduce explicit social actors, that is, embodied conversational agents, in these environments with which users can communicate and exchange information in intelligent and social ways in order to fulfill a need to establish relationships with their environments?

Some notes are in order. Firstly, it is not unusual to contribute personality characteristics to a room, a house, a mall, a street or square, to a town or even to a landscape or an other natural environment. At least one may think that thoughts and activities (i.e., interactions with the environment) are influenced by the particular environment. We won't go into that here. Secondly, it is useful to distinguish between situations. Different circumstances require different kinds of interactions. Sometimes we want to see things arranged in an efficient way. Sometimes we are more concerned with the partner's satisfaction when arranging things. Sometimes arranging itself is entertaining. Both interaction and information exchange can be goals, e.g., when we enter conversations with our children or colleagues. Efficiency has not always priority. A third note, as mentioned above, concerns the future. It is already the case that a large part of the professional population in Western countries spends the day with discussion, meetings and knowledge exchange and spends lots of time interacting with computers. The need to do this in the office will decrease and home, work and mobile situations will more and more resemble each other. Interaction forms require mixtures of efficiency, social relationship, and entertaining aspects. Our hypothesis is that people prefer to be able to interact with their 'own', personalized (but not only in the current technical sense, i.e., aimed at efficiency) and non-anonymous environment.

Although the SRCT perspective makes us aware that people react socially to computers, a more detailed view can make clear many nuances. To start with, there is no such thing as *the* computer. Its performance, as it shows in the interface, can be task oriented, it can be communication oriented and it can be oriented towards establishing and maintaining relationships. In Interpersonal Theory these types are the three tracks of conversational goals [Shechtman & Horowitz, 2003]. The task goal in human-to-human conversation is why the conversation is started, i.e., to accomplish a certain task and part of the interaction behavior is meant to reach this goal. The communication goals aim at making the interaction process run, e.g., by allowing smooth turn taking. The relationship goals of the conversational partners set the tone of the conversation. Two broad categories of relationship goals are distinguished: communion (behaviors oriented towards connecting with one another or disconnecting from another) and agency (behaviors oriented toward exerting influence or yielding to influence). Shechtman conducted experiments to study relationship behavior during keyboard human-computer interaction and (apparently) keyboard mediated human-human interaction. In the latter case participants used much more communion and agency relationship statements, used more words and spent more time in conversation.

Not all modalities that can be employed in human-computer interaction lend themselves to the same degree to the different types of performance that we distinguished above. In human-human interaction nonverbal cues play an important part in the relationship track of communication. Hence, we can ask whether we can recognize and interpret these communication aspects in human-computer interaction and whether they can play a similar role. From the SRCT perspective we know that humans react socially on social computer behavior and having the computer display more cues about its social behavior may strengthen the social reaction. Obviously, there will not necessarily be a need to consider your own computer, let alone, every computer, as a personal friend with whom you want to share your feelings. Nevertheless, there will be many situations, especially in a personal environment, where people will prefer communicating with systems that show knowledge of the user and display reactive and pro-active behavior that shows understanding of the particular context of the user, including its mood and emotions. To do this we need other modalities in interaction and presenting information than just menu-based graphical user interfaces.

2.5   Embodied conversational agents and multimodality

In the previous sections we saw some examples of embodied conversational agents or virtual humans. Embodied conversational agents (ECAs) have become a well-established research area. Embodied agents are agents that are visible in the interface as animated cartoon characters or animated objects resembling human beings. Sometimes they just consist of an animated talking face, displaying facial expressions and, when using speech synthesis, having lip synchronization. These agents are used to inform and explain or even to demonstrate products or sequences of activities in educational, e-commerce or entertainment settings. We saw examples, Karin knowing how to inform theater visitors and Jacob assisting students. Experiments have shown that ECAs can increase the motivation of a student or a user interacting with the system. Lester et al. [1997] showed that a display of involvement by an embodied conversational agent motivates a student in doing (and continuing) his or her learning task. Some examples of embodied conversational agents are shown in Figure 2.13. From left to right we see: Jennifer James, a car saleswoman who attempts to build relationships of affection, trust and loyalty with her customers, Karin, informing about theater performances and selling tickets, Steve, educating a student about maintaining complex machinery, and Linda, a learning guide.

Figure 2.13.   Examples of 2D and 3D embodied agents.

In this section we will discuss the intelligence and nonverbal interaction of embodied conversational agents. We will look at the role of gestures and the role of gaze. Displaying emotions, in particular through facial expressions is another issue that will be discussed. Finally, we have a few words about ECA design that allows the development of interpersonal relationships.

2.5.1   Intelligence and nonverbal interaction

Embodiment allows more multimodality, therefore making interaction more natural and robust. Several authors have investigated nonverbal behavior among humans and the role and use of nonverbal behavior to support human-computer interaction. See e.g. [Cassell et al., 2000] for a collection of chapters on properties and impact of embodied conversational agents (with an emphasis on coherent facial expressions, gestures, intonation, posture and gaze in communication) and for the role of embodiment (and small talk) on fostering self-disclosure and trust building.

Current ECA research deals with improving intelligent behavior of these agents, but also with improving their verbal and nonverbal interaction capabilities. Improving intelligent behavior requires using techniques from artificial intelligence, in particular natural language processing. Domain knowledge and reasoning capabilities have to be modeled. Agent models have been developed that allow separation between the beliefs, desires and intentions of an agent. Together with dialogue modeling techniques rudimentary natural language interaction with such agents is becoming possible.

What role do gestures play in communication and why should we include them in an agent's interaction capability? Categories of gestures have been distinguished. Well known is a distinction in consciously produced gestures (emblematic and propositional gestures) and the spontaneous, unplanned gestures (iconic, metaphoric, deictic and beat gestures). Gestures convey meanings and are primarily found in association with spoken language. Different views exist on the role of gestures in communication. Are they for the benefit of the gesturer or for the listener? Gestures convey extra information [Kendon, 1980] about the internal mental processes of the speaker: "... *an alternative manifestation of the process by which ideas are encoded into patterns of behavior which can be apprehended by others as reportive of ideas.*" Observations show that natural gestures are related tot the information structure (e.g., the topic-focus distinction) and (therefore) the prosody of the spoken utterance. In addition they are related to the discourse structure and therefore also to the regulation of interaction (the turn taking process) in a dialogue. Apart from these viewpoints on embodiment, we can also emphasize the possibility of an embodied agent to walk around, to point at objects in a visualized domain, to manipulate objects or to change a visualized (virtual) environment. In these cases the embodiment can provide a point of the focus for interaction. When, for example, we introduce a guide in our virtual environments this is a main issue and more important than detailed facial expressions and the gestures discussed above.

2.5.2 The role of gaze

For believability and naturalness embodied conversational agents should also display life-like forms of non-verbal communication. In our environment, the face of Karen was designed to make control over its features possible. In the version of Karen that is currently accessible on the web, some changes in facial expressions are hard-coded to accompany some fixed elements in the interaction. For instance, Karin will look down at the table with performances when pointing out that more information can be found there. Currently a lot of research is going on that is specifically aimed at improving the non-verbal communication skills of Karin and other agents. This not only includes the use of facial expressions but also of gaze, gestures and posture.

Getting a system that behaves naturally in this respect involves tight coordination of the facial animation driver with many parameters of the dialogue manager, with the mental state of the character and its model of the user and subtle aspects of the linguistic utterance that is produced or attended to. Consider in this respect the functioning of gaze in human-human conversations [Argyle & Cook, 1976; Torres et al., 1997]. Gazing away from or towards the interlocutor can function as an important emotional signal as well as a signal to hand over the turn or avoid the turn to be taken over. As a function in the organization of turn-taking behavior, the timing of mutual gaze (eye-contact) correlates with the information-structure of the utterances (its topic-focus articulation).

In an experiment, we investigated the effects of different styles of gaze of Karin on the conversation. We had forty-eight subjects each make two reservations with different style versions. We videotaped the conversations, clocked the time they spent on the task, and had them fill in a questionnaire after they had made the reservations. It appeared that participants that had conversed with a version in which common gaze behavior was implemented (looking away and towards users and beginnings and ends of turns, respectively) appreciated their conversation significantly better than the other participants in most respects. They not only were more satisfied overall, they found it easier to use than a version with the minimal amount of eye-movements, appreciated the personality of the agent better and thought the head movements were more natural. They were also the fastest, on average, to complete the task. For more details and more results we refer to [Heylen et al., 2003]. This short summary already shows the important effects that can be achieved by paying attention to the non-verbal language signals of embodied conversational agents.

2.5.3   Emotional behavior, personality, friendship

Facial expressions and speech are the main modalities to express nonverbal emotion. Human beings do not express emotions using facial expressions and speech only. Generally they have their emotions displayed using a combination of modalities that interact with each other. We cannot consider one modality in isolation. Facial expressions are combined with speech. There are not only audio or visual stimuli, but also audio-visual stimuli when expressing emotions. A smile gesture will change voice quality, variations in speech intensity will change facial expression, etc. Attitude, mood and personality are other factors that make interpretation and generation of emotional expressions even less straightforward. In addition we can have different intensities of emotion and the blending of different emotions in an emotional expression. We should consider combinations and integration of speech, facial expressions, gestures, postures and bodily actions. It should be understood that these are displays and that they should follow from some emotional state that has been computed from sensory inputs of a human interactant, but also from an appraisal of the events that happen or have happened simultaneously or recently. A usual standpoint is that of appraisal theory, the evaluation of situations and categorizing arising affective states. It should be understood that what exactly is said and what exactly is done in a social and emotional setting is not part of the observations above. The importance of the meaning of words, phrases and sentences, uttered and to be interpreted in a specific context is not to be diminished. In Figure 2.14 we display Cyberella, an embodied agent, developed at DFKI in Saarbrücken. This agent is working as a receptionist. For example, she can provide directions to the office of a staff member. However, since she has been provided with an affective model, she also reacts emotionally to a visitor's utterances when appropriate [Gebhard, 2001].

Figure 2.14.   Cyberella, a virtual receptionist.

One of the issues we investigated was how aspects of personal attraction or friendship development [Stronks et al., 2002] can be made part of the design of an embodied agent that is meant to provide an information service to a human partner. As a 'lay psychologist', we all know that people that you like (or your friends) are able to help you better, teach you better, and generally are more fun to interact with, than people that you don't like. However, 'liking' is person dependent. Not everybody likes the same person, and one person is not liked by everyone. These observations sparked our interest in the application, effects, and design of a 'virtual friend'. An agent that observes it's user, and adapts it's personality, appearance and behavior according to the (implicit) likes and dislikes of the user, in order to 'become friends' with the user and create an affective interpersonal relationship. This agent might have additional benefits over a 'normal' embodied conversational agent in areas such as teaching, navigation assistance and entertainment.

There is extensive knowledge about human interpersonal relationships in the field of personality and social psychology. Aspects of friendship that need to be considered in ECA design are gender (e.g., activity-based men's friendship vs. affectively-based women's friendship), age, social class and ethnic background. Effects of friendship on interaction include increase of altruistic behavior, a positive impact on task performance and an increase in self-disclosure. Interpersonal attraction is an important factor in friendship. It is governed by positive reinforcements, and similarity between subjects is a key factor. Similarity of attitudes, personality, ethnicity, social class, humor, etc., reinforces the friendship relationship. Other issues are physical attractiveness (the 'halo effect') and reciprocity of liking (whether we think that the other person likes us). In [Stronks et al., 2002] we discussed the translation of the main aspects of human-human friendship to human-ECA friendship and how we can incorporate this translation in the design process of an ECA, using a scenario-based design. One observation is that it is important to distinguish between the initial design of an ECA and the possibility to change the ECA characteristics according to an adaptation strategy based on knowledge obtained by interacting with a particular user.

2.5.4 Humor in embodied conversational agents

In previous years researchers have discussed the potential role of humor in the interface. Humans use humor to ease communication problems and in a similar way humor can be used to solve communication problems that arise with human-computer interaction. For example, humor can help to make the imperfections of natural language interfaces more acceptable for the users and when humor is sparingly and carefully used it can make natural language interfaces much friendlier. During these years the potential role of embodied conversational agents was not at all clear, and no attention was paid to their possible role in the interface.

Humans employ a wide range of humor in conversations. Humor support, or the reaction to humor, is an important aspect of personal interaction and the given support shows the understanding and appreciation of humor. There are many different support strategies. Which strategy can be used in a certain situation is mainly determined by the context of the humorous event. The strategy can include smiles and laughter, the contribution of more humor, echoing the humor and offering sympathy. In order to give full humor support, humor has to be recognized, understood and appreciated. These factors determine our level of agreement on a humorous event and how we want to support the humor.

Humor plays an important role in interpersonal interactions. From the many CASA experiments we may extrapolate that humor will play a similar role in human-computer interactions. This has been confirmed with some specially designed experiments. There is not yet much research going on into embodied agents that interpret or generate humor in the interface. In [Nijholt, 2002] we discuss how useful it can be, both from the point of view of humor research and from the point of view of embodied conversational agent research, to pay attention to the role of humor in the interaction between humans and the possibility to translate it to the interactions between humans and embodied conversational agents. Graphics, animation and speech synthesis technology make it possible to have embodied agents that can display smiles, laughs and other signs of appreciation of the interaction or explicitly presented or generated humor. There are many applications that can profit from being able to employ such embodied agents. The designer of the interface can decide when in certain scenarios of interaction agents should display such behavior. However, much more in the line of research on autonomous (intelligent and emotional) agents we rather have an agent understand why the events that take place generate enjoyment by its conversational partner and why it should display enjoyment because of its appreciation of an humorous situation.

2.6 Conclusions

In this chapter we discussed the role of multimodality in human-computer interaction and in environments that know how to interpret human interactions and human-related events through multi-sensory perception. Examples of multimodal interfaces were shown. We emphasized the role of visualization in the interface, allowing us to consider interactions in virtual environments and their counterparts in real environments. Near term and long term roadmaps illustrating research issues until 2010 were presented. We zoomed in on the role of virtual humans in multimodal interfaces and virtual environments. We hardly were able to discuss interaction tools based on movement sensors, data gloves, eye trackers, haptic devices or physiological measurements. Several small-sized projects using such tools and devices are in progress in our research group. Another issue we did not discuss is the role of emerging standards and toolkits for designing virtual humans. They are concerned with the generation of gestures, facial expressions and body movements. Mark-up languages are being developed that allow designers to describe these nonverbal expressions. We think that our agent-oriented approaches, our layered software architectures and our attempts to model multimodality on a sufficiently abstract level will allow us to integrate known and not yet considered modalities in the current ideas and models of fusion and coordination.

Acknowledgments

In this chapter we surveyed part of our research on multimodal interfaces in the last three years. Many students and researchers contributed to this research. In particular we would like to thank: Betsy van Dijk, Rieks op den Akker, Dirk Heylen, Job Zwiers, Ivo van Es, Jeroen van Luin, Bas Stronks, Wauter Bosma, Natasa Jovanovic, Dennis Hofs and Marc Evers. Hendri Hondorp took care of the final text editing and formatting of this chapter. Harry Bunt (Tilburg), Oliviero Stock (Trento) and Gerhard Rigoll (München) were helpful in obtaining some of the pictures included in this chapter.

References

Argyle, M., and M. Cook [1976]. *Gaze and Mutual Gaze*. Cambridge University Press, Cambridge.

Broersen, A., and A. Nijholt [2002]. Developing a virtual piano playing environment. In *Proc. IEEE International Conference on Advanced Learning Technologies (ICALT 2002)*, V. Petrushin, P. Kommers, Kinshuk, and I. Galeev (eds.), Kazan, Russia, pages 278–282.

Bunt, H., and R.-J. Beun (eds.) [2001]. *Cooperative Multimodal Communication*. CMC'98 Selected Papers, Springer.

Bunt, H., M. Kipp, M.T. Maybury, and W. Wahlster [2003]. Fusion and coordination for multimodal interactive information presentation. Chapter in *Intelligent Information Presentation*, O. Stock & M. Zancanaro (eds.), Kluwer Academic Publishers.

Cassell, J., J. Sullivan, S. Prevost, and E. Churchill (eds.) [2000]. *Embodied Conversational Agents*. The MIT Press.

Darken, R.P, and J.L. Silbert [1996]. Way finding strategies and behaviors in virtual worlds. In *Proc. CHI*, pages 142–149.

Evers, M., and A. Nijholt [2000]. Jacob - an animated instruction agent for virtual reality. In *Advances in Multimodal Interfaces - ICMI 2000*, Proc. Third International Conference on Multimodal Interfaces, Beijing, China, Lecture Notes in Computer Science 1948, T. Tan, Y. Shi, and W. Gao (eds.), Springer-Verlag, Berlin, pages 526–533.

Gebhard, P. [2001]. Enhancing embodied intelligent agents with affective user modelling. *UM2001, 8th International Conference*, J. Vassileva and P. Gmytrasiewicz, (eds.), Berlin, Springer.

Heylen, D., I. van Es, B. van Dijk, and A. Nijholt [2003]. Experimenting with the gaze of a conversational agent. Chapter in *Natural, Intelligent and Effective Interaction in Multimodal Dialogue Systems*, J. van Kuppevelt, L. Dybkjaer, and N.O. Bernsen (eds.), Kluwer Academic Publishers.

Hofs, D., R. op den Akker, and A. Nijholt [2003]. A generic architecture and dialogue model for multimodal interaction. Submitted for publication.

Höök, K., et al. [1988]. Towards a framework for design and evaluation of navigation in electronic spaces. Personal deliverable for the EC.

Hospers, M., E. Kroezen, A. Nijholt, R. op den Akker, and D. Heylen [2003]. Developing a generic agent-based intelligent tutoring system and applying it to nurse education. In *Proc. IEEE International Conference on Advanced Language Technologies (ICALT '03)*, Athens, Greece.

Johnston, M., P. Cohen, D. McGee, S. Oviat, J. Pittman, and I. Smith [1997]. Unification-based multimodal integration. In *Proc. of the 35th Annual ACL Conference*, New Jersey, pages 281–288.

Johnston, M., and S. Bangalore [2000]. Finite-state multimodal parsing and understanding. In *Proc. of COLING-2000*, Saarbrücken, Germany.

Kendon, A. [1980]. Gesticulation and speech: Two aspects of the process of utterance. In *The Relation of Verbal and Nonverbal Communication*, M.R. Key (ed.), Mouton, The Hague, the Netherlands.

Lester, J.C., et al. [1997]. The persona effect: Affective impact of animated pedagogical agents. *CHI '97 Human Factors in Computing Systems*, ACM, pages 359–356.

Luin, J. van, R. op den Akker, and A. Nijholt [2001]. A dialogue agent for navigation support in virtual reality. Extended abstracts *ACM SIGCHI Conference CHI 2001: Anyone. Anywhere.* ACM, J. Jacko and A. Sears (eds.), Seattle, pages 117–118.

Maybury, M., and W. Wahlster (eds.) [1988]. *Readings in Intelligent User Interfaces*. Morgan Kaufmann Press.

McCowan, I., S. Bengio, D. Gatica-Perez, G. Lathoud, F. Monay, D. Moore, P. Wellner, and H. Bourlard [2003]. Modeling human interaction in meetings. In *Proc. IEEE ICASSP*, Hong Kong.

Mikic, I., K. Huang, and M. Trivedi [2000]. Activity monitoring and summarization for an intelligent meeting room. In *Proc. IEEE Workshop on Human Motion*, Austin, Texas.

Nigay, L., and J. Coutaz [1995]. A generic platform for addressing the multimodal challenge. In *Proc. ACM CHI*, pages 98–105.

Nijholt, A., and J. Hulstijn [2000]. Multimodal interactions with agents in virtual worlds. Chapter 8 in *Future Directions for Intelligent Information Systems and Information Science*, N. Kasabov (ed.), Physica-Verlag, Springer, Heidelberg, pages 148–173.

Nijholt, A. [2002]. Embodied agents: A new impetus to humor research. *The April Fools Day Workshop on Computational Humour*, O. Stock, C. Strapparava, and A. Nijholt (eds.), In Proc. Twente Workshop on Language Technology 20 (TWLT 20), Trento, Italy, pages 101–111.

Nijholt, A., J. Zwiers, and B. van Dijk [2003]. Maps, agents and dialogue for exploring a virtual world. Chapter in *Web Computing*. J. Aguilar, N. Callaos, and E.L. Leiss (eds).

Oviat, S., P. Cohen, L. Wu, J. Vergo, L. Duncan, B. Suhm, J. Bers, T. Holzman, T. Winograd, J. Landay, J. Larson, and D. Ferro [2000]. *Designing the User Interface for Multimodal Speech and Gesture Applications: State-of-the-Art Systems and Research Directions for 2000 and Beyond*. Report.

Potter, D. (WP5-Team) [2003]. *Future Workspaces: A Strategic Roadmap for Defining Distributed Engineering Workspaces of the Future*. IST-2001-38346 deliverable.

Reeves, B., and C. Nass [1996]. *The Media Equation*. Cambridge University Press, Cambridge.

Shechtman, N., and L.M. Horowitz [2003]. Media inequality in conversation: how people behave differently when interacting with computers and people. In *Proc. SIGCHI-ACM CHI 2003: New Horizons*, ACM, New York, pages 281–288.

Stronks, B., A. Nijholt, P. van der Vet, and D. Heylen [2002]. Designing for friendship: Becoming friends with your ECA. In *Proc. Embodied Conversational Agents - Let's Specify and Evaluate Them!*, A. Marriott, C. Pelachaud, T. Rist, and Zs. Ruttkay (eds.), Bologna, Italy, pages 91–97.

Torres, O., J. Cassell, and S. Prevost [1997]. Modeling gaze behavior as a function of discourse structure. In *Proc. First International Workshop on Human Computer Conversations*. Bellagio, Italy.

Zobl, M., F. Wallhoff, and G. Rigoll [2003]. Action recognition in meeting scenarios using global motion features. In *Proc. IEEE International Workshop on Performance Evaluation of Tracking and Surveillance*.

Chapter 3

FROM STEREOTYPES TO PERSONAL PROFILES VIA VIEWER FEEDBACK

Srinivas Gutta, Kaushal Kurapati, and David Schaffer

Abstract   For a Personal Video Recorder (PVR) to provide an enriched TV experience to the user, personalization, achieved via a recommender engine, is the key. One of the thorny problems facing a recommender system is that of a *cold start*: how does one capture the user preferences quickly and effectively and provide user-specific personalization? To address the cold start problem, we propose a stereotype-enabled personalization framework that transforms a user's TV profile from a stereotypical, initial profile, to a personalized, more relevant one. The stereotypes have been derived from a sample set of users who have been contributing their TV viewing histories for periods ranging from five months to two years. We conducted three sets of experiments, each with a different set of stereotypes applied to all the users. The best performance is in the range of 11% error. This performance compares favorably with the best we have got to date on recommenders trained on user-specific data.

Keywords   Stereotypes, TV recommender, cold-start problem, bootstrapping.

3.1   Introduction

The overarching vision of ambient intelligence is the creation of a seamless digital environment that is constantly aware of the presence and context of users and is sensitive, adaptive and responsive to their needs, habits, interests, gestures and emotions. Ambient intelligence stems from the union of three key areas ubiquitous/pervasive computing, ubiquitous communication, intuitive and intelligent user interfaces. Ambient systems are expected to be non-intrusive, be present everywhere yet invisible. We advance in this chapter one such system that is adaptive and responsive to the needs of the user. Specifically, the system described below recommends content of interest based on the users viewing preferences.

W. Verhaegh et al. (eds.), Algorithms in Ambient Intelligence, 55-69.
© 2004 *Kluwer Academic Publishers. Printed in the Netherlands.*

Personal Television is here via a new class of devices called personal video recorders (PVRs). For a PVR to provide an enriched TV experience to the user, personalization is the key. PVRs need to be equipped with sophisticated recommender systems that track and recognize user preferences and help them select good content to fill the hard disk. This chapter presents the research that was done in the general area of recommender systems and more specifically, in the areas of *effective bootstrapping of recommender systems and learning via user feedback*.

Much work has been done in the area of recommender systems and they have been applied to a wide range of disciplines. Many systems have been built in recent years to help users deal with large quantities of information coming from various sources: e-mail (Maxims [Lashkari et al., 1994]), usenet news (NewT [Sheth & Maes, 1993]), the web (Letizia [Lieberman, 1997], Syskill and Webert [Pazzani et al., 1996], movies (MovieLens [Sarwar et al., 2001]), music (PATS [Pauws & Eggen, 2002]), and TV (TV-Advisor [Das & Ter Horst, 1998], PTV [Cotter & Smyth, 2000], 3-way-TV-Recommender [Gutta et al., 2000; Kurapati et al., 2001]). TV-Advisor and one prong of 3-way TV recommender make use of explicit techniques to generate recommendations for a TV viewer. Such techniques require the user to take the initiative and explicitly specify their interests, in order to get high quality recommendations. Implicit techniques, on the other hand, lessen the burden on the user and try to infer the user's preferences from a viewer's TV viewing history. The 3-way-TV-recommender [Gutta et al., 2000; Kurapati et al., 2001] uses 3 sources of user information: explicit, implicit and any feedback the user might give on individual shows.

Irrespective of the type of technique used, all of them suffer from the following problems: (a) new viewers are required to fill in lengthy questionnaires specifying their preferences at a coarse level of granularity (explicit), (b) they derive a profile completely unobtrusively from observing viewing behaviors (implicit) and thus require a long time to become accurate and/or (c) rating history needs to be acquired before comparing a against a sufficient number of other users (collaborative). The question then becomes, how to bootstrap a TV recommender system *quickly* and *effectively*? This is the crux of the '*cold start problem*'.

We propose a stereotypes-based personalization framework to address this problem. Stereotypes are a set of pre-derived profiles designed to reflect the 'stereotypical' patterns of TV shows watched by real viewers. For example, a person watching sitcoms (situation comedies), news and action shows can be captured by a combination of stereotypes catering to each of these viewing patterns: Comedy-buff + NewsJunkie + ActionPerson. A stereotype is usually defined in terms of clusters where each cluster consists of a particular segment of TV-shows exhibiting a specific pattern. A new viewer then chooses the stereotype(s) believed to be closest to his/her own interests to jump-start his/her profile. While the examples above appear to be simple genre-based clusters, we wish to make no prior assumptions as to how TV viewing patterns will cluster. Such assumptions are the basis of the explicit prong. The hope of this research is that real viewing patterns will induce fewer and more meaningful clusters that will simplify the task of specifying one's interests for most viewers. After the initialization, the profile adjusts and 'evolves' towards the specific, personal viewing behavior of each individual user, depending on his/her recording pattern, and the feedback given on shows.

The chapter is organized as follows: Sections 2 and 3 provide specific details regarding the generation of stereotypes and the profile transformation framework. Extensive experiments that were carried out are discussed in Section 4. Conclusions from our work are presented in Section 5, including the future directions for this research.

3.2   Stereotype generation

The process of deriving stereotypes-clusters of TV shows that are 'similar' to one another-begins with the application of an unsupervised data-clustering algorithm such as 'k-means' to the view history data set. The algorithm proceeds by partitioning the example data set into clusters such that points (TV shows) in one cluster are closer to the mean (centroid) of that cluster than any other cluster. The mean of the cluster becomes the representative TV show for the entire cluster. To determine closeness of a TV show to a cluster, we need to be able to compute distances between TV shows. In the following sub-section we describe the distance metric that has been used in the clustering algorithm. The following sub-sections also describe the clustering algorithm and the clustering results.

3.2.1   Distance metric for symbolic features

All clustering methods use some kind of distance metric to quantify the distinction between the various examples in a sample data set and decide on the extent of a cluster. To be able to cluster TV shows, we need to compute distances between any two TV shows in different viewers' view histories. TV shows that are 'close' to one another tend to fall into one cluster. It is relatively straightforward to define distances between numerical valued vectors: Euclidean distance, Manhattan distance, and Mahalanobis distance are some of the methods most commonly used. However, we cannot use those methods in the case of TV show vectors because TV shows comprise of 'symbolic' feature values. For instance, two TV shows such as "Friends", which aired on NBC at 8 pm on March 22, 2001, and "Simpsons" which aired on FOX at 8 pm on March 25, 2001, can be represented by the following feature vectors.

Channel: NBC   Channel: FOX
Air-date: 2001-03-22   Air-date: 2001-03-25
Air-time: 2000   Air-time: 2000
Title: Friends   Title: Simpsons

One cannot use any known numerical distance metric to compute the distance between "NBC" and "FOX" for instance. Therefore, in order to compute distances between symbolic features we use the Modified Value Difference Metric (MVDM) that takes into account the overall similarity of classification of all instances for each possible value of each feature [Cost & Salzberg, 1993]. Using this method, a matrix defining the distance between all values of a feature is derived statistically, based on the examples in the training set. We have adopted the MVDM for our purpose of computing distance between feature values of two TV shows. According to MVDM, the distance δ between two TV shows or between two attribute values is given in the equations below. In these equations, X and Y correspond to TV shows, small x and y to attribute values, m to the number of classes, and n to the number of features.

$$\delta(X,Y) = \sum_{f=1}^{n} \delta(x_f, y_f)$$

$$\delta(x_f, y_f) = \sum_{i=1}^{m} \left| \frac{C_i(x_f)}{C(x_f)} - \frac{C_i(y_f)}{C(y_f)} \right|$$

For our case, we rewrite the equation as shown below to deal specifically with the classes *watched* (w): shows watched by the user, and *not-watched* (nw): shows not watched by the user.

$$\delta(V_1, V_2) = \left| \frac{C_1^w}{C_1} - \frac{C_2^w}{C_2} \right| + \left| \frac{C_1^{nw}}{C_1} - \frac{C_2^{nw}}{C_2} \right|$$

In the above equation, V_1 and V_2 are two possible values for the feature under consideration, e.g. $V_1 = $ NBC, $V_2 = $ FOX, for the feature 'channel'. The distance between the values is a sum over all classes, into which the examples are classified. C_1^i is the number of times V_1 (NBC) was classified into class i ($i = $ 'w' implies class watched) and C_1 is the total number of times V_1 occurred in the data set.

The idea behind the metric is that the attribute values are similar if they occur with the same relative frequency for all classifications. The term C_1^i / C_1 represents the likelihood that the central residue will be classified as i given that the feature in question has value V_1. Thus, we say that two values are similar if they give similar likelihoods for all possible classifications. Thus distance between two TV shows is the sum of the distances between corresponding feature values of the two TV-show vectors.

A small portion of the distance table for the values associated with the attribute 'channel' would help explain the distance metric better. Table 1 below
shows the number of occurrences of each value for each class. Table 2 displays the distances between these feature values computed from the counts in
Table 1. The values shown in Table 1 have been taken from the composite view
history of all users that were providing data to us. Intuitively, NBC and ABC
should be 'close' to one another since they occur mostly in the class watched
and do not occur (ABC has a small not-watched component) in the class not-
watched. Table 2 confirms this with a small (non-zero) distance between NBC
and ABC. ESPN, on the contrary, occurs mostly in the class not-watched and
hence should be 'distant' to both NBC and ABC, for this data set. Table 2
shows the distance between NBC and ESPN to be 1.875, out of a maximum
possible distance of 2.0. Similarly, the distance between ABC and ESPN is
high: 1.872.

Table 3.1.   Number of occurrences of "Channel" feature values for each class.

	classes	
feature values	*watched*	*not watched*
NBC	353	0
ESPN	1	18
ABC	145	5

Table 3.2.   Value distance table for "Channel" feature values computed using MVDM.

	NBC	ESPN	ABC
NBC	0	1.895	0.066
ESPN	1.895	0	1.828
ABC	0.066	1.828	0

3.2.2   Clustering algorithm

We derive stereotypes by applying an unsupervised clustering algorithm, 'k-
means', to a composite view history data set that is a collection of all the shows
watched by our sample set of users. The algorithm we used to generate clusters
of TV shows is shown below in Figure 1.

Start with $k = 2$ clusters
repeat
    increment cluster size k to $k+1$
    initialize k clusters (say, the first k TV shows in the view history)
    repeat
        (re)compute cluster means (μ_i)
        for each show in view history pool
            if closest cluster to show $\neq$ current cluster of show
            then move show to closest cluster
    until (no shows have moved from clusters)
until (classification performance improves OR an empty cluster is found)
output k, the stable cluster size, and the clusters' contents

Figure 3.1. k-means algorithm used to cluster TV shows.

A key step in the clustering algorithm of Figure 1 is the computation of *symbolic mean* of a cluster. For numerical features, the mean is the value that minimizes the variance. Extending the concept to symbolic features, we can define the mean of a cluster by finding the show that minimizes intra-cluster variance [Cost & Salzberg, 1993] (and hence the radius or the extent of the cluster),

$$Var(J) = \sum_{i \in J}(x_i - x_\mu)^2 \quad R(J) = \sqrt{Var(J)}$$

where $R(J)$ is a cluster radius, J is a cluster of TV shows, x_i is a symbolic feature value for show i, and x_μ is a feature value from one of the TV shows in J such that it minimizes $Var(J)$. Computationally, each show in J is tried as x_μ and the show that minimizes the variance becomes the mean for the symbolic feature under consideration in cluster J. There are two types of mean computation that are possible: show-based mean and feature-based mean.

In the feature-based case, the cluster mean is made up of feature values drawn from the examples in the cluster because the mean for symbolic attributes must be one of its possible values. It is important to note that the cluster mean, however, might be a 'hypothetical' TV show. The feature values of this 'hypothetical show' could include a channel value drawn from one of the examples (say, NBC) and the title value drawn from another of the examples (say, BBC World News, which, in reality never airs on NBC).

Alternately, in the formula for the variance, x_i could be the TV-show i itself and similarly x_μ is the show in cluster J that minimizes the variance over the set of shows in J. In this case, the distance between the shows and not the individual feature values is the relevant metric to be minimized. Also, the resulting mean in this case is *not* a hypothetical show, but is a show picked right from the set *J*. We have implemented both versions for the mean computation.

3.2.3 Clustering results

We had view histories for a total of 10 users. We divided these 10 users into 2 sets. The first set consisted of 7 users (A, C, D, F, G, H and I) and the second set consisted of 3 users (J, K and O). We used a total of 1,496 unique shows corresponding to the view histories of the 7 users as input to our clustering process.

After experimenting with a wide range of parameters (number of initial shows per cluster, etc.), we arrived at a set of 18 clusters that seemed to reasonably reflect the viewing patterns of the sample user set that we used to cluster the TV shows. This was observed by eyeballing the formed clusters against the TV shows. These clusters were the basis for deriving the stereotypical profiles used in our experiments, the results of which are reported in section 4. We used a subset of shows from our pooled view history to test the classification accuracy of the clustering process. For each show in the test set, we compute the cluster closest to it and compare the class labels for the cluster and the show under consideration. The percentage of matched class labels is the accuracy of the clustering process. The accuracy of cluster classification, into watched and not-watched, is 98.5%. There were 15 clusters labeled watched and 3 labeled not-watched. A cluster is labeled positive if it has more shows coming from the actual view histories of all users 'watched' (hence, positive), than from the set of randomly picked 'not-watched' (hence, negative) shows. The positive clusters tend to be the exact representations of parts of viewing patterns of the sample users that were used in the clustering process. They also tend to be 'tighter', i.e., smaller in size and adhering to a particular pattern of TV viewing (conforming to a genre, or a specific day + time combination, or channel, etc.). The negative clusters tend to be larger and lack particular focus in viewing tendencies. This should be expected because the negative shows (not-watched shows) were picked by uniform random sampling of the TV schedule database and hence do not conform to a focused, specific viewing pattern.

Following are the key details on the clusters labeled positive.

- The most popular categories among clusters are 'crime drama' and 'drama'. There are five clusters spanning both these categories. Again, finer distinctions such as 'science fiction' (X-files), 'fantasy' (Touched by an Angel), and 'medical' (ER, Gideon's Crossing), in addition to the base 'drama' or 'crime drama' separate clusters from one another.

- The second most popular category mix among clusters are 'comedy, situation'. The four clusters with this category mix seem to be further differentiated among themselves as per 'channel' (NBC or CBS or other: TBS, WPIX, Fox, etc.) or day + time combination.

- The third most popular category mix among clusters is 'Talk, Magazine, News'. The categories of 'game' (Jeopardy! and Who Wants to be a Millionaire) and 'biography' also find place in these clusters, albeit sparsely.

- Finally, there is one cluster that has 'Children, Animated' as its dominant theme and another cluster, which has a sprinkling of 'Comedy' and 'Drama, Fantasy', etc. in it. This last cluster, with miscellaneous categories mixed in it, has to do mainly with channel distinction than genre distinction.

3.3 Personalization framework

As discussed, all recommender systems face the cold-start problem: how to bootstrap a recommender system quickly and effectively? We wished to estimate of how effective it might be to initialize with stereotypes and then have the profiles adapt to a better and better approximation of the true profile by viewer-feedback. Without the luxury of real volunteers to do this experiment, we simulated it. The framework for these simulations is shown in Figure 2.We have taken the approach of seeding a user's initial profile with a stereotypical profile. In order to 'simulate' the user feedback, we used ground-truth data we had acquired from users in an earlier test [Kurapati et al., 2001]. Using this approach we acquired estimates of the error rates for randomly selected initial profiles and the reduction in errors as feedback accumulated.

A user's profile is initialized with a combination of stereotypes (making up the positive and negative view histories). In reality, the user will choose the stereotypes that appear closest to his/her TV preferences. In our experiments, we have chosen the stereotypes, mostly at random, on the user's behalf. We used the Bayesian recommender [Kurapati et al., 2001] in our experiments, but any other TV show recommender can be used in practice: the recommender is a black-box in the scenario of this framework (see Figure 2).

The system first computes the recommender scores for all the shows in the user's ground-truth set based on the stereotype-initialized user profile. Then the errors between the ground-truth and the recommender scores form the basis for simulating the feedback. The ground-truth (GT) shows are sorted in a descending order on the basis of the square of the error between the ground-truth and the recommender score. The GT was collected from the users, on several shows based on the question: whether they would watch this show? The answer choices for the users were: $+1$: yes I would watch this show, -1: no I would not watch this show, 0: may be I would watch this show, and 'do not know' this show. The shows that the users marked 'do not know' were

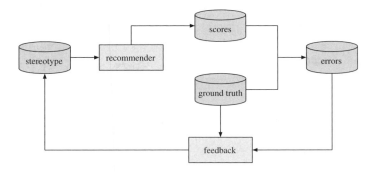

Figure 3.2. Framework for profile transformation: stereotypes to personal profiles.

eliminated from the experiments we describe in this document since they do not provide any basis for comparing recommendation scores.

In each iteration of the profile transformation process, the show with the largest squared error is picked as the candidate for feedback. Depending on that show's GT value (what the user said about that show), the simulated feedback is generated and applied to update the user profile. The simulated feedback follows the following empirical algorithm: if the GT is +1, the user loves the show and hence the feedback is put at +3. Feedback of +3 implies that all of this show's features are incremented by +3 in the user profile. The positive counts are updated because the GT value is +1 (the user loves the show, hence the show is reinforced on the positive side). Similarly, if the GT value is −1, the user presumably hates the show and all the negative feature counts pertaining to this show are updated in the user profile. The steps involved in the profile transformation framework are listed in Figure 3. The algorithm to simulate feedback based on ground-truth is listed in Figure 4.

The flexibility of our framework is that it can work with any recommender system, which is essentially a black box as far as the profile transformation is concerned. Furthermore, any number of empirical schemes to simulate the impact of user feedback on the profile can be used within the context of our framework. The feedback scheme we considered was symmetric: the magnitude of the 'force' applied to a profile's features is the same for ground-truth of +1 and −1. However, other schemes such as asymmetric feedback can be considered and tested with our framework.

3.4 Experiments

In this section we present the results of the experiments we conducted with our profile transformation framework on the data from ten real users. We initialized the profiles for each of the ten users with various stereotypical profiles and observed the rate of progression of the mean squared error with feedback

initialize the user profile with a stereotypical profile
compute recommendation scores for ground-truth shows based on initial
    profile
compute errors $(GT - recom\_score)^2$ for each show & total sum squared error
repeat
        sort (descending) GT shows based on individual show errors
        pick show with largest error as candidate for feedback
        calculate simulated feedback value (Figure 4 below)
        update user profile counts based on simulated feedback value
        recompute recom. scores for GT shows based on updated profile
        recompute individual show errors and total sum squared error
        print trace per iteration of current mean sum squared error
while (num_iterations < number of GT shows or as specified)

Figure 3.3.   Steps in the profile transformation framework.

---

cycle. First we describe the experimental user data used in our experiments. Finally we present the experimental results and discuss the trends in them.

3.4.1   Data composition

We have conducted the profile transformation experiments over a sample set of ten real users. These users have contributed their view histories for periods ranging from five months to two years. We used 7 users' view histories to construct the stereotypical profiles for our experiments. We then tested the profile transformation framework by testing on 'unseen' data of three users: K, J, and O. The number of ground-truth shows that could be used for our experiments varied from user to user. This was mainly due to the variable number of shows marked by each user as 'do not know'. The minimum number of ground-truth shows used in our experiments was 70 for user K and the maximum number was for 267 for user F. We eliminated any duplicate shows present in the ground-truth data.

In the profile transformation iterative loop, we limited the experiments to run for as many iterations as the number of shows being considered in the ground-truth for a particular user. We also restricted the number of times each show in the ground-truth data could be chosen as the candidate show for automatic feedback, to five so as to prevent the process from getting stuck in a local minima. Our intuition is that this parameter dictates the rate of progression of error, but in the current set of experiments being reported in this chapter,

for the candidate show for feedback (FB), retrieve ground truth (GT) value
if (GT == 1)
　　FB = +3　　　// user loves show; reinforce pos. feature counts thrice
elseif (GT == −1)
　　FB = −3　　　// user hates show; reinforce neg. feature counts thrice
elseif ((GT == 0) and (recom_score > 0.5))
　　FB = +2　　　// user is unsure on the show, but recommender is pos., so
　　　　　　　　// reinforce positive counts, but only twice
elseif ((GT == 0) and (recom_score < −0.5))
　　FB = −2　　　// user is unsure on the show, but recommender is neg., so
　　　　　　　　// reinforce negative counts, but only twice
elseif ((GT == 0) and (0.25 < recom_score < 0.5))
　　FB = +1　　　// user is unsure on the show, and recommender is mildly
　　　　　　　　// pos., so reinforce positive counts, but only once
elseif ((GT == 0) and (−0.5 < recom_score < −0.25))
　　FB = −1　　　// user is unsure on the show, and recommender is mildly
　　　　　　　　// neg., so reinforce negative counts, but only once
elseif ((GT == 0) and (−0.25 < recom_score < 0.25))
　　FB = 0　　　　// user is unsure and so is the recommender;
　　　　　　　　// do nothing in this iteration.

Figure 3.4.　Empirical algorithm to compute simulated feedback value and update user profile feature counts, based on ground-truth.

we have not evaluated the sensitivity of the error rate to changes on that input factor.

3.4.2　Selection of stereotypes for profile initialization

In a real deployment, users would choose the clusters of TV shows that seem to reflect their viewing behavior to construct their seed stereotypical profile. Before calling in our users to do the same for us, we decided to test our profile transformation framework with stereotypes that were randomly constructed from various cluster combinations. We built stereotypical profiles out of combinations of three, four, and five cluster sets. We randomly selected three clusters and labeled them as 'positive clusters'. Next we automatically selected a set of three clusters such that they were farthest from the positive cluster set. These were labeled as 'negative clusters'. Together, the three positive and three negative clusters formed a stereotypical profile. The same process applies to cluster sets of size four and five.

3.4.3   Experimental runs

To evaluate the profile transformation framework, we ran three sets of experiments. We used the Bayesian TV show recommender [Gutta et al., 2000; Kurapati et al., 2001] to generate recommendation scores in the profile transformation process.

- Experiment 1: Stereotypes built from three positive and three negative clusters were used as seed profiles. The stereotype selection process was repeated ten times, with different sets of three clusters being considered each time. The same set of stereotypes were applied to all users.

- Experiment 2: Same as Experiment 1 except that the stereotypes consist of four positive and four negative clusters.

- Experiment 3: Same as Experiment 1 except that the stereotypes consist of five positive and five negative clusters.

The errors reported are normalized based on the number of ground-truth shows that could be used in the experiments for each user. The normalization of the total sum-squared error gives the mean squared error. We further normalize the mean-squared error to adjust for the errors being computed on a $[-1.0, 1.0]$ scale, to arrive at the percentage errors.

Cold-start performance.   Our goal in constructing this stereotype-based profile transformation framework was to address the 'cold-start' problem. Our intuition was to achieve a quick and effective way of initializing TV-recommender systems via stereotypes. To that extent, we observed the 'initial % errors' for the ten users in each experiment.

User K comes out top with best initial error ranging between 28 to 32% for experimental runs one through three. This means that stereotypes start out at a point that is very close to some of the best performing recommender systems we have built to date. If the stereotype was not chosen properly, then the initial error could be around 60%. On an average over all users and runs, the stereotypes seem to start out at an error of 40%. The best start need not necessarily mean that stereotype would yield the minimum error over a period of time. Similarly, a bad start need not lead to worse error rates in the long run. From our experiments, we could only find a couple of instances when the best start (user G, five positive + five negative clusters and user K, three positive + three negative clusters) yielded the best or the second best overall minimum error. The users' appetite for and perception of a 40% average initial, out-of-the-box error needs to be tested out in focus groups for us to get a good handle on the issue of whether these initial error rates are acceptable or not. We believe that given more view histories, drawn from a wider population pool, as input to the clustering algorithms, the stereotypes would better reflect the typical viewer's tastes leading to a better out-of-the-box performance.

Best performance. Table 3 below gives the overall best performances for all users and stereotypes (constructed from 3+3, 4+4, and 5+5 clusters). The best performance is the minimum of all the minimum errors for a particular user, over all stereotypes that were generated using a specified number of clusters.

The overall conclusion is that performance we obtain at this stage is the same as that was obtained if a recommender was trained on each user's view history [Kurapati et al., 2001]. For example, we observed earlier that using our Bayesian and Decision Tree based TV show recommenders, we had an error rate of 22% for user K. By using 3 positive and 3 negative clusters, for user K, with the profile transformation framework, we were able to drive the error down to 13%. Averaging across all users and all stereotypes used in our experiments (total of 30 data points: ten users, three experimental runs), we get the average best performance to be 26.7% error.

For all the users except users H and K, we observe that there is almost no difference in the best performances as the number of clusters that were used to build stereotypes increased. In general we observe that there is no marked improvement in the average performance when the number of clusters that constitutes a stereotype is increased from 6 (3 positive + 3 negative) to 8 (4 positive + 4 negative) and 10 (5 positive + 5 negative).

Table 3.3. Overall best performance across experimental runs.

best performance for runs 1,2 & 3	A	C	D	F	*user* G	H	I	J	K	O
experiment 1	27	24	26	17	27	11	29	39	13	33
experiment 2	30	25	25	19	26	28	28	38	22	36
experiment 3	28	27	27	18	26	30	30	38	20	34

Rate of personalization.   The question of how long it takes to get to the best minimum error points (shown above in Table 3) is worth exploring. The answer to this depends on how fast a user consumes TV shows. The average show-watching rate, across all users in our data set, is 10.8 shows/week. For the best performing users, F, H, K (Table 1), the rates are 19.9, 7.15, and 13.4 shows/week, respectively. User F is the closest to the typical US TV viewer, in our sample set. For these users, it took 210 (F), 135 (H), and 70 (K) shows to reduce the mean-squared error to their best minimum points. If these users were to watch at the rate they have been watching, and if they were to give feedback on every show they watched, then it would take the system 10.5, 18.8, and 5.22 weeks, respectively, to achieve the best performance. We believe that experimenting with various empirical feedback schemes and richer stereotypes can yield faster rates of personalization

3.5 Conclusion

We have developed a practical, viable, TV-recommender and profiling framework. This framework provides a solution to the cold start problem: how to jump start TV-recommender systems quickly and effectively? Our approach is to build a library of stereotypical TV viewer profiles, which reflect the viewing behavior of a majority of the population, and populate boxes (PVRs) with these profiles. Users can choose a collection of these stereotypes to initialize their profiles and start getting recommendations 'out-of-the-box'. In this chapter we quantified the 'out-of-the-box' performance for our initial set of stereotypes derived from a set of seven sample users.

The best initial error rates we got were around 30%. This is an excellent starting point for a recommender system; and from the user's perspective, the perceived performance out-of-the-box is very good (we have not validated that from user tests, but this is an educated guess).

The other important issue we investigated was to figure out how personalized-these stereotypes could become. We used user provided ground truth data to simulate feedback and guide the stereotypical initial profiles towards personal profiles. We measured the error rates over the ground truth data. The average best-case performance was found to be around 26.7%. The best-case performances for a couple of users ranged around 11% error.

The rate of personalization of stereotypes seemed to vary widely in our experiments. The three users (F, H, and K) who had the best results (error rates: 18%, 11%, and 13% respectively) required 10, 18, and 5 weeks respectively to get to that level of recommender accuracy. Given this wide range for rates of personalization on a limited data set, we feel further experimentation is warranted to determine the reasons for faster and slower personalization.

We observed that the error does not always progress in a monotonic manner. Nevertheless, the general tendency, we observed in our experiments, is towards a lower error rate with increasing feedback. We realize that the fluctuations in the errors might be a close reflection of the ways in which a multitude of users in the general population might deal with such a system (giving conflicting feedback, or less to no feedback at all).

We have identified several areas for improvement in our framework: build richer stereotypes from a wider and deeper pool of user data, such as from Nielsen Media Research, and experiment with asymmetric and accelerated feedback empirical schemes and identify those that work the best for a given situation.

References

Cost, S., and S. Salzberg [1993]. A weighted nearest neighbor algorithm for learning with symbolic features. *Int. J. Machine Learning*, 10:57–58.

Cotter, P., and B. Smyth [2000]. PTV - personalised TV guides. In *Proceedings of the 12th Conference on Innovative Applications of Artificial Intelligence*, IAAI, Austin, Texas.

Das, D., and H. ter Horst [1998]. Recommender systems for TV. In *Proceedings of the 15th National Conference of AAAI*.

Gutta, S., K. Kurapati, K.P. Lee, J. Martino, J. Milanski, D. Schaffer, and J. Zimmerman [2000]. TV content recommender system. In *Proceedings of the 17th National Conference of AAAI*, Austin, Texas.

Kurapati, K., S. Gutta, D. Schaffer, J. Martino, and J. Zimmerman, [2001]. A multi-agent TV recommender. In *Proceedings of the Workshop on Personalization in Future TV, User Modeling*, Sonthofen, Germany.

Lashkari, Y., M. Metral, and P. Maes [1994]. Collaborative interface agents. In *Proceedings of the National Conference on Artificial Intelligence*, AAAI, Seattle.

Lieberman, H. [1997]. Autonomous interface agents. In *Proceedings of Conference on Human Interaction*, Atlanta.

Pauws, S., and B. Eggen [2002]. PATS - realization and evaluation of an automatic playlist generator. In *Proceedings of the 3rd International Conference on Music Information Retrieval*, Paris, France.

Pazzani, J., M. Muramatsu, and D. Billsus [1996]. Syskill and Webert - identifying interesting web sites. In *Proceedings of the 13th National Conference of AAAI*, pages 54–61.

Sarwar, B.M., G. Karypis, J.A. Konstan, and J. Riedl [2001]. Item-based collaborative filtering recommendation algorithms. In *Proceedings of the 10th International World Wide Web Conference (WWW10)*, Hong Kong.

Sheth, B., and P. Maes [1993]. Evolving agents for personalized information filtering. In *Proceedings of Ninth Conference on Artificial Intelligence for Applications*, IEEE Computer Press.

Chapter 4

CUBYHUM:
ALGORITHMS FOR QUERY BY HUMMING

Steffen Pauws

Abstract   Query by humming is an interaction concept in which the identity of a melody
has to be revealed fast and orderly from a given sung input using a large database
of known melodies. In short, it tries to detect the pitches in a sung melody and
compares these pitches with symbolic representations of the known melodies.
Melodies that are similar to the sung pitches are retrieved. Approximate pattern
matching in the melody comparison process compensates for the errors in the
sung melody by using classical dynamic programming. A filtering method is
used to save computation in the dynamic programming framework. This paper
presents the algorithms for pitch detection, note onset detection, quantisation,
melody encoding and approximate pattern matching as they have been implemented in the CubyHum software system.

Keywords   Music retrieval, query by humming, approximate pattern matching.

4.1   Introduction

Typically, people listen to music separately from gaining knowledge about
the name of the performer, the composer or the title of the song. Because
song titles and melodies are not learnt associatively, recalling a song title from
a given melody or vice versa is notoriously difficult [Peynirçioglu, Tekcan,
Wagner, Baxter & Shaffer, 1998]. Obviously, it is hard to find music without
knowing it by heart. The interaction concept of query by humming makes it
possible to retrieve a song when the user ponders a catchy tune without being
able to name the song. It allows the user to sing any melodic passage of a
song, while the system seeks the song containing that melody fast and orderly.
To this end, the system requires symbolic representations of the song melodies
consisting of a sequence of musical notes (e.g., their pitch names) and the time
onset of each note.

W. Verhaegh et al. (eds.), Algorithms in Ambient Intelligence, 71-87.
© 2004 *Kluwer Academic Publishers. Printed in the Netherlands.*

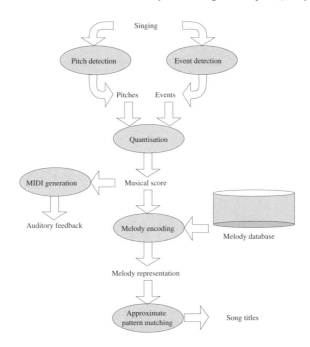

Figure 4.1.   The algorithmic framework of query by humming as implemented in CubyHum.

The algorithmic steps for query by humming are illustrated in Figure 4.1 as they are realised in the CubyHum system. First, the pitch is estimated from the singing by a technique called sub-harmonic summation (SHS). Second, musical events and corresponding timing information are found in the singing such as note onsets and gliding tones using signal processing techniques. Then, the pitch and timing information are quantised into musical notes, which transcribes the singing input into its formal musical notation or score. From this score, a melody can be synthesised for auditory feedback by using MIDI technologies. Approximate pattern matching on a key- and tempo-invariant melody representation allows the comparison of melodies that are distorted in various ways, since people are inaccurate in remembering and reproducing a melody. In particular, we have defined a distance between any two variable-length melodies. It comes down to finding an optimal alignment between melodies by minimising the total sum of costs that are assigned to their differences. This problem can be easily solved in a dynamic programming framework, which is however impractical in terms of running time performance for large melody databases. Therefore, a filter mechanism quickly discards passages in the melody database that cannot contain an approximate match.

4.2 Pitch detection

Pitch is a percept that is defined as the characteristic of a sound that gives the sensation of being high or being low. For a complex tone (as the human voice), the pitch corresponds mainly with the fundamental frequency of the signal. However, the correlation between fundamental frequency and pitch is not perfect; pitch perception is also influenced by the harmonics of the sound, amongst other things.

We use the sub-harmonic summation (SHS) method [Hermes, 1988] to estimate the pitch in the singing. This method stems from the theory that each spectral peak contributes to the perception of a pitch if there exists a harmonic relationship between the two. More particularly, peaks that have an integral factor in frequency with a pitch candidate contribute to that pitch, taking into account that higher peaks contribute less than lower peaks do. All these contributions add up in a sub-harmonic summation. The maximum of this sum result is the estimate of the pitch. Even when a fundamental frequency (i.e., the first harmonic) is missing in the signal, while other harmonics are present, this mechanism creates a (virtual) pitch of about that typically produced by that fundamental. The algorithm has been implemented as outlined in the original paper [Hermes, 1988], explained by the following expression,

$$H(s) = \sum_{n=1}^{N} h^{n-1} W(s + \log_2 n) |S(s + \log_2 n)|,$$

where $s = \log_2 f$ denotes the logarithmic frequency, $H(s)$ represents the sub-harmonic sum spectrum, N (e.g., 15) denotes the number of harmonics, n is the compression rank, h (e.g., 0.84) denotes the decreasing factor, $W(s)$ is an arctangent function representing the transfer function of the auditory sensitivity filter, and $|S(s + \log_2 n)|$ denotes the compressed amplitude spectrum representation. A pitch estimate is then the value of for which $f = 2^s$ is the maximum.

4.3 Event detection

Once the continuous pitches have been identified, the time locations at which a note starts (the onset time) and ends (the offset time) have to be found. To date, no algorithm has been developed that reliably detects the wide range of possible note onsets in performance data from different singing styles. For the current purpose, note onsets are defined as vowel onsets. Consequently, the singing is assumed to consist of short, relatively isolated syllables, preferably comprising a lengthened unvoiced fricative and a long mid vowel (e.g., /fa/-/fa/-/fa/). Note onsets are then characterised by an abrupt rise in energy over a broad frequency range. The sustained note has a relatively steady spectral shape representing the formants of the vowel used. Though note offsets can be identified to some extent by the fall of energy in especially the higher frequencies, they are less clearly defined. This is due to the exponential decay of the amplitude of a note making a note already inaudible while it is still physically present.

Several standard signal processing techniques are used to segment the signal into note onset and offset times (see Figure 4.2). First, the short-term energy method is used to detect silent parts in the singing. Subsequently, each non-silent part is provided to the other three methods in succession. We assume a digital signal blocked in frames $x(n)$, for $n = 0, \ldots, N - 1$, that is first pre-emphasised by the filter $1 - 0.95z^{-1}$. Pre-emphasis compensates for the -6dB/octave decay in voiced speech due to the radiation from the lips.

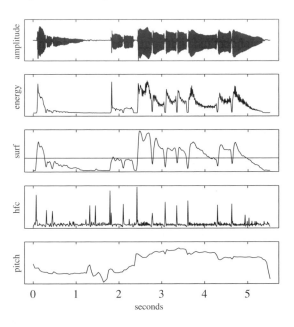

Figure 4.2. The waveform produced by a male person singing the first melody line of the Beatles' song 'Yesterday' of 12 notes by using the syllables 'na-na'. The short-term energy method indicates regions of silence and singing for isolated notes; it detects 9 note onsets. The Surf method indicates the same 9 note onsets by looking at the positive zero-crossings in the surf contour. The high-frequency content method can detect all 12 note onsets by peak picking; there are some spurious peaks that can result in 'false alarms'. The pitch method can detect gliding note onsets by looking how the pitch contour fluctuates over time.

4.3.1   Short-term energy method

The short-term energy method is a straightforward method to distinguish singing from silence and hence to detect note onsets and offsets. To that end, the signal is blocked into non-overlapping frames of 10 msecs. The short-term energy E_k in frame k is calculated by

$$E_k = \sum_{n=0}^{N-1} x(n)^2.$$

The short-time energy is normalised by a maximum short-term energy found in a running window of the signal. Adaptive threshold values are used to determine note onsets and note offsets, in which the note onset threshold (e.g., 0.02) is defined to be higher than the note offset threshold (e.g., 0.01). This is done to avoid an on-off oscillation of a marginal signal (e.g., a weak fricative).

4.3.2 Surf method

The Surf onset detection algorithm has been adopted from the techniques of Schloss [Schloss, 1985]. The signal is passed through a first-order high pass filter and blocked into frames of 20 msecs, with a frame shift of 10 msecs. The frames are used to compute a smoothed amplitude envelope of the signal that represents the higher frequencies. This envelope $y(k)$ is made out of the sequence of average absolute values of the signal within each frame k. The slope of the envelope is computed by a 5-point second-order polynomial fitting procedure [Rabiner & Juang, 1993]. Since a note onset is characterised by an abrupt rise of higher frequencies of the signal, we looked at positive zero-crossings of the slope contour to find these onset times.

4.3.3 High-frequency content method

The high-frequency content method has been adopted from Masri and Bateman [Masri & Bateman, 1996]. It aims at revealing both changes in overall energy and the energy concentration at higher frequencies. The signal is blocked and Hanning-windowed into frames of 20 msecs, with a frame shift of 10 msecs.

An M-point FFT is used to produce a short-time DFT $X_k(m)$. The short-time energy in frame k is computed as the sum of the squared magnitude of each FFT bin,

$$E_k = \sum_{m=m_0}^{M/2+1} |X_k(m)|^2,$$

where m_0 denotes the lowest FFT bin that is taken into account. Only the FFT bins are considered that fall within a frequency band of 400 Hz and higher.

The short-time higher frequency content H_k in frame k is a weighted version of E_k, linearly biased to the higher frequencies,

$$H_k = \sum_{m=m_0}^{M/2+1} m \cdot |X_k(m)|^2.$$

A detection function is computed that combines each pair of consecutive frames; it is the product of the rise in high frequency energy between two frames and the current normalised high frequency content,

$$D_k = \frac{H_k}{H_{k-1}} \cdot \frac{H_k}{E_k}.$$

The first ratio represents the rise in high frequency content. The second ratio represents the normalised high frequency content for the current frame k. Their product (i.e., D_k) peaks prominently at abrupt increase in high frequency energy content. If it surpasses a given threshold, we say that the detection function has found a note onset.

4.3.4 Pitch method

The pitch method is a way to segment gliding notes spanning several pitches into note onset and offset times. To find a sequence of gliding pitches, we use two consecutive windows superimposed on the array of pitch frames. If the median pitch in the foremost window falls beyond 100 cents (a semitone) of the median pitch of the hindmost window, we say that a new note has started in the foremost window. The hindmost window becomes the foremost window and a new foremost window is created. If the median pitches do not differ by 100 cents, the foremost window moves one frame and the hindmost window grows one frame. The foremost window has a fixed size of 3 pitch frames (120 msecs), which also determines the minimal duration of a gliding note. Finding note onset and offset times in gliding pitch has the advantage that the user has some freedom in singing: notes do not need to be sung in an isolated manner but can be 'thread together'. However, a long gliding note (due to portamento or glissando) is segmented into a ascending or descending sequence of shorter notes.

4.4 Quantisation

Quantisation means the division of the pitch (tone) and time continuum into discrete steps. Time quantisation is not further discussed, since quantised duration is not used in the melody comparison. Instead, the inter-onset-interval (IOI) is used as timing information, which is the time difference between two successive note onsets.

The median pitch between a note onset and offset is used to quantise the musical pitch value for each note using the equally tempered musical scale tuned at $A_4 = 440$Hz (A-440). Music theory states that musical pitch is represented in categories along scales in terms of semitones and cents. These categories are relative measures based on frequency ratios. Knowing that an octave is a frequency ratio of 2:1, the semitone is one-twelfth of an octave ($\sqrt[12]{2} \approx 1.05946$)

and a cent is 1/100 of a semitone. Now, notes on the equally tempered scale relative to A-440 occur at multiples of 100 cents; they can be expressed as a distance in cents from 8.176 Hz and have a total order. For instance, the middle C ($C_4 = 261.63$Hz) is 6000 cents (or there about). To calculate the discrete musical pitch p of a median pitch f, we use the frequency ratio $R = f/8.176$ and

$$p = \lfloor 12 \cdot \log_2 R + 0.5 \rfloor.$$

The musical pitch is then represented by an integer value. By allowing an integer range between 0 and 127, we have essentially the MIDI convention to encode musical pitch.

For singing inevitably deviates from the A-440 standard, the tuning is adapted to the singing in due course by changing the reference pitch (which is at 8.176 Hz, at first) after each sung note.

4.5 Melody representation

Without any assistance, people start singing in any preferred key. Therefore, all melodies have to be encoded in a representation that is invariant to key. A melody representation that is invariant to key is an interval representation; a musical interval is the distance between two succeeding notes expressed in semitones. In particular, a melody sequence $S = s_1 s_2 \ldots s_N$ comprising absolute pitches is transformed in a sequence $S = \cdot (s_2 - s_1)(s_3 - s_2) \ldots (s_N - s_{N-1})$, where the dot '$\cdot$' represents a special start element since no interval is associated with the first note in a melody.

Only nine interval categories are defined: the unison, four ascending and four descending intervals. Intervals spanning 1 to 2 semitones are grouped as people often mix intervals of that size in their singing. As shown in Table 4.1, they are encoded by an integer between -4 and 4 making up an alphabet Σ. Intervals larger than 6 semitones are not further distinguished. It is well-known that intervals larger than 5 semitones and greater are rare (only 10%) in musical melodies from all over the world [Dowling & Harwood, 1986]. In addition, large intervals are difficult to sing accurately.

Temporal information is kept by storing the real value of the inter-onset-interval (IOI) of each note to each corresponding interval category. These data are used to make melody comparison invariant to global tempo; the melody distance is defined in terms of ratios of consecutive IOIs (see Section 4.6.3).

4.6 Melody comparison

Melody comparison comes down to finding an approximate match of one relatively short melodic sequence (say, 10-15 notes for a sung query) in a second longer melodic sequence (say, 300 notes for a vocal melody of a pop song) that resides in a database with many more melodic sequences. To this end, we

Table 4.1. The interval representation for melodies (st = semitone).

interval name	*interval size*	*integer code*
desc. perfect fifth and greater	< -6 st	-4
desc. perfect/augm. fourth	-5 or -6 st	-3
desc. minor/major third	-3 or -4 st	-2
desc. minor/major second	-1 or -2 st	-1
unison	0 st	0
asc. minor/major second	1 or 2 st	1
asc. minor/major third	3 or 4 st	2
asc. perfect/augm. fourth	5 or 6 st	3
asc. perfect fifth and greater	> 6 st	4

need an appropriate melody distance measure that (1) assigns different costs to different local differences between melodic sequences, that (2) meets some invariance principles and that (3) agrees with human expectation. As will be explained in the next sections, the computation of the melody distance comes down to the minimisation of the sum of costs that are assigned to local differences between two melodic sequences. This minimisation is done by dynamic programming. First, we will introduce the notation used and the edit distance that will be used later on to speed up the melody comparison in a filter technique.

4.6.1   Notation

We adopt the following notation for comparing melodic sequences: let $Q = q_1 q_2 \ldots q_M \in \Sigma^M$ be a query pattern sequence of length $|Q| = M$ and $S = s_1 s_2 \ldots s_N \in \Sigma^N$ a sequence of length $|S| = N$, with $M \ll N$. Σ is a finite alphabet of interval categories. Its size is represented by $|\Sigma| = \sigma$. Here, we use the alphabet $\Sigma = \{-4, -3, \ldots, 3, 4\}$.

We denote s_j as the j-th element of S for an integer $1 \leq j \leq N$. We denote $S_{i \ldots j} = s_i \ldots s_j$ as a subsequence of S, which is the empty subsequence ε if $i > j$. The *prefixes* of S are the $N + 1$ subsequences $S_{1 \ldots j}$ for $0 \leq j \leq N$. Likewise, the *suffixes* of S are $S_{j \ldots N}$ for $1 \leq j \leq N + 1$.

A subsequence $S_{i \ldots j}$ is termed an *exact* match of Q in S, if Q equals $S_{i \ldots j}$. It is termed an *approximate* match if at least one element in Q is different from the corresponding element in $S_{i \ldots j}$ or vice versa. The number of different elements allowed between two sequences is denoted by k and consequently the error level is denoted by $\alpha = k/M$. We speak of a *k-approximate* match, if at most k elements in Q are different from the corresponding elements in $S_{i \ldots j}$.

In addition, we define a tabular function L_S, which is specific to the sequence S, that provides the IOI for a given j-th element of S. In particular, $L_S(s_j) := t_j$, where t_j is the IOI for s_j.

4.6.2 Edit distance

The traditional way to compare two sequences is to allow particular differences (or errors) of single elements to occur in the sequences while computing their distance, denoted as $ed : \Sigma^* \times \Sigma^* \to \mathbb{R}_0^+$. Thus, $ed(Q,S)$ represents a distance definition between Q and S. The types of differences can be deletions, insertions and replacements of single elements that are necessary to transform one sequence into the other. A cost (or penalty) is associated with each transformation (or difference). A cost may be a constant (e.g., a unit cost for each transformation) or any value function that computes the difference between two elements in its context. When we restrict the costs to be unit, the match will be based on the unit-cost edit distance, that is, the minimal number of deletions, insertions and replacements to transform the sequence Q into the sequence S [Wagner & Fischer, 1974].

The unit-cost edit distance model can be used in two different ways.

1. *Minimal distance problem.* Finding an approximate match of Q in S that has minimal edit distance.

2. *k-difference problem.* Finding an approximate match (or all approximate matches) of Q in S that has (or have) at most k different elements with Q (i.e., at most an edit distance of k with Q).

The computation of the edit distance can be easily solved by using classical dynamic programming for sequences of the same length [Wagner & Fischer, 1974] and for sequences of different lengths [Sellers, 1980].

4.6.3 Melody distance

A melody distance model must account for local pitch and duration differences of a sung melody with respect to a melody in the database. For that purpose, different costs are assigned to different local pitch and duration differences. To compute a melody distance between the two melodic sequences, we minimise the sum of these costs while aligning both melodic sequences (or parts of them) by means of dynamic programming.

Hereunder, we enumerate the most important local differences between melodies. The ones that have to do with musical pitch are shown in Figure 4.3.

1. An *interval change* occurs if a single interval is sung too flat or too sharp. This may result into a change of key of the whole succeeding melody line.

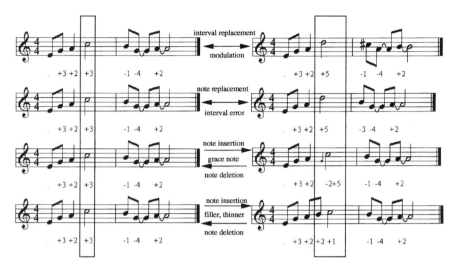

Figure 4.3. Typical local differences between melodies. Underneath each musical staff, the interval sizes in semitones are shown.

2. A *note replacement* means replacing one note for another note. Replacing one note affects the interval to that note and the interval from that note.

3. A *note insertion* means the singing of an additional note (e.g., a filler or a grace note).

4. A *note deletion* means the forgetting of singing a note (e.g., a thinner note).

5. A *duration error* is the lengthening or shortening of a note (without changing global tempo).

4.6.4 Dynamic programming solution

The dynamic programming approach to compute the melody distance $D(Q,S)$ between two melodic sequences Q and S is done by filling a matrix $(D_{0...M,0...N})$. The entry $D_{i,j}$ holds the minimal melody distance between the two prefixes $Q_{1...i}$ and $S_{1...j}$. The algorithm to construct the matrix is done by using the following recurrent formula in which costs are assigned to pitch differences and to duration differences

$$D_{i,j} = \min \begin{cases} D_{i-1,j} + 1 + K \cdot \left| \frac{L_Q(q_i)}{L_Q(q_{i-1})} \right| \quad \text{(interval insertion)} \\[2ex] D_{i-2,j-1} + 1 + K \cdot \left| \frac{L_Q(q_{i-1}) - L_Q(q_i)}{L_Q(q_{i-2})} - \frac{L_S(s_j)}{L_S(s_{j-1})} \right| \\ \quad \text{if } q_{i-1} + q_i = s_j, \ i > 2 \quad \text{(note insertion)} \\[2ex] D_{i-1,j-1} + \frac{1}{\sigma}|q_i - s_j| + K \cdot \left| \frac{L_Q(q_i)}{L_Q(q_{i-1})} - \frac{L_S(s_j)}{L_S(s_{j-1})} \right| \\ \quad \text{(interval change or no error)} \\[2ex] D_{i-1,j-2} + 1 + K \cdot \left| \frac{L_Q(q_i)}{L_Q(q_{i-1})} - \frac{L_S(s_{j-1}) - L_S(s_j)}{L_S(s_{j-2})} \right| \\ \quad \text{if } q_i = s_{j-1} + s_j, \ j > 2 \quad \text{(note deletion)} \\[2ex] D_{i,j-1} + 1 + K \cdot \left| \frac{L_S(s_j)}{L_S(s_{j-1})} \right| \quad \text{(interval deletion)} \end{cases} \tag{4.1}$$

where $\sigma = 9$ denotes the size of the alphabet, and K denotes a constant that represents the relative contribution of duration costs versus that of interval costs to the computation of the melody distance. We determined $K = 0.2$ empirically using a test set of sung melodies.

The following set of initial boundary conditions and special cases is used

$$\begin{aligned} D_{0,0} &= 0 \\ D_{1,0} &= 1 \\ D_{i,0} &= D_{i-1,0} + 1 + K \cdot \left| \frac{L_Q(q_i)}{L_Q(q_{i-1})} \right| \\ D_{i,1} &= D_{i-1,0} \\ D_{0,j} &= 0 \\ D_{1,j} &= D_{0,j-1} \end{aligned} \tag{4.2}$$

The rationale of the recurrent formula (4.1) is, first, that intervals between melodies are penalised by their absolute difference, $|q_i - s_j|$. If the pitch intervals are equal, there is no cost involved. If they are not equal, we speak about an interval change that may result in a modulation (key-change) of one melody in comparison to the other. The interval cost is normalised by the size of the alphabet σ so that it will never reach a cost of 1 or higher. Additional to this interval cost, there is a duration cost for shortening or lengthening a note. This cost is expressed by the absolute difference of ratios of consecutive inter-onset-intervals. This method makes the computation of the melody distance invariant to global tempo. A note replacement is not explicitly accounted for, but it can be interpreted as two interval changes in series since it involves two succeeding intervals.

Second, if $q_{i-1} + q_i = s_j$ or $q_i = s_{j-1} + s_j$, we speak of a note insertion or note deletion, respectively. A note insertion implies that the sum of the sizes of the two intervals setting up the additional note equals the size of the original interval (thus, $q_{i-1} + q_i = s_j$). A note deletion implies that the size of the new interval due to the forgotten note equals the sum of the sizes of the two original intervals (thus, $q_i = s_{j-1} + s_j$). A cost of 1 is associated with these differences. The duration cost penalises longer durations of inserted or deleted notes more than smaller durations; it thus favours grace notes for thinner and filler notes.

Interval insertions and deletions are differences that cannot be accounted for by the other schemes. Their costs are 1 plus a varying durational cost. The duration cost is based on the motivation that the deletion of an interval can be seen as replacing a note with a nullified note of zero-length. Likewise, an interval insertion is similar to replacing a zero-length note with a note of a non-zero length.

The initial boundary conditions and special cases in (4.2) express

1. the possibility that Q starts at any position in S,

2. the fact that the used duration ratios do not exist at the very start of a sequence and

3. the fact that the sequences start with a special start symbol.

The filling of the matrix $(D_{0...M,0...N})$ starts at $D_{0,0}$ and ends at $D_{M,N}$ in either a column-wise top-to-bottom manner or a row-wise left-to-right manner. By keeping track of each local minimisation decision in the matrix in a pointer structure, one can reveal the optimal alignment between Q and a subsequence of S. The entry in the column $(D_{M,0...N})$ holding the minimal distance value refers to the end of an optimal alignment. By tracing back the pointers, one can recover all local minimisation decisions in reverse order that resulted in this minimal value and, hence, the starting point of the optimal alignment. Likewise, one can find multiple optimal alignments, if there are several.

Since we have to compute all entries of the matrix and the computation of each entry $D_{i,j}$ is a constant factor, the worst and average case time complexity is $O(M \cdot N)$. Note that this computation has to be done for each melody in the database. In principle, if we compute the matrix column-wise or row-wise, only the current column (or row) and the previous two need to be stored; only $3 \cdot \min(M,N)$ cells are required. Since $M < N$, the space required is $O(M)$.

4.6.5   An index method: Filtering

Chances are small that a query pattern Q is highly similar to many melodic passages S in the database. Leaving out subsequences in S that cannot have a sufficiently high similarity with Q saves the computation of complete columns in the dynamic programming matrix. For instance, index methods quickly retrieve subsequences in S that might be highly similar to Q. When these subsequences in S are identified, they still need to be evaluated by using (4.1) and (4.2) to ensure whether or not they really have a high match with Q.

Current index methods are based on the k-difference problem between Q and S using the unit-cost edit distance model. One of these index methods is known as 'filtering': subsequences in S that meet a well-defined necessary (but not sufficient) 'filtration' condition with respect to Q are candidate for further evaluation, given a pre-defined error level $\alpha = k/M$. All other subsequences are discarded. It is conceivable that discarded subsequences in S can still have a low melodic distance with Q, as the filtering is based on the edit distance. To alleviate this discrepancy, the error level α has to be set appropriately.

The used filtering method is the Chang and Lawler's LET (Linear Expected Time) algorithm [Chang & Lawler, 1994]. It discards a subsequence of S when it can be inferred that it does not contain a k-approximate match with Q. This can be done by observing that a subsequence in S having a k-approximate match with a pattern Q of length M is at least of length $M - k$ and is a concatenation of at most $k + 1$ longest subsequences of Q with intervening (non-matching) elements. So, the LET 'filtration' condition says that any subsequence in S of $k + 1$ concatenated longest subsequences of Q that is shorter than $M - k$ can be discarded. The remaining subsequences are further evaluated using (4.1) and (4.2).

The LET algorithm uses a suffix tree on Q to determine the longest subsequences of Q in S in linear time. A suffix tree on a sequence Q is a special data structure that forms an ordered representation of all suffixes of Q. A suffix tree can be built in linear $O(M)$ time and needs $O(M)$ space [McCreight, 1976][Ukkonen, 1995]. It works by traversing S in a linear fashion (from left to right) and maintains the longest subsequence of Q at each element in S using the suffix tree on Q. When this subsequence cannot be extended any further, it starts a new subsequence of Q at the next element. Note that there is an intervening element defined between any two longest subsequences of Q in S. These elements are called *markers* in S.

An additional result of partitioning S in this way using Q is the number of markers in S. This quantity is also known as the *maximal matches* distance between S and Q. This distance has been proven to be a lower bound for the unit-cost edit distance [Ukkonen, 1992].

Example 4.1. Let $Q = abcba$ ($M = 5$) and $S = adaaabdbadbbb$ ($N = 13$). The partition of S as a concatenation of longest subsequences of Q intervened by markers is a-a-ab-ba-b-b, since a, ab, ba and b are all (longest) subsequences of Q in S. The markers have been omitted at positions 2, 4, 7, 10 and 12 in S. The *maximal matches* distance between Q and S equals 5. By allowing $k = 1$ difference, the regions a-a and b-b are discarded since they are of length $3 < M - k = 4$. On the other hand, the regions a-ab, ab-ba and ba-b need to be further evaluated since their lengths are $M - k = 4$.   □

4.6.6 Heuristic adjustments

By using the *maximal matches* distance between a subsequence in S and Q as a lower bound for their edit distance, we can use two heuristic rule-out methods by recognising that S can have repetitive subsequences and that repetitive subsequences do not need to get evaluated over and over again. Repetition in a melodic sequence is common; a melody can contain similar passages referring to the tune of the chorus or the individual phrases of a stanza, for instance.

1. *LET-H1*: all non-overlapping subsequences in S with equal *maximal matches distances* normalised by the length of the subsequence to Q are maintained. From this set, only one subsequence is subjected to further evaluation; all others are discarded.

2. *LET-H2*: only the subsequence in S with the minimal *maximal matches* distance normalised by the length of the subsequence to Q is chosen for further evaluation; all others are discarded.

It must be emphasised that these heuristic extensions make the filter no longer working correctly, since approximate matches in S are discarded on purpose. To find a balance in correctness (heuristic) level, filtration efficiency and melody comparison performance, we empirically set $\alpha = 0.25$ while using method LET-H1. As shown in Section 4.6.7, this provides us a 64% to 89% reduction in computing columns during dynamic programming for pattern sequences Q with a length of 12. In practice, the LET algorithm was found to be too permissive in providing still too many similar subsequences for further evaluation. In contrast, LET-H2 was found to be far too stringent by discarding relevant subsequences. Some subsequences in S that were discarded by LET-H2 turned out to have a high melodic similarity with Q.

4.6.7 Filtering experiment

In order to assess the filtration efficiency of the three filtering methods for typical problem instances, we conducted experiments with a varying error level α using a database with 510 popular melodies[1], each containing 285 notes on average. The filtering methods were LET, LET-H1 and LET-H2. All sequences were made out of the alphabet Σ of 9 interval categories as shown in Table 4.1. The patterns Q were constructed with varying lengths ($M = 10$, 12, 14). They were either randomly chosen excerpts from the database (the melodic sequences) or randomly compiled from the alphabet (the random sequences).

---

[1]The melody database contained 510 vocal monophonic melodies from songs of the Beatles (185), ABBA (73), the Rolling Stones (67), Madonna (38), David Bowie (34), U2 (33), Prince (23), Michael Jackson (20), Frank Sinatra (20) and the Police (17).

A measure for *filtration efficiency* is the number of elements that are discarded divided by the total number of elements,

$$filtration\ efficiency = \frac{N - N_e}{N},$$

where N denotes the total number of elements and N_e denotes the number of elements that need further evaluation. In order to decrease random variations, we have determined the averages of 250 independent runs with different patterns.

The results are shown in Table 4.2. The random sequences are more stringently filtered since they show little resemblance with the structure in popular melodies. It is clear that the filtration efficiency of LET has a steep drop at an error level α between 0.2 and 0.3. The use of the heuristics in LET-H1 and LET-H2 boosted the filter efficiency at each error level. An error level α of 0.25 is an appropriate parameter value when using one of the filter approaches.

Table 4.2. *Filtration efficiency* simulated for different parameters of a problem instance ($|\Sigma| = 9$). Parameter combinations that resulted in zero filtration efficiency are not shown.

M	k	α	melodic sequences			random sequences		
			LET	LET-H1	LET-H2	LET	LET-H1	LET-H2
10	1	0.10	0.99	1.00	1.00	1.00	1.00	1.00
	2	0.20	0.81	0.90	0.97	0.97	0.98	0.99
	3	0.30	0.22	0.37	0.76	0.35	0.49	0.85
	4	0.40	0.03	0.06	0.24	0.04	0.07	0.26
12	1	0.08	1.00	1.00	1.00	1.00	1.00	1.00
	2	0.17	0.93	0.96	0.98	1.00	1.00	1.00
	3	0.25	0.53	0.64	0.89	0.81	0.89	0.96
	4	0.33	0.11	0.16	0.45	0.14	0.23	0.52
	5	0.42	0.02	0.04	0.13	0.02	0.03	0.12
14	1	0.07	1.00	1.00	1.00	1.00	1.00	1.00
	2	0.14	0.98	0.99	0.99	1.00	1.00	1.00
	3	0.21	0.77	0.83	0.94	0.96	0.97	0.99
	4	0.28	0.28	0.38	0.70	0.45	0.58	0.86
	5	0.36	0.06	0.08	0.24	0.06	0.08	0.25

4.7 Conclusion

CubyHum is a software system in which query by humming is realised by linking algorithms from various fields: speech signal processing, music processing and approximate pattern matching. In short, it tries to detect the pitches in a sung melody and compares these pitches with symbolic representations of melodies in a large database. Melodies that are similar to the sung pitches are retrieved. Approximate pattern matching in the melody comparison process compensates for the errors in the sung melody (e.g., sharp or flat notes, wrong tempo) by using classical dynamic programming. A filtering technique saves much of the computing necessities involved in dynamic programming.

It may be evident that there are at least three factors that influence the retrieval performance of a today's query by humming system:

1. the quality and the style of the singing produced in the sung melody by the user,

2. the performance of the signal processing front-end to deliver the correct pitches and the correct timing information of the sung melody,

3. the robustness of approximate pattern matching to the discrepancies between the sung melody and the melodies in the database.

The quality of singing is definitely affected by singing education, singing experience and familiarity with the song. Less familiar songs are sung worse than familiar songs. And, trained singers are better in singing the correct intervals and in singing at a steady pulse than the general public [Pauws, 2003]. This imposes constraints on the required technology for query by humming.

If users sing from memory and at will, they tend to do that by mixing various singing styles such as singing with and without lyrics, humming, whistling, producing percussive sounds and using ornamentations such as portamento and vibrato. Each singing style produces specific sound characteristics and cues for pitch, note onset and note offset detection. Singing by using isolated syllables is the preferred singing style from a signal processing point of view, as it provides abrupt signal changes that indicate note onsets. Humming and whistling are most troublesome, as the use of a nasal consonant /m/ for humming and the pitch gliding effect in whistling tend to blur note onsets and offsets. The use of portamento and vibrato makes pitch detection less reliable as they obscure the target pitch. When considering both note onset detection and pitch detection, today's best signal processing techniques produce 15% error rate for syllable-singing, 21% error rate for singing using lyrics and 23% error rate for whistling [De Mulder, Martens, Pauws, Lesaffre, Leman, De Baets & De Meyer, 2003]. There is definitely a need for more accurate signal processing techniques to detect the correct pitches in all kinds of singing.

Approximate pattern matching for melody comparison must account for the local differences between the sung melody and the melodies in the database that are either due to the user singing performance and the signal processing front-end. One way to account for part of these differences is the melody representation used based on interval categories; it is a compromise for both the lack of singing accuracy and the lack of accuracy of pitch detection algorithms.

Also, the types of local differences have been identified and cost functions have been assigned to them. This inventory made it possible to model melody comparison as a precisely stated mathematical problem in a discrete domain to be solved optimally. Today's precision using the present melody distance model can reach about 50% for a sung melody using a database of 816 popular rock melodies [De Mulder, Martens, Pauws, Lesaffre, Leman, De Baets & De Meyer, 2003]. Further experimentation with singing data will result in a better cost assignment in the melody distance model and consequently will improve retrieval performance.

Lastly, there is a lot to gain with respect to speed in the melody comparison process by applying filter techniques. Faster filter techniques for the present melody comparison problem have already been developed [Van Vuuren, Egner, Korst & Pauws, 2003].

References

Chang, W., and E. Lawler [1994]. Sublinear approximate string matching and biological applications. *Algorithmica,* 12(4/5):327–344.

De Mulder, T., J.P. Martens, S. Pauws, M. Lesaffre, M. Leman, B. De Baets, and H. De Meyer [2003]. Benchmarking front-ends for a query-by-melody system. Submitted to ISMIR 2003.

Dowling, W.J., and D.L. Harwood [1986]. *Music Cognition.* Academic Press, New York.

Hermes, D.J. [1988]. Measurement of pitch by subharmonic summation. *Journal of Acoustical Society of America*, 83(1):257–264.

Masri, P., and A. Bateman [1996]. Improved modelling of attack transients in music analysis-resynthesis. In *Proceedings of International Computer Music Conference (ICMC 96)*, Hong-Kong, pages 100–103.

McCreight, E. [1976]. A space-economical suffix tree construction algorithm. *Journal of ACM,* 23(2):262–272.

Pauws, S.C. [2003]. How good do you sing and know a song when you sing a song? Submitted to ISMIR 2003.

Peynirçioglu, Z.K., A.I. Tekcan, J.L. Wagner, T.L. Baxter, and S.D. Shaffer [1998]. Name or hum that tune: Feeling of knowing for music. *Memory & Cognition*, 26(6):1131–1137.

Rabiner, L.R., and B. Juang [1993]. *Fundamentals of Speech Recognition.* Prentice-Hall Inc.

Schloss, W. [1985]. *On the Automatic Transcription of Percussive Music: From Acoustic Signal to High Level Analysis.* Ph.D. Thesis, Department of Music, Report No. STAN-M-27, Stanford University, CCRMA.

Sellers, P.H. [1980]. The theory and computation of evolutionary distances: Pattern recognition. *Journal of Algorithms*, 1:359–373.

Ukkonen, E. [1992]. Approximate string matching with q-grams and maximal matches. *Theoretical Computer Science*, 92(1):191–211.

Ukkonen, E. [1995]. Constructing suffix trees on-line in linear time. *Algoritmica*, 14(3):249–260.

Vuuren, M. van, S. Egner, J. Korst, and S. Pauws [2003]. Approximate pattern matching: An efficient search method for melody retrieval. Invited paper for *TALES of the disappearing computer*, June 1-4, 2003, Santorini, Greece.

Wagner, R.A., and M.J. Fischer [1974]. The string-to-string correction problem. *Journal of the Association of Computing Machinery*, 21(1):168–173.

Chapter 5

PERSONALIZED MULTIMEDIA SUMMARIZATION

Lalitha Agnihotri and Nevenka Dimitrova

Abstract   Summarization and abstraction are our survival tools in this age of information explosion and availability. Ability to summarize will be seen as essential part of intelligent behavior of the consumer devices.

We introduce the notion of video summarization, and provide definitions of the different flavors of summaries: Video skim, highlights, and structured multimedia summary. We present different features and methods for automatic video content analysis for the purpose of summarization: color analysis using Superhistograms, transcript extraction and analysis, superimposed and overlaid text detection, face detection, commercial detection. All these different types of video content analysis are used to produce multimedia summaries. We use audio, visual, and text information for selecting important elements of news stories for multimedia news summary.

We present a method for surface level summarization and its applications: a talk show browser and a content-based video recorder called Video Scout. We also discuss a method for news story segmentation and summarization as an example of structured video summarization.

Summaries presented to users should be personalized. Our initial study shows that personal preferences include implicit features such as viewing history, summary usage history, and explicit preferences such as topics, location, age, gender, profession, hobbies, allocated time, consumption preferences (auditory vs. visual). We believe that personalized summarization will provide essential tools for access to relevant information everywhere at any time in the context of ambient intelligence.

Keywords   Video analysis, program summary, user preferences.

5.1   Introduction

The amount of audiovisual content is expanding at an ever increasing rate and our available time to consume all of the desirable video content is decreas-

W. Verhaegh et al. (eds.), Algorithms in Ambient Intelligence, 89-111
© 2004 *Kluwer Academic Publishers. Printed in the Netherlands.*

ing. The increased amount of video content coupled with the decreasing time available to view it makes it impossible to view all of the potentially desirable content in its entirety. Accordingly, viewers are increasingly selective regarding the content they want to view. In order to accommodate viewer demands with little available time, techniques have been developed for video summarization to obtain compact representation of the original video for subsequent browsing and viewing. Video summaries are very important for content preview before the viewer decides to invest his/her time. Also, condensed form is desirable when the user has available only limited time of the original movie or program length. Video summaries can be used in two modes: browsing for new content and in a recollection mode when the user is trying to remember the content of a certain TV program or a movie.

In this chapter we introduce the notion of video summarization, and provide definitions of different flavors of summaries. We present different features and methods for automatic video content analysis for the purpose of summarization. Color information is very important for characterizing scenes in video content. We present a compact representation of video based on color Superhistograms. Superimposed and overlaid text act as 'meta-level' channels for providing information in addition to the underlying video signal. Automatically detecting videotext, analyzing the time and position as well as its content enables inference of genre information, commercial location, important frames, and program boundary. We present a method for videotext extraction and genre classification. Closed captions represent the transcript of the spoken audio and provide valuable information for segmenting and summarizing the video. We present a method for surface level summarization and its implementations in a talk show browser and in a content-based video recorder called Video Scout. All these different types of video content analysis are used to produce multimedia summaries.

The presentation of a multimedia summary can be based on the available time, location, task, device capabilities. Further, the summaries presented should depend on personal preferences of the user. Our initial study shows that personal preferences include implicit features such as viewing history, summary usage history, and explicit preferences such as topics of interest, location, age, gender, profession, hobbies, time allocated for watching TV, aspirations, consumption preferences (auditory vs. visual), abstract vs. concrete personality. We believe that personalized summarization will provide essential tools for access to relevant information everywhere at any time in the context of ambient intelligence.

5.1.1 Related work

Information available to consumers continues to increase, while human cognitive abilities remain about the same. Additionally, human preferences for the form and content of information are often idiosyncratic, and may even drift over time. Therefore, it is of high scientific interest to provide technologies that select and summarize information in a personalized but content-preserving way. Such summaries can serve as friendly indexes into the complete content, or as trained sentinels watching for unusual but desired events, or as gentle reminders of content that has migrated into media that are more difficult to browse.

Existing automatic video summarization methods can and do already shorten videos or create another representation of them, such as selected images, image collages, extracted text, etc. Most such summarization research is specialized by genre, with the bulk of the emphasis on news [Hauptmann & Witbrock, 1998; Merialdo et al., 1999; Merlino et al., 1997; Merlino & Maybury, 1999] and sports [Chang et al., 2001], although a few researchers have investigated the issues of structure- and content-preserving video summaries more generically [Agnihotri et al., 2001; Christel et al., 1998; Li et al., 2001; Lee et al., 2000; Smith & Kanade, 1997; Sundaram et al., 2002; Uchihashi et al., 1999].

Summarization appears to be more current and active among researchers working on speech [Arons, 1997] and printed text [Firmin & Chrzanowski, 1999; Mani & Maybury, 1999]; in particular, there have been several workshops hosted by the Association for Computational Linguistics on text summarization. In contrast, current video summaries have been largely limited to a visual table of contents illustrated with key frames or to a sequence of selected shots ('skims'), with very little work on generating a summary using all the modalities of visual, aural, and textual sources from the video. Furthermore, there is no work in personalizing the summary based on a user profile or on a user's environmental context, no work on how best to match video extraction and abstraction techniques to user preferences, and little work on measuring the results.

5.2 Definitions

Video summarization is the process of condensing content into a shorter descriptive form. There is a variety of flavors that have been considered under the topic of summarization: video skimming, highlights, and various types of multimedia summaries. Next, we distinguish between local summaries for part of a program (e.g. for a scene), global summaries for the entire program, and meta-level summaries of a collection of programs.

Video skim is a temporally condensed form of the video stream that preferably preserves the most important information. A method for generating visual skims based on scene analysis and using the grammar of film language is presented by Sundaram et al. [2002]. Ma et al. [2002] proposed an attention model that includes visual, audio, and text modalities for summarization of videos.

Video highlights is a form of summary that aims at including the most important events in the video. Various methods have been introduced for extracting highlights from specific subgenres of sports programs: goals in soccer video [Dagtas et al., 2000], hits in tennis video, touch down in football, important events in car racing video [Petkovic et al., 2002] and others.

Multimedia video summary is a collection of audio, visual, and text segments that preserve the essence and the structure of the underlying video (e.g. pictorial summary, story boards, surface summary). Uchihashi et al. [1999] present methods for automatically creating pictorial summaries of videos using image and audio analysis to find relative importance of segments. The output consists of static images linked to the video so that users can interact with it. *Surface-level summarization* looks for cues that have been predefined based on the structure of the program. For example, Agnihotri et al. [2001] present a surface summarization method for a talk shows that includes representative elements for the host portion and each of the guests. *Entity-level summarization* approaches build an internal representation of video, modeling 'video entities' and their relationships. These approaches tend to represent patterns of connectivity in the video to help determine what is salient. Relationships between entities include: Similarity (color similarity, similar faces) and co-occurrence. Li et al. [2001b] presented a method of clustering frames with similar color in order to generate summaries of programs. *Discourse-level* approaches model the global structure of the video and its relation to communicative goals. This structure can include threads of topics as they are revealed in the video. Aner & Kender [2002] introduce mosaic-based scene representation for clustering of scenes into physical settings.

Meta-level summaries provide an overview of a whole cluster of related videos. For example, a meta summary of all available news items from Web and TV sources is provided by the MyInfo system [Haas et al., 2002]. Summary of the news items is extracted by the reportage analysis and presented according to a personal profile.

5.3   Features for summarization

In this section we elaborate the different features that have been developed so far for summarization of programs. Figure 5.1 displays the core elements of a summarization system in terms of low, mid, and high-level layers. Different features are extracted at the low-level layer from each stream. In the visual domain, the system extracts color, edge, and shape. In the audio domain the system extracts different parameters, such as average energy, bandwidth, etc. In the transcript domain, different keywords are extracted.

Mid and high-level features are generated via integration of information. Mid-level features consist of family histograms, faces, and videotext in the visual domain; audio classification in the audio domain [Li & Kuo, 2000a]; and cues and categories in the transcript domain. High-level features correspond to the division between the actual program (that needs be summarized) and the non-program, i.e., the commercials. We call this coarse program segmentation. Once we know program vs. non-program content, we need to further perform macrosegment structure analysis to uncover more information about the program segments. Classification such as host vs. anchor segment and anchor vs. reportage segments are examples of such analysis. Once we have all the features we identify the key elements to be included in the summary and rank them based on their importance. The program is summarized by selecting the top ranked key elements. The multimedia summary generated is personalized using a user profile and is then presented to the user.

5.3.1   Family histogram

An image histogram is a one-dimensional vector representing the color values and the frequency of their occurrence in the image. Family histograms and Superhistograms are color representations of video segments and full length videos respectively. We introduced the notion of Superhistograms [Agnihotri & Dimitrova, 2000; Dimitrova et al., 1999] which is a compact representation of video. The computation of Superhistogram consists of keyframe detection, color quantization, histogram computation, histogram family comparison and merging, ranking of the histogram families to extract a Superhistogram. A *family* of frames is a set of frames (not necessarily contiguous) that exhibits uniform features (e.g. color, texture, composition). Here we use color histogram representations for our exploration of family of contiguous frames for scene boundary detection. Our concept of family histograms is based on computing frame histograms, finding the differences between consecutive histograms and merging similar histograms.

Family histograms can be used to segment videos into visually uniform color segments. The underlying assumption is that a TV program has a consistent color palette, which can be derived as a family of merged individual shot histograms. The method computes color histograms for individual shots. These could be the keyframes obtained from the cut-detection process. It then merges the histograms into a single cumulative histogram called a family histogram based on a comparison measure. This family histogram represents the color union of the all the shots in the family. As new shots are added, the

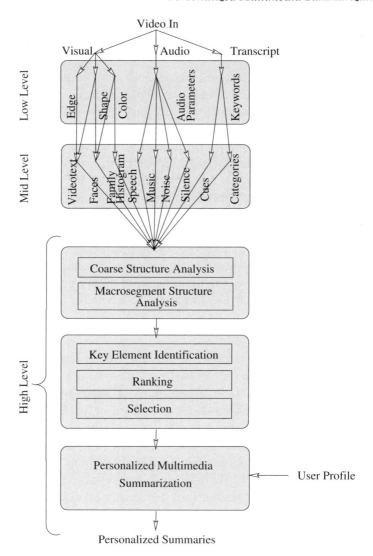

Figure 5.1.   The three layered Segmentation and Summarization module.

family histogram accumulates the new colors from the respective shots. However, if the histogram of a new frame is different from any of the previously constructed family histograms, a new family is formed. Figure 5.2 shows the frames that have been clustered together as separate families. The time progresses along the x-axis and the family number is along the y-axis.

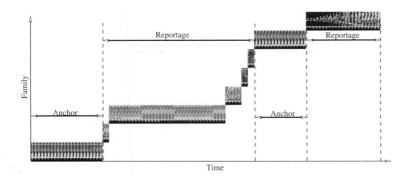

Figure 5.2.   Family histogram clustering of a news program.

5.3.2   Videotext

The textual information present within the frames of a video gives important semantic cues with multiple uses in summarization, indexing, and retrieval; it often appear in fixed positions on the screens, as in the case of game scores, highlights important video segments. The goal of videotext detection is to find regions in video frames, which correspond to text overlay (superimposed text), i.e., the anchor name in a news program and scene text (e.g., "hotel" street signs, etc.). Text analysis is related to detecting and characterizing the superimposed text on video frames. We can apply an optical character recognizer on the detected regions, which results in a transcript of the superimposed text on the screen. This can be used for video annotation, indexing, semantic video analysis, and search. For example, the origin of a broadcast is indicated by a graphic station logo in the right-hand top or bottom of the screen. Such station logo, if present, can be automatically recognized and used as annotation. From the transcript, a look-up database of important TV names, public figures, can be created. These names are associated with topics and categories, e.g., Bill Clinton is associated with "president of the U.S.A." and "politics". We can link names to faces if there is a single face detected in an image. Naming can be solved by using a "name" text region under the face that has certain characteristics of text length and height. Names can also be inferred from discourse analysis (e.g., in news, the anchors are passing the token to each other: "and Jim now back to you in New York".) Anchor/correspondent names and locations in a news program are often displayed on the screen and can be recognized by extracting the text showing in the bottom one-third of the video frame. Further, in music videos, musician names and music group names, and in talk shows, talk show hosts and guests, and other TV personalities are also introduced and identified in a similar fashion. So, by detecting the text box and recognizing the text, the video can be indexed based on a TV personality or a location. This information can then be used for retrieving news clips based on proper names or locations. For example, in the case of the personal profile indicating a preference to news read by a particular newscaster, information obtained using superimposed text analysis can help in detecting and tagging the news for later retrieval. Sports programs can be indexed by extracting the scores and team or player names.

We developed a method for text detection that uses edge information in the input images to detect character regions and text regions [Agnihotri & Dimitrova, 1999]. The method has 85% recall and precision for CIF resolution. The first step of videotext detection is to separate the color information that will be processed for detecting text: R frame of an RGB image or Y component for an image in the YUV format. The frame is enhanced and edge detection is performed. An edge filtering is performed next in order to eliminate frames with too many edges. The resulting edges are then merged to form connected components. If the connected components satisfy size and area restrictions, they are accepted for the next level of processing. If connected components lie within row and column thresholds of other connected components, they are merged to form text boxes. The text boxes are extracted from the original image and local threshold is performed to obtain text as black on white. This is then passed onto an optical character recognizer to generate text transcripts.

Figure 5.3, shows examples of edge images and extracted text areas. The text detection can be further used to string together text detected across multiple frames to generate the text pattern: scrolling, fading, flying, static etc. Scrolling text could possibly mean ending credits and flying text could mean that the text is a part of a commercial.

5.3.3   Face

Face detection is important in video summarization because people are most interested in people. The summary should reflect the presence of people including stars, celebrities, politicians in the selected key elements in the video.

Various methods have been proposed for face detection. A survey can be found in [Chellappa et al., 1995]. Those approaches can be assigned into one of the two broad categories: (i) feature-based methods, which operate by searching for different facial features and using their spatial relationship to locate faces (ii) classification-based methods which try to detect the presence of a face as a whole by classifying subimages of a given image into the categories of face or non-face subimages.

We used the face detection method described by Wei & Sethi [1999] in order to classify and recognize different genres [Dimitrova et al., 2001]. The method employs feature-based top-down scheme. It consists of the following

Figure 5.3. The original sub-image (top), edge image, accepted connected components, and locally thresholded image containing text as black on white (bottom).

steps: (i) Skin-tone region extraction, (ii) Pre-processing, (iii) Face candidate selection, and (iv) Decision making. Through manually labeling the skin-tone pixels of a large set of color images, a distribution graph of skin-tone pixels in YIQ color coordinate is generated. A half ellipse model is used to simulate the distribution and filter skin-tone pixels of a given color image Morphological operations are applied to skin-tone regions to smooth each region, break narrow isthmuses and remove thin protrusions and small isolated regions. Shape analysis is applied to each region and those with elliptical shapes are accepted as candidates. Iterative partition process based on k-means clustering is applied to rejected regions to decompose them into smaller convex regions and see if more candidates can be found. Finally, possible facial features are extracted and their spatial configuration is checked to decide if the candidate is truly a face.

5.3.4 Audio classification

The purpose of audio segmentation and classification is to divide the audio signal into portions of different classes (e.g. speech, music, noise, or combinations thereof) [Li et al., 2000b]. The first step is to partition a continuous bit-stream of audio data into non-overlapping segments, such that each segment is homogenous in terms of its class. Each audio segment is then classified, using low-level audio features such as bandwidth, energy, pitch, mel-frequency cepstral coefficients (MFCC), linear predictive coding coefficients (LPC), and zero-crossings (ZCR) into seven mid-level audio categories. The seven audio categories used in our experiments include silence, single speaker speech, music, environmental noise, multiple speakers' speech, simultaneous speech and music, and simultaneous speech and noise.

5.3.5   Transcript analysis

Transcript analysis can give semantic information about the video which is complimentary to the audiovisual analysis. Surface analysis with time information can reveal essential clues about the program structure. Keyword spotting has been used for news indexing and retrieval. Script analysis can be instrumental in role identification. Semantic analysis using thesauri and discourse analysis can enable semantic annotation and indexing of narrative programs. In the rest of the chapter we will give instances of how we used transcript analysis for commercial detection, for program summarization, and categorization.

Transcripts can be generated using multiple methods including speech to text conversion, closed captions (CC), or third party program transcription. In the United States, FCC regulations mandate insertion of closed captions in the broadcast. In the analog domain CC are inserted in the Vertical Blanking Interval. In the digital domain there are different standards for encoding closed captions. A complete time-stamped program transcript can be generated for all the programs that have closed captions embedded. The time-stamps are used to align the CC data with the related portion of the program. The transcripts also contain all the standard ASCII printable characters (ASCII value 32-127) that are not used as control characters. This means that the transcript in the United States contains the double ('>>') and triple arrows ('>>>') that can be used to identify specific portions of the transcript, for example the change in topic or speaker. Table 5.1 shows an example of a extracted closed caption text. The first column is the time stamp in milliseconds relative to the beginning of the program and the second is the closed captions extracted from the input video.

5.4   Structured program summarization

The summarization of a structured program is a three-step process. The first step consists of segmentation of program content from non-program content such as commercials, future program announcements etc. The second step is identification of semantically meaningful pieces that are complete in themselves. For a news program, this is an individual story. For a sports game it is a concept of 'a play' and 'break' [Xie et al., 2002]. For a talk show it is the segment that starts from the entry of the guest, the interaction of the host and the

Table 5.1. Sample extracted closed caption text.

time	closed caption
29863	an earlier decision and voted
31264	to require background checks
32567	to buy guns at gun shows.
34970	But did the senate really make
36141	the gun laws tougher?
38205	No one seems to agree on that.
40549	Linda Douglass is
41549	on capitol hill.
43613	>>Reporter: The senate debate
44815	dissolved into a frenzy

guest and the 'exit' of the guest or the entry of the next guest. Once the individual segments have been identified, the next step is the identification of content elements that will be included in the summary. For a news program, this could be the segment where the news story is being introduced by the anchor. In this section we present examples of structure program summarization.

A technical challenge in summarizing different programs is to use visual, audio, and textual cues to segment the program. Based on the application, a summary needs to be generated which includes audio, video and text from the program. Certain visual attributes are more prominent than certain audio attributes. The problem is how to reconcile the meaning of the different domains. How do we determine what is the most salient/descriptive/essential part of a segment. For example, if there is a story about the president, then the president giving his statement is the crux of the story and needs to be included in the summary. For a story that contains a short interview with the 'victim' and long interviews with relatives, neighbors etc., we need to find the small piece that contains the interview with the 'victim'. In text people have used the first few sentences. In news, the video associated with the first few sentences show the anchor that is not the novel element in the story. For an ideal summary we need the one segment which is the heart of the story. In the audio domain, segments preceded by long pause are more important. In the news program, however, this could mean some technical difficulty or a shot coming back to the reporter. The technical challenge is how to select visual, audio, and textual elements to create a comprehensive summary. The next problem after getting the 'right' audio and 'right' video is that people can get disoriented when the video being shown is out of sync with the audio being played. The problem thus is multifold: what segments to select and how to combine.

5.4.1   Commercial detection and boundaries

Producing summarized video representations of a TV broadcast requires reliable methods for isolating program segments out of broadcast material. We explored commercial detection methods in the uncompressed as well as compressed visual domain. In the literature there are many methods that have been proposed for detecting commercials [Blum, 1992; Bonner & Faerber, 1982; Agnihotri et al., 2003a; Iggulden et al., 1997; Li & Kuo, 2000a; Lienhart et al., 1997a; McGee & Dimitrova, 1999; Nafeh, 1994; Novak, 1988].

There are different families of algorithms that can be used for commercial boundary detection based on low and mid-level features. Also, the features can be extracted in either uncompressed or in compressed domain. We have considered the following features: (i) Unicolor frames (In this respect our video testing material is from countries where unicolor frames play an important role in commercial break editing.) (ii) High change in visual activity, computed using cut distance (i.e. distance between consecutive abrupt shot changes), (iii) Letterbox format, i.e. if the video material is presented in a 4:3 vs. 16:9 aspect ratio.

We performed an extensive analysis of the available features for a data set of eight hours of TV programs from various genres. Then we divided the set of features into two classes: (i) features that can aid in determining the location of the commercial break (triggers) and (ii) features that can determine the boundaries of the commercial break (verifiers). In the first step, the algorithm checks for triggers. The algorithm, then verifies if the detected segment is a commercial break. In our model we use the two types of features in a Bayesian Network, where the first layer comprises of the features that act as triggers, and the second layer comprises of the features that act as verifiers. In addition, we used genetic algorithms for parameter fine tuning and optimization of the final performance [Agnihotri et al., 2003a].

5.4.2   Talk show summarization

Talk show summarization determines the boundaries of program segments as well as commercial breaks and extracts a program summary from a complete broadcast. This system uses closed captions to segment, summarize, and index talk show videos [Agnihotri et al., 2001], whose structure is primarily determined by the time devoted to various guests. Various textual keywords, a database of other textual cues, and an inference engine is used to determine guest arrival times, guest identity, guest area of expertise, and the presence of commercial advertisements. Within the context of program summarization, the process of categorization is used to infer additional information about the subject of conversation in the program. For example, categorization is used to infer the main topic of a particular segment of the program. In the case of talk show summarization, categorization is used to infer the guest area of expertise. Four different summaries are then always produced, since it is not yet known how to generate only those most preferred by a given user.

The first is a purely textual summary, assembled from templates and extracted closed captioned text; see Figure 5.4. Italicized text are templates, bold text is inferred by the inference engine, and plain text is the close captioned text determined by the algorithm to be the most relevant excerpt. The second is a high-level table of contents which lists guests and their associated clock times and which omits commercials; see Table 5.2. This can be used as index into the video. The third selects the most relevant keyframes for a segment and generates a visual and textual tableau, as shown in Figure 5.5. It also stores for each guest a preview, that is, the portion of the video in which the guest is introduced. A fourth and purely graphic summary, called the 'yadda yadda barcode' is in Figure 5.6. It visualizes the speaking pattern of the host and guests and shows the location of commercials.

Summary of *The Late Show with David Letterman*

There were 3 guests featured in **The Late Show with David Letterman.**

The first guest was **Brooke Shields** *whose specialty is in the field of* **movie.**
Our first guest is a talented actress who stars in a brand-new film. It's called Black and White. It opens on Wednesday.

The second guest was **Oliver Platt** *from the field of* **movie.**
Our next guest is a talent and prolific actor. His latest film, Ready to Rumble, opens on Friday.

The last guest was **Joni Mitchell** *who has made a livelihood in the field of* **music.**
Our next guest is a legendary and influential singer- songwriter whose new CD is a collection of classic songs about love and, consequently, heartache. The CD is entitled both sides now.

Figure 5.4.   Summary of *The Late Show with David Letterman.*

Two retrieval methods were implemented to enable searching. The first, called Video Scout [Jasinschi et al., 2001], uses the output of the summarizer to enable the user of a home video storage (like TiVo) to view only segments and/or guests they are interested in, specified by keyword 'magnets'; see Figure 5.7. The second, Talkshow Miner, accumulates summary data in a relational database accessible over the web, where users can then specify via standard database queries those segments they wanted to see clips from.

Table 5.2.   Table of contents of *The Tonight Show with Jay Leno*.

Jay Leno	11:35pm – 12:35am	The Tonight Show with Jay Leno
segment 1	11:35 – 11:48	Jay Leno, host
segment 2	11:51 – 11:56	Jay Leno, host
segment 3	12:00 – 12:12	Tom Hanks, movie
segment 4	12:16 – 12:24	John Glenn, politics
segment 5	12:28 – 12:32	Puff Daddy, music

Summary visualization

The first guest was *Tom Hanks* whose specialty is in the field of movie.

The second guest was *John Glenn* from the field of politics.

The last guest was *Puff Daddy* from the field of music.

Figure 5.5.   Speaker-guest visualization of the talk show summary.

5.4.3   News summarization

Summarization of structured program consists of segmentation of individual stories and then identification of key elements to be included in the summary.

Segmentation.   We have developed a high-level segmentation method, in which we first find the commercial breaks in a particular news program, and then we perform story segmentation within the news portion. For stories, we use the story break markup ('>>>') in the closed captioning. This method has been used in the literature before [Merlino et al., 1997]. For commercials, we use a text transcript-based commercial detector. In part, this relies on the absence of closed captioning for 30 seconds or more, and in part, it relies on the news anchors using cue phrases to segue to/from the commercials, such as, "coming up after the break" and "welcome back". We look for onset cues such as "right back", "come back", "up next" and "when we return", in conjunction

Figure 5.6. Yadda yadda barcode for *The Tonight Show with Jay Leno*.

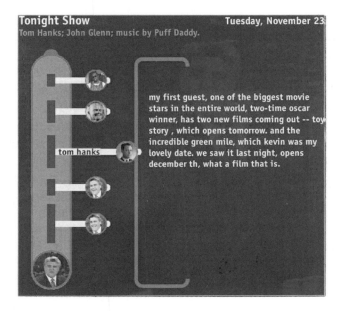

Figure 5.7. Interface for Video Scout: Expanded view and textual summary of user-selected program segment.

with offset cues, such as "welcome back" and the "new speaker" markup ('> >'). We tested commercial detection on four financial news and four talk show programs, totaling 360 minutes, with 33 commercials totaling 102 minutes. Our algorithm detected 32 commercials totaling 104 minutes. Of these, 25 were exactly right. Only one commercial was completely missed. We detected 4 extra minutes spread out over seven commercials. The resulting recall and precision are 98%and 96% respectively.

In addition we have developed a single descent method for story segmentation that relies on multiple cues: audio, visual and transcript. The single descent method relies on unimodal and multimodal segment detection. Unimodal — within the same modality — segment detection means that a video segment exhibits 'same' characteristic over a period of time using a single type of modality such as camera motion, presence of certain objects such as videotext or faces or color palette in the visual domain. Multi-modal segment detection means that a video segment exhibits a certain characteristic taking into account attributes from different modalities. Next, we use multimodal pooling as a method to determine boundaries based on applying votes from multiple modalities. In the single descent method, the idea is to start at the top of the stacked uniform segments and perform a single pass through the layers of unimodal segments that in the end yields the merged segments. In this process of descending down through the different attribute lines, we perform simple set operations such as union and intersection. For example, one approach is to start with the textual segments as the dominant attributes and then combine them with the audio and visual segments.

Story summarization.   Each broadcast news story must be summarized in order to present the summary for browsing. Although there are different forms of summaries, in our case a summary consists of a selection of 'key-elements' from the transcript, audio, and visual track. For example, key elements might include: a summary sentence of text and a representative image from the reportage. The key elements are selected based on computation of importance value. The key element importance value is computed as a deterministic linear function of low, mid and high level video features contained within the various frames of the news story segment. Alternatively, the importance function can be generated using a probabilistic framework (e.g. Bayesian Belief Network).

For selection of key elements from the transcript, the IBM TextMiner document summarizer is applied. The goal is to select the single best sentence in the 'document' [Textminer]. 'Best' in this context is some weighted metric involving the 'salience' (position) of the sentence in the document, its length, and other factors. Usually the first sentence of a news story is selected; since this sentence is normally both a comprehensive summary and a good introduction to the story. However, sometimes a non-useful sentence occurs first ("Hello, I'm Dan Rather."), this exception is often caught by TextMiner.

We also use a TextMiner engine for document (story) classification. It works on the basis of frequency of occurrence of words in the story. The classifier was trained off-line with a corpus of labeled exemplar stories. The corpus was composed of news stories from CBS, NBC, ABC etc. In all there were 686 stories that were classified as one of the following topics: weather, sports, traffic, closing, future announcements, local news, headlines, finance, commercials, and miscellaneous.

In order to find a representative visual key element, we find a representative keyframe for each news story. Each story is composed of an anchor shot followed by reportage shot(s). The anchor shot is the same for all stories, so it does not provide any value. In order to select an image from only the reportage, an anchorperson detector is used. Basically, it finds the face, which is the largest face in view in the majority of the frames of the entire news program. For news programs we have empirically determined that outdoor shots are more important for news stories than indoor shots. We use the indoor/outdoor detector developed by Naphade et al. [2002]. Subject to these constraints, we select a frame that is deemed to be the most 'interesting' by the algorithm that considers other attributes such as color, etc. Figure 5.8 shows an example of the summarization process for a news story.

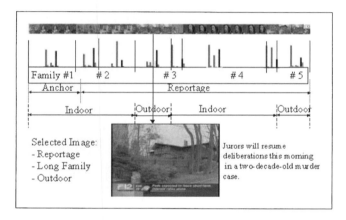

Figure 5.8. Example of news story summarization.

5.5 Personalized summarization

We all perceive things differently. When searching for content of interest we want to be presented with things that are most interesting and appealing to us. One-size-fits-all type of content analysis and retrieval will break down when the amount of content explodes beyond our ability to search it quickly and easily even with the most advanced tools. Content analysis and search needs to be personalized based on what is inside (semantics), how it is presented (form), where and when it is presented (context).

5.5.1   User study

We explored the fundamental issues around personalized summarization in a brainstorm session [Agnihotri et al., 2003b]. We examined four major questions: who needs summarization and why, what should summaries contain, how should summaries be personalized, and how can results be validated. The resulting ideas were then clustered by using the method of 'affinity diagrams' [Beyer & Holtzblatt, 1998]. The study suggests that user preferences should be derived from explicit user statements about age, gender, profession, hobbies, personality category, aspirations, topics, location, time allocated for media consumption, and media type preferences, and from implicit trends inferred from viewing histories and summary usage.

The study found that users fell into at least two classes with different needs, professionals and home users. Videos could be classified as produced or live-captured. Produced videos can be ranked by the level of their editing. People would use summaries to browse, search, plan future viewing, and organize viewing of past videos. A critical factor is user environment, with mobile users having devices with restricted resources. Generally, summaries could be expected to be viewed at a fixed time of day. Summary content should be hierarchically organized, and indexable by elements that are genre-specific. Some media seem better suited for certain type of summaries: text for financial, video for sports, audio for music, static visual for instructional content. A knowledge of user attention level (e.g., if driving), user activity, and the available devices and communication bandwidths to a server are all critical for summary usefulness.

User profiles can be obtained passively by recording any prior searches and any access patterns to prior summaries, although the required granularity of detail of this historical information is unknown. Actively, personal information and preferences for content and presentation should be gathered, but perhaps some of this can be bypassed by asking for more generic personality patterns. Summaries should be evaluated on both their content and their fit to their users with regard to information value, degree of personalization, accommodation of user time and task needs, and user satisfaction; this can be elicited by first presenting a summary and then presenting the actual video, and asking how well the summary did. More objectively, summary recall and precision can be measured against hand-labeled ground truth.

Major obstacles remain. There is no available method for an all-genre summarization method. It is difficult to map user profiles to user needs, or ultimately to the video content filters and to the presentation formats. However, there may be some intermediate psychological constructs that can reduce user classes and user interfaces to a few verifiable generic types —if they can be found. It is unlikely that summaries can be done in real-time on small devices. A methodology for measuring user satisfaction and then determining from such measures what needs to be improved is still undeveloped.

5.5.2 Requirements

We need to differentiate between media elements vs. content specific elements summarization. The personalization session of the workshop concluded unanimously that summary is user context dependent. The personal profile should be comprehensive and include implicitly derived elements from user behavior and explicitly provided personal information. The validation session revealed that both content requirements and user requirements should be validated. The workshop suggested that the more important research advances will result from tackling the 'more human' issues related to personalization and validation. In particular, it is imperative to develop a methodology for evaluating multimedia summaries. In the literature the methods have covered the content aspects of summarization for generic summaries. However, now more than ever before, it is important for summarization to be personalized to cover user aspects: preferences, context, time, location, and task.

5.5.3 Research issues

The main question is whether the multimedia summary generated for programs is user dependent. If so what is the level of personalization that is required? Does the personalization need to occur for the display of the summary also? If the answer to the above questions is yes, then the research in this area will be to find what are all the elements that make up the personal profile: What are the tangible facts about a person and the tastes (which are intangible) that shape person's likes and dislikes. We will need a process to map the personal profile attributes to video content representation and the values from different annotators. The profiles used so far contain text attributes only. For the purpose of personalized video summarization text may or may not be enough. If text is not enough, we will need to explore different audio and video features that should be included in a personal profile. A framework for modeling the user's likes and dislikes will be explored. Additionally, there exist issues for the profile representation.

We need a framework that captures the personal preferences, creates summaries, updates the preferences and the summaries and evolves over time. Ideally, we also need a process to deal with evolving user preferences.

Another area of research is how the needs of the user differ based on the genre of the program. For example, in a talk show, is it be sufficient to show text summary and a few keyframes containing the images of the guests. Versus, in a music program, both audio and video segments may need to be presented. Does the presentation of the summary need to be temporally consistent? What tasks are the summaries be mostly used for: in deciding whether or not to watch a program or in order to skim the programs, or else in order to find the part of the program that is of interest to the user and how does this effect the summary produced?

5.6   Conclusions and future work

Ability to cope with information explosion will be one of our fundamental tools in the digital content era. Automatic content summarization and abstraction will be essential in consumer access to information.

In this chapter we surveyed different video summarization techniques: color analysis using family histograms, transcript extraction and analysis, superimposed and overlaid text detection, face detection, and audio classification. We have shown how to use audio, visual, and text information for selecting important elements of news stories for multimedia news summary. We gave examples of structured program summarization such as news programs and talk shows.

We explored aspects of personalized multimedia summarization. Our research indicates that personal preferences such as viewing history, summary usage history, and explicit preferences such as topics, location, age, gender, profession, hobbies, allocated time, consumption preferences (auditory vs. visual) are very important for video summarization. Personalized multimedia summaries take different rendering based on the content and media preferences of the user as well as context of the user. There are many open research questions remaining in this area. One set of questions is related to all the information that should be included in the personal profile that enables effective personalization. Even when the elements of the personal profile are known the question is how to map the personal profile attributes to video content representation and the values from different audio, visual and text annotators. Additionally, there exist issues for the profile representation. Conceivably the user's preferences are evolving and we need to capture this aspect in the representation model as well as usage model. And, a very important question is how to evaluate the summaries. How do we create methodology for consistent personalized multimedia summarization evaluation?

There are many ways to create a summary. There will be lots of ways to personalize the summary for the user. The problem is to analyze and evaluate what is important to users in order to perform the personalization automatically so that we can capture users' requirements and not only what the technology today is capable of achieving.

References

Agnihotri, L., and N. Dimitrova [1999]. Text detection for video analysis. In: *Proc. of the IEEE Workshop on Content-Based Access of Image and Video Libraries (CBAIVL'99)*, pages 109–113.

Agnihotri, L., and N. Dimitrova [2000]. Video clustering using Superhistograms in large video archives. In: *Proc. Fourth International Conference on Advances in Visual Information Systems (Visual 2000)*, pages 62–93.

Agnihotri, L., K. Devara, T. McGee, and N. Dimitrova [2001]. Summarization of video programs based on closed captioning. In: *Proc. SPIE Conf. on Storage and Retrieval in Media Databases*, San Jose, CA, pages 599–607.

Agnihotri, L., N. Dimitrova, T. McGee, S. Jeannin, D. Schaffer, and J. Nesvadba [2003a]. Evolvable visual commercial detectors. In: *Proc. IEEE Conference on Vision and Pattern Recognition*, Madison, WI.

Agnihotri, L., N. Dimitrova, J. Kender, and J. Zimmerman [2003b]. User study on personalized multimedia summarization. In: *Proc. of the International Conference on Multimedia and Expo*, submitted.

Aner, A., and J.R. Kender [2002]. Video summaries through mosaic-based shot and scene clustering. In: *Proc. European Conf. on Computer Vision*, Denmark.

Arons, B. [1997]. Speechskimmer: A system for interactively skimming recorded speech. *ACM Transactions on Computer-Human Interaction*, 4(1):3–38.

Beyer, H., and K. Holtzblatt [1998]. *Contextual Design: Defining Customer-Centered Systems*. Morgan and Kaufmann, San Francisco, CA.

Blum, D.W. [1992]. *Method and Apparatus for Identifying and Eliminating Specific Material from Video Signals*. US patent 5,151,788.

Bonner, E.L., and N.A. Faerber [1982]. *Editing System for Video Apparatus*. US patent 4,314,285.

Chang, S.-F., D. Zhong, and R. Kumar [2001]. Video real-time content-based adaptive streaming of sports videos. In: *Proc. of the IEEE Workshop on Content-Based Access of Image and Video Libraries (CBAIVL'01)*.

Chellappa, R., C.L. Wilson, and S. Sirohey [1995]. Human and machine recognition of faces: A Survey. In: *Proc. of the IEEE*, 83(5):705–740.

Christel, M.G., M.A. Smith, C.R. Taylor, and D.B. Winkler [1998]. Evolving video skims into useful multimedia abstractions. In: *Proc. of the ACM Conference on Computer Human Interaction (CHI'98)*, pages 171–178.

Dagtas, S., T. McGee, and M. Abdel-Mottaleb [2000]. Smart Watch: An automated video event finder. In: *Proc. ACM Multimedia'2000*, Los Angeles, CA.

Dimitrova, N., J. Martino, L. Agnihotri, and H. Elenbaas [1999]. Color super-histograms for video representation. In: *Proc. of the International Conference on Image Processing (ICIP'99)*, pages 314–318.

Dimitrova, N., L. Agnihotri, and G. Wei [2001]. Video classification using object tracking. *International Journal of Image and Graphics, Special Issue on Image and Video Databases*, 1(3):487–506.

Dimitrova, N., L. Agnihotri, and R. Jainschi [2003]. Temporal video boundaries. In: *Video Mining*, A. Rosenfeld, D. Doermann, and D. Dementhon (eds.), Kluwer, pages 63–92.

Firmin, T., and M.J. Chrzanowski [1999]. An evaluation of automatic text summarization systems. In: *Advances in Automatic Text Summarization*, I. Mani and M.T. Maybury (eds.), MIT Press, pages 391–401.

Gould, J.D., and C. Lewis [1985]. Designing for usability: Key principles and what designers think. *Communications of the ACM*, 28(3):300–311.

Haas, N., R. Bolle, N. Dimitrova, A. Janevski, and J. Zimmerman [2002]. Personalized news through content augmentation and profiling. In: *Proc. IEEE ICIP*.

Hauptmann, A.G., and M.J. Witbrock [1998]. Story segmentation and detection of commercials in broadcast news video. In: *Proc. Advances in Digital Libraries Conference (ADL'98)*, pages 168–179.

Iggulden, J., K. Fields, A. McFarland, and J. Wu [1997]. *Method and Apparatus for Eliminating Television Commercial Messages*. US Patent 5,696,866.

Jasinschi, R.S., N. Dimitrova, T. McGee, L. Agnihotri, J. Zimmerman, and D. Li [2001]. Integrated multimedia processing for topic segmentation and classification. In: *Proc. of IEEE Intl. Conf. on Image Processing (ICIP)*, Greece.

Kurapati, K., S. Gutta, D. Schaffer, J. Martino, and J. Zimmerman [2001]. A multi-agent TV recommender. In: *Proc. of User Modeling 2001: Personalization in Future TV Workshop*.

Lee, H., A. Smeaton, P. McCann, N. Murphy, N. O'Connor, and S. Marlow [2000]. Fischlar on a PDA: A handheld user interface for video indexing, browsing and playback system. In: *Proc. of the Sixth ECRIM Workshop: User Interfaces for All*.

Li, Y., and C.C.J. Kuo [2000a]. Detecting commercial breaks in real TV programs based on audiovisual information. In: *Proc. SPIE on Internet Multimedia Management System*, vol. 4210, Boston, pages 225–236.

Li, D., I.K. Sethi, N. Dimitrova, and T. McGee [2000b]. Classification of general audio data for content-based retrieval. *Pattern Recognition Letters*, 22(5):533–544.

Li, Y., W. Ming, C.-C. Jay Kuo [2001]. Semantic video content abstraction based on multiple cues. In: *Proc. ICME*, Japan, pages 804–808.

Lienhart, R., C. Kuhmunch, and W. Effelsberg [1997a]. On the detection and recognition of television commercials. In *Proc. IEEE International Conference on Multimedia Computing and Systems*, pages 509–516.

Lienhart, R., S. Pfeiffer, and W. Effelsberg [1997b]. Video abstracting. *Communications of the ACM*, 40(12):55–62.

Ma, Y.-F., L. Lu, H.J. Zhang, and M. Li [2002]. A user attention model for video summarization. In: *Proc. ACM Multimedia*, Juan Les Pin.

Mani, I., and M.T. Maybury [1999]. *Advances in Automatic Text Summarization*. MIT Press.

Merlino, A., D. Morey, and M. Maybury [1997]. Broadcast news navigation using story segmentation. In: *Proc. of the Fifth ACM International Conference on Multimedia (ACMMM'97)*, pages 381–391

Merlino, A., and M. Maybury [1999]. An empirical study of the optimal presentation of multimedia summaries of broadcast news. In: *Advances in Automatic Text Summarization*, I. Mani and M.T. Maybury, (eds.), MIT Press, pages 391–401.

Merialdo, B., K.T. Lee, D. Luparello, and J. Roudaire [1999]. Automatic construction of personalized tv news program. In: *Proc. of the Seventh ACM International Conference on Multimedia (ACMMM'99)*, pages 323–331.

McGee, T., and N. Dimitrova [1999]. Parsing TV program structures for identification and removal of non-story segments. In: *Proc. SPIE Conference on Storage and Retrieval for Image and Video Databases VII*.

Nafeh, J. [1994]. *Method and Apparatus for Classifying Patterns of Television Programs and Commercials Based on Discerning of Broadcast Audio and Video Signals*. US patent 5,343,251.

Naphade, M.R., I. Kozintsev, and T.S. Huang [2002]. A factor graph framework for semantic video indexing. *IEEE Transactions on Circuits and Systems for Video Technology*, 12(1):40–52.

Novak, A.P. [1988]. *Method and System for Editing Unwanted Program Material from Broadcast Signals*. US patent 4,750,213.

Petkovic, M., V. Mihajlovic, W. Jonker [2002]. Multi-modal extraction of highlights from TV formula 1 programs. In: *Proc. IEEE Conf. on Multimedia and Expo*, Lausanne.

Smith, M., and T. Kanade [1997]. Video skimming and characterization through the combination of image and language understanding techniques. In: *Proc. of the IEEE Computer Society Conference on Computer Vision and Pattern Recognition (CVPR'97)*, pages 775–781.

Sundaram, H., L. Xie, S.-F. Chang [2002]. A utility framework for the automatic generation of audio-visual skims. In: *Proc. ACM Multimedia*, Juan Les Pin.

IBM Intelligent Miner for Text.

Uchihashi, S., J. Foote, A. Girgensohn, and J. Boreczky [1999]. Video Manga: Generating semantically meaningful video summaries. In: *Proc. ACM Multimedia*, pages 383–392.

Wei, G., and I.K. Sethi [1999]. Face detection for image annotation. In: *Proc. of Pattern Recognition in Practice VI*, Vlieland, The Netherlands.

Xie, L., S.-F. Chang, A. Divakaran, and H. Sun [2002]. Structure analysis of soccer video with hidden Markov models. In *Proc. Interational Conference on Acoustic, Speech and Signal Processing (ICASSP-2002)*, Orlando, FL, May 13-17.

Yahiaoui, I., B. Merialdo, and B. Huet [2001]. Generating summaries of multi-episode video. In: *Proc. ICME*, Japan, pages 792–796.

Chapter 6

FEATURES FOR AUDIO CLASSIFICATION

Jeroen Breebaart and Martin F. McKinney

Abstract   Four audio feature sets are evaluated in their ability to differentiate five audio classes: popular music, classical music, speech, background noise and crowd noise. The feature sets include low-level signal properties, mel-frequency spectral coefficients, and two new sets based on perceptual models of hearing. The temporal behavior of the features is analyzed and parameterized and these parameters are included as additional features. Using a standard Gaussian framework for classification, results show that the temporal behavior of features is important for automatic audio classification. In addition, classification is better, on average, if based on features from models of auditory perception rather than on standard features.

Keywords   Audio classification, automatic content analysis

6.1   Introduction

Developments in Internet and broadcast technology enable users to enjoy large amounts of multimedia content. With this rapidly increasing amount of data, users require automatic methods to filter, process and store incoming data. Examples of applications in this field are automatic setting of audio equalization (e.g., bass and treble) in a playback system, automatic setting of lighting to correspond with the mood of the music (or vice versa), automatic cutting, segmenting, labeling, and storage of audio, and automatic playlist generation based on music similarity or some other user specified criteria. Some of these functions will be aided by attached *metadata*, which provides information about the content. However, due to the fact that metadata is not always provided, and because local processing power has increased tremendously, interest in *local* automatic multimedia analysis has increased. A major challenge in this field is the automatic classification of audio. During the last decade, several authors have proposed algorithms to classify incoming audio data based on different algorithms [Davis & Mermelstein, 1980; Wold et al., 1996; Spina &

W. Verhaegh et al. (eds.), Algorithms in Ambient Intelligence, 113-129
© 2004 *Kluwer Academic Publishers. Printed in the Netherlands.*

Zue, 1996; Scheirer & Slaney, 1997; Spina & Zue, 1997; Scheirer, 1998; Zhang et al., 1998; Wang et al., 2000a; Wang et al., 2000b; Zhang & Kuo, 2001; Li et al., 2001]. Most of these proposed systems combine two processing stages. The first stage analyzes the incoming waveform and extracts certain parameters (features) from it. The feature extraction process usually involves a large information reduction. The second stage performs a classification based on the extracted features.

A variety of signal features have been proposed for general audio classification. A large portion of these features consists of low-level signal features, which include parameters such as the zero-crossing rate, the signal bandwidth, the spectral centroid, and signal energy [Davis & Mermelstein, 1980; Wold et al., 1996; Scheirer & Slaney, 1997; Scheirer, 1998; Wang et al., 2000a; Wang et al., 2000b]. Usually, both the averages and the variances of these signal properties are included in the feature set. A second important feature set which is inherited from automatic speech recognizers consists of mel-frequency cepstral coefficients (MFCC). This parametric description of the spectral envelope has the advantage of being level-independent and of yielding low mutual correlations between different features for both speech [Hermansky & Malayath, 1998] and music [Logan, 2000]. Classification based on a set of features that are uncorrelated is typically easier than that based on features with correlations.

Both low-level signal properties and MFCC have been used for general audio classification schemes of varying complexity. The simplest audio classification tasks involve the discrimination between music and speech. Typical classification results of up to 95% correct have been reported [Toonen Dekkers & Aarts, 1995; Scheirer & Slaney, 1997; Lu & Hankinson, 1998]. The performance of classification schemes usually decreases if more audio classes are present [Zhang et al., 1998; Zhang & Kuo, 2001]. Hence, the use of features with high discriminative power becomes an issue. In this respect, the MFCC feature set seems to be a powerful signal parameterization that outperforms low-level signal properties. Typical audio classes that have been used include clean speech, speech with music, noisy speech, telephone speech, music, silence and noise. The performance is roughly between 80 and 94% correct [Foote, 1997; Naphade & Huang, 2000a; Nahphade & Huang, 2000b; Li et al., 2001].

For the second stage, a number of classification schemes of varying complexity have been proposed. These schemes include Multivariate Gaussian models, Gaussian mixture models, self-organizing maps, neural networks, k-nearest neighbor schemes and hidden Markov models. Some authors have found that the classification scheme does not influence the classification accuracy [Scheirer & Slaney, 1997; Golub, 2000], suggesting that the topology of the feature space is relatively simple. An important implication of these results is that, given the current state of audio classifiers, perhaps further advances could be made by developing more powerful features or at least understanding the feature space, rather than building new classification schemes.

Thus, our focus here is on features for classifying audio. We compare the two existing feature sets most commonly used, low-level signal properties and the MFCC, with two new feature sets and evaluate their performance in a general audio classification task with five classes of audio. The two new feature sets, described in detail below, are based on perceptual models of auditory processing. Additionally, a more advanced method of describing temporal feature behavior will be discussed which extends the traditional way of including mean and variance of feature trajectories.

6.2   Method

Our audio classification framework consists of two stages: feature extraction followed by classification. We compare four distinct feature extraction stages to evaluate their relative performance while in each case using the same classifier stage. The feature sets (described below) are: (1) standard low-level (SLL) signal properties; (2) MFCC; (3) psychoacoustic (PA) features including roughness, loudness and sharpness; and (4) an auditory filter representation of temporal envelope (AFTE) fluctuations. The audio database consists of a subset of a larger audio database (approximately 1000 items). Two volunteers listened to all tracks and classified the audio according to 21 pre-defined audio categories. Furthermore, a rating was given of how well each audio item matched the audio category. From these ratings, a 'quintessential' audio database was made of all tracks that had the same label for both volunteers and had a sufficiently high rating. Finally, five general audio classes were obtained by combining the 21 audio classes: classical music, popular music (including jazz, country, folk, electronica, latin, rock, rap, etc), speech (male, female, English, Dutch, German and French) crowd noise (applauding and cheering) and background noise (including traffic, fan, restaurant, nature, etc). The number of files in each general audio class is given in Table 6.1.

The classification process begins with the extraction of a set of features, i.e., feature vectors, from each sound file. Feature vectors are calculated on consecutive 32768-sample frames (743 ms at 44.1 kHz sampling rate) with a hop-size of 24576. The choice of a 743-ms frame length was based on a finding of Spina & Zue [1996]. Using a Gaussian-based classification mechanism to classify audio into several categories, they operated on MFCC and found that performance increased as the analysis frame size increased to about 700 msec and then saturated (and decreased a little) with further increases. The resulting feature vectors are grouped into classes based on the type of audio.

Table 6.1. Audio database by class.

class name	files
popular music	175
classical music	35
speech	31
noise	25
crowd noise	31

The resulting feature vectors from each class are divided into two groups, a training group and a test group: a randomly chosen 90% of the vectors are assigned to the training group and the remaining 10% are assigned to the test group.[1] An L-dimensional (where L is the length of each feature vector) Gaussian mixture model is then parameterized based on the *training* group. Subsequently, the predicted audio classes of the *test* group are compared to the actual audio classes to derive the classification performance. The controlled random division between training and test groups was performed 10 times. The average classification performance of these 10 divisions is used as the overall classification performance of the current feature set and model.

When classifying a feature vector from the test group, a feature vector $\mathbf{x}$ of length L with $\mathbf{x} \in \Re^L$ falls into one of J classes. The solution entails a rule for predicting the class membership based on the L features. This solution is based on the statistical properties of the training data which comprise a set of feature vectors $\mathbf{x}_{n,j}$ with their corresponding class membership j. It is assumed that the features in each class follow a multivariate Gaussian distribution with each class having its own mean vector and its own covariance matrix. Then the probability density in class j, $p(\mathbf{x}_j)$, is given by

$$p(\mathbf{x}_j) = p(\mathbf{x}|j) = p(\mathbf{x}, \mu_j, \mathbf{S}_j) = \frac{1}{\sqrt{(2\pi)^L |\mathbf{S}_j|}} \exp\left(-\frac{1}{2}(\mathbf{x} - \mu_\mathbf{j})^T \mathbf{S}_j^{-1} (\mathbf{x} - \mu_\mathbf{j})\right),$$

with $\mathbf{x}$ the feature vector, μ_j the average value for class j, which can be estimated from the training data:

$$\hat{\mu}_j = \frac{1}{N_j} \sum_{n=1}^{N_j} \mathbf{x}_{n,j},$$

---

[1] This method and the 90%-10% split of training and test data was used in an earlier study on music genre classification [Tzanetakis et al., 2001]. It is not clear that this is the optimal division of training and test data but we have not yet evaluated the effect of using different split sizes.

where N_j is the number of training vectors belonging to class j and $\mathbf{x}_{n,j}$ the n-th learning vector for class j. The within-class covariance matrix $\mathbf{S}_j$ can be estimated by

$$\hat{\mathbf{S}}_j = \frac{1}{N_j - 1} \sum_{n=1}^{N_j} (\mathbf{x}_{n,j} - \hat{\mu}_j)(\mathbf{x}_{n,j} - \hat{\mu}_j)^T.$$

Classification of a new feature vector $\mathbf{x}$ is based on maximizing the discriminant function δ_j across classes J. The discriminant function for class j is given by

$$\delta_j(\mathbf{x}) = -\frac{1}{2}(\mathbf{x} - \mu_j)^T \mathbf{S}_j^{-1}(\mathbf{x} - \mu_j) - \frac{L}{2}\ln(2\pi) - \frac{1}{2}\ln|\mathbf{S}_j| + \ln p(j),$$

which can be rewritten as

$$\delta_j(\mathbf{x}) = -\frac{1}{2}D(\mathbf{x}, \mu_j, \mathbf{S}_j) - \frac{1}{2}\ln(|\mathbf{S}_j|) + \ln(p(j)) - \frac{L}{2}\ln(2\pi),$$

where $D(..)$ denotes the *Mahalanobis distance* from $\mathbf{x}$ to μ_j, and is given by

$$D(\mathbf{x}, \mu_j, \mathbf{S}_j) = (\mathbf{x} - \mu_j)^T \mathbf{S}_j^{-1}(\mathbf{x} - \mu_j).$$

In addition to evaluating each feature set by its classification performance we also look at the discriminating power of individual features. To do this, we calculate the *Bhattacharyya distance* between classes based on single features. The Bhattacharyya distance $M(i,j)$ is a symmetric normalized distance measure between two centroids based on the centroid means and (co)variances [Papoulis, 1991]:

$$M(i,j) = M(j,i) = \frac{1}{8}(\mu_i - \mu_j)^T \left(\frac{\mathbf{S}_i + \mathbf{S}_j}{2}\right)^{-1} (\mu_i - \mu_j) + \frac{1}{2}\ln\left(\frac{|\frac{1}{2}(\mathbf{S}_i + \mathbf{S}_j)|}{\sqrt{|\mathbf{S}_i|}\sqrt{|\mathbf{S}_j|}}\right).$$

A high Bhattacharyya distance for a particular feature means that the centroids are well separable along that feature (dimension). An interesting property of the Bhattacharyya distance is *additivity*: the distances between two joint distributions of statistically independent random variables equals the sum of the marginal distances. Thus, *as long as features are statistically independent*, the distance of a certain subset can directly be calculated by summing marginal Bhattacharyya distances.

Although the size of the feature sets differ, we performed classification using the same number of features from each set. We chose the best 9 features from each set following an iterative ranking procedure. First the feature space was reduced to one feature and for each feature, the overall misclassification rate was estimated based on Gaussian data assumptions. The expected misclassification rate between classes i and j, ε_{ij} is given by

$$\varepsilon_{ij} = p(i)p(error|i) + p(j)p(error|j).$$

The likelihood ratio $K(\mathbf{x})$ at position $\mathbf{x}$ is given by

$$K(\mathbf{x}) = \frac{p(\mathbf{x}|i)}{p(\mathbf{x}|j)}.$$

The decision boundary for classification is set at $K(\mathbf{x}) = 1$. If the class centroids μ_j are assumed to be known, and if the shape of the class clusters is normal and can be characterized by their covariance matrices $\mathbf{S}_j$, the expected error rates can be calculated. Following [Fukunaga, 1972], the upper bound (Chernoff bound) of a misclassification error between classes i and j, ε_{ij}, is then given by

$$\varepsilon_{ij} \leq \sqrt{p(i)p(j)}\exp\left(-M_{ij}\right),$$

with M_{ij} the Bhattacharyya distance between class i and j. The upper bound for the total misclassification rate ε is given by

$$\varepsilon \leq \sum_i^c \sum_{j>i}^c \varepsilon_{ij}.$$

The feature which gave the lowest estimated misclassification rate was ranked as the top feature. Next the same process was performed using a two-feature space that included the top-ranked feature and one of the remaining features. The feature that gave, along with the top-ranked feature the lowest estimate of misclassification was ranked second. This process was repeated until all features were ranked (note that this method does not guarantee that the optimal combination is found since the search method may result in order effects). The top nine features of each set were chosen and used for the classification results described below.

6.2.1   Features

It has been reported, for speech-music discrimination, that the 2nd-order statistics of features (over time) are better features for classification than the features themselves [Scheirer & Slaney, 1997]. Here we carry the temporal analysis one step further and include a parameterized analysis of the features' temporal fluctuations. To do this we subdivide the audio frame into 1024-sample (23-ms) subframes with a 512-sample overlap, calculate feature values for each subframe and take the fast Fourier transform (FFT) on the array of subsequent feature calculations. Next the power spectrum is calculated and normalized by the DC value to reduce correlations. Finally the frequency axis is summarized by summing the energy in four frequency bands: 1) 0 Hz (average across observations), 2) 1-2 Hz (on the order of musical beat rates), 3) 3-15 Hz (on the order of speech syllabic rates), and 4) 20-43 Hz (in the range of modulations contributing to perceptual roughness).

Low-level signal parameters. This feature set, based on standard low-level (SLL) signal parameters, includes: (1) root-mean-square (RMS) level, (2) spectral centroid, (3) bandwidth, (4) zero-crossing rate, (5) spectral roll-off frequency, (6) band energy ratio, (7) delta spectrum magnitude, (8) pitch, and (9) pitch strength. This set of features is based on a recent paper by Li et al. [2001].

The final SLL feature vector consists of 36 features:

1-9: DC values of the SLL feature set
10-18: 1-2 Hz modulation energy of the SLL feature set
19-27: 3-15 Hz modulation energy of the SLL feature set
28-36: 20-43 Hz modulation energy of the SLL feature set

MFCC. The second feature set is based on the MFCCs [Slaney, 1998]. Mel-frequency cepstrum coefficients represent a parameterized description of the (frequency-warped) power spectrum. They are often used in automatic speech recognizers due to the following properties:

- Compactness: they are able to represent the spectral envelope with only a few parameters.

- Independence: the cepstral coefficients are approximately uncorrelated for speech signals [Hermansky & Malayath, 1998] and music [Logan, 2000]. The discrete cosine transform (DCT) used in the MFCC algorithm is a good approximation of the optimal diagonalizing principle-component analysis (PCA) transform.

- Gain independence: except for the zeroth MFCC coefficient, which is a function of the overall signal level, the remaining MFCC coefficients do not depend on the input level.

The full MFCC feature vector consists of 52 features:

1-13: DC values of the MFCC coefficients
14-26: 1-2 Hz modulation energy of the MFCC coefficients
27-39: 3-15 Hz modulation energy of the MFCC coefficients
40-52: 20-43 Hz modulation energy of the MFCC coefficients

Psychoacoustic features. The third feature set is based on estimates of the percepts roughness, loudness and sharpness. Roughness is the perception of temporal envelope modulations in the range of about 20-150 Hz and is maximal for modulations near 70 Hz. Loudness is the sensation of intensity and sharpness is a perception related to the spectral density and the relative strength of high-frequency energy. For loudness and sharpness, we characterize the temporal behavior in the same manner as for the SLL and MFCC feature sets. The estimate of roughness, however, is not treated the same way. Because roughness is based on mid-frequency temporal envelope modulations, an accurate estimate can only be obtained for relatively long audio frames ($>\sim$ 180 msec). Thus, the temporal variation of roughness within an audio frame is represented by its mean and standard deviation over subframes of length $N_s = 8192$ (186 msec) with a hopsize of 4096.

Roughness.   Our model for roughness is based on those of Zwicker & Fastl [1999a] and Daniel & Weber [1997]. First we filter each frame of audio by a bank of gammatone filters [Patterson et al., 1995], bandpass filters based on the effective frequency analysis of the ear, which are spaced logarithmically between 125 and 10 kHz. Next, the temporal (Hilbert) envelope of each filter output is calculated by taking the FFT, setting the negative frequency components to zero, multiplying the positive frequency components by 2, taking the inverse FFT and finally the absolute value. A correlation factor is then calculated for each filter based on the correlation of its output with that from two filters above and below it in the filter bank. This measure was introduced to decrease the estimated roughness of bandpass noise. The roughness estimate is then calculated by filtering the power in each filter output with a set of bandpass filters (centered near 70 Hz) that pass only those modulation frequencies relevant to the perception of roughness [Zwicker & Fastl, 1999a], multiplying by the correlation factor and then summing across frequency and across the filter bank.

Loudness.   The loudness model is loosely based on the work of Zwicker & Fastl [1999b]. Here we assume that the maximum allowed sample value in the digital representation of the audio file corresponds to 96 dB SPL and we estimate the loudness level in sones. First, the power spectrum of the input frame is calculated and then normalized by subtracting (in dB) an approximation of the absolute threshold of hearing. This normalized power spectrum is then filtered by a bank of gammatone filters and summed across frequency to yield the power in each auditory filter, which corresponds to the internal excitation as a function of frequency. These excitations are then compressed, scaled and summed across filters to arrive at the loudness estimate.

Sharpness.   The psychoacoustic percept of sharpness is based primarily on the relative strength of high-frequency components [von Bismarck, 1974]. It is estimated here using an algorithm almost identical to that of loudness with the only differences being a weight applied to each filter before the final summation and an additional normalization factor. The weights are larger for filters at higher center frequencies and were optimized to fit the psychoacoustic data on sharpness [von Bismarck, 1974; Zwicker & Fastl, 1999c].

Jeroen Breebaart and Martin F. McKinney   121

The final psychoacoustic (PA) feature vector consists of 10 features:

  1: average roughness
  2: standard deviation of roughness
  3: average loudness
  4: average sharpness
  5: 1-2 Hz loudness modulation energy
  6: 1-2 Hz sharpness modulation energy
  7: 3-15 Hz loudness modulation energy
  8: 3-15 Hz sharpness modulation energy
  9: 20-43 Hz loudness modulation energy
  10: 20-43 Hz sharpness modulation energy

Auditory filterbank temporal envelopes. The fourth feature set is based on a model representation of temporal envelope processing by the human auditory system. Each audio frame is processed in two stages: (1) it is passed through a bank of gammatone filters, as in the PA feature set, which represent the spectral resolution of the peripheral auditory system and (2) a temporal analysis is performed by computing the modulation spectrum of the envelope (computed as in the roughness feature) of each filter output. In this implementation the filterbank includes every other critical band filter from 260-9795 Hz. Because the temporal analysis is performed directly on the entire 32768-sample frame we do not need to subdivide it into sub-frames as with the other features. The other features consist of only one value per audio frame and thus in order to evaluate their temporal behavior within a single frame, their values must be computed on a subframe basis. An advantage of being able to perform the temporal analysis directly at the level of the audio frame is that higher frequencies (up to the Nyquist frequency of the sampling rate) can be represented. After computing the envelope modulation spectrum for each auditory filter it is normalized by the average value (DC) and, parameterized by summing the energy in four frequency bands and taking the log: 0 Hz (DC), 3-15 Hz, 20-150 Hz, and 150-1000 Hz. The parameterized summary of high-frequency modulations is not calculated for some low-frequency critical band filters: a frequency band summary value is only computed for a critical band filter if the filter's center frequency is greater than the maximum frequency of the band. This process yields 62 features describing the auditory filterbank temporal envelopes (AFTE):

  1-18: DC envelope values of filters 1-18
  19-36: 3-15 Hz envelope modulation energy of filters 1-18
  37-52: 20-150 Hz envelope modulation energy of filters 3-18
  53-62: 150-1000 Hz envelope modulation energy of filters 9-18

6.3   Results

6.3.1   Standard low-level features (SLL)

The results for the standard low-level feature set are shown in Figure 6.1. The left panel shows the confusion matrix using the best 9 features of the SLL feature set. Classification performance is best for crowd noise with 99% correct classification and second best for classical music with 96% correct classification. Popular music is correctly classified in 80% of the cases, while in 20% of the cases it is classified as speech. Detection of background noise is not good (46% correct). It is often misclassified as classical music (28%) or crowd noise (21%). The overall classification accuracy is 82%.

The right panel shows the Bhattacharyya distance between all classes based on single features. Features 5 (spectral rolloff frequency) and 6 (band-energy ratio), and their second-order statistics (features 14, 15, 23, 24, 32, 33) show discriminative power between classical music and other classes. Furthermore, the 2-3 Hz and 3-15 Hz modulation energies of most features (feature numbers 19-27) contribute to discrimination between speech and background noise and between speech and crowd noise. Consistent with the confusion between speech and popular music in the classification results, no features show strong discrimination between popular music and speech. Only features 19 (3-15 Hz modulation energy of the signal RMS) and 28 (20-43 Hz modulation energy of the RMS) show some discriminative power. The small numbers above the x-axis at the right panel indicate the rank of the best 9 features.

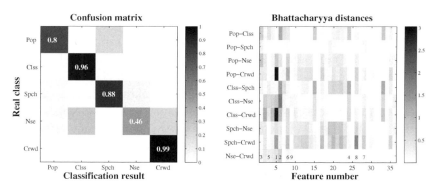

Figure 6.1.   *Standard low-level features*: Classification performance (left) and feature discrimination power, i.e., distance between classes as a function of feature (right). The numbers above the x-axis indicate the rank of the best 9 features.

6.3.2 Mel-frequency cepstral coefficients (MFCC)

Figure 6.2 shows the results for the MFCC feature set. The format of the figure is the same as Figure 6.1: the confusion matrix of classification using the best 9 features is shown in the left panel and the Bhattacharyya distances between classes based on single features are shown in the right panel. The overall classification accuracy using the best 9 MFCC features is 85%, which is better than the SLL feature set. However, some of the individual audio classes show worse classification accuracy. For example, classical music is correctly identified in 90% of all cases, compared to 96% for the SLL feature set. Furthermore, crowd noise is correctly recognized in 86% of the cases, compared to 99% for the SLL feature set. Classification of background noise shows a large increase in performance, at 75% for the MFCC feature set compared to only 46% for the SLL feature set.

The Bhattacharyya distances in the right panel show that the second MFCC feature, which is the 2nd discrete cosine transform coefficient of the input spectrum, is a powerful feature, especially for discriminating crowd noise from other classes. This feature can be interpreted as the relative levels of low- and high-frequency energy in the signal. Features 6-13, which describe the input spectrum at a fine detail level, do not contribute to the classification process. On the other hand, second-order statistics of the first few MFCCs contribute to the discrimination between various classes. As with SLL features, discrimination between popular music and speech and between background noise and crowd noise is poor. This is consistent with the low Bhattacharyya distances between those classes.

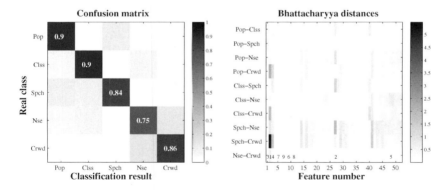

Figure 6.2. *Mel-frequency cepstral coefficients (MFCC)*: Classification performance (left) and feature discrimination power, i.e., distance between classes as a function of feature (right). The numbers above the x-axis indicate the rank of the best 9 features.

6.3.3   Psychoacoustic (PA) feature set

The results for the PA feature set are shown in Figure 6.3. The overall classification accuracy of this feature set is 84%. The confusion matrix shows that most classes were classified with an accuracy between 72 and 88% correct, with the exception of crowd noise which was classified correctly in 100% of the cases. The features that best discriminate between the classes are the 3-15 Hz modulation energy of the sharpness (feature 8), the average sharpness (feature 4), the average roughness (feature 1), the average loudness (feature 3) and the 3-15 Hz loudness modulation energy (feature 7). The panel of Bhattacharyya distances for individual class contrasts shows that feature 8 (3-15 Hz modulation energy of the sharpness) is key in the discrimination of speech from crowd noise, background noise and classical music. In addition, the average sharpness (feature 4) provides a relatively large distance between classical music and crowd noise.

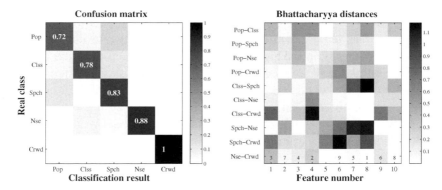

Figure 6.3. *Psychoacoustic features*: Classification performance (left) and feature discrimination power, i.e., distance between classes as a function of feature (right). The numbers above the x-axis indicate the rank of the best 9 features.

6.3.4   AFTE feature set

The feature analysis results for the auditory filter temporal envelope modulation feature vector are shown in Figure 6.4. The layout of the figure is the same as previous figures. The overall classification accuracy using the best 9 features is high (90%). Crowd noise is detected correctly in all cases and background noise and popular music are detected quite accurately (91%). Speech and classical music have lower scores (85% and 83%, respectively) and are both sometimes misclassified as popular music. Low and high Bhattacharyya distances (right panel) are somewhat scattered across features and audio classes, however there is a clear maximum for features 1-5 (steady-state values of the auditory filters 1-5 centered at 260-376 Hz) for the discrimination between popular music and crowd noise. Other than that, no other individual feature sticks out as a powerful discriminator; the high performance of the AFTE feature set is due to a combination of features.

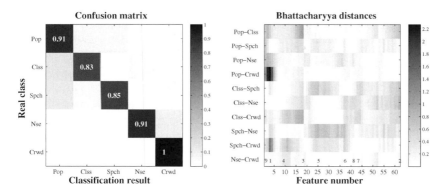

Figure 6.4. *Auditory filterbank temporal envelope*: Classification performance (left) and feature discrimination power, i.e., distance between classes as a function of feature (right). The numbers above the x-axis indicate the rank of the best 9 features.

6.3.5   Results summary

The results are summarized in Table 6.2. A comparison across all feature sets shows that, overall, the AFTE feature set are the most powerful for classification with our audio classes. For some individual classes, however, other feature sets perform slightly better: for classical music, the MFCC set performs the best with 90% classification; and for speech, the SLL set performs the best with 88% classification. Although it is not shown here, the performance of the AFTE feature set increases as more features are included. With the best 20 features, average classification performance increases to 95% with a 95% classification accuracy for classical music as well.

In comparing Bhattacharyya distances across features it is important to note that they are not normalized across feature sets. The MFCC set gives the single largest Bhattacharyya distance, 5.5 between the speech and crowd noise classes. Despite this large distance, the MFCC feature set is not the best basis for classifying speech or crowd noise: speech is often confused with popular and classical music and crowd noise is often confused with noise (see left panel of Figure 6.2). The PA and AFTE feature sets, on the other hand, give the lowest maximum Bhattacharyya distances at 1.2 and 2.2 respectively, but they are not the worst feature set overall. This combination of low Bhattacharyya distances and high classification performance may be due to a high correlation

Table 6.2. *Classification Results Summary.* Each entry gives the percent correct classification for the given audio class (top row) and feature set (left column). The right column shows, for each feature set, the average percent correct across all classes.

feature set	popular music	classical music	speech	noise	crowd noise	average
SLL	80%	96%	88%	46%	99%	82%
MFCC	90%	90%	84%	75%	86%	85%
PA	72%	78%	83%	88%	100%	84%
AFTE	91%	83%	85%	91%	100%	90%

between features and/or a better distribution of distances across features and audio classes.

6.4 Discussion

One can see from the ranking of the top nine features (see right panels of Figures 6.1–6.4) that temporal variations of the basic features are important for classification. In all cases, there are at least a few features in the top nine that incorporate temporal modulations. In addition, although we don't show the results here, performance of the SLL feature set is reduced to 71% overall if only the average values (DC) of the feature set are used for classification.

Our assumption of Gaussian-shaped clusters in the feature space may not be valid. Based on reasonably favorable results, it appears that it is not a bad assumption but we have not analyzed the feature space to the point where we can quantitatively evaluate this assumption. Classification performance could be further improved by such an analysis followed by the incorporation of perhaps more appropriate probability density functions.

Further improvements in classification performance could also come from changes to the classifier. For example, it is possible that sequential classification using fewer classes at each stage (i.e. grouping several classes initially) could result in improved performance. One could use different features, perhaps based on the Bhattacharyya distances between classes, for each sequential stage. In addition, as more powerful features for class discrimination are developed, different classification schemes (self-organizing maps, neural networks, k-nearest neighbor schemes and hidden Markov models) may begin to show differences in performance.

Finally, combinations of the best features from each set could also lead to improvements in classification performance. One could rank the features across sets in the same manner that we rank features within each feature set, and then choose the combination that yields the best performance.

6.5   Conclusions

We have shown that audio classification can be improved by developing and working with improved audio features. Our comparison of current feature sets for this purpose shows that, overall, the AFTE feature set is the most powerful. However, for classifying particular audio classes, namely classical music and speech, the SLL feature set performs best.

From our ranking of features we have also shown that temporal variations in features are important for audio class discrimination. In all of our feature sets, the nine top-ranked features include at least two features representing temporal fluctuations.

Finally, we have seen that the Bhattacharyya distance can be a useful measure for determining the power of a particular feature. However a high Bhattacharyya distance between two clusters does not necessarily guarantee good classification performance for those cluster classes. In order to better relate Bhattacharyya distance and classification performance, one must look at correlations between features and at the entire feature vs. distance space (right panels of Figures 6.1–6.4).

Future work will involve the development of new features, further analysis of the feature space to test the Gaussian assumption, examination of alternative classification schemes, and the incorporation of more audio classes.

Acknowledgments

The authors would like to thank Armin Kohlrausch of Philips Research for helpful comments on this manuscript and Nick de Jong and Fabio Vignoli of Philips Research for their assistance in building the audio database.

References

Bismarck, G. von [1974]. Sharpness as an attribute of the timbre of steady sounds. *Acustica*, 30:159–172.

Daniel, P., and R. Weber [1997]. Psychoacoustical roughness: Implementation of an optimized model. *Acustica·Acta Acustica*, 83:113–123.

Davis, S.B., and P. Mermelstein [1980]. Comparison of parametric representations for monosyllabic word recognition in continuously spoken sentences. *IEEE Transactions on Acoustics, Speech and Signal Processing*, ASSP-28:357–366.

Duda, R.O., and P.E. Hart [1973]. *Pattern classification and scene analysis*. Wiley, New York.

Foote, J. [1997]. A similarity measure for automatic audio classification. In *Proc. AAAI 1997 Spring Symposium on Intelligent Integration and Use of Text, Image, Video, and Audio Corpora*.

Fukunaga, K. [1972]. *Introduction to Statistical Pattern Recognition*. Academic press, New York, London.

Glasberg, B.R., and B.C.J. Moore [1990]. Derivation of auditory filter shapes from notched-noise data. *Hearing Research*, 47:103–138.

Golub, S. [2000]. *Classifying Recorded Music*. Master's thesis, University of Edinburgh. http://www.aigeek.com/aimsc/.

Hermansky, H., and N. Malayath [1998]. Spectral basis functions from discriminant analysis. In *International Conference on Spoken Language Processing*.

Li, D., I.K. Sethi, N. Dimitrova, and T. McGee [2001]. Classification of general audio data for content-based retrieval. *Pattern Recognition Letters*, 5:533–544.

Logan, B. [2000]. Mel frequency cepstral coefficients for music modeling. In *International Symposium on Music Information Retrieval*.

Lu, G., and T. Hankinson [1998]. A technique towards automatic audio classification and retrieval. In *4th Int. Conference on Signal Processing*, Beijing.

Naphade, M.R., and T.S. Huang [2000a]. A probabilistic framework for semantic indexing and retrieval in video. In *IEEE International Conference on Multimedia and Expo (I)*, pages 475–478.

Naphade, M.R., and T.S. Huang [2000b]. Stochastic modeling of soundtrack for efficient segmentation and indexing of video. In *Proc. SPIE, Storage and Retrieval for Media Databases*, San Jose, CA, pages 168–176.

Papoulis, A. [1991]. *Probability, Random Variables and Stochastic Processes*. McGraw-Hill series in electrical engineering. McGraw-Hill, New York.

Patterson, R.D., M.H. Allerhand, and C. Giguere [1995]. Time domain modeling of peripheral auditory processing: A modular architecture and software platform. *J. Acoust. Soc. Am.*, 98:1890–1894.

Scheirer, E., and M. Slaney [1997]. Construction and evaluation of a robust multifeature speech/music discriminator. In *Proc. ICASSP*, Munich, Germany, pages 1331–1334.

Scheirer, E.D. [1998]. Tempo and beat analysis of acoustical musical signals. *J. Acoust. Soc. Am.*, 103:588–601.

Slaney, M. [1998]. *Auditory Toolbox*. Technical Report 1998-010, Interval Research Corporation. http://rvl4.ecn.purdue.edu/m̃alcolm/interval/1998-010/.

Spina, M.S., and V.W. Zue [1996]. Automatic transcription of general audio data: Preliminary analysis. In *Proc. 4th Int. Conf. on Spoken Language Processing*, Philadelphia, PA.

Spina, M.S., and V.W. Zue [1997]. Automatic transcription of general audio data: Effect of environment segmentation on phonetic recognition. In *Proceedings of Eurospeech*, Rhodes, Greece.

Toonen Dekkers, R.T.J., and R.M. Aarts [1995]. *On a Very Low-Cost Speech-Music Discriminator*. Technical Report 124/95, Nat.Lab. Technical Note.

Tzanetakis, G., G. Essl, and P. Cook [2001]. Automatic musical genre classification of audio signals. In *Proceedings International Symposium for Audio Information Retrieval (ISMIR)*, Princeton, NJ.

Wang, H., A. Divakaran, A. Vetro, S.F. Chang, and H. Sun, [2000a]. *Survey on Compressed-Domain Features used in Video/Audio Indexing and Analysis*. Technical report, Department of electrical engineering, Columbia University, New York.

Wang, Y., Z. Liu, and J.C. Huang [2000b]. Multimedia content analysis using both audio and visual cues. *IEEE Signal Processing Magazine*, 17:12–36.

Wold, E., T. Blum, D. Keislar, and J. Wheaton [1996]. Content-based classification, search, and retrieval of audio. *IEEE Multimedia*, Fall:27–36.

Zhang, M., K. Tan, and M.H. Er [1998]. Three-dimensional sound synthesis based on head-related transfer functions. *J. Audio. Eng. Soc.*, 146:836–844.

Zhang, T., and C.C.J. Kuo [2001]. Audio content analysis for online audiovisual data segmentation and classification. *IEEE Transactions on Speech and Audio Processing*, 9:441–457.

Zwicker, E., and H. Fastl [1999a]. *Psychoacoustics: Facts and Models*, volume 22 of *Springer series on information sciences*, chapter Roughness, pages 257–264. Springer-Verlag, Berlin, 2nd edition.

Zwicker, E., and H. Fastl [1999b]. *Psychoacoustics: Facts and models*, volume 22 of *Springer series on information sciences*, chapter Loudness, pages 203–238. Springer-Verlag, Berlin, 2nd edition.

Zwicker, E., and H. Fastl [1999c]. *Psychoacoustics: Facts and models*, volume 22 of *Springer series on information sciences*, chapter Sharpness and Sensory Pleasantness, pages 239–246. Springer-Verlag, Berlin, 2nd edition.

Chapter 7

INFORMATION RETRIEVAL IN THE AUDIO DOMAIN

Matthew Harris, Jan Kneissler, and Frank Thiele

Abstract   Multimedia content in the form of non-textual data is becoming more and more abundant. This chapter addresses the problem of adequate natural and efficient access to this increasing amount of available content, sometimes referred to as the content bottleneck. We focus on the special case of spoken audio content and demonstrate how partly erroneous document information (e.g. from automatic speech recognizer transcripts) may be consistently incorporated into existing information retrieval infrastructure. Experiments and results on a standard spoken document retrieval task are presented.

Keywords   Spoken document retrieval, probabilistic vector space modeling, topic boundary detection.

7.1   Introduction

Today, content is available in large quantities and it will become even more abundant in the future. Finding the right piece of content will therefore become a critical issue for devices and services that store or deliver content. To make content easily accessible it has to be structured and annotated to support time-efficient searching and navigation. For audio/video content, using only the visual information already helps, and much has been done in Philips in this area. However, most video content is accompanied by audio and there are also devices that are solely dedicated to storing and delivering audio.

First retrieval features, purely based on the video signal, are already entering products. Using the audio signal will in general improve retrieval quality. Audio is also an important feature for navigation, and in some products it is the only one.

W. Verhaegh et al. (eds.), Algorithms in Ambient Intelligence, 131-150.
© 2004 *Kluwer Academic Publishers. Printed in the Netherlands.*

7.1.1   Information retrieval using spoken documents

Speaking in most generality, the purpose of information retrieval (*IR*) is, given a large set of information containers (= *documents*), to identify a subset containing exactly those documents that are *relevant* with respect to some representation of the user's requirements (= *query*).

In addition to the 'classical' scenario, where documents and queries are given in textual form (e.g. web search engines), there is an increasing need for retrieval involving other modalities like images, audio, and video.

While we deal with spoken documents in this chapter, there are other IR applications in the audio domain which are not related to speech content, e.g. identifying a specific speaker in a movie. Within Philips there has also been work on music retrieval ('query-by-humming') [Pauws, 2002] and audio fingerprinting ('name that tune') [Haitsma & Kalker, 2001].

Focusing on speech and text for queries as well as documents one obtains a matrix of four different scenarios (SDR = spoken document retrieval):

Table 7.1.   Information retrieval scenarios.

	queries	
documents	text	speech
text	web search	voice web
speech	SDR	SDR dialog system

One application using spoken queries is the LISy Newsfinder (presented at CRE2002 [Bauer et al., 2002]). The LISy system allows search in a large set of automatically recorded information sources (news broadcasts on TV) using queries spoken in natural language.

In this chapter we mainly target the bottom left corner of the table i.e. information retrieval of spoken documents using textual queries. The NIST's text retrieval conferences (TREC) introduced a standard evaluation task for this scenario [Garofolo et al., 2000]. For a simple application, 'textual' queries could also be generated by menus or a few buttons of a DVD recorder. A more advanced application of this scenario is question answering, where not only a document relevant to a specific question (e.g. "Who killed Abraham Lincoln?") is to be found, but also the required piece of information is extracted from the document and an answer is formulated.

To retrieve spoken content, the spoken input is converted to a textual representation using automatic speech recognition. Since speech recognition introduces errors, the retrieval accuracy will degrade compared to written documents. On the other hand, the speech recognizer does not produce a single transcript but rather a 'lattice' of alternatives what could have been said. Here, we investigated the impact of the speech recognition by comparing retrieval using manual reference transcriptions for the documents with retrieval using recognized documents.

7.2 Overview

A real life system for multimedia retrieval consists of a preprocessing and indexing part (offline) and a query processing part (online, possibly involving interaction). The document processing and retrieval comprises the following stages:

1. Segmentation of the acoustic signal → Section 3.2 (Acoustic methods).

2. Classification of the segments (e.g. according to gender, channel characteristics) → Section 3.3.

3. Transcription using automatic speech recognizer → Section 7.3.3.

4. Detection of story boundaries (i.e. topic changes) → Section 3.2 (Lexical and prosody methods).

5. Preparation of recognizer output (text or word lattices) for info retrieval → Sections 7.3.4 and 7.4.3.

6. Information retrieval → Sections 7.4.1 and 7.4.2.

In a dialog system for multimedia information retrieval, the processing of spoken queries also involves steps 2, 3, and 4 in its online part.

7.3 Content (pre-)processing

Information retrieval from spoken content involves additional steps on top of that for written documents. The speech must be converted into written document form to be able to carry out the further information retrieval steps.

7.3.1 Broadcast news aspects

In this chapter we consider broadcast news sources, and use the audio parts for our analysis. A news program contains a variety of different modes - reports, interviews, music, noise. The boundaries between such modes may also be topic boundaries. Broadcast news audio data has many aspects that pose challenges for automatic speech recognition systems.

- There are different speaking styles, ranging from 'read' speech, where a (grammatically correct) prepared text is read out, to completely (grammatically loose) spontaneous speech in an interview with someone on the street.

- There are different background noise conditions, ranging from a quiet TV studio, to background traffic noise from a street interview, to the cocktail party effect where other people are speaking in the background, etc.

- There are different microphone and recording characteristics, ranging from a high quality studio microphone to input from a mobile telephone (in a telephone interview).

- Speech segments are intermingled with music or noise segments, sometimes where the boundary is rather fuzzy.

7.3.2   Topic boundary detection

Real life data is not always already divided into documents, each addressing just one topic. With real life text data, a document may be a web page, or a paragraph in the text etc. With audio input, it is often a problem that it is not naturally divided into such segments with each segment addressing just one topic. For the information retrieval task, we require a database of documents, from which we must choose the relevant ones. The information retrieval results on the TREC data, given in Section 7.5.1, use hand segmented documents (i.e. the topic boundaries as provided by the NIST). This allows comparison with results from other sites that have worked on the TREC data. Acoustic methods were used to segment the audio data in the LISy system [Bauer et al., 2002]. More elaborate topic boundary detection schemes are summarized at the end of this section.

Acoustic methods.   An initial segmentation approach purely works with the acoustic input signal, without any automatic transcription of the input. A simple energy criterion can be used to find positions of pause in the speech signal. Pauses may mark sentence boundaries, and may also mark speaker boundaries. This approach can also be used as starting point for the more involved topic boundary detection methods described below.

The Bayesian Information Criterion (BIC) is an effective algorithm to find speaker boundaries and changes in acoustic conditions. BIC finds the most likely position of an acoustic change, and gives a criterion to determine whether the change at this point is significant or not. This simple method has proven very effective in detecting speaker changes in the broadcast news stream [Harris et al., 1999]. In our system, it was used to find gender changes, so the speech recognizer knows when to switch between its gender dependent models.

Here we describe how BIC is used to find exactly *one* speaker change in an interval, and refer to [Chen & Gopalakrishnan, 1998] for more details. Suppose we have a sequence of features representing the speech data

$\{x_i \in \mathbb{R}^d, i = 1 \ldots N\}$. We suppose that features generated from *one* speaker speaking in *one* set of background conditions can be modeled by *one* multivariate Gaussian distribution. The mean and covariance matrix of this Gaussian should clearly be the sample mean and sample covariance. We now compare two scenarios:

1. Only one speaker speaks in the passage $x_1 \ldots x_N$

2. One speaker speaks for the first t frames $x_1 \ldots x_t$, and another for the remaining frames $x_{t+1} \ldots x_N$.

The two scenarios translate to the hypotheses:

1. $x_i \sim \mathcal{N}(\mu, \Sigma)$, $i = 1 \ldots N$,
   where μ and Σ are estimated on $x_1 \ldots x_N$.

2. $x_i \sim \mathcal{N}(\mu_1, \Sigma_1)$, $i = 1 \ldots t$,
   $x_i \sim \mathcal{N}(\mu_2, \Sigma_2)$, $i = t+1 \ldots N$
   where (μ_1, Σ_1) and (μ_2, Σ_2) are estimated on $x_1, \ldots, x_t$ and $x_{t+1}, \ldots, x_N$ respectively.

In the first hypothesis, all N vectors are modeled by one Gaussian, and in the second, the first t are modeled by one Gaussian, and the last $N - t$ are modeled by another. The log likelihood ratio of these two hypotheses is

$$R(t) = N \log |\Sigma| - t \log |\Sigma_1| - (N - t) \log |\Sigma_2|, \qquad (7.1)$$

and the time of most probable speaker change is the value $\hat{t}$ of t for which $R(t)$ is maximum.

Modeling N vectors by two Gaussians rather than one can always give a better fit, as one uses twice as many parameters. The improvement gained by this increase in parameters can be offset. $\text{BIC}(t)$ is defined to be

$$\text{BIC}(t) = R(t) - \lambda \alpha(d) \log N, \qquad (7.2)$$

where $\lambda \in \mathbb{R}$ and $\alpha(d)$ is half the difference in the number of parameters used in the two hypotheses (which is a function of the dimension d of the feature vectors).[1] We say there was a speaker change at $\hat{t}$ if $\text{BIC}(\hat{t}) > 0$. There are some arguments for the choice of $\lambda = 1$, however, varying λ can change the sensitivity to speaker change (and noise).

---

[1] As we choose symmetric Gaussians for the two hypotheses, we have $2\alpha(d) = d + \frac{1}{2}d(d+1)$.

Lexical and prosody methods. More sophisticated topic detection methods start with text (possibly from a speech recognizer), divided into blocks. The topic boundaries are assumed to only occur at the block boundaries. Topic boundary detection done on a word level is too noisy, and would result in imprecise topic boundaries. The blocks obtained using the acoustic methods as discussed before can be used as a starting point. There are also other approaches, e.g. [Carter & Gransden, 2000; Shriberg et al., 2000; Hearst, 1994].

Given the input blocks, the problem is one of labeling each block with a topic, which also defines the topic boundaries. There are two general approaches to topic boundary detection - lexical and prosody methods. Usually, these two approaches are combined in some way.

Lexical methods. Methods which just use text information (and no other information such as prosody in the input sound file) we call 'lexical methods'. Several different lexical approaches are possible.

- *Determining lexical similarity between text blocks.* Measures of 'lexical similarity' between different blocks of text are created. Such measures consider the number of words (or word stems, see Section 7.3.4) in common between blocks. The utilized similarity function are typically of the form given in (7.3) in Section 7.4.1. The topic boundaries are placed at positions where neighboring blocks have a low similarity [Hearst, 1994; Choy 2000].

- *Language model approach using Hidden Markov Models.* Language models describing word usage for various different topics are trained. (A language model gives the probability of seeing a particular word sequence for the given topic.) We now label each sentence, depending on the language model scores for the various topic language models. We model it such that when in a particular topic, it is more likely to stay in that topic than to spring to a new topic (otherwise the tagging would be too noisy). To do this, we use a Hidden Markov Model [Mulbregt et al., 1999; Tur et al., 2001; Shriberg et al., 2000; Stolcke et al., 1999].

- *Boundary word spotting.* Certain words are more likely to appear near a topic change, and other words are less likely. We increase the probability of a topic change at sentence boundaries where more topic turn words are seen, and where fewer non-topic words are seen [Beeferman et al., 1999].

Prosody methods. Prosody methods use features extracted from the speech signal. Such features include silence length between words, changes in energy between words, changes in phoneme length, etc. The different prosody features are combined to give the highest predictive value for topic change.

As mentioned, most authors combine both lexical and prosody methods. Detecting topic changes is quite an active area of research. See for example [Tur et al., 2001; Shriberg et al., 2000; Stolcke et al., 1999].

7.3.3 Automatic speech recognition

The speech recognizer converts the speech signal into text. The basic principle is to compare representations of the signal (*features*) with an *acoustic model* that has been trained on large amounts of speech. The speech recognition system has several aspects:

- *Feature extraction.* The input sound signal is converted into a sequence of feature vectors containing the information relevant to a speech recognizer. Each feature vector corresponds to 10 ms of speech.

- *Acoustic model.* Statistical models are trained for each phoneme. The model of a recognizable word is the concatenation of the relevant phoneme models. For each utterance, one can use these models to find the probability that the utterance was a particular word or word sequence.

  The acoustic model can be adapted from the general models (trained on many speakers) to the speaker and condition at hand. This can bring a significant improvement to the recognition performance.

- *Language model.* Gives the probability of seeing a particular word sequence. It introduces 'statistical knowledge' about the language being spoken, to make nonsense recognitions less likely.

- *Search.* The actual recognition tries to find the word sequence which has most probably been spoken. Statistical knowledge and heuristic methods restrict the huge *search space* of all possible hypotheses to a reasonable subspace. Still, an efficient search is by no means trivial, see [Aubert, 1999; Aubert & Blasig, 2000; Schramm & Aubert, 2000] for details. By *pruning* of the search space, the time demand of search can be traded off against accuracy. Another important property of the search, exploited in this work, is the possibility to write out (parts of the) search space to a *word lattice* which also carries information about the probability of the hypotheses.

Automatic speech recognition using gender dependent acoustic models.
The recognition was improved substantially on the LISy system [Bauer et al., 2002] by using different acoustic models on the different acoustic blocks. A simple gender detection was carried out on each block, and then a male acoustic model was used on the male blocks, and a female acoustic model on the

female blocks. In the recognition system used for the broadcast news transcription evaluation, the acoustic models were adapted to each individual speaker in the data.

For a more detailed description of the Philips speech recognition system used in the international broadcast news evaluations see [Beyerlein et al., 2002].

7.3.4 Word mappings

For information retrieval purposes, inflections and declinations of words are of minor significance. In most cases it is even necessary not to distinguish between different word forms (e.g. if the query contains the word "election", it is advisable to also consider documents with the words "elections", "elect", "elected" or even "ballot"). Thus, during the indexing/retrieval process different words might be treated as identical objects (called *terms*). A term in the info retrieval context may even correspond to phrases (sequences of words), e.g. "the White House". There are different ways to proceed from word level to term level:

- Stemming: words are mapped to their stems; for English there exist fairly simple rule-based stemming approaches (e.g. the Porter [1980] stemmer).

- Lemmatizing: Similar to stemming, but uses linguistic database (e.g. [Wordnet] distinguishes between "occupant" and "occupancy" which the Porter stemmer would map to the same term "occup").

- Mapping to congruence classes according to the synonym relation.

In addition to these, most IR systems allow NULL-mapping of words (called stop word list removal), i.e. neglect words that are supposed to be of little discriminatory power (like "is", "a", etc.).

7.4 Information retrieval in uncertain domains

Classical information retrieval deals with the necessity of finding a subset of *relevant* documents out of a large collection according to a query. Best known examples are search engines for the world wide web. In this classical setup, documents and queries are *exact* in the sense that they are produced without potential error sources (web queries are typically typed, documents are either manually written or automatically composed, e.g. from database entries). However for multimedia documents or spoken queries we have to apply methods that have intrinsic uncertainties (see Section 7.3.3). In order to deal with non-perfect representations of documents and/or queries we propose a probabilistic extension of the information retrieval paradigm.

We will give a new, probabilistic approach to IR based on a well established IR method called vector space modeling (VSM). In the following subsection, we will give a very brief introduction to the basic (non-probabilistic) vector space modeling approach. We will not discuss the more advanced features (latent semantic analysis, blind relevance feedback, see e.g. [Manning & Schütze, 1999]) 'sitting on top' of the basic VSM machinery. It should also be noted, that there are other approaches to IR (e.g. coming from the direction of language modeling [Ponte & Croft, 1998]) that make an intrinsic use of probabilities. However, we are looking for a probabilistic version of the VSM idea in order not to sacrifice its two major advantages:

- the ability of handling huge document collections,

- the compliance with efficient incremental document database updates.

In Section 7.4.2, we will extend the classical VSM setup to the case of probabilistic input, tributing to these two principles.

7.4.1 The vector space modeling approach (VSM)

This very common method for retrieval performed on large collections of documents is based on the following principles:

1. Documents are compositions of 'atomic' units, called *terms*; these units are unique and comparable (i.e. deciding whether two terms are identical is assumed trivial). Apart from this requirement, terms may be anything: words, word stems, phrases, objects (in an image/video), concepts, entities, etc.

2. Documents and queries are regarded as bags of terms, i.e. the only information that is used (for retrieval) is which terms occur and how often. A bag of terms is coded as a vector of integers corresponding to the list of occurrence counts (filling in zeros for the non-occurring terms) with respect to a fixed linear ordering of all terms (*vector representation* of documents and queries).

3. The relevance of a document with respect to a query is modeled as real-valued function, depending on the vector representation of the query, the document and all (other) documents in the database.

A very simple example for such a function is the angle (or equivalently its cosine) between the document and query vector:

$$\cos\phi(\mathbf{d}, \mathbf{q}) \;=\; \frac{\mathbf{d} \cdot \mathbf{q}}{|\mathbf{d}|\,|\mathbf{q}|} \;=\; \sum_{\text{terms } t} \frac{d_t}{|\mathbf{d}|}\frac{q_t}{|\mathbf{q}|} \qquad (7.3)$$

A very popular generalization is to replace the inner product by a general scalar product $\langle \mathbf{d} | \mathbf{q} \rangle = \sum_{i,j} g_{ij} d_i q_j$, usually using a diagonal metrics $g_{ij} = \delta_{ij} r_i$. The values on the diagonal are usually defined by $r_i := -\ln(n(i)/n_d)$, where $n(i)$ denotes the number of documents in the database that contain the term i and n_d is the total number of documents (*inverse document frequency*).

Most VSM systems use a variation of the vector-norm-based length normalization and transformations of term counts (in order not to over-weight terms occurring many times in a document). Thus, for many information retrieval systems, the built-in similarity function S looks on an abstract level like this:[2]

$$S(\mathbf{d}, \mathbf{q}) \ := \ \sum_{\text{terms } t} f_1 \left(d_t, \frac{|\mathbf{d}|}{\langle |\mathbf{d}| \rangle} \right) \cdot f_2(q_t, |\mathbf{q}|) \cdot f_3 \left(\frac{n(t)}{n_d} \right) \qquad (7.4)$$

The choice of the functions f_1, f_2, f_3 is a matter of heuristic nature; however there are a few reasonable restrictions that can be made:

- f_1 factorizes into a count weighting part f and a length normalization part g:
$$f_1(x, y) = f(x) \cdot g(y),$$

- $f(0) = 0$ (to keep the document vectors sparse), $f(1) = g(1) = 1$ (scaling normalization),

- $f(x)$ and $f_2(x, y)$ are monotonously increasing but sub-linear functions (w.r.t. x),

- $g(x)$ behaves asymptotically like $1/x$ for $x \to \infty$,

- $f_3(1) = 0$, f_3 is decreasing in $[0, 1]$ (frequent terms are less relevant) typically with a steep negative slope at 0 and a gentle slope at 1.

Since in most applications the queries consist only of a few words, length normalization and count transformations have no effect on the query side, so f_2 is chosen trivially: $f_2(q_t, |\mathbf{q}|) := q_t$. Many IR systems take the logarithm or an iterated logarithm as document term transformation, e.g. $f(x) = \log_2(1 + \log_2(1 + x))$. The document frequency weighting function f_3 is commonly also based on the logarithm: $f_3(x) = -\ln(x)$, i.e. $f_3(\frac{n(t)}{n_d}) = \ln(\frac{n_d}{n(t)})$. The length normalization factor is typically of the form $g(y) = \frac{1}{b+(1-b)y}$ with a parameter $b \in [0, 1]$.

---

[2] Note that the length of the document vector $|\mathbf{d}|$ is normalized with respect to the mean length $\langle |\mathbf{d}| \rangle$ (averaged over the full document collection).

A classical example for a vector space modeling similarity function is the so-called OKAPI metrics [Schäuble, 1997]:

$$S(\mathbf{d}, \mathbf{q}) := \sum_{\text{terms } t} \frac{d_t}{0.25 + 0.75 \frac{|\mathbf{d}|}{\langle |\mathbf{d}| \rangle}} \cdot q_t \cdot \ln\left(\frac{0.5 + n_d - n(t)}{0.5 + n(t)}\right) \quad (7.5)$$

7.4.2 The probabilistic VSM approach

Let us first define the setup for probabilistic IR, pursuant to the three paradigms given in the previous section: documents and queries are still — in principle — representable by bags of terms, however we are not given the 'real' documents/queries itself but we rather obtain a bunch of probability distributions P_i over the set of all possible bags of terms, where the index i is running over all documents and queries[3]. For a given bag-of-term vector $\mathbf{b}$ the value of the i-th distribution function $P_i(\mathbf{b})$ models the probability that $\mathbf{b}$ is equal to the bag of terms corresponding to the document i.

The probabilistic IR problem can be reduced to the deterministic case in a simple but reasonable way: given a deterministic similarity function S (as in the previous section), just define a similarity function $\hat{S}$ between probability distributions of bags of terms to be defined as the expectation value of S (under the joint product distribution):

$$\hat{S}(P_i, P_j) := \langle S \rangle_{P_i, P_j} = \sum_{\mathbf{b}_1, \mathbf{b}_2} P_i(\mathbf{b}_1) P_j(\mathbf{b}_2) S(\mathbf{b}_1, \mathbf{b}_2).$$

In principle we are hereby done, but there are a few restrictions/approximations required to make the approach applicable. First let us require that the distributions factor with respect to terms:

$$P_i(\mathbf{b}) := \prod_{\text{terms } t} P_{i,t}(b_t). \quad (7.6)$$

The expression $P_{i,t}(k)$ just is the probability that term t occurs exactly k times in document i. To formulate it in a sloppy way: we model distributions of bags of terms by bags of distributions of terms (or to be more precise: by collections of independent one-dimensional distributions of term occurrence counts, one for each possible term).

Next let us assume that the deterministic similarity function S decomposes as follows:

$$S(\mathbf{d}, \mathbf{q}) = \sum_{\text{terms } t} f_1(d_t) f_2(q_t) r_t, \quad (7.7)$$

---

[3]Throughout this section, there is no need to distinguish between queries and documents, so we stop here mentioning queries explicitly.

where f_1, f_2 depend only the term's counts and the relevance r_t depends only on the term. Then we may derive[4]:

$$\hat{S}(P_i, P_j) \;=\; \sum_{\text{terms } t} \langle f_1 \rangle_{P_{i,t}} \langle f_2 \rangle_{P_{j,t}} r_t \qquad (7.8)$$

This means, that we can use the classical search engine machinery, storing the document database in a sparse term-document matrix and evaluating a query by multiplying the corresponding vector with the matrix. Only the way in which the document/query vectors are constructed differs: instead of counting terms and applying the transformation functions f_1, f_2, we have to estimate the expectation values of f_1, f_2, respectively.

However, there are two features in the general VSM setup, that contradict our composition assumption (7.7):

- the term's relevance weights r_t are estimated using inverse document frequencies (see (7.4)), which depend (weakly) on d_t: if $d_t \neq 0$ the number of documents containing t is higher (by 1) compared to $d_t = 0$,

- the function f_1 usually involves a length normalization factor, i.e. depends on $|\mathbf{d}|$ and the mean document length $\langle |\mathbf{d}| \rangle$ (averaged over the whole document set).

These two blemishes may only be overcome effectively by approximations. The first inaccuracy is negligible for large document collections: we simply determine for each term t its document frequency distribution $P_t(k)$ = probability that exactly k documents contain term t at least once, and use an expectation value in the fashion of the last term of (7.4):

$$r_t = \sum_k P_t(k) f_3 \left(\frac{k}{n_d} \right). \qquad (7.9)$$

The problem with length normalization can be approximately solved by first estimating the documents' lengths[5], and averaging over all documents. Then, in (7.8), a document's length together with average document length are treated as fixed characteristics of the document and document collection respectively, not depending any more on the underlying term count distributions P_i.

---

[4] We have to require absolute convergence of the series involved, in order to swap summation over terms and summation over bags of terms. This can be assured by making the realistic assumption that $P_{i,t}(k) = 0$ for almost all pairs (t, k), i.e. for each document, there exists an upper bound for the number of terms in it.

[5] This may involve another approximation: the estimate of the document length is defined as the expectation value of the vector norm; yet this may be hard to compute and we prefer taking the vector norm of the expectation values of the vector components. Under the premise (7.6) this is exact for the $L1$-norm ('city-block metric'), but not necessarily for other norms (the Euclid norm, for instance).

7.4.3 Building probabilistic bags of terms from a speech recognizer's output

In order to make the described probabilistic IR scenario applicable to tasks with spoken queries and/or documents, we still have to explain, how a speech recognizer's output should be interpreted as a probabilistic bag of terms.

As mentioned in Section 7.3.3 the speech recognizer allows a dump of the search space which is constructed during the recognition. The resulting word lattice contains word hypotheses in form of edges in an oriented graph. Acoustic and language model scores define a probability distribution on the set of outgoing edges at each vertex. This defines a probability for every path through the lattice (product of the branching probabilities). The recognized text (or *first-best transcription*) is the path with highest probability. The *word-graph confidence measure* [Wendemuth et al., 1999; Wessel et al., 1998] of an edge is defined as the sum of the probabilities of all paths going through that edge (see Figure 7.1). It can be seen as an estimate of the probability that the path that has been 'spoken in reality' meets this edge.

There is one principle problem when using the word-graph confidences for our purposes: the probabilities for two edges e_1, e_2 are not independent; the conditional probability for passing e_2, after e_1 has been passed, may differ significantly from e_2's a-priori probability.[6] Yet if the lattices are *dense* enough and the two edges are 'far enough apart' on the time axis, the assumption of independence is approximately justified.

In view of the factorization requirement made in (7.6), we have to hope that the effect of neighboring words not obeying the independence assumption is negligible. With increasing number of words in a document, the number of close neighbors (growing linearly) vanishes in the set of all possible pairings (growing quadratically), so at least for long documents this hope is realistic.

In order to get the distribution of the number of occurrences for a word w, all we have to do is to collect the probability for every individual occurrence of w, and then construct the joint occurrence distribution out of it. Yet, there is a little complication: in general the mapping from lattice edges to word occurrences is many-to-one. This is due to different reasons:

- there are parallel hypothesis for the same word (differing by history, time boundaries, pronunciation),

- different word hypothesis are collapsed by the word mapping of Section 7.3.4.

---

[6]If e_2 lies temporally before e_1, it is even impossible to pass e_2 after e_1 in the graph, but the statement also applies to pairs of edges in the 'correct' ordering.

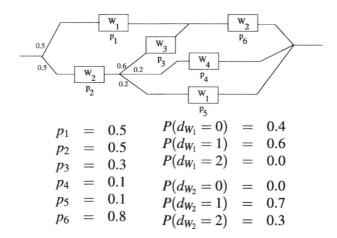

$$
\begin{array}{ll}
p_1 = 0.5 & P(d_{W_1} = 0) = 0.4 \\
p_2 = 0.5 & P(d_{W_1} = 1) = 0.6 \\
p_3 = 0.3 & P(d_{W_1} = 2) = 0.0 \\
p_4 = 0.1 & \\
p_5 = 0.1 & P(d_{W_2} = 0) = 0.0 \\
p_6 = 0.8 & P(d_{W_2} = 1) = 0.7 \\
         & P(d_{W_2} = 2) = 0.3
\end{array}
$$

Figure 7.1. Example word graph with word confidences p_i due to the branching factors. For W_1 and W_2 the resulting occurrence probability distribution is given (all edges are assumed to be oriented from left to right.)

So, before constructing the occurrence distribution, there is a collecting step in which parallel edges for the same term are detected and glued together, summing up the probabilities.

7.5 Experiments

7.5.1 Uncertainty at document side: Spoken document retrieval

The TREC-8 spoken document retrieval task [Voorhees & Harman, 1999] consists of 21,754 news broadcast stories collected over a period of 6 months. Since story boundaries are provided, step 4 of Section 7.2 is not necessary. The material comprises of about 390 hours of audio material. As test material 50 queries (e.g. "List documents relevant to David Filo and Jerry Yang, who were the creators of YAHOO! on the internet!") are provided, together with relevance judgments (i.e. a 50×21754 matrix with entries in $\{0, 1\}$). The vector space dimension (number of terms from recognizer lexicon, i.e. after Porter stemming and stop word removal) is about 33000.

We ran 4 different speech recognizer setups on the full audio material, shown in Table 7.2.

The scenarios vary from 'fast' to 'very fast' only differing in the size of the speech recognizer's search space. A 'normal' real time factor[7] for a large

---

[7] A *real time (RT) factor* of n means that a document of length t seconds is recognized in $n \cdot t$ seconds.

Table 7.2. Overview of the four different speech recognizer runs.

	1	2	3	4
real time (RT)-factor	3.8	2.4	1.1	0.5
word error rate	27.9	28.7	32.2	40.7
lattice error rate	17.5	19.9	26.8	38.8
lattice density	301	170	69	31
branching factor	2.9	2.7	2.3	2.1

vocabulary news broadcast transcription system lies in the order of 10. Note that our 3.8×RT system (on a Dec AlphaStation XP1000, 667 MHz) produced a word error rate comparable to the 'reference' recognizer transcripts (28.0%) provided with the TREC-8 material which has been produced by the NIST at about 10×RT (in 1999).

The three last lines in Table 7.2 give information on the word lattices that have been produced during the recognition. The lattice error rate gives the minimal word error rate of all paths through the graph. The branching factor is the average number of outgoing edges per vertex. Lattice density is the ratio of the number of lattice edges to the number of words in the reference text. For higher RT-factors, the increased portion of the search space that is being considered during speech recognition allows to produce denser word lattices with lower lattice error rates. In doing so, we expect to obtain larger benefits from taking word lattice information into account for the high RT-factor runs.

In retrieval tasks, the agreed measure for judging the quality of a system is mean average precision (MAP). It is defined as area under the precision-recall curve, averaged over all queries in the test material.[8]

In Figure 7.2, we plot mean average precision over speech recognition performance for a retrieval system using blind relevance feedback and the OKAPI term weighting metric of (7.5). The reference transcriptions provided by the NIST are supposed to have a word error rate of 9.0% which give rise to the data point on the left.[9] One may see that there is a strong correlation between retrieval quality and recognizer performance with a rather gentle slope of 0.35.

---

[8]Given a number n and a retrieval ranking, precision is defined as number of relevant documents among the first n documents in the ranking divided by n; recall is defined as number of relevant documents among the first n divided by total number of relevant documents. By varying the working point n, one obtains the precision-recall curve.

[9]The NIST reference transcriptions are derived from closed caption transcriptions and hence contain errors. A 10 hour subset was manually transcribed and used to determine the closed caption error rate. The word error rates in Table 7.2 were also measured on that subset using the manual transcriptions.

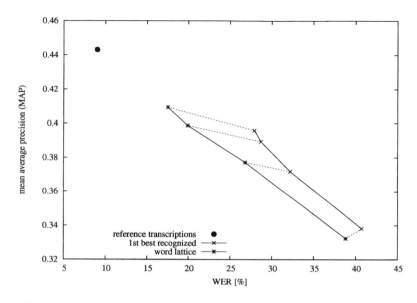

Figure 7.2. Dependence of retrieval performance (in terms of mean average precision) on word error rate for the TREC-8 SDR task.

We also included the performance of retrieval on the word lattices into the plot, using the lattice error rate as ordinate and connecting points corresponding to the same real time factor by dotted lines.

It should be noted that taking the lattices of the $0.5 \times$RT-factor run into account even degrades retrieval performance, while positive (and increasing with RT-factor) improvements are observed for the other experiments. Apparently, there is a turn-over point (however in the range of relatively 'poor' lattices already) beyond which the additional information in word lattices starts becoming beneficial.

7.5.2 Uncertainty at query side: Voice portal application

We have also applied our search engine to a text classification task for the purpose of call steering based on the OASIS database collected by BTexact Technologies (see [Edginton et al., 1999; Chou et al., 2000; Durston et al., 2001]). The goal is to obtain an automated opening dialog between customers and a call center by putting a general question (e.g. "How may I help you?") and then routing the customer to an appropriate sub-service according to her reply. The data consists of recordings and transcriptions of the first customer utterance in operator assistance calls to BT, which are to be recognized and assigned to one of a set of 19 classes representing different services that the

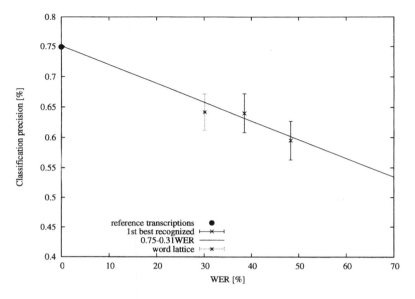

Figure 7.3. Dependence of classification performance on word error rate for the OASIS call steering task.

callers should be re-directed to. Since there are no speaker or topic changes in this scenario, steps 1, 2, and 4 of Section 7.2 are not required.

In addition, we have perfect transcriptions of the 'documents' (the training material) but possibly erroneous transcriptions of the spoken queries (the customer's utterances). Under these circumstances, the first-best precision (i.e. the fraction of correctly routed queries) is the appropriate measure.

In Figure 7.3, we plot the achieved first-best precisions for different word error levels (perfect query transcriptions corresponding to 0% correspond to the dot on the *y*-axis).

Here again,we observe a linear (within error bars) correlation with a slope of about 0.3. The data point for probabilistic retrieval on word lattices (on rather sparse lattices however, having densities in the order of 10), falls slightly off the fitted line, but not as much as it is the case for the SDR task.

7.5.3 Evaluating the word-graph confidence measure

The heuristic measure for word occurrence probabilities, introduced in Section 7.4.3 relies on approximations and depends on search parameters (lexicon size and pruning thresholds).

Having perfect transcriptions for all documents of the voice portal application, we are able to evaluate the accuracy of the word-graph confidence measure.

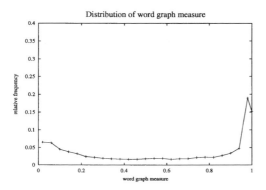 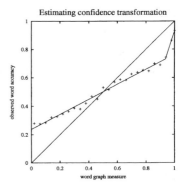

Figure 7.4. Words grouped into 26 classes according to word-graph measure; observed distribution of word graph measure (left side) and observed word accuracy (right side).

Therefore, the interval $[0, 1)$ is divided into 25 subintervals of same length. Together with the remaining value 1.0 (which is assigned to a significant number of words) this defines 26 word confidence classes. The observed distribution over these classes is shown in Figure 7.4.

Measuring word accuracies within these classes, we observe that the data points deviate significantly but also consistently from the diagonal. Transforming word level confidence values in the test data according to the piecewise linear function in Figure 7.4 yields a small (about 1% percent relative) precision gain compared to the untransformed lattices.

7.6   Conclusions

In this chapter, we consider the problem of accessing large amounts of multimedia content. For the special case of speech data, we describe the full pre-processing chain from segmentation up to indexing. In order to allow information retrieval using error-prone sources, we extend the classical vector space modeling approach formally to cope with stochastic/uncertain input on both document and query side. In experiments with either spoken documents or spoken queries, we observe a strong correlation with gentle slope between speech recognizer accuracy and retrieval performance. Improvements by applying the developed probabilistic info retrieval machinery on word lattices follow approximately the same correlation with respect to word error rates. In other words, with no additional speech recognition effort, the probabilistic approach is able to pull more relevant information out of the word lattices than is available in the first-best recognized texts alone.

Acknowledgments

We would like to thank Mark Farrell, David Attwater, James Allen and Peter Durston from BT not only for providing the OASIS databases but also for their continuous support and helpful discussions, Anne Kienappel and Dietrich Klakow for setting up the speech recognizer for the call routing task and Xavier Aubert for his help in optimizing the speech recognition search environment for the four SDR runs. We would like to give special thanks to Mark Farrell for suggesting the use of confidence transformations.

References

Aubert, X. [1999]. One pass cross word decoding for large vocabularies based on a lexical tree search organization. In *Proc. Eurospeech*, Budapest, Hungary, pages 1559–1562.

Aubert, X., and R. Blasig [2000]. Combined acoustic and linguistic look-ahead for one-pass time-synchronous decoding. In *Proc. ICSLP*, Beijing, China, Vol. 3, pages 802–805.

Bauer, G., M. Harris, A. Kellner, D. Klakow, J. Kneissler, T. Portele, E. Thelen, and F. Thiele [2002]. *LISy - Speech Based Content Management – Information Dealer*. Demonstration at Philips Corporate Research Exhibition (CRE).

Beeferman, D., A. Berger, and J. Lafferty [1999]. Statistical models for text segmentation. *Machine Learning*, 34:177–210.

Beyerlein, P., X. Aubert, R. Haeb-Umbach, M. Harris, D. Klakow, A. Wendemuth, S. Molau, H. Ney, M. Pitz, and A. Sixtus [2002]. Large vocabulary continuous speech recognition of broadcast news - The Philips/RWTH approach. *Speech Communications*, 37:109–131.

Carter, D., and I. Gransden [2000]. Resource limited sentence boundary detection. In *Proc. Eurospeech*, Aarlborg, Denmark, Vol. 1, pages 443–446.

Chen, S., and P. Gopalakrishnan [1998]. Speaker, environment and channel change detection and clustering via the Bayesian information criterion. In *Proc. of the DARPA Broadcast News Transcription and Understanding Workshop*, Virginia.

Chou, W., D.J. Attwater et al [2000]. Natural language call steering for service applications. In *Proc. ICSLP*, Beijing, China, Vol. 4, page 382.

Choy, F. [2000]. Advances in domain independent linear text segmentation. In *Proc. of NAACL*, Seattle.

Durston, P.J., M. Farrell, D. Attwater, J. Allen, H.-K.J. Kuo, M. Afify, E. Fosler-Lussier, and C.-H. Lee [2001]. OASIS natural language call steering trial. In *Proc. Eurospeech*, Vol. 2, pages 1323–1326.

Edgington, M., D.J. Attwater, and P.J. Durston [1999]. OASIS - a framework for Spoken Language Call Steering. In *Proc. Eurospeech*.

Garofolo, J., G. Auzanne, and E. Voorhees [2000]. *The TREC Spoken Document Retrieval Track: A Success Story*, NIST publication, http://www.nist.gov/speech/tests/sdr/sdr2000/papers/01plenary1.pdf.

Haitsma, J.A., and A.A.C. Kalker [2001]. Audio fingerprinting: A way to identify music. *EBU Network Seminar*, Geneva, 16 slides, 26–28 November.

Harris, M., X. Aubert, R. Haeb-Umbach, and P. Beyerlein [1999]. A study of broadcast news audio stream segmentation and segment clustering. In *Proc. Eurospeech*, Vol. 3, pages 1027–1030.

Hearst, M. [1994]. Multi-paragraph segmentation of expository text. *Proc. of ACL*.

Manning, C., and H. Schütze [1999]. *Foundations of Statistical Natural Language Processing*, Chapter 15, MIT Press, Cambridge, London.

Mulbregt, P. van, I. Carp, L. Gillick, S. Lowe, and J. Yamron [1999]. Segmentation of automatically transcribed broadcast news. In *Proc. of the DARPA Broadcast News Workshop*, pages 77–80.

Pauws, S. [2002]. *Query by Humming: The Algorithms*. Technical Note 2001/140, Philips Research Laboratories.

Ponte, J.M., and W.B. Croft [1998] A language modelling approach to information retrieval. In *Proc. 21st ACM SIGIR*.

Porter, M.A. [1980]. An algorithm for suffix stripping. *Program*, 14:130–137.

Salton, G., and M. McGill [1983]. *Introduction to Modern Information Retrieval*. McGraw-Hill, New York.

Schäuble, P. [1997]. Multimedia Information Retrieval: Content-Based Information Retrieval from Large Text and Audio Data Bases. Kluwer Academic Publishers.

Schramm, H., and X. Aubert [2000]. Efficient integration of multiple pronunciations in a large vocabulary decoder. In *Proc. ICASSP*, Vol. 3, Istanbul, Turkey, pages 1659–1662.

Shriberg, E., A. Stolcke, D. Hakkani-Tur, and G. Tur [2000]. Prosody-based automatic segmentation of speech into sentences and topics. *Speech Communication*, 32(1-2):127–154.

Stolcke, A., E. Shriberg, D. Hakkani-Tur, G. Tur, Z. Rivlin, and K. Somnez [1999]. Combining words and speech prosody for automatic topic segmentation. In *Proc. DARPA Broadcast News Workshop*, Herndon, VA, pages 61–64.

Tur, G., D. Hakkani-Tur, A. Stolcke, E. Shriberg [2001]. Integrating prosodic and lexical cues for automatic topic segmentation. *Computational Linguistics*, 27(1):31–57.

Voorhees, E., and D. Harman [1999]. *Overview of the Eighth Text REtrieval Conference (TREC-8)*, Maryland. NIST publication, http://trec.nist.gov/pubs/trec8/t8_proceedings.html.

Wendemuth, A., G. Rose, and J.G.A. Dolfing [1999]. Advances in confidence measures for large vocabulary. In *Proc. ICASSP*, Phoenix, AZ, Vol. 1, page 1.

Wessel, F., K. Macherey, and R. Schlueter [1998]. Using word probabilities as confidence measures. In *Proc. ICASSP*, Vol. 1, pages 225–228.

Wordnet. http://www.cogsci.princeton.edu/~wn/.

Chapter 8

APPROACHES IN MACHINE LEARNING

Jan van Leeuwen

Abstract   Machine learning deals with programs that learn from experience, i.e. programs
that improve or adapt their performance on a certain task or group of tasks over
time. In this tutorial, we outline some issues in machine learning that pertain to
ambient and computational intelligence. As an example, we consider programs
that are faced with the learning of tasks or concepts which are impossible to
learn exactly in finitely bounded time. This leads to the study of programs that
form hypotheses that are 'probably approximately correct' (PAC-learning), with
high probability. We also survey a number of meta-learning techniques such as
bagging and adaptive boosting, which can improve the performance of machine
learning algorithms substantially.

Keywords   Machine learning, computational intelligence, models of learning, concept
learning, learning in the limit, PAC learning, VC-dimension, meta-learning, bagging, boosting, AdaBoost, ensemble learning.

8.1 Algorithms that learn

Ambient intelligence requires systems that can learn and adapt, or otherwise
interact intelligently with the environment in which they operate ('situated intelligence'). The behavior of these systems must be achieved by means of intelligent algorithms, usually for tasks that involve some kind of learning. Here
are some examples of typical learning tasks:

- select the preferred lighting of a room,

- classify objects,

- recognize specific patterns in (streams of) images,

- identify the words in handwritten text,

- understand a spoken language,

- control systems based on sensor data,

W. Verhaegh et al. (eds.), Algorithms in Ambient Intelligence, 151-166
© 2004 *Kluwer Academic Publishers. Printed in the Netherlands.*

- predict risks in safety-critical systems,

- detect errors in a network,

- diagnose abnormal situations in a system,

- prescribe actions or repairs, and

- discover useful common information in distributed data.

Learning is a very broad subject, with a rich tradition in computer science and in many other disciplines, from control theory to psychology. In this tutorial we restrict ourselves to issues in *machine learning*, with an emphasis on aspects of algorithmic modeling and complexity.

The goal of machine learning is to design programs that learn and/or discover, i.e. automatically improve their performance on certain tasks and/or adapt to changing circumstances over time. The result can be a 'learned' program which can carry out the task it was designed for, or a 'learning' program that will forever improve and adapt. In either case, machine learning poses challenging problems in terms of algorithmic approach, data representation, computational efficiency, and quality of the resulting program. Not surprisingly, the large variety of application domains and approaches has made machine learning into a broad field of theory and experimentation [Mitchell, 1997].

In this tutorial, some problems in designing *learning algorithms* are outlined. We will especially consider algorithms that learn (or: are trained) *online*, from examples or data that are provided one at a time. By a suitable feedback mechanism the algorithm can adjust its hypothesis or the model of 'reality' it has so far, before a next example or data item is processed. The crucial question is how good programs can become, especially if they are faced with the learning of tasks or concepts which are impossible to learn exactly in finite or bounded time.

To specify a learning problem, one needs a precise *model* that describes what is to be learned and how it is done, and what measures are to be used in analyzing and comparing the performance of different solutions. In Section 2 we outline some elements of a model of learning that should always be specified for a learning task. In Section 3 we highlight some basic definitions of the theory of learning programs that form hypotheses that are 'probably approximately correct' [Kearns & Vazirani, 1994; Valiant, 1984]. In Section 4 we mention some of the results of this theory (see also [Anthony, 1997]). In Section 5 we discuss meta-learning techniques, especially bagging and boosting. For further introductions we refer to the literature [Cristianini & Shawe-Taylor, 2000; Mendelson & Smola, 2003; Mitchell, 1997; Poole et al., 1998] and to electronic sources [COLT].

8.2 Models of learning

Learning algorithms are normally designed around a particular 'paradigm' for the learning process, i.e. the overall approach to learning. A computational learning model should be clear about the following aspects.

Learner.   Who or what is doing the learning. In this tutorial: an algorithm or a computer program. Learning algorithms may be embedded in more general software systems e.g. involving systems of agents or may be embodied in physical objects like robots and ad-hoc networks of processors in intelligent environments.

Domain.   What is being learned. In this tutorial: a function, or a concept. Among the many other possibilities are: the operation of a device, a tune, a game, a language, a preference, and so on. In the case of concepts, sets of concepts that are considered for learning are called *concept classes*.

Goal.   Why the learning is done. The learning can be done to retrieve a set of rules from spurious data, to become a good simulator for some physical phenomenon, to take control over a system, and so on.

Representation.   The way the objects to be learned are represented *c.q.* the way they are to be represented by the computer program. The *hypotheses* which the program develops while learning may be represented in the same way, or in a broader (or: more restricted) format.

Algorithmic technology.   The algorithmic framework to be used. Among the many different 'technologies' are: artificial neural networks, belief networks, case-based reasoning, decision trees, grammars, liquid state machines, probabilistic networks, rule learning, support vector machines, and threshold functions. One may also specify the specific learning paradigm or discovery tools to be used. Each algorithmic technology has its own learning strategy and its own range of application. There also are *multi-strategy* approaches.

Information source.   The information (training data) the program uses for learning. This could have different forms: positive and negative examples (called *labeled examples*), answers to queries, feedback from certain actions, and so on. Functions and concepts are typically revealed in the form of labeled instances taken from an *instance space X*. One often identifies a concept with the set of all its positive instances, i.e. with a subset of *X*. An information source may be *noisy*, i.e. the training data may have errors. Examples may be *clustered* before use in training a program.

Training scenario.   The description of the learning process. In this tutorial, mostly *on-line learning* is discussed. In an on-line learning scenario, the program is given examples one by one, and it recalculates its hypothesis of what it learns after each example. Examples may be drawn from a random source, according to some known or unknown probability distribution. An on-line scenario can also be *interactive*, in which case new examples are supplied depending on the performance of the program on previous examples. In contrast, in an off-line learning scenario the program receives all examples at once. One often distinguishes between

- *supervised learning:* the scenario in which a program is fed examples and must predict the label of every next example before a teacher tells the answer.

- *unsupervised learning:* the scenario in which the program must determine certain regularities or properties of the instances it receives e.g. from an unknown physical process, all by itself (without a teacher).

Training scenarios are typically finite. On the other hand, in *inductive inference* a program can be fed an unbounded amount of data. In *reinforcement learning* the inputs come from an unpredictable environment and positive or negative feedback is given at the end of every small sequence of learning steps e.g. in the process of learning an optimal strategy.

Prior knowledge.   What is known in advance about the domain, e.g. about specific properties (mathematical or otherwise) of the concepts to be learned. This might help to limit the class of hypotheses that the program needs to consider during the learning, and thus to limit its 'uncertainty' about the unknown object it learns and to *converge* faster. The program may also use it to *bias* its choice of hypothesis.

Success criteria.   The criteria for successful learning, i.e. for determining when the learning is completed or has otherwise converged sufficiently. Depending on the goal of the learning program, the program should be *fit* for its task. If the program is used e.g. in safety-critical environments, it must have reached sufficient accuracy in the training phase so it can decide or predict reliably during operation. A success criterion can be 'measured' by means of *test sets* or by theoretical analysis.

Performance.   The amount of time, space and computational power needed in order to learn a certain task, and also the quality (accuracy) reached in the process. There is often a trade-off between the number of examples used to train a program and thus the computational resources used, and the capabilities of the program afterwards.

Computational learning models may depend on many more criteria and on specific theories of the learning process.

8.2.1 Classification of learning algorithms

Learning algorithms are designed for many purposes. Learning algorithms are implemented in web browsers, pc's, transaction systems, robots, cars, video servers, home environments and so on. The specifications of the underlying models of learning vary greatly and are highly dependent on the application context. Accordingly, many classifications of learning algorithms exist based on the underlying *learning strategy*, the type of *algorithmic technology* used, the ultimate *algorithmic ability* achieved, and/or the *application domain*.

8.2.2 Concept learning

As an example of machine learning we consider *concept learning*. Given a (finite) instance space X, a concept c can be identified with a subset of X or, alternatively, with the Boolean function $c(x)$ that maps instances $x \in X$ to 1 if and only if $x \in c$ and to 0 if and only if $x \notin c$. Concept learning is concerned with retrieving the definition of a concept c of a given concept class C, from a *sample* of positive and negative examples. The information source supplies noise-free instances x and their *labels* $c(x) \in (0,1)$, corresponding to a certain concept c. In the training process, the program maintains a hypothesis $h = h(x)$ for c. The training scenario is an example of on-line, supervised learning:

Training scenario: The program is fed labeled instances $(x, c(x))$ one-by-one and tries to learn the unknown concept c that underlies it, i.e. the Boolean function $c(x)$ which classifies the examples. In any step, when given a next instance $x \in X$, the program first *predicts* a label, namely the label $h(x)$ based on its current hypothesis h. Then it is presented the true label $c(x)$. If $h(x) = c(x)$ then h is right and no changes are made. If $h(i) \neq c(x)$ then h is wrong: the program is said to have made a *mistake*. The program subsequently *revises* its hypothesis h, based on its knowledge of the examples so far.

The goal is to let $h(x)$ become consistent with $c(x)$ for all x, by a suitable choice of learning algorithm. Any correct $h(x)$ for c is called a *classifier* for c.

The number of mistakes an algorithm makes in order to learn a concept is an important measure that has to be minimized, regardless of other aspects of computational complexity.

Definition 8.1. Let C be a finite class of concepts. For any learning algorithm A and concept $c \in C$, let $M_A(c)$ be the maximum number of mistakes A can make when learning c, over all possible training sequences for the concept.

Let $Opt(C) = \min_A(\max_{c \in C} M_A(c))$, with the minimum taken over all learning algorithms for C that fit the given model.   □

$Opt(C)$ is the optimum ('smallest') mistake bound for learning C. The following lemma shows that $Opt(C)$ is well-defined.

Lemma 8.1 (Littlestone, 1987). $Opt(C) \leq \log_2(|C|)$.
Proof. Consider the following algorithm A. The algorithm keeps a list L of all possible concepts $h \in C$ that are consistent with the examples that were input up until the present step. A starts with the list of all concepts in C. If a next instance x is supplied, A acts as follows:

1. Split L in sublists $L_1 = \{d \in L | d(x) = 1\}$ and $L_0 = \{d \in L | d(x) = 0\}$. If $|L_1| \geq |L_0|$ then A predicts 1, otherwise it predicts 0.

2. If a mistake is made, A deletes from L every concept d which gives x the wrong label, i.e. with $d(x) \neq c(x)$.

The resulting algorithm is called the 'Halving' or 'Majority' algorithm. It is easily argued that the algorithm must have reduced L to the concept to be found after making at most $\log_2(|C|)$ mistakes.   □

Definition 8.2 (Gold, 1967). An algorithm A is said to identify the concepts in C *in the limit* if for every $c \in C$ and every allowable training sequence for this concept, there is a finite m such that A makes no more mistakes after the mth step. The class C is said to be learnable in the limit.   □

Corollary 8.2. *Every (finite) class of concepts is learnable in the limit.*   □

8.3   Probably approximately correct learning

As a further illustration of the theory of machine learning, we consider the learning problem for concepts that are impossible to learn 'exactly' in finite (bounded) time. In general, insufficient training leads to weak classifiers. Surprisingly, in many cases one can give bounds on the size of the training sets that are needed to reach a good *approximation* of the concept, with high probability. This theory of 'probably approximately correct' (PAC) learning was originated by Valiant [1984], and is now a standard theme in *computational learning*.

8.3.1   PAC model

Consider any concept class C and its instance space X. Consider the general case of learning a concept $c \in C$. A PAC learning algorithm works by learning from instances which are randomly generated upon the algorithm's request by an external source according to a certain (unknown) distribution $\mathcal{D}$ and which are labeled ($+$ or $-$) by an oracle (a teacher) that knows the concept c. The hypothesis h after m steps is a random variable depending on the sample of size m that the program happens to draw during a run. The performance of the algorithm is measured by the bound on m that is needed to have a high probability that h is 'close' to c regardless of the distribution $\mathcal{D}$.

Definition 8.3. The error probability of h w.r.t. concept c is: $Err_c(h) = Prob(c(x) \neq h(x)) =$ 'the probability that there is an instance $x \in X$ that is classified incorrectly by h'. □

Note that in the common case that always $h \subseteq c$, $Err_c(h) = Prob(x \in c \wedge x \neq h)$. If the 'measure' of the set of instances on which h errs is small, then we call h ε-good.

Definition 8.4. A hypothesis h is said to be ε-good for $c \in C$ if the probability of an $x \in X$ with $c(x) \neq h(x)$ is smaller than ε: $Err_c(h) \leq \varepsilon$. □

Observe that different training runs, thus different samples, can lead to very different hypotheses. In other words, the hypothesis h is a *random variable* itself, ranging over all possible concepts in C that can result from samples of m instances.

8.3.2 When are concept classes PAC learnable

As a criterion for successful learning one would like to take: $Err_c(h) \leq \varepsilon$ for every h that may be found by the algorithm, for a predefined tolerance ε. A weaker criterion is taken, accounting for the fact that h is a random variable. Let $Prob_S$ denote the probability of an event taken over all possible samples of m examples. The success criterion is that

$$Prob_S(Err_c(h) \leq \varepsilon) \geq 1 - \delta,$$

for predefined and presumably 'small' tolerances ε and δ. If the criterion is satisfied by the algorithm, then its hypothesis is said to be 'probably approximately correct', i.e. it is 'approximately correct' with probability at least $1 - \delta$.

Definition 8.5 (PAC-learnable). A concept class C is said to be *PAC-learnable* if there is an algorithm A that follows the PAC learning model such that

for every $0 < \varepsilon, \delta < 1$ there exists an m such that for every concept $c \in C$ and for every hypothesis h computed by A after sampling m times:

$$Prob_S(h \text{ is } \varepsilon\text{-good for } c) \geq 1 - \delta,$$

regardless of the distribution $\mathcal{D}$ over X.   □

As a performance measure we use the minimum sample size m needed to achieve success, for given tolerances $\varepsilon, \delta > 0$.

Definition 8.6 (Efficiently PAC-learnable). A concept class C is said to be *efficiently PAC-learnable* if, in the previous definition, the learning algorithm A runs in time polynomial in $\frac{1}{\varepsilon}$ and $\frac{1}{\delta}$ (and $\ln|C|$ if C is finite).   □

The notions that we defined can be further specialized, e.g. by adding constraints on the representation of h. The notion of efficiency may then also include a term depending on the size of the representation.

8.3.3   Common PAC learning

Let C be a concept class and $c \in C$. Consider a learning algorithm A and observe the 'probable quality' of the hypothesis h that A can compute as a function of the sample size m. Assume that A only considers *consistent* hypotheses, i.e. hypotheses h that coincide with c on all examples that were generated, at any point in time. Clearly, as m increases, we more and more 'narrow' the possibilities for h and thus increase the likelihood that h is ε-good.

Definition 8.7. After some number of samples m, the algorithm A is said to be ε-*close* if for every (consistent) hypothesis h that is still possible at this stage: $Err_c(h) \leq \varepsilon$.   □

Let the total number of possible hypotheses h that A can possibly consider be finite and bounded by H.

Lemma 8.3. *Consider the algorithm A after it has sampled m times. Then for any $0 < \varepsilon < 1$:*
$$Prob_S(A \text{ is not } \varepsilon\text{-close}) < He^{-\varepsilon m}.$$

Proof. After m random drawings, A fails to be ε-close if there is at least one possible consistent hypothesis h left with $Err_c(h) > \varepsilon$. Changing the perspective slightly, it follows that:

$$
\begin{aligned}
&Prob_S(A \text{ is not } \varepsilon\text{-close}) \\
=\ &Prob_S(\text{after } m \text{ drawings there is a consistent } h \text{ with } Err_c(h) > \varepsilon) \\
\leq\ &\sum_{h:Err_c(h)>\varepsilon} Prob_S(h \text{ is consistent}) \\
=\ &\sum_{h:Err_c(h)>\varepsilon} Prob_S(h \text{ correctly labels all } m \text{ instances}) \\
\leq\ &\sum_{h:Err_c(h)>\varepsilon} (1-\varepsilon)^m
\end{aligned}
$$

$$\leq \sum_{h:Err_c(h)>\varepsilon} e^{-\varepsilon m}$$

$$\leq He^{-\varepsilon m},$$

where we use that $(1-t) \leq e^t$. □

Corollary 8.4. *Consider the algorithm A after it has sampled m times, with h any hypothesis it can have built over the sample. Then for any* $0 < \varepsilon < 1$:

$$Prob_S(h \text{ is } \varepsilon\text{-good}) \geq 1 - He^{-\varepsilon m}.$$

□

8.4 Classes of PAC learners

We can now interpret the observations so far. Let C be a finite concept class. As we only consider consistent learners, it is fair to assume that C also serves as the set of all possible hypotheses that a program can consider.

Definition 8.8 (Occam-algorithm). An *Occam-algorithm* is any on-line learning program A that follows the PAC-model such that (a) A only outputs hypotheses h that are consistent with the sample, and (b) the range of the possible hypotheses for A is C. □

The following theorem basically says that Occam-algorithms are PAC-learning algorithms, at least for finite concept classes.

Theorem 8.5. *Let C be finite and learnable by an Occam-algorithm A. Then C is PAC-learnable by A. In fact, a sample size M with*

$$M > \frac{1}{\varepsilon}\left(ln\frac{1}{\delta} + ln|C|\right)$$

suffices to meet the success criterion, regardless of the underlying sampling distribution $\mathcal{D}$.
Proof. Let C be learnable by A. The algorithm satisfies all the requirements we need. Thus we can use the previous Corollary to assert that after A has drawn m samples,

$$Prob_S(h \text{ is } \varepsilon\text{-good}) \geq 1 - He^{-\varepsilon m} \geq 1 - \delta,$$

provided that $m > \frac{1}{\varepsilon}(ln\frac{1}{\delta} + ln|C|)$. Thus C is PAC-learnable by A. □

The sample size for an Occam-learner can thus remain polynomially bounded in $\frac{1}{\varepsilon}$, $\frac{1}{\delta}$ and $ln|C|$. It follows that, if the Occam-learner makes only polynomially many steps per iteration, then the theorem implies that C is even *efficiently* PAC-learnable.

While for many concept classes one can show that they are PAC-learnable, it appears to be much harder sometimes to prove efficient PAC-learnability. The problem even hides in an unexpected part of the model, namely in the fact that it can be NP-hard to actually determine a hypothesis (in the desired representation) that is consistent with all examples from the sample set.

Several other versions of PAC-learning exist, including versions in which one no longer insists that the probably approximate correctness holds under every distribution $\mathcal{D}$.

8.4.1 Vapnik-Chervonenkis dimension

Intuitively, the more complex a concept is, the harder it will be for a program to learn it. What could be a suitable notion of complexity to express this. Is there a suitable characteristic that marks the complexity of the concepts in a concept class C. A possible answer is found in the notion of Vapnik-Chervonenkis dimension, or simply VC-dimension.

Definition 8.9. A set of instances $S \subseteq X$ is said to be 'shattered' by concept class C if for every subset $S' \subseteq S$ there exists a concept $c \in C$ which separates S' from the rest of S, i.e. such that

$$c(x) = \begin{cases} + & \text{if } x \in S', \\ - & \text{if } x \in S - S'. \end{cases}$$

$\square$

Definition 8.10 (VC-dimension). The VC-dimension of a concept class C, denoted by $VC(C)$, is the cardinality of the largest finite set $S \subseteq X$ that is shattered by C. If arbitrarily large finite subsets of X can be shattered, then $VC(C) = \infty$.

$\square$

VC-dimension appears to be related to the complexity of learning. Here is a first connection. Recall that $Opt(C)$ is the minimum number of mistakes that any program must make in the worst-case, when it is learning C in the limit. VC-dimension plays a role in identifying hard cases: it is lowerbound for $Opt(C)$.

Theorem 8.6 (Littlestone, 1987). *For any concept class C: $VC(C) \leq Opt(C)$.*

$\square$

VC-dimension is difficult, even NP-hard to compute, but has proved to be an important notion especially for PAC-learning. Recall that finite concept classes that are learnable by an Occam-algorithm, are PAC-learnable. It turns out that this holds for *infinite* classes also, provided their VC-dimension is finite.

Theorem 8.7 (Vapnik, Blumer et al.). *Let C be any concept class and let its VC-dimension be $VC(C) = d < \infty$. Let C be learnable by an Occam-algorithm A. Then C is PAC-learnable by A. In fact, a sample size M with*

$$M > \frac{\gamma}{\varepsilon}(\ln\frac{1}{\delta} + d\ln\frac{1}{\varepsilon})$$

suffices to meet the success criterion, regardless of the underlying sampling distribution $\mathcal{D}$, for some fixed constant $\gamma > 0$. □

VC-dimension can also be used to give a lowerbound on the required sample size for PAC-learning a concept class.

Theorem 8.8 (Ehrenfeucht et al.). *Let C be a concept class and let its VC-dimension be $VC(C) = d < \infty$. Then any PAC-learning algorithm for C requires a sample size of at least $M = \Omega(\frac{1}{\varepsilon}(\log\frac{1}{\delta} + d))$ to meet the success criterion.* □

8.5 Meta-learning techniques

Algorithms that learn concepts may perform poorly because e.g. the available training (sample) set is small or better results require excessive running times. Meta-learning schemes attempt to turn weak learning algorithms into better ones. If one has several weak learners available, one could apply all of them and take the best classifier that can be obtained by combining their results. It might also be that only one (weak) learning algorithm is available. We discuss two meta-learning techniques: bagging and boosting.

8.5.1 Bagging

Bagging [Breiman, 1996] stands for '*bootstrap aggregating*' and is a typical example of an *ensemble* technique: several classifiers are computed and combined into one. Let X be the given instance (sample) space. Define a bootstrap sample to be any sample X' of some fixed size n obtained by sampling X uniformly at random *with* replacement, thus with duplicates allowed. Applications normally have $n = |X|$. Bagging now typically proceeds as follows, using X as the instance space.

1. For $s = 1, \ldots, b$ do:

    – construct a bootstrap sample X_s

    – train the base learner on the sample space X_s

    – let the resulting hypothesis (concept) be $h_s(x) : X \rightarrow \{-1, +1\}$.

2. Output as 'aggregated' classifier:

$$h_A(x) = \text{the majority vote of the } h_s(x) \text{ for } s = 1 \ldots b.$$

Bagging is of interest because bootstrap samples can avoid 'outlying' cases in the training set. Note that an element $x \in X$ has a probability of only $1 - (1 - \frac{1}{n})^n \approx 1 - \frac{1}{e} \approx 63\%$ of being chosen into a given X_s. Other bootstrapping techniques exist and, depending on the on the application domain, other forms of aggregation may be used. Bagging can be very effective, even for small values of b (up to 50).

8.5.2 Boosting weak PAC learners

A 'weak' learning algorithm may be easy to design and quickly trained, but it may have a poor expected performance. Boosting refers to a class of techniques for turning such algorithms into arbitrarily more accurate ones.

Boosting was first studied in the context of PAC learning [Schapire, 1990]. Suppose we have an algorithm A that learns concepts $c \in C$, and that has the property that for some $\varepsilon < \frac{1}{2}$ the hypothesis h that is produced always satisfies $Prob_S(h$ is ε-good for $c) \geq \gamma$, for some 'small' $\gamma > 0$. One can boost A as follows. Call A on the same instance space k times, with k such that $(1 - \gamma)^k \leq \frac{\delta}{2}$. Let h_i denote the hypothesis generated by A during the i-th run. The probability that *none* of the hypotheses h_i found is ε-good for c is at most $\frac{\delta}{2}$. Consider $h_1, \ldots, h_k$ and test each of them on a sample of size m, with m chosen large enough so the probability that the *observed* error on the sample is not within ε from $Err_c(h_i)$ is at most $\frac{\delta}{2k}$, for each i. Now output the hypothesis $h = h_i$ that makes the *smallest* number of errors on its sample. Then the probability that h is not 2ε-good for c is at most: $\frac{\delta}{2} + k \cdot \frac{\delta}{2k} = \delta$. Thus, A is automatically boosted into a learner with a much better confidence bound. In general, one can even relax the condition on ε.

Definition 8.11 (Weakly PAC-learnable). A concept class C is said to be *weakly PAC-learnable* if there is an algorithm A that follows the PAC learning model such that

for some polynomials p, q and $0 < \varepsilon_0 = \frac{1}{2} - \frac{1}{p(n)}$ there exists an m such that for every concept $c \in C$ and for every hypothesis h computed by A after sampling m times:

$$Prob_S(h \text{ is } \varepsilon_0\text{-good for } c) \geq \frac{1}{q(n)},$$

regardless of the distribution $\mathcal{D}$ over X.   □

Theorem 8.9 (Schapire). *A concept class is (efficiently) weakly PAC-learnable if and only if it is (efficiently) PAC-learnable.* □

A different boosting technique for weak PAC learners was given by Freund [1995] and also follows from the technique below.

8.5.3 Adaptive boosting

If one assumes that the distribution $\mathcal{D}$ over the instance space is not fixed and that one can 'tune' the sampling during the learning process, one might use training scenarios for the weak learner where a larger weight is given to examples on which the algorithm did poorly in a previous run (thus outliers are not circumvented, as opposed to bagging.) This has given rise to the '*adaptive boosting*' or AdaBoost algorithm, of which various forms exist (see e.g. [Freund & Schapire, 1997; Schapire & Singer, 1999]). One form is the following:

1. Let the sampling space be $Y = \{(x_1, c_1), \ldots (x_n, c_n)\}$ with $x_i \in X$ and $c_i \in \{-1, +1\}$ (c_i is the label of instance x_i according to concept c).

2. Let $\mathcal{D}_1(i) = \frac{1}{n}$ (the uniform distribution).

3. For $s = 1, \ldots, T$ do:

   - train the weak learner while sampling according to distribution $\mathcal{D}_s$
   - let the resulting hypothesis (concept) be h_s
   - choose α_s (we will later see that $\alpha_s \geq 0$)
   - update the distribution for sampling

   $$\mathcal{D}_{s+1}(i) \leftarrow \frac{\mathcal{D}_s(i)e^{-\alpha_s c_i h_s(x_i)}}{Z_s}$$

   where Z_s is a normalization factor chosen so $\mathcal{D}_{s+1}$ is a probability distribution on X.

4. Output as final classifier: $h_B(x) = \text{sign}(\sum_{s=1}^{T} \alpha_s h_s(x))$.

The AdaBoost algorithm contains weighting factors α_s that should be chosen appropriately as the algorithm proceeds. Once we know how to choose them, the values of $Z_s = \sum_{i=1}^{n} \mathcal{D}_s(i)e^{-\alpha_s c_i h_s(x_i)}$ follow inductively. A key property is the following bound on the error probability $Err_{\text{uniform}}(h_B)$ of $h_B(x)$.

Lemma 8.10. *The error in the classifier resulting from the AdaBoost algorithm satisfies:*

$$Err_{\text{uniform}}(h_B) \leq \prod_{s=1}^{T} Z_s.$$

Proof. By induction one sees that

$$\mathcal{D}_{T+1}(i) = \mathcal{D}_1 \frac{e^{-\sum_s \alpha_s c_i h_s(x_i)}}{\prod_s Z_s} = \frac{e^{-c_i \sum_s \alpha_s h_s(x_i)}}{n \cdot \prod_s Z_s},$$

which implies that

$$\frac{1}{n} \cdot e^{-c_i \sum_s \alpha_s h_s(x_i)} = (\prod_{s=1}^{T} Z_s) \mathcal{D}_{T+1}(i).$$

Now consider the term $\sum_s \alpha_s h_s(x_i)$, whose sign determines the value of $h_B(x_i)$. If $h_B(x_i) \neq c_i$, then $c_i \cdot \sum_s \alpha_s h_s(x_i) \leq 0$ and thus $e^{-c_i \sum_s \alpha_s h_s(x_i)} \geq 1$. This implies that

$$
\begin{aligned}
Err_{\text{uniform}}(h_B) &= \frac{1}{n} |\{i | h_A(x_i) \neq c_i\}| \\
&\leq \frac{1}{n} \sum_i e^{-c_i \sum_s \alpha_s h_s(x_i)} \\
&= \sum_i (\prod_{s=1}^{T} Z_s) \mathcal{D}_{T+1}(i) \\
&= \prod_{s=1}^{T} Z_s.
\end{aligned}
$$

$\square$

This result suggests that in every round, the factors α_s must be chosen such that Z_s is minimized. Freund & Schapire [1997] analyzed several possible choices. Let $\varepsilon_s = Err_{\mathcal{D}_s}(h_s) = Prob_{\mathcal{D}_s}(h_s(x) \neq c(x))$ be the error probability of the s-th hypothesis. A good choice for α_s is

$$\alpha_s = \frac{1}{2} \ln(\frac{1 - \varepsilon_s}{\varepsilon_s}).$$

Assuming, as we may, that the weak learner at least guarantees that $\varepsilon_s \leq \frac{1}{2}$, we have $\alpha_s \geq 0$ for all s. Bounding the Z_s one can show:

Theorem 8.11 (Freund and Schapire). *With the given choice of α_s, the error probability in the classifier resulting from the AdaBoost algorithm satisfies:*

$$Err_{\text{uniform}}(h_B) \leq e^{-2\sum_s(\frac{1}{2} - \varepsilon_s)^2}.$$

$\square$

Let $\varepsilon_s < \frac{1}{2} - \theta$ for all s, meaning that the base learner is guaranteed to be at least slightly better than fully random. In this case it follows that $Err_{\text{uniform}}(h_B) \leq$

$e^{-2\theta^2 T}$ and thus AdaBoost gives a result whose error probability decreases exponentially with T, showing it is indeed a boosting algorithm.

The AdaBoost algorithm has been studied from many different angles. For generalizations and further results see [Schapire, 2002]. In recent variants one attempts to reduce the algorithm's tendency to overfit [Kwek & Nguyen, 2002]. Breiman [1999] showed that AdaBoost is an instance of a larger class of '*a*daptive *r*eweighting and *combin*ing' (arcing) algorithms and gives a game-theoretic argument to prove their convergence. Several other adaptive boosting techniques have been proposed, see e.g. Freund [2001]. An extensive treatment of ensemble learning and boosting is given by e.g. Meir & Rätsch [2003].

8.6 Conclusion

In creating intelligent environments, many challenges arise. The supporting systems will be 'everywhere' around us, always connected and always 'on', and they permanently interact with their environment, influencing it and being influenced by it. Ambient intelligence thus leads to the need of designing programs that learn and adapt, with a multi-medial scope. We presented a number of key approaches in machine learning for the design of effective learning algorithms. *Algorithmic learning theory* and *discovery science* are rapidly developing. These areas will contribute many invaluable techniques for the design of ambient intelligent systems.

References

Anthony, M. [1997]. Probabilistic analysis of learning in artificial neural networks: the PAC model and its variants. In *Neural Computing Surveys*, 1:1–47. (see also: http://www.icsi.berkeley.edu/~jagota/NCS).

Blumer, A., A. Ehrenfeucht, D. Haussler, and M.K. Warmuth [1989]. Learnability and the Vapnik-Chervonenkis dimension. *Journal of the ACM*, 36:929–965.

Breiman, L. [1996]. Bagging predictors. *Machine Learning*, 24:123–140.

Breiman, L. [1999]. Prediction games and arcing algorithms. *Neural Computation*, 11:1493–1517.

COLT. *Computational Learning Theory*. Archives, web sites and other resources available at http://www.learningtheory.org.

Cristianini, N., and J. Shawe-Taylor [2000]. *Support Vector Machines and Other Kernel-Based Learning Methods*. Cambridge University Press, Cambridge (UK).

Ehrenfeucht, A., D. Haussler, M. Kearns, and L. Valiant [1989]. A general lower bound on the number of examples needed for learning. *Information and Computation*, 82:247–261.

Freund, Y. [1995]. Boosting a weak learning algorithm by majority. *Information and Computation*, 121:256–285.

Freund, Y. [2001]. An adaptive version of the boost by majority algorithm. *Machine Learning*, 43:293–318.

Freund, Y., and R.E. Schapire [1997]. A decision-theoretic generalization of on-line learning and an application to boosting. *Journal of Computer and Systems Sciences*, 55:119–139.

Gold, E.M. [1967]. Language identification in the limit. *Information and Control*, 10:447–474.

Kearns, M.J., and U.V. Vazirani [1994]. *An Introduction to Computational Learning Theory*. The MIT Press, Cambridge, MA.

Kwek, S., and C. Nguyen [2002]. *i*Boost: boosting using an *instance*-based exponential weighting scheme. In: T. Elomaa, H. Mannila, and H. Toivonen (eds.), *Machine Learning: ECML 2002*, Proc. 13th European Conference, Lecture Notes in Artificial Intelligence, vol. 2430, Springer-Verlag, Berlin, pages 245–257.

Littlestone, N. [1987]. Learning quickly when irrelevant attributes abound: a new linear-threshold algorithm. *Machine Learning*, 2:285–318.

Meir, R., and G. Rätsch [2003]. An introduction to boosting and leveraging. In: S. Mendelson and A.J. Smola (eds.), *ibid*, pages 118–183.

Mendelson, S., and A.J. Smola (Eds) [2003]. *Advanced Lectures on Machine Learning*. Lecture Notes in Artificial Intelligence, vol. 2600, Springer-Verlag, Berlin.

Mitchell, T.M. [1997]. *Machine Learning*. WCB/McGraw-Hill, Boston, MA.

Paliouras, G., V. Karkaletsis, and C.D. Spyropoulos (Eds.) [2001]. *Machine Learning and its Applications*, Advanced Lectures. Lecture Notes in Artificial Intelligence, vol. 2049, Springer-Verlag, Berlin.

Poole, D., A. Mackworth, and R. Goebel [1998]. *Computational Intelligence - A Logical Approach*. Oxford University Press, New York.

Schapire, R.E. [1990]. The strength of weak learnability. *Machine Learning*, 5:197–227.

Schapire, R.E. [2002]. The boosting approach to machine learning - An overview. In *MSRI Workshop on Nonlinear Estimation and Classification*. (available at: http://www.research.att.com/~schapire/publist.html).

Schapire, R.E., and Y. Singer [1999]. Improved boosting algorithms using confidence-rated predictions. *Machine Learning*, 37:297–336.

Skurichina, M., and R.P.W. Duin [2002]. Bagging, boosting and the random subspace method for linear classifiers. *Pattern Analysis & Applications*, 5:121–135.

Valiant, L.G. [1984]. A theory of the learnable. *Communications of the ACM*, 27:1134–1142.

Chapter 9

MACHINE LEARNING FOR AMBIENT INTELLIGENCE: BOOSTING IN AUTOMATIC SPEECH RECOGNITION

Carsten Meyer and Peter Beyerlein

Abstract   An important aspect of Ambient Intelligence is a convenient user interface, supporting several user-friendly input modalities. Speech is one of the most natural modalities for man-machine interaction. Numerous applications in the context of Ambient Intelligence — whether referring to a single input modality or combining different ones — involve some pattern classification task. Experience shows that for building successful and reliable real life applications, advanced classification algorithms are needed providing maximal accuracy for the underlying task. In this chapter, we investigate whether a generic machine learning technique, the boosting algorithm, can successfully be applied to increase the accuracy in a 'large-scale' classification problem, namely large vocabulary automatic speech recognition. Specifically, we outline an approach to implement the AdaBoost.M2 algorithm for training of acoustic models in a state-of-the-art automatic speech recognizer. Detailed evaluations in a large vocabulary name recognition task show that this 'utterance approach' improves the best test error rates obtained with standard training paradigms. In particular, we obtain additive performance gains when combining boosting with discriminative training, one of the most powerful training algorithms in speech recognition. Our findings motivate further applications of boosting in other classification tasks relevant for Ambient Intelligence.

Keywords   Machine learning, boosting, AdaBoost.M2, automatic speech recognition, maximum likelihood training, discriminative training.

9.1   Introduction

An important feature of Ambient Intelligence is a user-friendly interface, supporting and combining various convenient input modalities. A number of applications of Ambient Intelligence involve some classification problem, relating to a single input modality as well as combining different modalities. For

W. Verhaegh et al. (eds.), Algorithms in Ambient Intelligence, 167-183
© 2004 *Kluwer Academic Publishers. Printed in the Netherlands.*

example, when addressing a TV show without knowing its precise title, the input speech has to be converted into text, which in turn has to be matched against a TV database. When offering a number of services, e.g. from playing songs to controlling the shopping list, the requested action or service has to be identified, e.g. by speech input, touch panels or eyeball tracking. Or, for personalized services, the individual user has to be identified, probably by its voice combined with video input and weight sensors.

One of the most natural input modalities for man-machine interaction is speech. However, in complex tasks like large vocabulary speech recognition or spontaneous speech, the recognition accuracy of state-of-the-art recognizers is still not sufficient to ensure a robust and reliable use in real life applications.

This raises two questions: first, what are generic methods to improve the accuracy for classification tasks in a given input modality (e.g. speech), and second, what are effective methods for an accurate combination of different input modalities? In this chapter, we suggest to use a generic machine learning technique called 'boosting' for addressing both questions, and investigate its performance in a large vocabulary automatic speech recognition task, namely proper name recognition.

9.1.1   Boosting: Idea and previous work

Boosting is a general method to improve the accuracy of almost any learning algorithm [Schapire 1990]. The underlying idea is to sequentially train and combine a collection of classifiers in such a way that the later classifiers focus more and more on hard-to-classify examples. To this end, in the well-known AdaBoost algorithm [Freund & Schapire, 1997], a probability distribution is introduced and maintained on the input space. Initially, every training example gets the same weight. In the following iterations, the weights of hard-to-classify examples are increased, according to the classification result of the current classifier on the training set. Using the calculated training weights, a new classifier is trained. This process is repeated, thus producing a set of individual ('base') classifiers. As in discriminative model combination [Beyerlein, 1998], which combines arbitrary models into a log-linear distribution, the output of the final classifier is determined from a linear combination of the individual classifier scores. However, the weights of the combination are given by AdaBoost theory (analytically minimizing an upper bound on the training error of the final classifier), whereas in discriminative model combination, the weights are determined experimentally (minimizing the empirical training error).

AdaBoost has been successfully applied to a variety of classification tasks, improving the classifier's accuracy and generalization properties. Examples include text and speech categorization [Schapire, 2000], document routing [Iyer et al., 2000], text filtering [Schapire et al., 1998b], call classification [Rochery et al., 2002], 'ranking' problems [Freund et al., 1998], tagging [Abney et al., 1999], parsing [Henderson & Brill, 2000], word sense disambiguation [Escudero et al., 2000], and image retrieval [Tieu & Viola, 2000]; for an overview, see e.g. [Schapire, 1999].

The experimental success of boosting was also supported by theoretical analysis [Schapire et al., 1998a], showing that AdaBoost is especially effective at increasing the *margins* of the training examples, i.e. the difference between the classifier score for the correct label and the score for the closest incorrect label.

However, to the best of our knowledge, most applications of boosting so far have focused on systems with a rather moderate number of classes and internal degrees of freedom. It is particularly interesting to investigate whether boosting can be successfully applied also to 'large scale' classification problems, involving thousands of classes and hundreds of thousands of internal parameters. An important example for such a scenario is large vocabulary automatic speech recognition, involving tens of thousands of words to be recognized and up to a million of internal parameters.

Previous work applying boosting to acoustic model training addressed the problem of classifying individual feature vectors to phone symbols [Cook & Robinson, 1996; Schwenk, 1999; Zweig & Padmanabhan, 2000], resulting in considerable computational effort. In a recent work [Meyer, 2002], it was proposed to apply AdaBoost to *utterance* classification, i.e. to the mapping of the whole feature vector sequence to the corresponding word sequence. This 'utterance approach' is computationally much less expensive than boosting applied to single feature vectors. For maximum likelihood training, the standard training paradigm in speech recognition, the approach has been shown to improve recognition accuracy [Meyer, 2002].

Yet another popular training paradigm in acoustic model training, which has been proven to be very effective in improving recognition accuracy, is *discriminative training*. In contrast to maximum likelihood training, discriminative training is directly related to the decision rule of the speech recognizer and tries to maximize class separability [Juang & Katagiri, 1992; Bahl et al., 1986]. An important aspect for practical applications is that the number of parameters of the acoustic model is not increased, as opposed to boosting. This renders discriminative training especially attractive for speech recognition. Thus, in order to evaluate the effectiveness of boosting in acoustic model training, its performance should be compared to discriminative training, and ideally both methods should be combined.

9.1.2   Contribution of our work

In this chapter, we provide experimental evidence that utterance-level boosting significantly improves recognition accuracy of a state-of-the-art speech recognizer in a large vocabulary name recognition task, even when applied in combination with discriminative training. In particular, we experimentally analyze the effect of boosting and discriminative training in terms of classification margins. The results of our study — and work from other sites — demonstrate the relevance of boosting for classification tasks in the context of Ambient Intelligence. Experimental results have previously been published in [Meyer & Beyerlein, 2002].

The remainder of this chapter is organized as follows. In the next section we review the maximum likelihood and discriminative training paradigms for acoustic model training. Then, in Section 9.3, we describe the standard AdaBoost algorithm and our utterance approach. Experimental results are presented in Section 9.4. First, we give baseline results for maximum likelihood as well as discriminative training (Section 9.4.1). In Section 9.4.2 we apply the boosting algorithm to maximum likelihood models. The combination of boosting and discriminative training is discussed in Section 9.4.3. We summarize our findings in Section 9.5 and conclude in Section 9.6 with further potential applications of boosting in the context of Ambient Intelligence.

9.2   Criteria for acoustic model training

In this section, we briefly review the basic classification and training criteria in automatic speech recognition.

For decoding a word sequence y' (out of a set of possible word sequences y), given a spoken utterance x (acoustic observation), we apply Bayes decision rule:

$$y' \quad = \quad \arg\max_y p(y|x) \tag{9.1}$$

$$= \quad \arg\max_y \left(p(x|y) \cdot p(y) \right). \tag{9.2}$$

In (9.2), the term $p(x)$ was omitted due to maximizing over y. The term $p(x|y)$ denotes the probability for observing an acoustic feature sequence x, given a word sequence y, and is called 'acoustic model'. The term $p(y)$ measures the prior probability for the word sequence y and is called 'language model'. In automatic speech recognition (ASR), both probability models are approximated on training data, by employing a range of thousands to millions of parameters.

Apart from using sufficient and appropriate data for a robust parameter estimation, there are two major lines for improving acoustic model performance. The first is a suitable parameterization of the acoustic model, capturing as close as possible the characteristics of speech, for example context information (see

[Odell, 1995] for an overview). The second one is to use an adequate training criterion for acoustic parameter estimation; this second issue is the topic of this chapter.

Maximum likelihood training. The standard approach in ASR is the maximum likelihood (ML) criterion. Given a set of training utterances x_i, $i = 1, \ldots, N$ with spoken (correct) word sequences y_i, the criterion amounts to:

$$F_{ML}(\theta) = \sum_{i=1}^{N} \log p_\theta(x_i|y_i),$$

where θ represents the set of acoustic model parameters. ML training maximizes this criterion, i.e. the likelihood for the correct word sequence to generate the acoustic observation. Competing word hypotheses y are not taken into account. Due to incorrect modeling assumptions and insufficient training data, this results in sub-optimal models yielding non-optimal recognition accuracy.

Discriminative training. A second training paradigm that is more directly related to the classification rule (9.1) is *discriminative training*. Several approaches have been investigated in the literature. 'Minimum classification error' (MCE) training [Juang & Katagiri, 1992] directly minimizes a smoothed function of the sentence error rate, by gradient descent methods. Another approach aims at maximizing the (empirical) mutual information between the acoustic observations and the corresponding word sequences ('MMI training', [Bahl et al., 1986]):

$$F_{MMI}(\theta) = \sum_{i=1}^{N} \log \frac{p_\theta(x_i|y_i)}{\sum_y p_\theta(x_i|y)p(y)}. \tag{9.3}$$

By simultaneously decreasing the likelihood of competing hypotheses y to generate the observed acoustics, discriminative training optimizes class separability. However, the denominator in (9.3) — in general approximated by data obtained from a recognition pass on the training corpus — renders the training process computationally extremely involved and time-intensive, since equation (9.3) can only be solved in a complex iteration process, each iteration requiring a recognition on the training data (the same holds for MCE training). The computations can be simplified by further restricting the denominator to the recognized text. The resulting algorithm, called 'corrective training' (CT) gives however only slight improvements if the training error is very low. An extension of the CT algorithm, called 'rival training' (RT) has been proposed [Meyer & Rose, 2000], which is computationally less expensive than lattice–based discriminative training methods like MMI or MCE, but gives significantly better performance than CT. Instead of a set of competing hypotheses, RT employs only the best scored *incorrect* hypothesis (the 'rival') in the denominator of (9.3), if it is sufficiently 'close' to the correct hypothesis.

However, for maximum likelihood as well as discriminative training, there is no direct relation to generalization performance on independent test data. This motivated us to investigate the performance of boosting in acoustic model training.

9.3 The AdaBoost algorithm

9.3.1 AdaBoost.M2

The AdaBoost algorithm was presented for transforming a 'weak' learning rule into a 'strong' one [Schapire 1990], given a set of labeled training pairs (x_i, y_i), where $x_i \in X$ denotes the input patterns and $y_i \in Y = \{1, \ldots, k\}$ the (correct) label from a set of k labels. In multi-class classification ($k > 2$), the AdaBoost.M2 version [Freund & Schapire, 1997] is commonly used. Ada-Boost.M2 (in the following simply referred to as AdaBoost) is applicable when the classifier defines a mapping $h_t : X \times Y \to [0,1]$, which may be regarded e.g. as providing a confidence score for each label. The basic algorithm is outlined in Figure 9.1.

Input:	example sequence $(x_1, y_1), \ldots, (x_N, y_N)$ with $x_i \in X$ and $y_i \in Y = \{1, \ldots, k\}$
Init:	define $B = \{(i, y) : i \in \{1, \ldots, N\}, y \neq y_i\}$
	and $D_1(i, y) = 1/|B| \quad \forall \quad (i, y) \in B$, else 0
Repeat:	1. train weak learner using distribution D_t.
	2. get weak hypothesis $h_t : X \times Y \to [0,1]$ and calculate pseudo-loss
	$\varepsilon_t = \frac{1}{2} \sum D_t(i, y)(1 - h_t(x_i, y_i) + h_t(x_i, y))$
	3. set $\beta_t = \frac{\varepsilon_t}{1-\varepsilon_t}$
	4. update distribution D_t: $D_{t+1}(i, y) = \frac{D_t(i,y)}{Z_t} \beta_t^{\frac{1}{2}(1+h_t(x_i,y_i)-h_t(x_i,y))}$,
	where Z_t is a constant normalizing D_{t+1}.
Output:	final hypothesis: $H(x) = \arg\max_{y \in Y} \sum_t (\ln \frac{1}{\beta_t}) h_t(x, y)$.

Figure 9.1. The AdaBoost.M2 algorithm.

AdaBoost maintains a distribution $D_t(i, y)$ over the example/label pairs (x_i, y) (being 0 for the correct label y_i: $D_t(x_i, y_i) = 0$). This distribution is updated according to the output of the current classifier on the training set: weights for example/label pairs belonging to confidently classified examples are reduced relative to those of misclassified examples. The update rule is designed to guarantee upper bounds on the training and generalization error rates [Freund & Schapire, 1997; Mason et al., 1997]. In each iteration t, a new classifier is trained with respect to the distribution D_t. In recognition, the scores of the individual classifiers are linearly combined, with weights being inversely related to the classifiers' training error, to give the final output (Figure 9.1).

9.3.2   Utterance Approach in ASR

In our utterance approach to speech recognition [Meyer, 2002], we define the input patterns x_i to be the sequence of feature vectors corresponding to utterance i, and y to be one possible output (word sequence) of the speech recognizer (y_i being the correct word sequence for utterance i). In isolated word recognition, the label space Y is simply defined by the recognition lexicon. It is, however, convenient to restrict the label space — for each utterance individually — to the most likely hypotheses, as determined e.g. by a baseline recognition on the training corpus [Zweig & Padmanabhan, 2000]. This is mandatory for applying the utterance approach to continuous speech recognition. For the function h_t we choose the 'a posteriori' confidence measure approximating the posterior probability $p(y|x_i)$. It is calculated on basis of the N-best list L_i obtained for utterance i [Rüber 1997]:

$$h_t(x_i, y) = \frac{p(x_i|y)^\lambda}{\sum_{z \in L_i} p(x_i|z)^\lambda}. \tag{9.4}$$

Here, λ is a parameter introduced since the recognizer provides only scores $(-\log p(x_i|y))$ up to some scaling factor. λ essentially controls the decay of confidence values in the N-best list. We use AdaBoost.M2 to weight the training utterances used in subsequent maximum likelihood and discriminative training of Gaussian mixture density Hidden Markov Models (HMMs; see Section 9.4.1). To this end, the weights $D_t(i, y)$ calculated by AdaBoost.M2 (Figure 9.1) are summed up to give an utterance weight $w_t(i)$ for each training utterance [Schwenk, 1999; Zweig & Padmanabhan, 2000]:

$$w_t(i) = \sum_{y(\neq y_i)} D_t(i, y).$$

The next parameter set θ for the acoustic model is then trained with respect to the calculated utterance weights, arriving at the following criteria for boosted maximum likelihood training:

$$F_{ML,t}(\theta) = \sum_{i=1}^{N} w_t(i) \log p_\theta(x_i|y_i), \tag{9.5}$$

and boosted maximum mutual information training:

$$F_{MMI,t}(\theta) = \sum_{i=1}^{N} w_t(i) \log \frac{p_\theta(x_i|y_i)}{\sum_y p_\theta(x_i|y)p(y)}. \tag{9.6}$$

9.4   Experimental results

9.4.1   Baseline models

Setup.   We performed experiments on a telephone-bandwidth large vocabulary isolated word recognition task based on *SpeechDat(II) German* material, consisting of city, company, first and family names and other single
words. We created three isolated word training corpora of different size: The
'SMALL' training corpus consists of 9k utterances (about 2.1h of speech), the
'MEDIUM' corpus of 18k utterances (about 4.3h of speech) and the 'LARGE'
corpus of 40k training utterances (about 9.7h of speech). For evaluation, we
used a test corpus of 10k isolated word utterances (about 3.5h of speech).

We employed standard feature extraction using mel-frequency cepstral coefficients (MFCC) [Davis & Mermelstein, 1980], optionally including a linear
discriminant analysis (LDA). The acoustic model is made of context dependent
HMM based phone models ('triphones'), with state-clustering applied for parameter reduction. For each state, the probability density function is assumed
to be a continuous Gaussian mixture density distribution. In recognition (and
in rival training), we used a lexicon consisting of about 10k words. For more
detailed information on acoustic modeling we refer to [Odell, 1995] and on the
setup to [Meyer & Rose, 2000].

Results.   Word error rates (WER) on the test corpus are presented in Table 9.1. Part A shows evaluation results for ML training as a function of the
number of densities and the amount of training data used. For ML training on
the 'SMALL' corpus without LDA, our lowest WER was 11.28%, using 74k
densities. Using more acoustic parameters in ML training resulted in overfitting. The test error rate can be significantly improved by using more training
data and applying LDA. Our best WER with ML training was 6.6% (training
on the 'LARGE" corpus, 104k densities, with LDA).

Part B of Table 9.1 presents results for applying rival training (RT) to selected ML models, in dependence of the number of RT iterations. In our experiments, RT improved the recognition accuracy by about 10% relative, using
the same amount of training data and the same number of densities.

Margin analysis.   Figure 9.2 shows the cumulative distribution of margins (difference between the confidence measure of the correct class and the
strongest confidence measure of a wrong class) on the training corpus for rival
training as a function of the iteration number. The margin of a classification example (x, y) is a number in $[-1, +1]$ and is positive if and only if the example
is classified correctly. Moreover, the magnitude of the margin can be interpreted as a measure of confidence in the prediction. In a theoretical analysis,
Schapire et. al. [1998a] proved that larger margins on the training set translate

Table 9.1. Baseline word error rates (WER, in %) on the test corpus for maximum likelihood (ML, top) and rival training (RT, bottom) on the 'SMALL', 'MEDIUM' and 'LARGE' training corpora (see text), in dependence of the number of densities ('# dens.') of the acoustic model and the number of RT iterations ('# it.').

a) maximum likelihood training (ML)

train corpus	LDA	# dens.	WER
'SMALL'	no	53k	11.34
	no	74k	11.28
	no	94k	11.71
'MEDIUM'	no	33k	10.15
	yes	35k	8.00
	yes	62k	7.66
	yes	101k	7.23
'LARGE'	yes	104k	6.64

b) rival training (RT)

train corpus	# it.	LDA	# dens.	WER
'MEDIUM'	3	yes	35k	7.71
	10	yes	35k	7.14
	15	yes	35k	7.23
	20	yes	35k	7.10
'LARGE'	17	yes	104k	5.94

into a superior upper bound on the generalization error. The margin analysis of Figure 9.2 shows that RT continuously increases the margins of the training patterns[1]. Note, however, that even for more than 10 iterations the margins are still increased, although the test error rate is not improved anymore.

9.4.2 Boosting maximum likelihood models

On selected ML models, we iterated the AdaBoost.M2 algorithm as explained in Section 9.3. In view of the linearity of the ML re-estimation equations, the utterance weights $w_t(i)$ were normalized to a mean value of 1.0.

---

[1] The discontinuity at margin 1.0 (margin 1.0 $\hat{=}$ 100%) stems from the fact that due to the inherent pruning applied in speech recognition, for a considerable portion of training utterances (30-40%) the recognition output consists of only a single hypothesis (N-best list of length 1). This leads to a confidence value and margin of exactly 1.0.

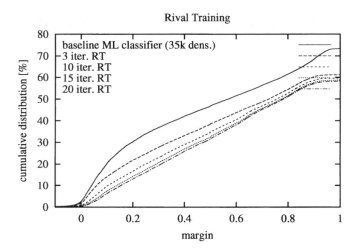

Figure 9.2. Cumulative distribution of margins on the training corpus for maximum likelihood (ML) and rival training (RT) up to 20 iterations. Margins are calculated on basis of the
confidence measure (9.4) with $\lambda = 0.005$, where the label space for each utterance has been
restricted to the most likely hypotheses. Baseline model: 35k densities, training on 'MEDIUM'
corpus, with LDA. Difference to 100% at margin 1.0: See the footnote on page 175.

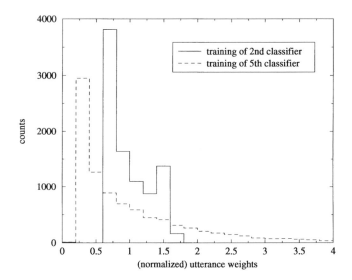

Figure 9.3. (Normalized) utterance weight histograms for boosting the ML baseline system
with 53k densities, trained on the 'SMALL' training corpus, without LDA. For the first classifier,
all utterance weights are 1.0.

Figure 9.3 shows example histograms for the calculated utterance weights. A margin analysis on the training corpus for the combined classifier is presented in Figure 9.4. It shows that boosting not only reduces the training error (up to 60% relative), but also increases the margins of correctly classified examples in the low margin regime.

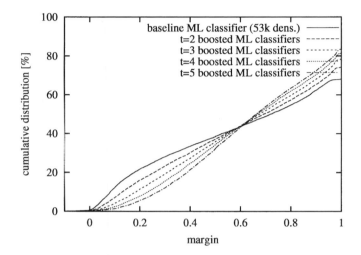

Figure 9.4. Cumulative distribution of margins on the training corpus, boosting a maximum likelihood (ML) trained baseline model (53k densities, training on 'SMALL' corpus, without LDA) up to $t = 5$ iterations ($\lambda = 0.005$). Difference to 100% at margin 1.0: See the footnote on page 175.

Table 9.2 presents test error rates for the final, boosted classifier, combining base classifier confidence scores (9.4) according to

$$H(x) = \arg\max_{y \in Y} \sum_t (\ln \frac{1}{\beta_t}) h_t(x, y).$$

We see that boosting leads to a significant improvement of the baseline word error rate. For example, boosting the ML baseline model with 53k densities, trained on the 'SMALL' training corpus (without LDA) for 5 iterations, the test error rate is improved by about 10% relative. Compared to increasing the acoustic resolution (i.e. number of densities) in standard ML training (Table 9.1), boosting however appears advantageous mostly for high accuracy acoustic models, where a further increase of parameters in ML training results in overfitting.

It is interesting to compare the results obtained by boosting to those achieved by combining non-boosted models. To this end, we calculated word error rates obtained by linearly combining acoustic scores from (non-boosted) ML models with different acoustic resolution. Comparing results for classifier ensembles

Table 9.2. Boosting maximum likelihood trained models: Word error rates (WER, in %) on the test corpus, boosting various ML baseline systems as indicated. t is the boosting iteration index ($t = 1$: baseline system). 'tot. # dens.' refers to the number of densities of the final (combined) classifier.

'SMALL' training corpus

baseline system	λ	t	tot. # dens.	WER
53k dens.,	0.005	1	53k	11.34
no LDA		2	102k	10.78
		3	148k	10.30
		4	193k	10.17
		5	237k	10.24
	0.01	1	53k	11.34
		2	103k	10.83

'MEDIUM' training corpus

35k dens.,	0.005	1	35k	8.00
LDA		2	68k	7.55
		3	101k	7.35
	0.01	1	35k	8.00
		2	68k	7.61

with a similar (total) number of densities, we found that boosting clearly outperforms the combination of non-boosted models. Further details are given in [Meyer, 2002].

On the other hand, Table 9.1 reveals that the improvements obtained by boosting are of the same order than those obtained by RT. This motivates the combination of both training paradigms.

9.4.3 Combining Boosting and Discriminative Training

The goal of this section is to investigate whether boosting can be used to further improve the performance of discriminatively trained models. To this end, we performed experiments using the baseline model with 35k densities (including LDA), trained on the 'MEDIUM' training corpus with 10 iterations of rival training. The baseline test WER for this model is 7.14% (Table 9.1). The resulting N-best list of a recognition pass on the training corpus was fed into the AdaBoost.M2 algorithm to calculate utterance weights $w_t(i)$ similar to Section 9.4.2. A second (boosted) classifier was trained on the reweighted

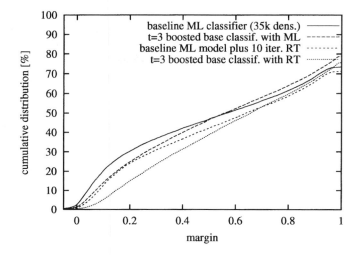

Figure 9.5. Cumulative distribution of margins on the training corpus, for boosting applying maximum likelihood (ML) and rival training (RT). Baseline model: 35k densities, training on 'MEDIUM' corpus, with LDA (ML training: solid line, plus 10 iterations RT: short-dashed line). Boosting up to $t = 3$ iterations ($\lambda = 0.005$) a) applying ML training (long-dashed line), b) applying RT (dotted line). Difference to 100% at margin 1.0: See the footnote on page 175.

training data by first applying ML training (9.5), followed by 20 iterations of rival training (9.6). This was repeated for the third classifier.

The margin analysis for this training process, Figure 9.5, shows that boosting in addition to rival training further increases the margins for training patterns classified with low margin.

Evaluation results for combining boosting and rival training are presented in Table 9.3. Again we see that boosting significantly reduced the word er-

Table 9.3. Boosting Rival Trained models: Word error rates (WER, in %) on the test corpus, combining boosting and rival training (RT). t is the boosting iteration index. 'tot. # dens.' refers to the number of densities of the final (combined) classifier.

'MEDIUM' training corpus

baseline system	λ	t	tot. # dens.	WER
35k dens.,	0.005	1	35k	7.14
LDA		2	68k	6.81
		3	101k	6.56

ror rate compared to the baseline system, demonstrating that boosting can be successfully applied also in combination with discriminative training.

Combining boosting and rival training, we arrived at a WER of 6.6% on the test corpus (using the 'MEDIUM' training corpus consisting of 18k utterances, 101k densities). Thus, both training methods resulted in an additive word error rate reduction of 18% relative compared to the ML baseline model (test WER: 8.0%, 35k densities). Since by increasing the acoustic resolution (number of densities) of the baseline model, the test WER can be further improved even by ML training, we again remark that boosting is mostly appropriate for high accuracy models, after fully exploiting the potential of increased acoustic resolution in maximum likelihood and discriminative training.

On the other hand, in view of expensive training data, the superiority of advanced training methods like boosting and discriminative training is clearly seen: to achieve a test WER of 6.6% by ML training with a similar number of densities (104k), training has to be performed on 41k utterances ('LARGE' training corpus), which is more than twice the training material.

9.5   Summary

We presented an experimental evaluation of boosting applied to maximum likelihood and discriminative training of Hidden Markov Model based speech recognizers. Specifically, we applied the well-known AdaBoost.M2 algorithm to calculate utterance weights used in acoustic model training of subsequent boosted classifiers. In a large vocabulary isolated word recognition task we obtained significant performance improvements compared to the baseline model, applying maximum likelihood training as well as in combination with discriminative training. We argued that both boosting and discriminative training increase the classification margins for training patterns classified with low margin. This effect was additive when combining boosting and discriminative training.

Boosting maximum likelihood models, the error rate reduction was comparable to that obtained by discriminative training, however at the expense of a considerable increase in recognizer complexity (i.e. number of densities of the final classifier). On the other hand, in combination with discriminative training, we obtained additive performance gains, suggesting an effective combination of both training paradigms.

Our results indicate that boosting is mostly relevant for high accuracy acoustic models, which fully exploit the potential of an increased acoustic resolution (i.e. number of densities of the acoustic model). In this case, further increasing the number of densities does not improve test performance in the context of standard training, due to overfitting. Boosting, on the other hand, resulted in further significant test error rate reductions, for the maximum likelihood as well as for the discriminative training criterion. Moreover, by combining boosting and discriminative training, we needed less than half the amount of training material to achieve a similar performance as standard maximum likelihood training.

9.6 Discussion and conclusions

Our experimental results indicate that boosting can be successfully applied even in 'large-scale' classification tasks, involving large numbers of candidate classes and internal parameters of the classifier. This was demonstrated in a large vocabulary automatic speech recognition task (proper name recognition). We obtained significant performance improvements even in the context of advanced acoustic model training paradigms, namely discriminative training. This is another evidence for the relevance of boosting to achieve high performance in advanced classification tasks. Some interesting applications relevant for Ambient Intelligence have been investigated by other sites, see e.g. in [Schapire, 2000] and [Schapire et al., 2002] for text categorization, [Schapire et al., 1998b] for text filtering, [Freund et al., 1998] for 'ranking' problems and [Tieu & Viola, 2000] for image retrieval. Other interesting applications include voice recognition, dialogue act classification, query by humming, and image and gesture recognition.

Another relevant issue for Ambient Intelligence is the combination of different input modalities. A standard paradigm for combining different knowledge sources are model combination techniques, e.g. discriminative model combination [Beyerlein, 1998]. By directly increasing their weights in the training database, the boosting algorithm further adds the advantage of 'reinforcing' the influence of hard-to-classify training examples.

Acknowledgment

It is a pleasure to thank Dietrich Klakow for valuable comments on the manuscript.

References

Abney, S., R.E. Schapire, and Y. Singer [1999]. Boosting applied to tagging and PP attachment. In *Proc. of the Joint SIGDAT Conference on Empirical Methods in Natural Language Processing and Very Large Corpora*, College Park, Maryland, pages 38–45.

Bahl, L.R., P.F. Brown, P.V. de Souza, and R.L. Mercer [1986]. Maximum mutual information estimation of hidden Markov model parameters for speech recognition. In *Proc. Intern. Conference on Acoustics, Speech and Signal Processing (ICASSP-86)*, Tokyo, Japan, pages 49–52.

Beyerlein, P. [1998]. Discriminative model combination. In *Proc. International Conference on Acoustics, Speech and Signal Processing (ICASSP-98)*, Seattle, WA, pages 481–484.

Cook, G.D., and A.J. Robinson [1996]. Boosting the performance of connectionist large vocabulary speech Recognition. In *Proc. International Conference on Spoken Language Processing (ICSLP-96)*, Philadelphia, PA, pages 1305–1308.

Davis, S.B., and P. Mermelstein [1980]. Comparison of parametric representations for monosyllabic word recognition in continuously spoken sentences. *IEEE Trans. ASSP*, 28:357–366.

Escudero, G., L. Marquez, and G. Rigau [2000]. Boosting applied to word sense disambiguation. In *Proc. 12th European Conf. on Machine Learning*, pages 129–141.

Freund, Y., and R.E. Schapire [1997]. A decision-theoretic generalization of on-line learning and an application to boosting. *Journal of Computer and System Sciences*, 55:119–139.

Freund, Y., R. Iyer, R.E. Schapire, and Y. Singer [1998]. An efficient boosting algorithm for combining preferences. In *Machine Learning: Proc. 15th International Conference (ICML-98)*.

Henderson, J.C., and E. Brill [2000]. Bagging and boosting a treebank parser. In *Proc. of the First Meeting of the North American Chapter of the Association for Computational Linguistics (NAACL-2000)*, Seattle, WA, pages 34–41.

Iyer, R.D., D.D. Levis, R.E. Schapire, Y. Singer, and A. Singhal [2000]. Boosting for document routing. In *Proc. 9th International Conference on Information and Knowledge Management*.

Juang, B.H., and S. Katagiri [1992]. Discriminative learning for minimum error classification. *IEEE Transactions on Signal Processing*, 40:3043–3054.

Mason, L., P. Bartlett, and M. Golea [1997]. *Generalization error of combined classifiers*. Technical report, Department of Systems Engineering, Australian National University.

Meyer, C., and G. Rose [2000]. Rival training: Efficient use of data in discriminative training. In *Proc. International Conf. on Spoken Language Processing (ICSLP-00)*, Beijing, China, pages 632–635.

Meyer, C. [2002]. Utterance-level boosting of HMM speech recognizers. In *Proc. International Conf. on Acoustics, Speech and Signal Processing (ICASSP-02)*, Orlando, FL, pages 109–112.

Meyer, C., and P. Beyerlein [2002]. Towards "large margin" speech recognizers by boosting and discriminative training. In *Machine Learning: Proc. of the Nineteenth International Conference (ICML-02)*, Sydney, Australia, pages 419–426.

Odell, J.J. [1995]. *The Use of Context in Large Vocabulary Speech Recognition*. Ph.D. thesis, University of Cambridge 1995, England.

Rochery, M., R. Schapire, M. Rahim, N. Gupta, G. Riccardi, S. Bangalore, H. Alshawi, and S. Douglas [2002]. Combining prior knowledge and boosting for call classification in spoken language dialogue. In *Proc. International Conference on Acoustics, Speech and Signal Processing (ICASSP-02)*, Orlando, FL, pages 29–32.

Rüber, B. [1997]. Obtaining confidence measures from sentence probabilities. In *Proc. EUROSPEECH*, Rhodes, Greece, pages 739–742.

Schapire, R.E. [1990]. The strength of weak learnability. *Machine Learning*, 5:197–227.

Schapire, R.E., Y. Freund, P. Bartlett, and W.S. Lee [1998a]. Boosting the margin: A new explanation of the effectiveness of voting methods. *The Annals of Statistics*, 26:1651–1686.

Schapire, R.E., Y. Singer, and A. Singhal [1998b]. Boosting and Rocchio applied to text filtering. In *Proc. 21st Annual Int. Conf. on Research and Development in Information Retrieval*.

Schapire, R.E. [1999]. Theoretical views of boosting and applications. In *Proc. 10th International Conference on Algorithmic Learning Theory*, Tokyo, Japan.

Schapire, R.E., and Y. Singer [2000]. BoosTexter: A boosting-based system for text categorization. *Machine Learning*, 39:135–168.

Schapire, R.E., M. Rochery, M. Rahim, and N. Gupta [2002]. Incorporating prior knowledge into boosting. In *Machine Learning: Proc. of the Nineteenth International Conference (ICML-02)*, Sydney, Australia, pages 538–545.

Schwenk, H. [1999]. Using boosting to improve a hybrid HMM/neural network speech recognizer. In *Proc. International Conference on Acoustics, Speech and Signal Processing (ICASSP-99)*, Phoenix, AZ, pages 1009–1012.

Tieu, K., and P. Viola [2000]. Boosting image retrieval. In *Proc. of the IEEE conference on Computer Vision and Pattern Recognition*.

Zweig, G., and M. Padmanabhan [2000]. Boosting Gaussian mixtures in an LVCSR system. In *Proc. International Conference on Acoustics, Speech and Signal Processing (ICASSP-00)*, Istanbul, Turkey, pages 1527–1530.

Chapter 10

EXCHANGE CLUSTERING AND EM ALGORITHM FOR PHRASE CLASSIFICATION IN TELEPHONY APPLICATIONS

Sven C. Martin

Abstract   This chapter presents two approaches how to automatically find useful phrases that extract semantic meaning from user utterances in natural language dialogue applications. The presented algorithms are based on exchange clustering with a word-error like criterion and on the expectation-maximization algorithm, respectively, and work on annotated training texts. The methods are applied to the Philips TABA corpus of train timetable enquiries, and the resulting error rates of the semantic tags are computed from a reference assignment.

Keywords   Automated enquiry systems, grammar learning, k-means clustering, expectation maximization, TABA.

10.1   Introduction

Speech is a very natural and intuitive way of requesting information. Picking up the telephone receiver, dialing a number and stating a question does not need any technical understanding at all. Numerous existing telephone services are a proof of the profitability of this concept. However, running a telephone call center is still quite expensive. Costs can be reduced by automating the handling of incoming phone calls using speech recognition, e.g. by automated call routing to a human expert operator for a requested service, the automated servicing of a FAX request, or even an automated database query, as in the example of a train timetable enquiry system. Many automated systems have come into existence in the recent years. However, most of them employ strict hierarchical menus, like

> "Please give your destination station."
> "Canterbury."
> "Please give your departure station."

W. Verhaegh et al. (eds.), Algorithms in Ambient Intelligence, 185-197.
© 2004 *Kluwer Academic Publishers. Printed in the Netherlands.*

> "Oxford."
> "Please give the day of your departure."
> "Tomorrow."
> "Please give your departure time."
> "Eleven o'clock a.m."

This kind of dialogue is quite unnatural and wearisome. Philips was the first company that employed a dialogue system that allows natural, fluent, and unrestricted speech access [Souvignier et al., 2000], e.g. to telephone directory information [Kellner et al., 1997], or train timetable enquiries [Aust et al., 1995]. The system allows queries from experienced users like

> "I'd like to go from Oxford to Canterbury
> at eleven o'clock tomorrow."

to rather talkative dialogues like

> "I want to visit my grandmother at Canterbury."
> "From where do you want to go to Canterbury?"
> "From Oxford, tomorrow."
> "At what time do you want to leave from Oxford
> tomorrow?"
> "At eleven o'clock."

The Philips system uses a technique known as concept spotting or chunk parsing. Of the fluent user utterance, only those parts are processed that are semantically useful in the context of the application. All *phrases*, i.e. word sequences, that share the same type of semantic information are assigned to a *concept*, e.g. the phrase "to Canterbury" belongs to the destination train station concept, and the phrase "at eleven o'clock" to the train departure time concept in a train timetable enquiry system. Phrases whose semantic meaning is useless for the application, e.g. "I want to visit my grandmother", are ignored. Usually, finding phrases and assigning them to an appropriate concept is done by hand and encoded in some formalism, e.g. stochastic context-free grammars in the case of the Philips system. Due to the many ways of expressing information in fluent speech (far more than can be thought of from the examples above), this is a weary, time-consuming, and thus expensive task. There are several attempts to automate similar problems such as finding appropriate keywords for call routing (e.g. [Bellegarda & Silverman, 2000; Georgila et al., 2000; Ries et al., 1995]), apart from an immense number of approaches to learning general natural language grammars that have a far broader scope than needed here (some of them described in [Charniak, 1993; Chen, 1996]). All of these methods learn useful phrases and words from annotated training corpora, i.e. utterance transcriptions or other texts along with the respective semantic interpretations encoded in some way.

Our first attempt to automatically find semantically meaningful phrases from an annotated corpus for the Philips spoken dialogue system was an adaptation of the concept of salient fragments, introduced by Gorin [Gorin, 1996] and refined by Arai et al. [Arai et al., 1999] for the well-known AT&T "How may I help you" call routing task (where incoming calls are automatically routed according to the key phrases, or "fragments" as they are called here, that appear in the caller's utterance). The basic idea is to group phrases according to their context and call-type similarities into classes, and, in a second step, to generalize phrases by replacing frequent subphrases by the class of that subphrase. However, the adaptation for our purposes failed mainly due to overgeneralization and a mismatch between the phrase grouping criterion (a probability-based heuristics) and our assessment criterion (error rate).

From the lessons learned we devised the first algorithm, presented in Section 10.2 of this chapter, that does not generalize at all, and whose selection of useful phrases is based on exchanging phrases between the various concepts until a criterion similar to error rate is minimized. An alternative method, presented in Section 10.3, estimates the likelihood that a concept appears with a given phrase, and finally assigns the phrase to the most likely concept. Experiments follow in Section 10.4, where the performance of both methods is matched against a simple baseline and a perfect supervised method. Conclusions are drawn in Section 10.5.

10.2   Exchange clustering

As stated in the introduction, the training material consists of an annotated corpus. Here, an annotated corpus is a list of tagged sentences (a.k.a. utterances, turns). A tagged sentence consists of two parts. First, the collection of the phrases that appear in the sentence, in arbitrary order. Second, the collection of tags, one for each semantic meaning that appears in the sentence, in arbitrary order. The connection of words to phrases, and the tagging of sentences is performed in some way of manual or automated preprocessing. See Figure 10.1(a) for an example of a tagged sentence. Note that from the annotation it is not clear which of the phrases in the sentence text is responsible for any one of the tags of the sentence. This allows the quick and easy manual tagging of a corpus, or to obtain tags automatically: a machine may get the meaning of an utterance it cannot interpret from a different source (e.g. a reformulation of the utterance) but does not have any information later, when that machine tries to learn new meaningful phrases from such utterances, which phrases of the first utterance bear that meaning. The relation between phrases and tags is exactly what is to be learned by the classification algorithm.

More formally, let $\bar{w}$ denote a phrase that appears in the corpus, and k any tag. An algorithm is needed that assigns a unique meaning (a tag k) to a phrase

$\bar{w}$, i.e. that finds an appropriate mapping $\bar{w} \mapsto k(\bar{w})$ or indicates that a certain phrase has no useful meaning at all (in this case it is mapped to a special tag named "__VOID__"). See Figure 10.1(b) for a sample assignment. If such a mapping (of yet unknown quality) is found, it can be applied to the phrases of a corpus sentence, and the resulting tags (if not "__VOID__") are matched against the tags in the annotation. The degree of mismatch is a measure of quality of the mapping. To achieve a good quality, the algorithm has to minimize the mismatch.

To formalize the measurement of mismatch, each tag set of an annotated training sentence s is seen as a vector whose components give the frequency $N(k,s)$ of tag k in that sentence s (where k may be any tag that appears in the corpus, apart from the __VOID__ tag, so that all vectors contain counts for all tags and thus all have the same length). There is one such vector from the reference assignments given by the training data, with counts $N_{\text{true}}(k,s)$, and one from the current mapping, with counts $N_{\text{current}}(k,s)$. The criterion F that measures the mismatch is the sentencewise squared Euclidean distance between these vectors:

$$F = \sum_{s,k}(N_{\text{true}}(k,s) - N_{\text{current}}(k,s))^2. \tag{10.1}$$

See Figure 10.1(c) for a sample criterion evaluation of a single sentence. The squared Euclidean distance is selected as criterion due to its handy mathematical properties. Other distance measures may also be suitable. Further, this criterion is close to the *tag error rate*. An error rate, a.k.a. edit distance or Levenshtein distance, is the minimum number of insertions, deletions, and substitutions needed to transform an erroneous word sequence into a correct one, divided by the number of words in the correct word sequence. It is the standard measure of quality in speech recognition (mismatch between recognized and actually spoken utterance). The tag error rate is the mismatch between the tags that come from the mapping and the tags that come from the annotation (where the tags are in the same order as the corresponding phrases appear in the sentence). The tag error rate might be used directly as criterion for the algorithm. However, it is computationally quite expensive (it contains a minimization problem), and it requires some sequential order of the phrases and the tags, something not provided for in the training.

The algorithm used to derive the mapping $\bar{w} \mapsto k(\bar{w})$ is an exchange clustering algorithm that is a generalization of k-means clustering [Duda & Hart, 1973, pp. 227–228]. An exchange clustering algorithm is used to partition a set of items into a fixed number of clusters, or classes, by moving an item from one cluster to another until some criterion is optimized. Exchange clustering is a greedy algorithm but has been successfully applied to finding word classes in language modeling for speech recognition [Martin et al., 1998]. Here, the set of items is the set of all phrases that appear in the training corpus, a cluster corresponds to the phrases that belong to the same concept (tag) (including a cluster for __VOID__ phrases), and the criterion to be optimized (here minimized) is the squared Euclidean distance F.

Initially, all phrases are assigned to the __VOID__ class. In the exchange algorithm, each phrase is visited in some fixed order. It is temporarily assigned to each class, and the criterion F is evaluated for each temporary assignment. If the criterion indicates that another class suits better than the original, the phrase is moved to that class. Once all phrases have been visited, the algorithm commences with the first phrase again, until no moves have been observed in one such run.

For efficiency, the sum in (10.1) is computed only once at the beginning of the algorithm. For the successive moves, only those terms of (10.1) are taken out and recomputed that are actually affected by changing a tag k of some phrase $\bar{w}$. The flow diagram of the EXCHANGE algorithm is given in Figure 10.2.

10.3 EM algorithm

Statistical methods have been used in speech processing with great success [Jelinek, 1999]. Therefore, it is likely that such a method is also useful for attaching meaning to a phrase. Usually with these methods, probabilities are drawn from observations, and decisions are made based on these probabilities. If it is possible to estimate, from the annotated training corpora, the probability $p(k|\bar{w})$ that, if phrase $\bar{w}$ appears in some sentence, then it bears the semantic

(a) *text*   a:train from:<station> to:<station>
    tags   origin destination

(b) a:train $\rightarrow$ __VOID__
    from:<station> $\rightarrow$ origin
    to:<station> $\rightarrow$ __VOID__

(c) (origin)
    (destination)

$$\left\| \begin{pmatrix} 1 \\ 1 \\ 0 \\ \vdots \\ 0 \end{pmatrix}_{(true)} - \begin{pmatrix} 1 \\ 0 \\ 0 \\ \vdots \\ 0 \end{pmatrix}_{(current)} \right\|_2^2 = 1$$

Figure 10.1. (a) Sample tagged sentence, (b) sample (erroneous) assignment and (c) resulting error.

meaning of tag k, the mapping $\bar{w} \mapsto k(\bar{w})$ can be derived from the decision

$$k(\bar{w}) \stackrel{def}{=} \underset{k}{\mathrm{argmax}}\, p(k|\bar{w}) = \underset{k}{\mathrm{argmax}}\, p(k, \bar{w}),$$

i.e. a phrase $\bar{w}$ is mapped to its most likely meaning.

If we could count the number of times $N(k, \bar{w})$ that a phrase $\bar{w}$ bears the semantic meaning of tag k, it would be easy to estimate the probability $p(k|\bar{w})$ from these figures, e.g. by relative frequencies $p(k|\bar{w}) = N(k, \bar{w})/\sum_{k'} N(k', \bar{w})$. However, this information is not provided in the annotated training corpus. A tag k in a tagged sentence just states that there is a phrase in that sentence that bears the meaning of tag k. It does not say which one. Thus, the counts $N(k, \bar{w})$ cannot be directly computed. For such cases, where a statistics on events that cannot be directly observed is needed, the EM (expectation-maximization) algorithm [Dempster et al., 1977] has been developed. The EM algorithm is used with success in the training of hidden Markov models, where it is known as forward-backward or Baum-Welch algorithm, or in the training of stochastic context-free grammars, where it is known as inside-outside algorithm.

EXCHANGE:
        attach each different phrase $\bar{w}$ to $\_\_VOID\_\_$;
        compute initial values $N_{\mathrm{true}}(k, s)$ and $N_{\mathrm{current}}(k, s)$,
            and mismatch F;
    repeat
        for each different phrase $\bar{w}$ in corpus *do*
            for each tag k *do*
                detach phrase $\bar{w}$ from its current tag c,
                temporarily attach it to tag k,
                and compute difference in mismatch $\Delta F(k)$;
            end;
            if $\Delta F(k) < 0$ for some $k \neq c$ *then*
                attach $\bar{w}$ to k with minimum $\Delta F(k)$ and update F;
            else
                keep the original assignment of $\bar{w}$,
                along with the original F;
            endif;
        end;
    until no phrase $\bar{w}$ changed its tag c in this iteration;

Figure 10.2.   EXCHANGE algorithm.

Let y denote an instance of observable data that depends on unobservable data t. What is searched for is a joint probability distribution $p_\theta(t,y)$, where θ denotes a set of parameters that determine the characteristics of that distribution. The aim of the EM algorithm is to find a maximum-likelihood estimation of $p_\theta(y) = \sum_t p_\theta(t,y)$, i.e. some parameter set θ that maximizes the probability $p_\theta(y)$ of the observations on the training data. The core of the EM algorithm is the so-called Q-function

$$Q(\theta',\theta) = \sum_t p_{\theta'}(t|y) \cdot \log p_\theta(t,y).$$

The basic EM theorem is that for any two parameter sets θ' and θ

$$Q(\theta',\theta) > Q(\theta',\theta') \Rightarrow p_\theta(y) > p_{\theta'}(y)$$

holds [Jelinek, 1999, Section 9.2]. Thus, by maximizing $Q(\theta',\theta)$ (and thereby estimating the probability distribution $p_\theta(t,y)$), the likelihood of observations is also maximized. The EM algorithm now is to find for any initial parameter set $\theta^{[0]}$ a new parameter set

$$\theta^{[1]} = \underset{\theta}{\mathrm{argmax}}\, Q(\theta^{[0]},\theta).$$

Then it is guaranteed that $p_{\theta^{[1]}}(y) > p_{\theta^{[0]}}(y)$, and the algorithm continues to find an even better parameter set $\theta^{[2]}$ that maximizes $Q(\theta^{[1]},\theta)$. This is repeated until some suitable convergence criterion is met. Like the EXCHANGE algorithm, this is a greedy algorithm.

In the problem of estimating $p(k|\bar{w})$, the word sequence W of the sentence corresponds to the observed data y. Also known is the unordered list of tags $\mathcal{K}$ that appears in the sentence. The hidden data t is the actual sequence of tags $K \in \pi(\mathcal{K})$, where $\pi(\mathcal{K})$ denotes the set of permutations over the unordered list $\mathcal{K}$. Thus, the probability distribution searched for by the EM algorithm is

$$p_\theta(K,W) \approx \prod_{k,\bar{w}} p_\theta(k,\bar{w})^{N_K(k,\bar{w})},$$

where $p_\theta(k,\bar{w})$ is the joint probability that phrase $\bar{w}$ appears and that it has the meaning of tag k, and $N_K(k,\bar{w})$ is the frequency of that event in the current sentence, using the sequence of tags K. Since $p_\theta(k,\bar{w})$ is a discrete probability distribution, the set of parameters θ consists of the probabilities themselves, therefore it is valid to simply write $p(k,\bar{w})$ instead of $p_\theta(k,\bar{w})$.

Thus, the EM algorithm's Q-function is

$$
\begin{aligned}
Q(p,\tilde{p}) &= \sum_{K\in\pi(\mathcal{K})} p(K|W) \cdot \log[\tilde{p}(K,W)] \\
&= \sum_{K\in\pi(\mathcal{K})} p(K|W) \cdot \sum_{\bar{w},k} N_K(k,\bar{w}) \cdot \log[\tilde{p}(k,\bar{w})].
\end{aligned}
$$

where p denotes the initial probabilities and $\tilde{p}$ the probabilities that are to be optimized. Optimization is performed by setting the derivation $\partial Q(p,\tilde{p})/\partial \tilde{p}(k,\bar{w})$ to zero and to solve that equation for $\tilde{p}(k,\bar{w})$. However, since $\tilde{p}(k,\bar{w})$ is a probability and probabilities must sum up to 1, this normalization constraint is formulated using a Lagrange multiplier:

$$Q^*(p,\tilde{p}) = Q(p,\tilde{p}) - \mu \cdot \left(\sum_{\bar{w}',k'} \tilde{p}(\bar{w}',k') - 1 \right).$$

Starting from some probability distribution $p(K,W)$, the improved (in the sense of Maximum Likelihood) distribution $\tilde{p}(K,W)$ is gained by taking the partial derivatives

$$\frac{\partial Q^*(p,\tilde{p})}{\partial \tilde{p}(k,\bar{w})} = \sum_{K \in \pi(\mathcal{K})} p(K|W) \cdot \frac{N_K(k,\bar{w})}{\tilde{p}(k,\bar{w})} - \mu \overset{!}{=} 0$$

and

$$\frac{\partial Q^*(p,\tilde{p})}{\partial \mu} = \sum_{\bar{w}',k'} \tilde{p}(\bar{w}',k') - 1 \overset{!}{=} 0.$$

Solving these equations for $\tilde{p}(k,\bar{w})$ yields the estimation formula

$$\tilde{p}(k,\bar{w}) = \frac{N(k,\bar{w})}{\sum_{\bar{w}',k'} N(k',\bar{w}')}$$

where

$$N(k,\bar{w}) \overset{def}{=} \sum_{K \in \pi(\mathcal{K})} p(K|W) \cdot N_K(k,\bar{w})$$

is the sum of the counts $N_K(k,\bar{w})$ depending on the tag sequence K and weighted by the probability that this sequence actually describes the words W of the sentence. This estimation is valid for one single sentence. For the probability over all sentences of the training corpus, the count $N(k,\bar{w})$ (now written as $N_s(k,\bar{w})$) is computed separately for each sentence s and summed up over all sentences.

A sketch of the EM algorithm is given in Figure 10.3. Note that the estimation $\tilde{p}(k,\bar{w})$ is used in the next iteration for computing $p(K|W)$. The initial probabilities are uniform.

10.4 Experiments

10.4.1 Corpus preparation

The TABA corpus. For the experiments, we use the Philips TABA corpus [Aust et al., 1995] that consists of train table enquiries in German over the telephone. This corpus is divided into a training and a testing subcorpus. To see the effect of varying training corpus sizes, a 1K subcorpus of the training corpus is also used for training. A statistics on the training corpora can be found in Table 10.1. The corpus named "32K" is the full TABA training corpus. The original TABA test corpus comprises 2 hours of speech. The test corpus is subdivided into two corpora named "DEV" and "EVL", where the "DEV" corpus is usually used for optimizing (DEVeloping) recognition parameters, and the "EVL" (for EVaLuation) corpus as the hard test case.

TABA is an application where the phrases that belong to a concept are encoded in a hand-written stochastic context-free grammar. This grammar serves as reference. It is used for producing the tagging of the training and test texts. The grammar transforms a string of words into a string of meanings (e.g. this phrase denotes the destination train station) with values (e.g. the actual name of the destination station), or, rather, into a string of *concepts* with *attributes*. This sophisticated grammar assigns concepts to sentence inputs almost as correctly as a human would do in this limited domain. The TABA grammar consists of 34 concepts, 96 non-terminals (including concepts), and 1955 rules. Typical concepts are `origin` and `destination`, for phrases that denote the origin and destination stations, respectively, and `date` and `complete_time` for date and time information.

There are word sequences that belong to complex logic expressions, such as time and date, or database entries, such as station names. These complex logic expressions can be encoded in application-independent standard grammars, and it is thus not necessary to feed these expressions, or database entries,

---

***EM*:**

    initialize $p(k|\bar{w})$ with uniform probabilities;
    repeat
        set $\tilde{q} = 0$ and $\tilde{q}(k,\bar{w}) = 0 \; \forall k, \bar{w}$;
        for each training corpus sentence s *do*
            for each phrase $\bar{w} \in W_s$ and each tag $k \in \mathcal{K}_s$ *do*
                set $N_s(k,\bar{w}) = \sum_{K \in \pi(\mathcal{K}_s)} p(K|W_s) \cdot N_K(k,\bar{w})$;
                set $\tilde{q}(k,\bar{w}) = \tilde{q}(k,\bar{w}) + N_s(k,\bar{w})$ and $\tilde{q} = \tilde{q} + N_s(k,\bar{w})$;
        end;
    end;
    set $p(k,\bar{w}) = \tilde{q}(k,\bar{w})/\tilde{q} \; \forall k, w$;
    until convergence;
    determine mapping $k(\bar{w}) \overset{def}{=} \text{argmax}_k \, p(k,\bar{w})$;

Figure 10.3. EM algorithm.

Table 10.1.   Test and training corpora statistics (without sentence end marker).

	1K	32K	DEV	EVL
no. of text/tag lines	1024	33081	1000	1278
words	4098	110154	3135	3835
per line	4.00	3.33	3.14	3.00
different words	174	1462	220	215
concept tags	2320	61007	1699	2068
per line	2.27	1.84	1.70	1.62
different concept tags	30	34	31	28
words per concept tag	1.77	1.81	1.85	1.85

into the classification process. As a consequence, numbers, names of days and months, and station names are replaced by appropriate placeholders in the test and training texts.

Tagging.   Initially, a text line of the training and test corpora consists of the string of words of a user utterance. These text lines are parsed by the hand-written grammar and intertwined with lines containing the concept tags resulting from the parsing of the preceding text line, in the correct order. The order of the tags is not used for phrase learning but, however, for the assessment of its result. Table 10.1 gives some statistics on the prepared corpora.

Phrase generation and pruning.   A simple count-based phrase generation is performed in three steps. First, create a bigram statistics on the text; second, take the 10 most frequent bigrams as phrases; third, in the text, substitute the words of the phrase by the phrase itself. Using the 1K and 32K training texts as baseline, the three steps are repeated 10 times, thus producing 100 phrases from each text. Each of the 100 phrases consists of at most 4 words. Further, words that appear only once in a training corpus are removed, since they bear no statistical significance. The remaining words are seen as phrases of length 1. In this sense, there are 177 different phrases in the 1K corpus and 1006 different phrases in the 32K corpus subjected to phrase classification. Figure 10.1(a) shows an example training sentence after tagging and phrase processing.

10.4.2   Learning and evaluation

Using the EXCHANGE and EM algorithms, each phrase is assigned a tag, or it is marked __VOID__. Ambiguous long phrases are removed, i.e. those phrases that can be split into two subphrases that are assigned to different tags. Using the learned mappings, tag sequences are constructed from the sentences of the three corpora and matched against the reference tag sequences, and a tag error rate (TER, as described in Section 10.2) and sentence error rate (SER, the ratio of sentences with at least one tag error) is computed. With the EM algorithm, the convergence is reached once the tag error rate on the DEV corpus starts to rise, a sign of beginning overtraining.

10.4.3 Contrasting methods

For a better assessment of the phrase classification result, two further methods are applied.

Mutual Information. This is a simplification of Gorin's salient fragment selection [Gorin, 1996] that assigns tags to phrases without clustering. It contrasts the performance of the EXCHANGE and EM algorithms against a simpler but useful method. For each phrase, the value

$$m(\bar{w}) = \sum_k p(k, \bar{w}) \cdot \log \frac{p(k|\bar{w})}{p(k)}$$

derived from mutual information is computed, where

$$\frac{p(k|\bar{w})}{p(k)} = \frac{p(k, \bar{w})}{(\sum_{\bar{w}'} p(k, \bar{w}')) \cdot (\sum_{k'} p(k', \bar{w}))},$$

and the probabilities $p(k, \bar{w})$ are pure relative frequencies based on the count

$$N(k, \bar{w}) = \sum_s N_s(k) \cdot N_s(\bar{w})$$

with $N_s(k)$ denoting the number of times that tag k appears in sentence s, and $N_s(\bar{w})$ denoting the number of times that phrase $\bar{w}$ appears in sentence s. The phrases $\bar{w}$ with $m(\bar{w}) < 0.005$ are supposed to be meaningless and assigned the __VOID__ tag (where the threshold 0.005 comes from a rule of thumb). The remaining phrases are assigned to their most likely tag $k(\bar{w}) = \text{argmax}_k p(k|\bar{w}) = \text{argmax}_k p(k, \bar{w})$.

Correct Assignment. The phrases are directly fed into the TABA grammar. The grammar assigns a unique tag to each phrase. If that is not possible, the phrase is supposed to be __VOID__. Since the tagging of the test corpora also comes from the same grammar, this is the best possible assignment of phrases and contrasts the phrase clustering against the perfect outcome for the given fixed set of generated phrases. The error rates of the correct assignment are not zero since the generation of phrases in the corpora is purely frequency-based, as described in Section 10.4.1, and thus there is a mismatch between them and the phrases encoded in the hand-written grammar.

Table 10.2.   SER and TER results for (a) mutual information, (b) the EXCHANGE algorithm, (c) the EM algorithm, and (d) correct assignments, on TRAINING, DEV, and EVL corpora.

		TRAINING		DEV		EVL	
		SER	TER	SER	TER	SER	TER
1K	(a)	29.10	15.99	19.20	16.18	15.34	12.35
	(b)	11.91	6.53	13.20	10.63	8.76	7.65
	(c)	10.55	6.16	18.80	15.78	12.05	11.26
	(d)	8.40	4.59	14.70	10.76	9.08	7.10
32K	(a)	23.25	17.02	18.00	14.77	13.85	10.60
	(b)	13.30	10.55	11.80	9.89	9.94	9.73
	(c)	10.36	8.29	8.00	6.89	6.57	6.67
	(d)	9.23	7.57	6.50	5.75	5.95	6.39

10.4.4   Results

The EXCHANGE and EM algorithms never take more than 4 iterations. Error rate results can be seen in Table 10.2. Using the small training corpora, the clustering result matches the correct assignment (sometimes it is even a bit better, since the clustering assigns tags to phrase fragments that are rejected by the TABA grammar). The mutual information approach has a considerably worse performance, since the probabilities are estimated on sparse data. The same is true for the EM algorithm. Using large training corpora, however, the clustering is only halfways between mutual information and correct assignment. The large training corpora give a good statistical evidence for mutual information and the EM algorithm, but the large number of phrases obviously lead the clustering to dissatisfying local optima. Here it is the EM algorithm that comes close to the correct assignments.

Thus, given the phrases in the training corpus, the correct assignments are almost matched, in the case of little training data by the EXCHANGE algorithm, in the case of large training data by the EM algorithm.

Further research may work on the problem how to find better phrases in the training corpus, and how to find the semantic content of a phrase once it has been assigned to a tag (i.e. how to automatically locate e.g. the station name once a phrase has been assigned to the `origin` concept).

10.5   Conclusions

Two algorithms have been presented in this chapter that ease the time and cost intensive development of semantically meaningful phrases for new dialogue applications. One is based on exchange clustering, the other on the

EM algorithm. Both algorithms automatically learn phrases from an annotated training corpus that carry semantically useful meanings. They have been applied to the transcriptions of real phone calls collected by the TABA train time table enquiry application. The results from exchange clustering come close to a correct reference assignment on a small training corpus, while the same is true for the results of the EM algorithm on a large training corpus. Thus, the mapping from a phrase to its semantic meaning is developed rapidly and is closely tied to real data.

References

Arai, K., J. Wright, G. Riccardi, and A. Gorin [1999]. Grammar fragment acquisition using syntactic and semantic clustering. *Speech Communication*, 27:43–62.

Aust, H., M. Oerder, F. Seide, and V. Steinbiss [1995]. The Philips automatic train timetable information system. *Speech Communication*, 17(3–4):249–262.

Bellegarda, J., and K. Silverman [2000]. Toward unconstrained command and control: Data-driven semantic inference. In *Proc. Int. Conference on Speech and Language Processing*, Beijing, volume I, pages 258–261.

Charniak, E. [1993]. *Statistical Language Learning*. MIT Press, Cambridge, MA.

Chen, S. [1996]. *Building Probabilistic Models for Natural Language*. Ph.D. thesis, Harvard University, Cambridge, MA.

Dempster, A.P., N.M. Laird, and D.B. Rubin [1977]. Maximum likelihood from incomplete data via the EM algorithm. *Journal of the Royal Statistical Society*, 39(ser. B):1–38.

Duda, R.O., and P.E. Hart [1973]. *Pattern Classification and Scene Analysis*. Wiley, New York.

Georgila, K., N. Fakotakis, and G. Kokkinakis [2000]. Building stochastic language model networks based on simultaneous word/phrase clustering. In *Proc. Int. Conference on Speech and Language Processing, Beijing*, volume I, pages 122–125.

Gorin, A. [1996]. Processing of semantic information in fluently spoken language. In *Proc. 4th Int. Conference on Spoken Language Processing, Philadelphia, PA*, volume 2, pages 1001–1004.

Jelinek, F. [1999]. *Statistical Methods for Speech Recognition*. MIT Press, Cambridge, MA.

Kellner, A., B. Rueber, F. Seide, and B.-H. Tran [1997]. PADIS – an automatic telephone switchboard and directory information system. *Speech Communication*, 23:95–111.

Martin, S., J. Liermann, and H. Ney [1998]. Algorithms for bigram and trigram word clustering. *Speech Communication*, 24(1):19–37.

Ries, K., F. Buø, and Y.-Y. Wang [1995]. Improved language modeling by unsupervised acquisition of structure. In *Int. Conference on Acoustics, Speech, and Signal Processing*, volume 1, pages 193–196.

Souvignier, B., A. Kellner, B. Rueber, H. Schramm, and F. Seide [2000]. The thoughtful elephant: Strategies for spoken dialog systems. *IEEE Transactions on Speech and Audio Processing*, 8(1):51–62.

Part II

SYSTEM INTERACTION

Chapter 11

ALGORITHMS FOR AUDIO AND VIDEO FINGERPRINTING

Job Oostveen, Jaap Haitsma, and Ton Kalker

Abstract   Audio and video fingerprinting are technologies for identification of audio and video signals. They are based on extraction of *fingerprints*, relatively short bit-vectors representing the most essential perceptual characteristics, and comparison of these fingerprints with pre-computed fingerprints of known audio/video.

In this chapter we present the three algorithms behind Philips' fingerprinting technology, i.e., the fingerprint extraction algorithms (both for audio and for video) and the database search algorithm.

Keywords   Audio and video identification, robust features, fingerprinting.

11.1   Introduction

Recent years have seen a growing scientific and industrial interest in identification of multimedia objects by computing and matching *fingerprints* [Allamanche et al., 2000; Cheng, 2001; Fragoulis et al., 2001; Haitsma et al., 2001; Neuschmied et al., 2001; Oostveen et al., 2002]. The growing industrial interest is shown among others by a large number of (startup) companies (like Audiblemagic, Auditude, Moodlogic, Philips, Relatable, Shazam and Yacast) and the recent request for information on audio fingerprinting technologies by the International Federation of the Phonographic Industry (IFPI) and the Recording Industry Association of America (RIAA) [RIAA-IFPI, 2001]. The prime objective of multimedia fingerprinting is to provide an efficient mechanism to establish the perceptual equality of two multimedia objects: not by comparing the (typically large) objects themselves, but by comparing the associated fingerprints (small by design). The fingerprints serve as some sort of summary of the content. In most systems using fingerprinting technology, the fingerprints of a large number of multimedia objects are stored in a database along with their associated meta-data (e.g. name of artist, title and album). The fingerprints serve as an index to the meta-data. The meta-data of unidentified

W. Verhaegh et al. (eds.), Algorithms in Ambient Intelligence, 201-219.
© 2004 *Kluwer Academic Publishers. Printed in the Netherlands.*

multimedia content are then retrieved by computing a fingerprint and using this fingerprint as a query in the fingerprint/meta-data database. The advantage of using fingerprints instead of the multimedia content itself is three-fold:

- *reduced memory/storage requirements* as fingerprints are relatively small;

- *efficient comparison* as perceptual irrelevancies have already been removed from fingerprints; and

- *efficient searching* as the database to be searched is smaller.

As can be concluded from the above, a fingerprint system generally consists of two components: a method to extract fingerprints and a method to efficiently search for matching fingerprints in a fingerprint database. This chapter describes fingerprinting technologies for audio and video that are suitable for a large number of applications. After defining the concept of a fingerprint in Section 11.2 and elaborating on possible applications in Section 11.3, we focus on the technical aspects of the proposed fingerprinting algorithms; Fingerprint extraction is described in Section 11.4 and fingerprint searching in Section 11.5.

11.2   Fingerprinting concepts

11.2.1   Fingerprint definition

Recall that a fingerprint can be seen as a short summary of an audiovisual object. Therefore a fingerprint function F should map an audiovisual object X, consisting of a large number of bits, to a fingerprint of only a limited number of bits. Here we can draw an analogy with so-called hash functions, which are well known in cryptography. A cryptographic hash function H maps a (usually large) object X to a (usually small) hash value. A cryptographic hash function allows comparison of two large objects X and Y by just comparing their respective hash values $H(X)$ and $H(Y)$. Equality of the latter pair implies equality of the former, with only a very low probability of error. For a properly designed cryptographic hash function this probability is 2^{-n}, where n equals the number of bits of the hash value. At first one might think that cryptographic hash functions are a good candidate for fingerprint functions. However recall from the introduction that instead of strict bitwise equality, we are interested in perceptual similarity. For example, an original CD quality version of a song and an MP3 version at 128kb/s sound equal to a human listener, but their waveforms can be quite different. Although the two versions are perceptually similar they are mathematically quite different. Therefore cryptographic hash functions cannot decide upon perceptual equality of these two versions. Even worse, cryptographic hash functions are typically bit-sensitive: a single bit of difference in the original object results in a completely different hash value.

In order to be able to discriminate between different audiovisual objects, there must be a very high probability that dissimilar audiovisual objects result in dissimilar fingerprints. More mathematically, for a properly designed fingerprint function F, there should be a threshold T such that with very high probability $\|F(X) - F(Y)\| \leq T$ if objects X and Y are similar and $\|F(X) - F(Y)\| > T$ when they are dissimilar.

11.2.2 Fingerprint systems parameters

Having a proper definition of an audio fingerprint we now focus on the different parameters of an audio fingerprint system. The main parameters are:

- *Robustness:* Can an audiovisual clip still be identified after severe signal degradation? In order to achieve high robustness the fingerprint should be based on perceptual features that are invariant (at least to a certain degree) with respect to signal degradations. Preferably, a severely degraded signal still leads to very similar fingerprints. The false negative probability is generally used to express the robustness. A false negative occurs when the fingerprints of perceptually similar audio clips are too different to lead to a positive match.

- *Reliability:* Reliability refers to a low false positive probability, which is the probability that an object is incorrectly identified.

- *Fingerprint size:* To enable fast searching, fingerprints may need to be stored in RAM memory. Therefore the fingerprint size, usually expressed in bits per second or bits per object, determines to a large degree the memory resources that are needed for a fingerprint database server.

- *Granularity:* How long a segment of an audio- or video-signal is needed to identify it? Granularity requirements depend on the application. In some applications only the whole object needs to be recognized, in others one prefers to recognize short segments.

- *Search speed and scalability:* How long does it take to find a fingerprint in a fingerprint database and how does this speed scale with the size of the database? For the commercial deployment of fingerprint systems, search speed and scalability are key parameters.

These five basic parameters are strongly related. For instance, if one wants a finer granularity, one needs to extract more bits per frame to obtain the same reliability. This is due to the fact that the false positive probability is inversely related to the fingerprint size.

11.3   Applications

In this section we elaborate on a number of applications for audio and video fingerprinting.

11.3.1   Broadcast monitoring

Broadcast monitoring is probably the best known application for fingerprinting [Allamanche et al., 2000; Fragoulis et al., 2001; Haitsma et al., 2001; Neuschmied et al., 2001]. It refers to the automatic playlist generation of radio, television or web broadcasts for, among others, purposes of royalty collection, program verification, advertisement verification and people metering. Currently broadcast monitoring is still largely a manual process: i.e. organizations interested in playlists, such as performance rights organizations, have 'real' people viewing/listening to broadcasts and filling out scorecards. A large-scale broadcast monitoring system based on fingerprinting consists of several monitoring sites and a central site where the fingerprint server is located. At the monitoring sites fingerprints are extracted from all (local) broadcast channels. The central site collects the fingerprints from the monitoring sites. Subsequently, the fingerprint server, containing a huge fingerprint database, produces the playlists of all the broadcast channels.

11.3.2   Connected content

Connected content is a general term for consumer applications where content is somehow connected to additional and supporting information. For example, a service could be set up to identify unknown songs over a mobile phone. When a users hears a song he likes but doesn't know, he phones to this service. At the server side a fingerprint is extracted and matched. The user then receives a voice-, SMS- or email-message with the identity of the song and possibly some extra information. This business is actually pursued by a number of companies (among others Shazam and Philips. The audio signal in this application is severely degraded due to processing applied by radio stations, FM/AM transmission, the acoustical path between the loudspeaker and the microphone of the mobile phone, GSM speech coding and finally the transmission over the mobile network. Therefore, from a technical point of view, this is a very challenging application.

11.3.3   Enhanced personal video recorders

Fingerprinting can be used in several ways to enhance the functionality and increase the efficiency of personal video recorders (PVRs). A PVR may select programs for recording based on a personal profile. Because programs may be repeated several times this leads to inefficient usage of system resources.

Using fingerprints the recorder can compare the to-be-recorded program to already recorded programs and decide to stop the recording. Another possibility is content-based recording. When a viewer selects a program for recording, fingerprints of the program-start and program-end are loaded into the recorder. These fingerprints are used as trigger for recording start and stop. Moreover, for series with a fixed intro, fingerprinting can be used to automatically record all editions of the series.

11.3.4   Filtering technology for file sharing

Filtering refers to active intervention in content distribution. The prime example for filtering technology for file sharing was Napster. Starting in June 1999, users who downloaded the Napster client could share and download a large collection of music for free. Later, due to a court case by the music industry, Napster users were forbidden to download copyrighted songs. Therefore in March 2001 Napster installed an audio filter based on file names, to block downloads of copyrighted songs. The filter was not very effective, because users started to intentionally misspell filenames. Therefore, in May 2001 Napster introduced an audio fingerprinting system by Relatable, which aimed at filtering out copyrighted material even if it was misspelled.

Although from a consumer standpoint audio filtering could be viewed as a negative technology, there are also a number of potential benefits to the consumer. Firstly it can organize music song titles in search results in a consistent way by using the reliable meta-data of the fingerprint database. Secondly, fingerprinting can guarantee that what is downloaded is actually what it says it is.

11.3.5   Automatic music library organization

Nowadays many PC users have a music library containing several hundreds of songs. The music is generally stored in compressed format (usually MP3) on their hard-drives. When the songs are obtained from different sources, such as ripping from a CD or downloading from file sharing networks, such libraries are often not well organized. Meta-data may be inconsistent, incomplete or even incorrect. Assuming that the fingerprint database contains correct meta-data, audio fingerprinting can ensure correctness and consistency of the meta-data of the songs in the library, allowing easy organization based on, for example, album or artist.

11.4   Fingerprint extraction

11.4.1   Guiding principles

Fingerprints intend to capture the relevant perceptual features of an audio-visual object. At the same time extracting and searching fingerprints should be fast and easy, preferably with a small granularity to allow usage in highly demanding applications (e.g. mobile phone recognition). A few fundamental questions have to be addressed before starting the design and implementation of such a fingerprinting scheme. The most prominent question to be addressed is: what kind of features are the most suitable. A scan of the existing literature shows that the set of relevant features can be broadly divided into two classes: the class of semantic features and the class of non-semantic features. Typical elements in the former class are genre, beats-per-minute, distribution of scene changes, etcetera. These types of features usually have a direct interpretation, and are commonly used for classification, play-list generation and more. The latter class consists of features that have a more mathematical nature and are difficult for humans to 'read' directly from music. A typical element in this class is 'AudioFlatness' which is proposed in MPEG-7 as an audio descriptor tool [Allamanche et al., 2000]. For the work described in this chapter we have explicitly chosen to work with non-semantic features for a number of reasons:

1. Semantic features do not always have a clear and unambiguous meaning, i.e. personal opinions on such classifications differ. Moreover, semantics may actually change over time. For example, music that was classified as hard rock 25 years ago may be viewed as soft listening today. This makes mathematical analysis difficult.

2. Semantic features are in general more difficult to compute than non-semantic features.

3. Semantic features are not universally applicable. For example, beats-per-minute does not typically apply to classical music.

A second question to be addressed is the representation of fingerprints. One obvious candidate is the representation as a vector of real numbers, where each component expresses the weight of a certain basic perceptual feature. A second option is to stay closer in spirit to cryptographic hash functions and represent digital fingerprints as bit-strings. For reasons of reduced search complexity we have decided in this work for the latter option. The first option would imply a similarity measure involving additions/subtractions and most probably even multiplications, which is expected to be prohibitively complex, given the stringent scalability and search speed requirements. Fingerprints that are represented by bit vectors can be compared simply by counting bits. Given the expected application scenarios, we do not expect a high robustness for each

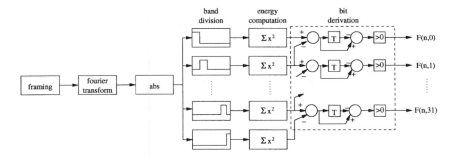

Figure 11.1.   Overview of the audio fingerprint extraction scheme.

and every bit in such a binary fingerprint. Therefore, in contrast to crypto-graphic hashes that typically have a few hundred bits at the most, we will al-low fingerprints that have a few thousand bits. Fingerprints containing a large number of bits allow extremely reliable identification even if the percentage of non-matching bits is relatively high.

A final question involves the granularity of fingerprints. In the applications that we envisage there is no guarantee that the audiovisual objects that need to be identified are complete. For example, in broadcast monitoring, any inter-val of 5 seconds is a unit of music that has commercial value, and therefore may need to be identified and recognized. Also, in security applications such as file filtering on a peer-to-peer network, one would wish that deletion of the first few seconds of an audio file would not prevent identification. In this work we therefore adopt the policy of fingerprint streams by dividing the signal into frames and deriving sub-fingerprints from the frames. These sub-fingerprints will, in general, not be large enough to identify the frames themselves, but a sufficiently large amount of consecutive sub-fingerprints (referred to as finger-print block), will allow robust and reliable identification of the corresponding segment.

11.4.2   Audio fingerprint extraction algorithm

In this section, we will describe our audio fingerprint extraction algorithm. It is based on the streaming approach as described in Section 11.4.1. It extracts 32-bit sub-fingerprints for every interval of 11.6 milliseconds. A fingerprint block consists of 256 subsequent sub-fingerprints, corresponding to a granu-larity of only 3 seconds.

For a detailed description of the algorithm, we refer to Figure 11.1.

The audio signal is first segmented into overlapping frames. The overlap-ping frames have a length of 0.37 seconds and are weighted by a Hanning window with an overlap factor of 31/32. This strategy results in the extraction of one sub-fingerprint for every 11.6 milliseconds. A spectral representation is computed by performing a Fourier transform on every frame. Due to the sensitivity of the phase of the Fourier transform to different frame boundaries and the fact that the Human Auditory System (HAS) is relatively insensitive to phase, only the absolute value of the spectrum, i.e. the power spectral density, is retained. In order to extract a 32-bit sub-fingerprint value for every frame, 33 non-overlapping frequency bands are selected. These bands lie in the range from 300Hz to 2000Hz (the most relevant spectral range for the HAS) and have a logarithmic spacing. Let us denote the energy of band m of frame n by $E(n,m)$ and the m-th bit of the sub-fingerprint of frame n by $F(n,m)$. The fingerprint bits are a thresholded version of the difference of the energy in neighboring (both in frequency and in time) frequency bands. The energy difference $D(n,m)$ is defined as (see also the gray block in Figure 11.1, where T is a delay element):

$$D(n,m) = E(n,m) - E(n,m+1) - (E(n-1,m) - E(n-1,m+1)).$$

Now, the corresponding fingerprint bit is formally defined as

$$F(n,m) = \begin{cases} 1 & \text{if} \quad D(n,m) > 0 \\ 0 & \text{if} \quad D(n,m) \leq 0 \end{cases}$$

Figure 11.2 shows an example of 256 subsequent 32-bit sub-fingerprints (i.e. a fingerprint block), extracted with the above scheme from a short excerpt of "O Fortuna" by Carl Orff. A '1' bit corresponds to a white pixel and a '0' bit to a black pixel. Figure 11.2.a and Figure 11.2.b show a fingerprint block from an original CD and the MP3 compressed (128kbps) version of the same excerpt, respectively. Ideally these two figures should be identical, but due to the compression some of the bits are retrieved incorrectly. These bit errors, which are used as the similarity measure for our fingerprint scheme, are shown in black in Figure 11.2.c.

The computing resources needed for the proposed algorithm are limited. Since the algorithm only takes into account frequencies below 2kHz the received audio is first down sampled to a mono audio stream with a sampling rate of 5kHz. The sub-fingerprints are designed such that they are robust against signal degradations. Therefore very simple down sample filters can be used without introducing any performance degradation. Currently 16-tap FIR filters are used. The most computationally demanding operation is the Fourier transform of every audio frame. In the down sampled audio signal a frame has a length of 2048 samples. If the Fourier transform is implemented as a fixed point real-valued FFT the fingerprinting algorithm has been shown to run efficiently on portable devices such as a PDA or a mobile phone.

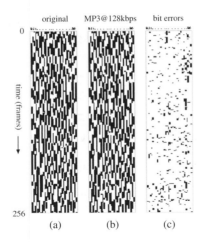

Figure 11.2. (a) Fingerprint block of original music clip. (b) Fingerprint block of a compressed version. (c) The difference between (a) and (b) showing the bit errors in black (BER=0.078).

11.4.3 Video fingerprint extraction algorithm

In this section, we present a feature extraction algorithm for robust video fingerprinting and we discuss some of the choices and considerations in the design of such an algorithm.

As we want our algorithm to be usable in CE devices, not only performance but also complexity are key issues in the design. For complexity reasons it is preferable to avoid complex operations, like DCT or DFT transformations. Therefore, we choose to compute features in the spatio-temporal domain. Moreover, to allow easy feature extraction from most compressed video streams as well, we choose features which can be easily computed from block-based DCT coefficients. Based on these considerations, the proposed algorithm is based on the mean luminance, computed over relatively large regions. This is also approach taken by [Abdel-Mottaleb et al., 1999]. We will choose our regions in a fairly simple way: the example algorithm in this chapter uses a fixed number of rectangular blocks per frame. In this way, the algorithm is automatically resistant to changes in resolution.

For a detailed description of our video fingerprint extraction algorithm, we refer to Figure 11.3.

Each frame is divided in a grid of 4 rows and 9 columns, resulting in 36 blocks. For each of these blocks, the mean of the luminance values of the pixels is computed. The mean luminance of block (r, c) in frame m is denoted $E(r, c, m)$. We apply a spatial filter with kernel $[\ -1\ \ 1\ ]$ on the mean luminance frame, consisting of 4×9 'super-pixels', and a temporal filter with

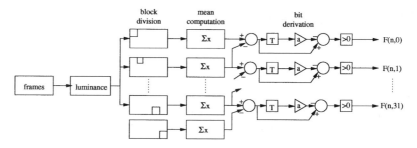

Figure 11.3.   Overview of the video fingerprint extraction scheme.

kernel $[\,-a\ 1\,]$. This leads to the 'differential' mean luminance $D(r,c,m)$

$$D(r,c,m) = E(r,c,m) - E(r,c,m+1) - a\,(E(r,c-1,m) - E(r,c-1,m+1)),$$

for $c = 1,\dots,8$ and $r = 1,\dots,4$.

The sign of the differential mean luminance constitutes the fingerprint bit $F(r,c,m)$ for block (r,c) in frame m. Thus, per frame we derive 32 fingerprint bits:

$$F(r,c,m) = \begin{cases} 1 & \text{if} \quad D(r,c,m) > 0; \\ 0 & \text{if} \quad D(r,c,m) \le 0. \end{cases}$$

The reason for parameter a in the temporal difference kernel, instead of a straightforward difference is the frequent occurrence of still regions in a video clip. If (a region in) a video is effectively a prolonged still image, the temporal differentiation is completely determined by noise, and therefore the extracted bits would be very unreliable. Inclusion of the parameter a circumvents this problem by not completely suppressing temporal DC.

This fingerprint definition has a number of important advantages:

- Only a limited number of bits is needed to uniquely identify short video clips with a low false positive probability

- the feature extraction algorithm has a very low complexity and it may be adapted to operate directly on the compressed domain, without a need for complete decoding.

- The robustness of these features with respect to geometry-preserving operations is very good

A disadvantage may be that for certain applications the robustness with respect to geometric operations (like zoom & crop) may not be sufficient. Experimental robustness results are presented in Section 11.4.6, below.

For our experiments we used $a = 0.95$ and a block size 120×80 pixels for NTSC video material. Matching is done on the basis of fingerprint bits extracted from 90 consecutive frames, i.e., $3 \times 30 \times 32 = 2880$ bits.

11.4.4 False positive analysis

Two audio or video signals are declared similar if at most a fraction α of the bits of the two derived fingerprint blocks is different (i.e., if the Hamming distance between the fingerprint blocks is at most αn, where n is the number of bits per fingerprint block). For fixed n, the value of α directly determines the false positive probability P_f, i.e. the probability that signals are incorrectly declared equal: the smaller α, the smaller the probability P_f will be. On the other hand, a small value of α will lead to an increased false negative probability P_n, (the probability that two signals are 'equal', but not identified as such).

We take a Neyman-Pearson approach to selecting the appropriate value of this threshold α. That is, we minimize the false negative probability subject to a maximum tolerable value of the false positive probability. This leads to choosing a value of α that achieves the bound on the false positive probability.

To derive a model for the false positive probability as a function of the threshold α, we assume that the fingerprint extraction process yields random i.i.d. (independent and identically distributed) bits. Later on we will correct the resulting expressions for the correlation which is present in the fingerprint bits.

Assuming i.i.d. fingerprint bits, the Hamming distance between two randomly selected fingerprint blocks will have a binomial distribution $B(n,p)$, where n equals the number of bits extracted and $p\ (=0.5)$ is the probability that a '0' or '1' bit is extracted. Since n is large in our application, the binomial distribution can be approximated by a normal distribution with a mean $\mu = np$ and standard deviation $\sigma = \sqrt{np(1-p)}$. For two randomly selected fingerprint blocks, the probability that the Hamming distance is at most αn, is given by:

$$P_f(\alpha) = \frac{1}{\sqrt{2\pi}\sqrt{np(1-p)}} \int_{(-\infty)}^{\alpha n} e^{-\frac{(x-np)^2}{2np(1-p)}} dx = \frac{1}{2}\mathrm{erfc}\left(\frac{(1-2\alpha)}{\sqrt{2}}\sqrt{n}\right).$$

$$(11.1)$$

However, in practice the sub-fingerprints have high correlation along the time axis. This correlation is due not only to the inherent time correlation in audio or video, but for audio it is also caused by the large overlap of the frames used in fingerprint extraction. Higher correlation implies a larger standard deviation, as shown by the following argument. Assume that the fingerprint bits are samples from a binary Markov process with alphabet $\{-1,1\}$ with transition probability q (the transition probability is the probability that a fingerprint bit extracted from a certain frame is different from the corresponding bit in extracted from the previous frame). Then one may easily show that $E[x_i x_{i+k}] = a^{|k|}$, where $a = 1 - 2q$. If the source Z is the exclusive-or of two such sequences X and Y, then Z is symmetric and $E[z_i z_{i+k}] = a^{2|k|}$. For N large,

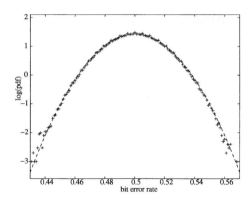

Figure 11.4. Comparison of the measured ('+') log-probability density function of the Hamming distance and the theoretical log-pdf (11.2).

the standard deviation of the average $\bar{Z}_N$ over N consecutive samples of Z can be approximately described by a normal distribution with mean 0 and standard deviation equal to

$$\sqrt{\frac{1+a^2}{N(1-a^2)}}.$$

Translating the above back to the case of fingerprints bits, a correlation factor a between subsequent fingerprint bits implies an increase in standard deviation for the Hamming distance by a factor

$$\sqrt{\frac{1+a^2}{1-a^2}}.$$

Next this model is used to determine the distribution of the Hamming distance between randomly selected real audio fingerprint blocks. A fingerprint database of 10,000 songs was generated. The transition probability of the fingerprint bits is determined from 100,000 randomly selected fingerprint blocks. It is measured to be $q \approx 0.07$, leading to $a = 2q - 1 \approx -0.86$ and to an increase of the standard deviation of the Hamming distance with a factor 2.7.

To verify the model, we also measured the relative Hamming distance (the Hamming distance divided by the number of bits) by matching 100,000 randomly selected pairs of fingerprint blocks from the same database. The standard deviation of the measured relative Hamming distance distribution on the same database was measured to be 0.0148, approximately 2.7 times higher than the 0.0055 one would expect from random i.i.d. bits. Figure 11.4 shows the log Probability Density Function (PDF) of the measured relative Hamming distance distribution and a normal distribution with mean of 0.5 and a standard deviation of 0.0148. The PDF of the Hamming distance is a close approximation to the normal distribution. For relative Hamming distances below 0.45 we observe some outliers, due to insufficient statistics. To incorporate the larger standard deviation of the Hamming distance distribution Formula (11.1) is modified by inclusion of a factor 3 (to stay at the conservative side of the computed factor 2.7):

$$P_f(\alpha) = \frac{1}{2}\text{erfc}\left(\frac{(1-2\alpha)}{3\sqrt{2}}\sqrt{n}\right). \qquad (11.2)$$

The threshold for the relative Hamming distance used during experiments was $\alpha = 0.35$. This means that out of 8192 bits at most 2867 bits are allowed to be different in order to decide that the fingerprint blocks originate from the same song. Using formula (11.2) we arrive at a very low false positive probability of $\text{erfc}(6.4)/2 = 3.6 \times 10^{-20}$.

11.4.5 Audio experimental robustness results

In this subsection we show the experimental robustness of the proposed audio fingerprinting scheme. That is, we try to answer the question of whether or not the BER between the fingerprint block of an original and a degraded version of an audio clip remains under the threshold α. We selected four short audio excerpts (Stereo, 44.1kHz, 16bps) from songs that belong to different musical genres: "O Fortuna" by Carl Orff, "Success has made a failure of our home" by Sinead o'Connor, "Say what you want" by Texas and "A whole lot of Rosie" by AC/DC. Table 11.1 lists all of the applied signal degradations and the average resulting bit error rates.

Thereafter the BERs between the fingerprint blocks of the original version and of all the degraded versions were determined for each audio clip. Almost all the resulting bit error rates are well below the threshold of 0.35, even for GSM encoding. The only degradations that lead to a BER above threshold are large linear speed changes. Linear speed changes in excess of $\pm2.5\%$ generally result in bit error rates higher than 0.35. This is due to misalignment of the framing (temporal misalignment) and spectral scaling (frequency misalignment). Appropriate pre-scaling (for example by exhaustive search) can solve this issue.

11.4.6 Video experimental robustness results

Extensive experiments with the algorithm described above are planned for the near future. In this chapter we report on the results of some initial tests. We have used a 10-second clip, taken from a Hollywood movie (with a resolution of 480 lines and 720 pixels per line). From this clip, we extracted the fingerprint. It is used as 'the database'. Subsequently, we processed the clip,

Table 11.1. Experimental bit error rates for the audio fingerprint extraction algorithm.

MP3 Encoding/Decoding	128 kbps	8.3%
	32 kbps	12.9%
Real Media Encoding/Decoding	20 kbps	16.7%
All-pass Filtering		2.0%
Amplitude Compression		7.9%
Equalization	10-band	5.5%
Echo addition		14.6%
Band-pass Filter	100Hz – 6000Hz	2.9%
Time Scale Modification	+4%	19.7%
(pitch unaffected)	-4%	19.3%
Linear Speed Change	+4%	43.3%
(pitch & tempo change)	-4%	45.1%
Re-sampling		0.0%
DA-AD Conversion	analog tape recorder	8.4%

and investigated how this influences the extracted fingerprint. The results are reported below in Table 11.2

Table 11.2. Experimental bit error rates for the video fingerprint extraction algorithm.

processing	*parameters*	*bit error rate*
MPEG-2 encoding	4 Mbps	2.8%
median filtering	3 × 3 neighborhood	1.5%
histogram equalization		8.9%
uniform (2D) scaling	80%	28%
	120%	22%
horizontal shifting	1 pixel	0.5%
	16 pixels	8.7%
	32 pixels	14.8%

The results indicate that the method is very robust against all processing which is done on a local basis, like for instance MPEG compression or median filtering. In general the alterations created by these processes average out within the blocks. Processing which changes the video more in a global fashion is more difficult to withstand. For instance, global geometric operations like scaling and shifting lead to far higher bit error rates. This behavior stems from the resulting misalignment of the blocks. A higher robustness could be obtained by using larger blocks, but this would reduce the discriminative power of the fingerprint.

11.5 Database search

11.5.1 Search algorithm

Finding extracted fingerprints in a fingerprint database is a non-trivial task. Instead of searching for a bit-exact fingerprint (easy!), the most similar fingerprint needs to be found. In this section we will introduce the problem of fingerprint matching and our solution. Although there is no difference between our audio and video database solutions, we will illustrate the exposition with numbers and examples from the proposed audio fingerprint scheme.

Consider a moderate size fingerprint database containing 10,000 songs with an average length of 5 minutes. This corresponds to approximately 250 million sub-fingerprints. To identify a fingerprint block originating from an unknown audio clip we have to find the most similar fingerprint block in the database. In other words, we have to find the position in the 250 million sub-fingerprints where the bit error rate is minimal. This is of course possible by brute force searching. However this takes 250 million fingerprint block comparisons. Using a modern PC, a rate of approximately of 200,000 fingerprint block comparisons per second can be achieved. Therefore the total search time for our example will be in the order of 20 minutes! This shows that brute force searching is not a viable solution for practical applications. We propose to use a more efficient search algorithm. Instead of calculating the BER for every possible position in the database, such as in the brute-force search method, it is calculated for a few candidate positions only. These candidates contain with very high probability the best matching position in the database.

In the simplest version of the improved search algorithm, candidate positions are generated based on the assumption that it is very likely that at least one sub-fingerprint is exactly equal to the corresponding sub-fingerprint in the database (i.e., it does not contain any bit errors) [Neuschmied et al., 2001; Haitsma et al., 2001]. If this assumption is valid, the only positions that need to be checked are the ones where one of the 256 sub-fingerprints of the query matches perfectly. In this way, the sub-fingerprints can be used as an index to the database. We will elaborate on this database structure, below. To illustrate the validity of the assumption, we determined the number of bit errors per sub-fingerprint for the fingerprints depicted in Figure 11.2. It indeed shows that there are 17 sub-fingerprints that do not contain any errors. If we assume that the 'original' fingerprint of Figure 11.2.a is indeed loaded in the database, its position will be among the selected candidate positions for the 'MP3@128kbps fingerprint' of Figure 11.2.b.

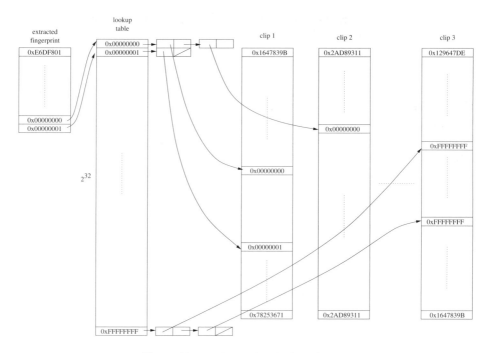

Figure 11.5.   Fingerprint database layout.

The positions in the database where a specific 32-bit sub-fingerprint is lo-cated are retrieved using the database architecture of Figure 11.5. The fin-gerprint database contains a lookup table (LUT) with all possible 32 bit sub-fingerprints as an entry. Every entry points to a list with pointers to the po-sitions in the real fingerprint lists where the respective 32-bit sub-fingerprint are located. In practical systems with limited memory a lookup table contain-ing 2^{32} entries is often not feasible, or not practical, or both. Furthermore the lookup table will be sparsely filled, because only a limited number of songs can reside in the memory. Therefore, in practice, a hash table [Cormen et al., 1998] is used instead of a lookup table. Let us again do the calculation of the average number of fingerprint block comparisons per identification for a 10,000-song database. Since the database contains approximately 250 mil-lion sub-fingerprints, the average number of positions in a list will be 0.058 ($= 250 \cdot 10^{6}/2^{32}$). If we assume that all possible sub-fingerprints are equally likely, the average number of fingerprint comparisons per identification is only 15 ($= 0.058 \times 256$). However we observe in practice that, due to the non-uniform distribution of sub-fingerprints, the number of fingerprint compar-isons increases roughly by a factor of 20. On average 300 comparisons are needed, yielding an average search time of 1.5 milliseconds on a modern PC. The lookup-table can be implemented in such a way that it has no impact on the search time. At the cost of a lookup-table, the proposed search algorithm is approximately a factor 800,000 times faster than the brute force approach.

The assumption that at least 1 sub-fingerprint is error-free almost always holds for audio signals with 'mild' audio signal degradations (See also Section 5.2). However, for heavily degraded signals the assumption is not always valid. For instance, after MP3 compression at 32 kbps, the fingerprint of the song of Figure 11.2 would violate this assumption. Some of the sub-fingerprints, however, contain only one error. So instead of only checking positions in the database where one of the 256 sub-fingerprints occurs, we can also check all the positions where sub-fingerprints occur which have a Hamming distance of one (i.e. one toggled bit) with respect to all the 256 sub-fingerprints. Rather than randomly toggling bits, we propose to estimate and use the probability that a fingerprint bit is received correctly. The sub-fingerprints are obtained by comparing and thresholding energy differences (see bit derivation block in Figure 11.1). If the energy difference is very close to the threshold, it is quite likely that the bit was received incorrectly (an unreliable bit). On the other hand, if the energy difference is much larger than the threshold the probability of an incorrect bit is low (a reliable bit). A list of likely sub-fingerprints is generated from the computed sub-fingerprints by toggling the N least-reliable bits. In practice the reliability information is not perfect (e.g. it happens that a bit with a low reliability is received correctly and vice-versa), but still the improvement of this approach is significant.

11.5.2   Database search experimental results

We measured how many of the generated candidate positions are pointing to the matching fingerprint block in the database for the same set of signal degradations used in the robustness experiments. We will refer to this number as the number of hits in the database. The number of hits has to be at least 1 to identify the fingerprint block and it can be at most 256 in the case that all sub-fingerprints generate a valid candidate position. First we determined the number of hits in case only the sub-fingerprints themselves are used to generate candidate positions (i.e. no soft decoding information is used). It was observed that the majority of the fingerprint blocks can be identified, because one or more hits occur. However a few fingerprint blocks, mainly originating from more severely degraded audio, such as at GSM with C/I of 4dB, do not generate any hits. This setting of the search algorithm can be used in applications, such as broadcast monitoring and automated labeling of MP3's, where only minor degradations of the audio are expected. After that we determined the number of hits with a setting that is used to identify heavily distorted audio as, for example, in the mobile phone application. Compared to the previous setting the 1024 most probable sub-fingerprints of every sub-fingerprint are additionally used to generate candidates. In other words, the 10 least reliable bits of every sub-fingerprint are toggled to generate more candidate positions. The resulting number of hits are far higher, and even the 'GSM C/I = 4dB fingerprint blocks' can be identified. Most of the fingerprint blocks with linear speed changes still do not have any hits. The BER of these blocks is already higher than the threshold and for that reason they cannot be identified even if hits occur. Furthermore one has to keep in mind that with appropriate pre-scaling, as proposed in Section 11.4.5, the fingerprint blocks with large linear speed changes can be identified rather easily.

11.6   Conclusions

In this chapter we presented algorithms for audio and video fingerprinting. The fingerprint extraction is based on dividing the signal in frames and extracting a 32 bit sub-fingerprint from every frame. The sub-fingerprints are generated by computing signal level differences along the frequency/spatial (for audio and video resp.) and the time axes. A fingerprint block, comprising a number of subsequent sub-fingerprints, is the basic unit that is used to identify a clip. The fingerprint database contains a two-phase search algorithm that is based on only performing full fingerprint comparisons at candidate positions pre-selected by a sub-fingerprint search. With reference to the parameters that were introduced in Section 2.2, the proposed system can be summarized as follows:

- Robustness: the fingerprints extracted are very robust.

- Reliability: The systems exhibit extremely low false positive probabilities.

- Fingerprint size: a fingerprint is 32 bit per frame, yielding a fingerprint size of 2.6kbit/s for audio and 1kbit/s for video

- Granularity: The technology allows reliable detection on 3-second segments

- Search speed and scalability: On a modern PC, the search algorithm allows handling dozens of requests per second for a database containing 20,000 songs.

Future research will focus on other feature extraction techniques, robustness w.r.t. scaling and optimization of the search algorithm.

Because of its demonstrated high level of robustness and the efficiency of the database approach, the resulting audio fingerprinting system is viable solution for all applications mentioned in Section 11.3. The video fingerprinting system is appropriate for applications where processing is constrained to compression, filtering, etc, but does include only limited (or known) changes of the geometry of the video.

References

Abdel-Mottaleb, M., G. Vaithilingam, and S. Krishnamachari [1999]. Signature-based image identification. In *SPIE conference on Multimedia Systems and Applications II*.

Allamanche, E., J. Herre, O. Helmuth, B. Fröba, and M. Cremer [2000]. AudioID: Towards content-based identification of audio material. In *Proceedings of the 110th Audio Engineering Society*.

Bancroft, J. [2000]. Fingerprinting: Monitoring the use of media assets. Omnibus Systems Limited. http://www.advanced-broadcast.com/.

Cheng, Y. [2001]. Music database retrieval based on spectral similarity. In *International Symposium on Music Information Retrieval (ISMIR)*.

Cormen, T., C. Leiserson, and R. Rivest [1998]. *Introduction To Algorithms*. MIT Press.

Fragoulis, D., G. Rousopoulos, T. Panagopoulos, C. Alexiou, and C. Papaodysseus [2001]. On the automated recognition of seriously distorted musical recordings. *IEEE Transactions on Signal Processing*, 49(4):898–908.

Haitsma, J., T. Kalker, and J.C. Oostveen [2001]. Robust audio hashing for content identification. In *International Workshop on Content-Based Multimedia Indexing*, pages 117–124.

Neuschmied, H., H. Mayer, and E. Battle [2001]. Identification of audio titles on the internet. In *Proceedings of International Conference on Web Delivering of Music*, pages 96–100.

Oostveen, J.C., A.A.C. Kalker, and J. Haitsma [2002]. Feature extraction and a database strategy for video fingerprinting. In *Recent Advances in Visual Information Systems, proceedings of the fifth international conference VISUAL 2002*, volume LNCS 2314, Springer Verlag, pages 117–128.

RIAA-IFPI [2001]. Request for information on audio fingerprinting technologies. http://www.ifpi.org/site-content/press/20010615.html.

Chapter 12

NEAR VIDEO-ON-DEMAND
WITH LIMITED CLIENT BANDWIDTH
AND DISTRIBUTED SERVERS

Wim F.J. Verhaegh, Ronald Rietman, and Jan Korst

Abstract   We investigate the option to implement a near-video-on-demand system in an access network in a distributed way, using the vast amount of available storage capacity at the end users to store the desired movie collection. An important constraint in the network is given by the limited upstream and downstream bandwidth of the end links between the users and the network. We use an improved version of fixed-delay pagoda broadcasting, which can take these constraints into account.

We present a feasible solution for a cable network, in which a fraction of the video data is injected higher up in the network, to improve response times. The solution requires only 18.5 MB of storage and an upstream bandwidth of 125 kb/s per user (200,000 users), as well as 84 MB of storage at each of the 500 fiber nodes, to implement a near-video-on-demand service of 1000 movies of 100 minutes each, with a response time of less than one second. Furthermore, we analyze the average number of transmission channels, and discuss how adding a little redundancy can make the system more robust.

Keywords   Video on demand, server, schedule, broadcasting, pagoda, bandwidth, storage.

12.1   Introduction

One of the most appealing networked multimedia services is that of video on demand, where any user can access any movie at any time. A straightforward way to implement this is by means of a large video server, which is placed centrally in a network, and transmits video streams to end users via one-to-one connections (unicast) on request. Alternatively, near-video-on-demand (NVoD) schemes are used [Hu, 2001; Korst et al., 2001], which reduce the required amount of transmission bandwidth by broadcasting streams according to a predefined scheme, from which the users can tap the stream they wish to

W. Verhaegh et al. (eds.), Algorithms in Ambient Intelligence, 221-237.
© 2004 *Kluwer Academic Publishers. Printed in the Netherlands.*

see. Using storage at the end user's site, for temporary storage of video data before playout, allows rather efficient broadcast schemes, where the worst-case response time (the maximum waiting time for a user to start watching) decreases exponentially in the number of channels allocated to a video stream. As more and more set-top boxes and other CE equipment contain (sufficiently large) hard disk drives, the required storage to allow this is becoming available.

This availability of storage at end users' sites raises the question whether it can also be employed to implement the video server, i.e., whether it is possible to use the end users' hard disk drives to store the offered video collection and to inject video streams into the network from the end users' sites. The aim of this chapter is to answer this question. We show that it is indeed viable to implement a near-video-on-demand service in a decentralized way, yielding very short response times, and using only little storage at the end users' sites.

The remainder of this chapter is organized as follows. First, in Section 12.2, we give some numbers of the target access network we consider, showing that the upstream and downstream bandwidth of the end links between the users and the network form the main communication bottleneck. Section 12.3 discusses an NVoD broadcast scheme that can take these restrictions into account. Next, Section 12.4 shows a feasible decentralized solution and its characteristic numbers. Finally, we determine the average number of used channels when video data is only transmitted if it is tapped, and we discuss how redundancy can be added to make the system more robust, in Sections 12.5 and 12.6, respectively.

12.2   Network assumptions

In this section we give the target network we consider and numbers associated with it. These numbers are some ball-park figures, and are typical for the kind of networks that we consider. We use the target network and its numbers as a running example in this chapter to do the calculations. Of course, the calculations can also be done for other numbers, to see the effect of choosing different parameter settings.

As a target network we consider a digital, tree-structured cable network as given in Figure 12.1, for a city of 200,000 homes.

The connections between the master headend down to the fiber nodes are implemented by optical fibers, of which we assume that their capacities are large enough. From each fiber node, four coax cables are leaving, each of which connects to 100 homes. We assume that the capacities of these coax cables form the main bottleneck of the network, where we assume an upstream and downstream capacity of about 400 kb/s and 20 Mb/s per individual home, respectively. Assuming a constant video transmission rate of 5 Mb/s, this implies that we can upstream 0.08 video channels and downstream 4 video channels per home. Having 200,000 homes, this gives a total upstream capacity

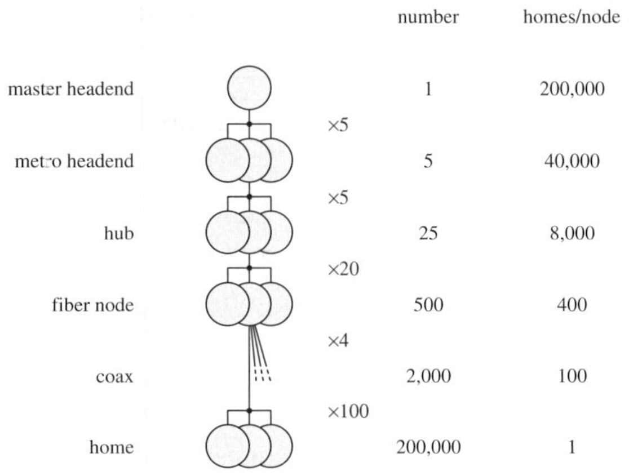

Figure 12.1. Characteristics of the target network.

of 16000 video channels. This already indicates that a true video-on-demand scheme using one-to-one connections is not feasible in a decentralized way. Hence we resort to a near-video-on-demand broadcast scheme. Furthermore, we have to take the limited downstream capacity into account. As mentioned, above the fiber nodes we assume no limitations on bandwidth, as the capacities of those connections can be made sufficiently large [Van Grinsven & Snijders, 2001].

Next, we assume for the time being that all homes are permanently connected, and that no failure at the nodes or data loss during transmission occurs. So, there is no redundancy needed for these purposes. We revisit this issue in Section 12.6.

A final assumption we make is that we want to have a collection of 1000 movies, which each last 100 minutes (6000 seconds). The size of a movie is hence 30 Gb, or 3.75 GB. We assume constant bit-rate movies, but the presented solution can easily be adapted to handle variable bit-rate movies as well.

12.3 Fixed-delay pagoda broadcasting

We use the fixed-delay pagoda broadcasting scheme of Pâris [2001]. This scheme is asymptotically optimal, meaning that the resulting response time for a given number of channels per video can be forced arbitrarily close to its theoretical minimum as given by Korst et al. [2001]. Furthermore, the scheme can easily handle limited client I/O bandwidth. Before explaining the details of how the scheme is computed in Section 12.3.1, we give a small example, shown in Figure 12.2. In this example, four transmission channels are used, of which the user can tap at most two simultaneously. We see that the scheme uses 11 blocks, i.e., a video is split into 11 blocks of equal size and equal

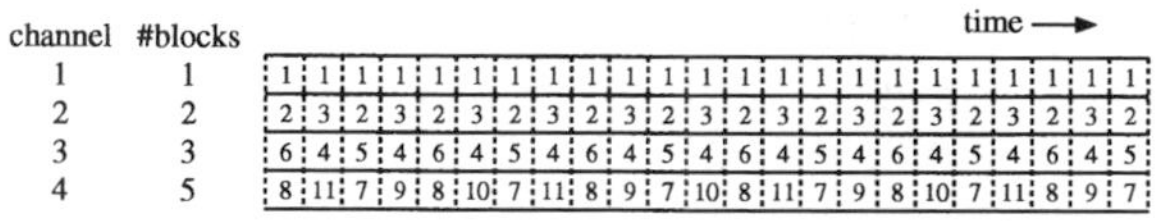

channel	#blocks																								
1	1	1	1	1	1	1	1	1	1	1	1	1	1	1	1	1	1	1	1	1	1	1	1	1
2	2	2	3	2	3	2	3	2	3	2	3	2	3	2	3	2	3	2	3	2	3	2	3	2
3	3	6	4	5	4	6	4	5	4	6	4	5	4	6	4	5	4	6	4	5	4	6	4	5
4	5	8	11	7	9	8	10	7	11	8	9	7	10	8	11	7	9	8	10	7	11	8	9	7

time ⟶

Figure 12.2. The fixed-delay pagoda broadcast scheme for four server channels and two client channels. Here, a movie is split into 11 unit-size blocks.

duration. As a result, the maximum waiting time for a user is a fraction $1/11$ of the duration of the movie, i.e., about 9 minutes.

Figure 12.3 shows how the retrieval takes place for a request at an arbitrary moment. It starts by tapping channels 1 and 2. When block 1 has been received from channel 1, this channel is no longer tapped, so channel 3 can start being tapped. After two time slots after the request, also channel 2 needs no longer be tapped, as both blocks 2 and 3 have been received from that channel. Now, channel 4 can start being tapped. In the above way, at most two channels are tapped at the same time, and all blocks arrive in time. A nice aspect of the pagoda scheme is that the times at which channels start and end being tapped, indicated by the grey overlay area in the figure, is independent of the moment of the request. We note that sometimes blocks may be received twice; the second reception can be discarded. We return to this inefficiency in Section 12.3.4.

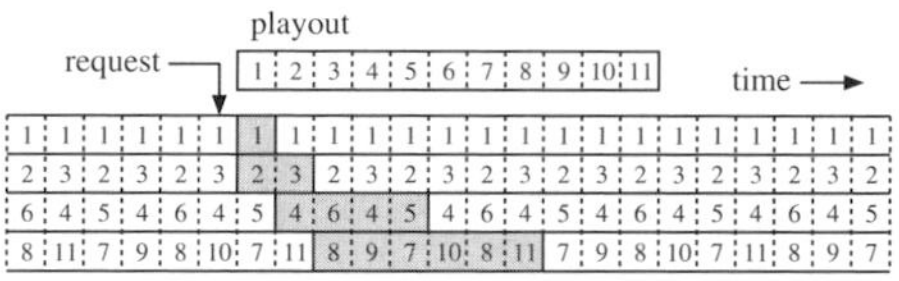

playout

| request ⟶ | 1 | 2 | 3 | 4 | 5 | 6 | 7 | 8 | 9 | 10 | 11 | time ⟶ |

1	1	1	1	1	1	1	1	1	1	1	1	1	1	1	1	1	1	1	1	1	1	1
2	3	2	3	2	3	2	3	2	3	2	3	2	3	2	3	2	3	2	3	2	3	2
6	4	5	4	6	4	5	4	6	4	5	4	6	4	5	4	6	4	5	4	6	4	5
8	11	7	9	8	10	7	11	8	9	7	10	8	11	7	9	8	10	7	11	8	9	7

Figure 12.3. Retrieval for a request at an arbitrary moment, indicated by the grey overlay. The shape of the overlay area is independent of the time slot in which the request takes place.

As the downstream link to a user has limited capacity, the tapping of the channels is to be done in the network, i.e., only the needed blocks are selected at the fiber node to be forwarded to the end user. This selection can be done by simply looking at the difference between the current time and the moment that the request took place. Based on this, the fiber node can determine which channels to forward to the user, as indicated by the grey overlay in Figure 12.3. Note that also at higher levels in the network already a selection can be made, e.g., a hub only has to forward the channels/blocks that will be consumed by any user in its sub-tree; the others do not have to be forwarded.

Key in the above NVoD scheme is that channel i starts being tapped after the tapping of channel $i-2$ has finished, thereby limiting the number of channels to be tapped to two. This means e.g. that for channel 4 one has to wait two time slots before one can start tapping the channel. As block 7 has to be received within 7 time slots after the request, this means that only 5 time slots are left to receive it, and hence it has to be transmitted with a period of at most 5, rather than 7. It is actually transmitted with a period of 4; the general structure of the broadcast scheme is explained next.

12.3.1   Computing the broadcast scheme

In this section we describe the general structure of the above broadcast scheme and how the scheme can be computed, for a given number c of server channels and a given number r of client channels. For simplicity reasons, we do not consider an offset as discussed by Korst et al. [2001] and Pâris [2001]; the equations can be adapted for this straightforwardly. Time points in this section are relative to the request time, unless stated otherwise.

We denote the start of the tapping segment in channel i by s_i, and the end by e_i. Then, in order not to exceed the maximum number r of channels that a user can receive, tapping in channel $i = r+1, \ldots, c$ is started after the tapping in channel $i - r$ has ended. Hence s_i is computed by

$$s_i = \begin{cases} 1 & \text{for } i = 1, \ldots, r \\ e_{i-r} + 1 & \text{for } i = r+1, \ldots, c. \end{cases}$$

Next, in channel i a consecutive series of blocks is transmitted, the lowest block number given by l_i and the highest one by h_i. The number of blocks transmitted in channel i is hence given by $n_i = h_i - l_i + 1$, and l_i is determined by

$$l_i = \begin{cases} 1 & \text{for } i = 1 \\ h_{i-1} + 1 & \text{for } i = 2, \ldots, c. \end{cases}$$

In order to receive each block in time, block k has to be transmitted in or before time slot k. If block k is transmitted in channel i, which starts being tapped in time slot s_i, this means that block k should be broadcast with a period of at most $k - (s_i - 1)$. Ideally, this period is exactly met for each block k, but it may be smaller.

The structure within a channel i in the pagoda scheme is computed as follows. First, channel i is divided into a number d_i of *sub-channels*. A good choice for this number of sub-channels is given by

$$d_i = \left\lceil \sqrt{l_i - (s_i - 1)} \right\rceil, \tag{12.1}$$

i.e., the square root of the optimal period of block l_i, rounded to the nearest integer (we return to this choice in Section 12.3.3). Each of these sub-channels gets a fraction $1/d_i$ of the time slots to transmit blocks, in a round-robin fashion. In other words, in time slot x, where we now consider x to indicate absolute time, sub-channel $x \bmod d_i$ can transmit a block. Here we number the sub-channels $0, 1, \ldots, d_i - 1$.

Now, if a block k is given a period p_k within a sub-channel of channel i, it is broadcast in channel i with a period of $p_k d_i$. Hence, as we must have $p_k d_i \leq k - (s_i - 1)$, this means that

$$p_k \leq \left\lfloor \frac{k - (s_i - 1)}{d_i} \right\rfloor.$$

By taking equal periods for all blocks within each sub-channel, we can trivially avoid collisions. So, if l_{ij} is the lowest block number in sub-channel j of channel i, this means that we choose a period

$$p_{ij} = \left\lfloor \frac{l_{ij} - (s_i - 1)}{d_i} \right\rfloor$$

for sub-channel j of channel i, and hence the number n_{ij} of blocks that we can transmit in this sub-channel (blocks $l_{ij}, \ldots, l_{ij} + n_{ij} - 1$) is given by $n_{ij} = p_{ij}$. The block numbers l_{ij} can be computed recursively by

$$l_{ij} = \begin{cases} l_i & \text{for } j = 0 \\ l_{i,j-1} + n_{i,j-1} & \text{for } j = 1, \ldots, d_i - 1. \end{cases}$$

The total number n_i of blocks transmitted in channel i can then be determined by

$$n_i = \sum_{j=0}^{d_i - 1} n_{ij},$$

with which we can compute $h_i = l_i + n_i - 1$.

Finally, we show how to compute the start and end times of the tapping of the channels. All sub-channels of channel i start being tapped at the same time, i.e. $s_{ij} = s_i$ for all j. Sub-channel j of channel i is ready after n_{ij} blocks, which takes at most $d_i n_{ij}$ time slots within channel i. Hence, the end of the tapping segment in sub-channel j is given by $e_{ij} = s_i - 1 + d_i n_{ij}$, and the tapping of channel i ends when its last sub-channel ends being tapped, at time slot $e_i = e_{i,d_i-1} = s_i - 1 + d_i n_{i,d_i-1}$.

12.3.2   An example channel

To exemplify the above, we add a fifth channel to the example of Figure 12.2; see also Figure 12.4. The first block in channel 5 is $l_5 = 12$ and the channel starts in time slot $s_5 = e_3 + 1 = 6$, so the number of sub-channels is $d_5 = \lceil \sqrt{12 - 5} \rceil = 3$. For sub-channel $j = 0$, the first block is $l_{5,0} = l_5 = 12$, hence we can transmit $n_{5,0} = p_{5,0} = \lfloor (12 - 5)/3 \rfloor = 2$ blocks in this sub-channel, being blocks 12 and 13. For sub-channel $j = 1$ we have $l_{5,1} = 14$, hence we can transmit $n_{5,1} = \lfloor(14-5)/3\rfloor = 3$ blocks in this sub-channel, being blocks 14, 15, and 16. For sub-channel $j = 2$ we have $l_{5,2} = 17$, hence we can transmit $n_{5,2} = \lfloor(17-5)/3\rfloor = 4$ blocks in this sub-channel, being blocks 17, 18, 19, and 20. The end of the segments in the sub-channels are given by $e_{5,0} = 5 + 3 \cdot 2 = 11$, $e_{5,1} = 5 + 3 \cdot 3 = 14$, and $e_{5,2} = 5 + 3 \cdot 4 = 17$, hence $e_5 = 17$.

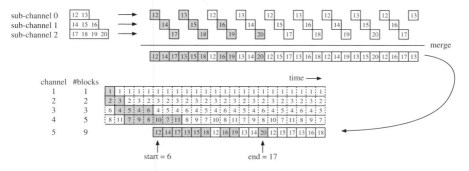

Figure 12.4. Adding a fifth channel, consisting of three sub-channels, to the example broadcast scheme of Figure 12.2.

12.3.3   On the number of sub-channels

The number d_i of sub-channels of channel i as given by (12.1) is generally good. The rationale behind this is as follows. If we choose $d_i = 1$ sub-channel, then all blocks in channel i will get the same period, which is inefficient for the blocks with the highest block number in this channel, as they are broadcast much more frequently than necessary. Choosing the other extreme, i.e., a sub-channel for each block, also results in all blocks having the same period in this channel. The square root of the period of the first block appears to be a good value between the two extremes, allowing the blocks to be transmitted with a period close to their desired one, in a relative sense.

Nevertheless, choosing a different value than the one given by (12.1) may result in a better solution, in terms of the number of blocks into which a movie can be split. To this end, we apply a first-order optimization by exploring per channel i a number of different values around the target value given in (12.1), calculating the resulting number of blocks that can be fit into channel i, and taking the number of sub-channels for which channel i can contain the highest number of blocks. Note that we do this per individual channel, i.e., we do not back-track to previous channels, to avoid an exponential run time for a straightforward implementation. This may lead to sub-optimal solutions, as choosing a different number of sub-channels in channel i to get a higher number of blocks in it may cause the end time e_i to increase, thereby increasing the start time

s_{i+r} of channel $i+r$, which may in turn decrease the number of blocks that can be fit into this channel. Nevertheless, this first-order optimization gives good results.

12.3.4   An improvement in starting new sub-channels

In the known pagoda broadcasting scheme [Pâris, 2001], the tapping of channel $i > r$ is started when that of channel $i - r$ has ended, i.e., when *all* sub-channels in channel $i - r$ have ended being tapped. A drawback of this is that the reception capacity is not always fully utilized, as we can see in Figure 12.5. In the figure, sub-channel 0 of channel 3 needs to be tapped for only

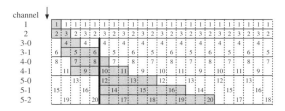

Figure 12.5.   The pagoda broadcasting scheme in a case with $r = 2$ reception channels, where channel 5 starts being tapped at the time when all sub-channels in channel 3 have ended being tapped.

two time slots to guarantee that all its blocks (block 4) have been received, but sub-channel 1 needs to be tapped for four time slots. As a result, the tapping of channel 5 only starts four time slots after the start of tapping channel 3, and only one block (block 9) is received in the time slot right after the end of tapping sub-channel 0 of channel 3 (as block 4 has already been received). Hence, the reception capacity is not fully used. Experiments for $r = 2$ and $c = 15$ show that this may result in a wasted reception capacity of about 0.55 channel (i.e., about 27%), which is quite severe.

A better schedule can be obtained by starting tapping some of the sub-channels of channel 5 already when sub-channel 0 of channel 3 has ended being tapped, and the remaining sub-channels of channel 5 when sub-channel 1 of channel 3 has ended being tapped, as indicated in Figure 12.6. Although the total number of blocks does not increase in this example, the impact for larger schemes can be significant.

To make the above approach work, we have to take care of two things. First, the number of sub-channels of channel $i > r$ has to be an integer multiple of the number of sub-channels of channel $i - r$, which is why we chose four sub-channels for channel 5 in Figure 12.6. Secondly, we have to make sure that after ending the tapping of a sub-channel in channel $i - r$, the newly tapped sub-channels in channel i use the same time slots, in order not to conflict with blocks transmitted in the other sub-channels of channel $i - r$. In the example

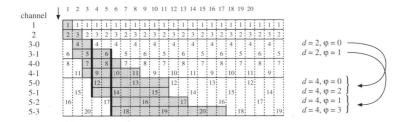

Figure 12.6. The improved pagoda broadcasting scheme in a case with $r = 2$ reception channels, where some sub-channels of channel 5 already start being tapped when the first sub-channel of channel 3 has ended being tapped.

of Figure 12.6, this means that sub-channels 0 and 1 of channel 5 must use the same time slots as allocated to sub-channel 0 of channel 3. The latter time slots are the even time slots, i.e, time slots x with $x \bmod 2 = 0$, so we allocate the time slots x with $x \bmod 4 = 0$ to sub-channel 0 of channel 5, and the time slots x with $x \bmod 4 = 2$ to sub-channel 1 of channel 5. In this way, the number of channels to be tapped simultaneously never exceeds r.

More formally, we introduce a phasing $\varphi_{ij} \in \{0, \ldots, d_i - 1\}$ for each sub-channel $j = 0, \ldots, d_i - 1$ of channel i. For channels $i = 1, \ldots, r$, the number d_i of channels can be chosen around its target value of (12.1), without any additional restriction. The phasing of the sub-channels of channel $i = 1, \ldots, r$ are simply assigned by

$$\varphi_{ij} = j.$$

The start time of tapping sub-channel j of channel $i = 1, \ldots, r$ is the same as in the original NVoD schedule, i.e.,

$$s_{ij} = s_i = 1,$$

and also the number of blocks per sub-channel is calculated as before.

For channels $i > r$, the number d_i of channels can again be chosen around its target value of (12.1), but now with the extra restriction that it should be a multiple of d_{i-r}. Next, whenever a sub-channel j' of channel $i - r$ ends being tapped, which happens in time slot $e_{i-r,j'}$, we start the tapping of d_i/d_{i-r} new sub-channels in channel i, numbered $j = j'd_i/d_{i-r}, \ldots, (j'+1)d_i/d_{i-r} - 1$, which all get a start time

$$s_{ij} = e_{i-r,j'} + 1.$$

The phasing of these new sub-channels is given by

$$\varphi_{ij} = \varphi_{i-r,j'} + kd_{i-r},$$

for $j = j'd_i/d_{i-r} + k$ with $k = 0, \ldots, d_i/d_{i-r} - 1$. This indeed gives us that the new sub-channels use the same time slots as the ended sub-channel, as

$$\varphi_{ij} \bmod d_{i-r} = \varphi_{i-r,j'}$$

Next, the number of blocks in sub-channel $j = j'd_i/d_{i-r}, \ldots, (j'+1)d_i/d_{i-r}-1$ is basically calculated in the same way as in the original schedule, i.e., we set

$$n_{ij} = p_{ij} = \left\lfloor \frac{l_{ij} - (s_{ij}-1)}{d_i} \right\rfloor.$$

Although the extra restriction on the choice of d_i for $i > r$ may give a performance penalty, the net effect of the above modification is positive. Experiments show that the effect is especially significant in case the number r of channels that can be received is low, as then wasting reception capacity is more severe. For instance, for $r = 2$ and $c = 15$ the new scheme gives over four times as many blocks to split a movie, resulting in a response time that is four times as small.

12.3.5   Some numbers and response times

Table 12.1 shows the number h_{cr} of blocks in which a movie can be split using c transmission channels and r reception channels. The series converge to power series, with bases of about 2.20, 2.55, 2.66, for $r = 2$, 3, and 4, respectively, and a base of $e \approx 2.72$, for $r = \infty$.

Table 12.1.   The values for h_{cr} for different values of c and r and an offset zero. The last column corresponds to having no limit on the number of client channels.

c	$r = 2$	$r = 3$	$r = 4$	$r = \infty$
1	1	1	1	1
2	3	3	3	3
3	6	8	8	8
4	11	18	20	20
5	21	41	47	50
6	42	94	115	127
7	85	224	286	328
8	172	544	729	859
9	357	1343	1892	2283
10	754	3356	4950	6112
11	1607	8456	13039	16459
12	3477	21435	34487	44484
13	7585	54543	91470	120485
14	16621	139131	243051	326795
15	36570	355433	646538	887124

Using the above values of h_{cr}, we can derive the maximum waiting time, which is given by $6000/h_{cr}$ seconds. So, for $c = 11$ and $r = 3$ we get a response time of $6000/8456 \approx 0.71$ s.

12.4   A feasible NVoD solution

For the remainder of this chapter, we aim at a maximum response time of about one second, and a limit of $r = 3$ channels to be tapped, so we use 11 transmission channels, splitting a movie into 8456 blocks, giving a response time of about 0.71 s.

12.4.1   Generating the transmission channels

If we would generate the 11 transmission channels of all 1000 movies at the homes, this would use 11000 out of the available 16000 channels. However, we can alternatively transmit a number of channels from the fiber nodes, thereby reducing the requirement on the scarce upstream bandwidth from the homes. If we select the first transmission channels per movie for this, then the corresponding storage requirements for the fiber nodes are limited, as the first transmission channels per movie concern a relatively low number of blocks.

As an example, if we transmit the first six NVoD channels from the fiber nodes, then we have to store a fraction $94/8456 \approx 0.011$ of each movie at the fiber nodes, which corresponds to $3750 \cdot 94/8456 \approx 42$ MB per movie. As we have 1000 movies and 500 fiber nodes, this can be stored in a memory module of 84 MB per fiber node.

The remaining storage, being a fraction $(8456 - 94)/8456 \approx 0.989$ of each movie, meaning about 3.7 GB, has to be distributed over the homes. If we do this evenly, this requires a storage capacity of $3700 \cdot 1000/200,000 \approx 18.5$ MB per home, which can also be done in memory modules. This even distribution can be realized by striping each movie into 200 stripes, and letting each home transmit a stripe of each of the NVoD channels 7–11. Figure 12.7 gives a graphical representation of how a movie is split into blocks and stripes. A fiber

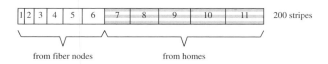

Figure 12.7. The way a movie is split into segments of consecutive blocks and how the segments to be transmitted from the homes are split into stripes. The picture is not to scale. The boundaries of the segments for the 11 NVoD channels are given by the values of h_{cr} in Table 12.1.

node can then generate the complete NVoD scheme by merging 200 'striped channels' per NVoD channel. Each fiber node has 400 homes connected to it, so it can generate the entire NVoD scheme of two movies. Note that each 'striped channel' has a bit rate of $5000/200 = 25$ kb/s, which gives a total upstream bit rate of 125 kb/s per home.

12.4.2 A system setup

The resulting system setup is shown in Figure 12.8. The upward arcs indicate the aggregation of all transmission channels and the corresponding bandwidth used. The downward arcs show the distribution of the channels and the corresponding worst-case bandwidth used. Here we assume that blocks/channels are only forwarded by a node if consumed by any user in its sub-tree. As each user taps at most three channels simultaneously, this implies that each coax has to carry at most 300 channels, and each fiber node has to forward at most 1200 channels, etc. To be able to do this selective forwarding, a node should keep track of all users in its sub-tree, and know where each user is in the reception process. Alternatively, selection can be done at only the fiber node, to keep the administration simple.

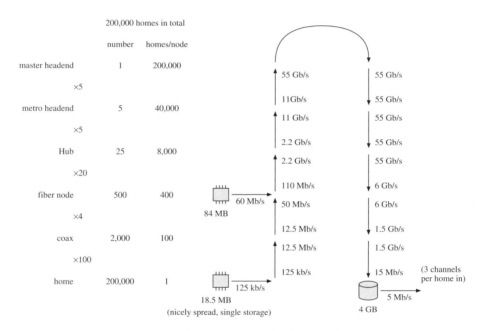

Figure 12.8. System setup for the derived solution.

The storage needed at the reception side, which is needed for reordering the blocks from the order in which they are tapped into the playout order, can simply be bounded by the size of a movie. This amount also allows a user to pause the movie for an unbounded time. If no pausing is allowed, calculations show that the storage requirement for reordering the blocks is about 35% of the movie size, i.e., about 1.3 GB, for $r = 3$, and about 32% and 37% for $r = 2$ and $r = \infty$, respectively.

12.4.3 Changing the system parameters

Although we made calculations for the numbers given in Section 12.2, one can easily redo the calculations for other settings of the system parameters. Most parameters, such as the number of movies, the length of the movies, and the number of homes feed linearly into the equations, and hence the effect of changing them is rather straightforward. The effect of the number of transmission channels on the maximum waiting time, on the other hand, is exponential.

A not so trivial relation is that between the storage requirements at the fiber and home nodes and the number of transmission channels. This storage appears to be relatively independent of the number of channels that is used. For instance, if we increase the number of channels to 12, then the response time is reduced to $6000/21435 \approx 0.28\,\mathrm{s}$. As a result, a movie is split into about 2.5 times as many blocks, and hence the blocks are about 2.5 times smaller. Therefore, we can choose the fiber nodes to generate one channel more, i.e., channels 1–7, and the homes to generate channels 8–12. The storage at a fiber node then equals $3750 \cdot 224/21435 \approx 39\,\mathrm{MB}$ per movie, which is roughly the same as the 42 MB required for 11 channels. The storage requirement at a home remains slightly less than a fraction 1/200 of a movie.

Calculations show that also the storage requirements for reordering the received blocks do not really depend on the number of used channels.

12.5 Selective broadcasting and the average number of channels

Generally, a drawback of broadcasting schemes is that unpopular movies get the same amount of bandwidth allocated as popular movies. To save on bandwidth for unpopular movies, we can decrease the number of used channels by not transmitting blocks that are not required to serve a user request. For an example, see Figure 12.9. As each sub-channel only is tapped by a user between its start and end time, a block only has to be transmitted if it falls within this interval for a certain user request. If there is no such request, the

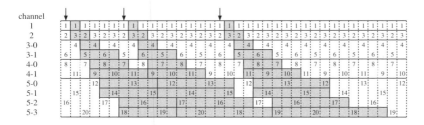

Figure 12.9. Three requests and the blocks that are needed to serve them, indicated by the numbers in the grey area.

block does not need to be transmitted, and the bandwidth can be used for other purposes. As a result, the average number of channels used simultaneously at the master headend level can be much lower than the worst-case number of 11000.

So, if a request occurs at time t, then sub-channel j of channel i should be active from time slot $t + s_{ij}$ until time slot $t + e_{ij}$, i.e., at time slots x for which $t + s_{ij} \leq x \leq t + e_{ij}$. The other way around, if at a time slot x it is sub-channel j's turn, then it has to transmit a block if and only if there has been a request at a time t for which $x - e_{ij} \leq t \leq x - s_{ij}$. If we assume a Poisson arrival process for the requests, with parameter λ, then the probability that channel i is active at a time slot occupied by sub-channel j is given by

$$1 - e^{-\lambda(e_{ij} - s_{ij} + 1)u},$$

where u is the length of a time slot. Dividing this by d_i, as sub-channel j occupies only one out of every d_i time slots, gives the fraction of a channel that this sub-channel uses. Adding this up over all sub-channels of all channels gives the expected number of used channels for a movie. Figure 12.10 shows this expected number of used channels for one movie and for different arrival rates (on a logarithmic scale), for the NVoD scheme of Section 12.4. We can conclude from the figure that selective transmission is indeed a good way to keep the used bandwidth for unpopular movies limited, so there is no need to transmit unpopular movies in a different way, e.g., by unicasting. This is favorable as one does not need to know whether or not a movie is popular, and the transmission of blocks automatically adapts if movies are popular during one part of the day, and less popular during another part.

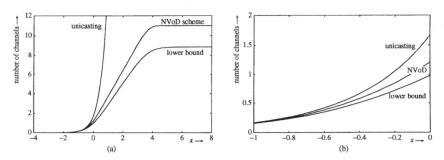

Figure 12.10. (a) The expected number of channels needed for a movie in the NVoD scheme of Section 12.4, for an arrival rate of 10^x clients per hour, compared to a unicasting solution, and compared to a lower bound for any adaptive transmission scheme as discussed next in the text. (b) The same picture zoomed in on the range $[-1, 0]$.

To determine a lower bound on the average number of used channels, we consider a fully adaptive transmission scheme, in which a block is only transmitted when necessary, and not earlier than strictly needed. This means that if a request arrives in time slot t, a block k is scheduled for transmission in time slot $t + k$, i.e., the time slot in which it is needed for playout. Then, all requests that arrive in time slots $t + 1, \ldots, t + k - 1$ can tap this transmission of block k too, i.e., the considered transmission of block k can be reused for as many other requests as possible. Only when a new request arrives in time slot $t + k$ or later, a new transmission of block k is scheduled. Note that although this schedule gives the lowest total (and hence also average) number of transmitted blocks, it can result in many blocks being transmitted in the same time slot, so there is no upper bound on the number of required channels. Without going into details, we mention that the average number of used channels in case of a Poisson arrival process can be determined by means of a Markov chain per block number. This results in a lower bound on the average number of channels given by

$$\ln\left(\frac{1 + \lambda(w + l)}{1 + \lambda w}\right),$$

where w is the maximum waiting time and l is the length of a movie. The lower line in Figure 12.10 gives this function for a maximum waiting time $w = 0.71\,\text{s}$ and movie length $l = 6000\,\text{s}$. We note that the chosen pagoda scheme performs not too bad compared to this lower bound; it is at most 28% higher.

Next, we give some rough estimates for the total number of channels needed on average for the collection of 1000 movies. We assume that there are a few very popular movies and many less popular movies, with a difference of a factor 100 in popularity between the most and least popular movie. This seems to be fair in practice when checking movie databases on the Internet, for instance. For a rough estimate of the popularity of the 1000 movies, we assume 31, 115, 200, 285, and 369 movies to have a probability of 0.01, 0.00316, 0.001, 0.000316, and 0.0001, of being selected, respectively. If we furthermore assume an arrival rate of 200,000 requests per 6000 seconds, i.e., users are more or less constantly watching movies, then the expected total number of used channels is about 5333 compared to the worst-case number of 11000. If the arrival rate is decreased by a factor 10, for instance since not all users will watch a movie, the number goes even further down to 2977. Note that these numbers are averages. Initial simulation results indicate a standard deviation of about 40 for both cases. Hence, if we bound the number of used channels in the first case to 5500 and do not admit new users if that would imply that this bound is exceeded, then the bound is about four times the standard deviation above the average. Assuming the number of used channels to more or less follow a Gaussian distribution, this results in a probability of the order of 10^{-8} that a user cannot be admitted.

12.6   Introducing redundancy

Finally, we touch upon the robustness of the NVoD system, where we focus on the set-top boxes at the homes. The broadcast system as presented in Section 12.4 apparently fails if the set-top box in any of the 200 homes that participate in broadcasting a movie does not deliver its share of five striped channels. There can be many reasons a set-top box fails to deliver its share, the most likely one being that the set-top box is switched off by the user. Another reason can be that the user temporarily needs the full upstream bandwidth for something more urgent. In the former case, the set-top box may be unavailable for a long time, in the order of days or weeks, so its upstream bandwidth can be used by other set-top boxes on the same coax. This means that also its broadcasting tasks can be taken over by another set-top box that is on the same coax. This redistribution of broadcasting tasks, during which the corresponding share is not available, is expected to take not much longer than a few minutes. In the latter case, the interruption is likely to be quite short, in the order of seconds or minutes. This can even be enforced by a bandwidth scheduler in the set-top box.

In any case, a share may be unavailable for a period of at most a few minutes at a time. The time a share is continuously available can be in the order of days or weeks: people are not expected to switch off their set-top box frequently and the interval between subsequent bursts of high upstream activity not related to the broadcasting of movies can be kept under control by a bandwidth scheduler. A pessimistic estimate of the fraction of time f that a share is not available is about 10 minutes per day, or about $f = 0.007$. If we assume that shares fail independently, this results in a failure for a movie for a fraction

$$f_{\text{fail}} = 1 - (1 - f)^{200} = 1 - 0.993^{200} \approx 0.75,$$

of the time, which is obviously too high. By adding redundancy, however, we can significantly bring down this movie failure rate.

We add redundancy by applying a Reed-Solomon encoding [Wicker & Bhargave, 1994], as an example. Instead of dividing each movie into 200 shares of striped channels, we divide it into $200 - p$ shares and p parity-like shares. As a result, the movie can be reconstructed if there are at least $200 - p$ out of the 200 shares of striped channels available, i.e., there is a movie failure only if more than p shares fail at the same time. The resulting 200 shares are distributed among the original 200 set-top boxes. These encoded striped channels are a factor $200/(200 - p)$ times as 'fat' as the bare striped channels we considered in Section 12.4. Without going into details, we mention that the results for $p = 10$, i.e., a redundancy of about 5%, are that the fraction of time the transmission of a movie fails is down to less than one in a million. Furthermore, the time between such failures is such that the probability that a viewer observes a hiccup during the duration of a movie is $1/20000$, and such a hiccup lasts about half a minute. Hence, this seems a viable solution. The costs to realize this is an increase of about 5% in required upstream bandwidth. Furthermore, the storage of a share also is 5% higher, and users need more storage if they are to take over the broadcast task of other users. For this latter, doubling the storage to about 37 MB per user should be sufficient. Also the fiber nodes need additional hardware, to perform the decoding of the two movies that are broadcast from the 400 set-top boxes below them. Since we choose to store a movie entirely in the subtree of a single fiber node, the fiber node can do the decoding, so the implementation of redundancy does not require any additional hardware and bandwidth above the fiber node level.

12.7 Conclusion

We have presented an efficient near-video-on-demand scheme that can take client bandwidth constraints into account. The NVoD channels can easily be constructed by following a simple algorithm. It gives very short response times for a limited number of channels. Next, we have presented a feasible distributed solution, in which the NVoD channels are injected partly at the users' sites, and partly at the fiber nodes. We have shown that this requires only little memory per user and fiber node to implement, and uses the scarce user upstream bandwidth economically. By making the NVoD scheme selective, i.e., only transmitting blocks that are needed, the NVoD scheme automatically adjusts its channel usage to the popularity of movies, thereby removing the need to treat unpopular movies in a different way. Finally, we indicated how adding a little redundancy can bring the system failure rate down to sufficiently low values.

References

Grinsven, P.A.M. van, and W.A.M. Snijders [2001]. *The Broadband Revolution: Survey of Access Network Technologies*. Technical Note NL-TN 2001/357, Philips Research Laboratories.

Hu, A. [2001]. Video-on-demand braodcasting protocols: A comprehensive study. In *Proceedings IEEE INFOCOM*, pages 508–517.

Korst, J., J. Aerts, M. de Jong, W. Michiels, and H. Hollmann [2001]. Near-video-on-demand strategies using periodic broadcast schedules and pre-recording. In *Proceedings Philips Workshop on Scheduling and Resource Management (SCHARM)*, pages 125–135.

Pâris, J.-F. [2001]. A fixed-delay broadcasting protocol for video-on-demand. In *Proceedings of the 10th International Conference on Computer Communications and Networks*, pages 418–423.

Wicker, S.B., and V.K. Bhargava (eds.) [1994]. *Reed-Solomon Codes and Their Applications*. IEEE Press.

Chapter 13

METHODS TO OPTIMALLY TRADE BANDWIDTH AGAINST BUFFER SIZE FOR A VBR STREAM

Edgar den Boef, Emile Aarts, Jan Korst, and Wim F.J. Verhaegh

Abstract   To reduce the peak bit-rate for transmitting a variable-bit-rate stream, one can prefetch and buffer data at the receiving side. Previous work shows how to minimize the required buffer size given the available bandwidth [Feng, 1997] and how to minimize the required bandwidth given the available buffer size [Salehi et al., 1998]. Instead of taking either bandwidth or buffer size fixed, we assume both to be decision variables with given cost coefficients. We explain our method [Den Boef et al., 2003a] and the method by Chang et al. [1998] and compare them. These methods find the optimal values by starting with a minimum value for either the bandwidth [Chang et al., 1998] or the buffer size [Den Boef et al., 2003a] and then increasing this value, while at the same time decreasing the value of the buffer size or the bandwidth, respectively. We conclude that our method has slightly better run times than the method by Chang et al. and uses about half the amount of memory.

Keywords   Resource management, bandwidth smoothing, buffer, trade-off, transmission schedule, variable bit rate.

13.1   Introduction

In an ambient intelligent environment devices are distributed and ubiquitous, and connected by wired or wireless network connections. To be able to run as many applications as possible in the environment while ensuring good quality of each application, smart usage of the network resources, such as bandwidth and buffer space, is required. When dealing with variable-bit-rate (VBR) streams, e.g. MPEG-encoded video streams, considerable gains in bandwidth requirements can be obtained by transmitting data in advance and buffering the data at the receiver, thereby smoothing the data stream. Several algorithms have already been described in the literature for the problem of de-

W. Verhaegh et al. (eds.), Algorithms in Ambient Intelligence, 239-258.
© 2004 *Kluwer Academic Publishers. Printed in the Netherlands.*

termining a transmission schedule for a single VBR stream from a server to a client with a given consumption scheme of the data. One of these algorithms minimizes the buffer at the client side for a given available bandwidth, and is called *rate-constrained bandwidth smoothing* (RCBS) [Feng, 1997]. *Buffer-size-constrained bandwidth smoothing* or minimum variability bandwidth allocation (MVBA) [Salehi et al., 1998] does the opposite; it minimizes the peak rate of the transmission schedule given the available buffer size. Instead of choosing either the bandwidth or buffer size fixed and minimizing the other, we consider the problem of finding an optimal trade-off between the two. In this chapter, we present two existing methods [Den Boef et al., 2003a; Chang et al., 1998] for determining the trade-off curve, and we attempt to compare both methods. As the problem constraints are all linear, the bandwidth-buffer trade-off curve is piecewise linear and can be described by its bend points. For a convex cost function of the resources, a solution with the lowest cost is then easily determined.

. An example of an application of the algorithms presented in this chapter is the following. Suppose a user connected to an intranet wants to view a live video stream that is supplied by an external supplier, e.g. the internet or a communication satellite. The video stream enters the intranet at a so-called gateway node where the user can reserve buffer space for the stream to use at a given cost. Then, it has to be transmitted over the intranet to the user, who has to pay for the reserved bandwidth of the intranet. Furthermore, the user has a given buffer size available at his own connection to the intranet, where the stream can also be buffered. The problem for the user is then to optimally balance the use of bandwidth of the intranet and the use of buffer space at the gateway node, such that his total costs are minimized.

Another application of the algorithms is found in the smoothing of multiple streams that simultaneously use a single bus and the buffers connected to it, as described in [Den Boef et al., 2003b]. It shows how this problem can be solved by repeatedly solving several single-stream problems. Besides the previously mentioned algorithms RCBS and MVBA, the trade-off algorithms presented in this chapter can be used for solving one of these single-stream problems.

Finally, Chang et al. [1999] extend their trade-off algorithm [Chang et al., 1998] into a setting where VBR data is transmitted over a network with multiple relay-servers.

The chapter is organized as follows. In Section 13.2 we give a description of the problem. In Section 13.3 we describe our algorithm that trades buffer size against bandwidth starting from a solution with minimum buffer size. Then, in Section 13.4 we describe the algorithm presented by Chang et al. [1998] for determining the bandwidth-buffer trade-off curve starting with minimum bandwidth. In Section 13.5 we compare both algorithms by their structure, theoretical complexity, computation time, and memory requirements. Finally, in Section 13.6 we present the conclusions of this chapter.

13.2   Problem description

In Section 13.2.1 we give the assumptions for the bandwidth-buffer trade-off problem. In Section 13.2.2 we introduce the notation used in this chapter. Then we give a formulation of the problem in Section 13.2.3.

13.2.1   Assumptions

We split up the time axis into a finite set of identical *time units*. A time unit can be chosen long, e.g. a minute, or short, e.g. 1/25 s, depending on the application of the model. We assume that there is no loss of data during transmission. With respect to buffering, we assume in this chapter that data can only be buffered at the receiver. Furthermore, we assume that a consumption scheme is given, which gives for each time unit the amount of data that is consumed. We assume that a supply scheme is not given, i.e., all data are supplied whenever required by the transmission schedule that is determined. The model and algorithms we present can be easily adapted to cases in which data can also or only be buffered at the supplier, and in which a supply scheme of the data is given; see [Den Boef et al., 2003a]. All data that arrive during a time unit has to be buffered at the receiver, even when it is consumed in the same time unit. Finally, the costs are assumed to be linear in the amount of bandwidth and buffer size.

13.2.2   Notation

As already mentioned the time axis is split up into time units. The moments in time between two consecutive time units are referred to as *time points*. $\mathcal{T} = \{0, 1, \dots, T\}$ denotes the set of time points, and $\mathcal{T}' = \{1, 2, \dots, T\}$ denotes the set of time units. Then, a time unit $t \in \mathcal{T}'$ is equivalent to the interval bounded by the time points $t - 1$ and t, i.e., the half-open interval $(t - 1, t]$. Let B represent the maximum amount of data that can be transmitted during a time unit. The capacity of the buffer at the receiver is given by M. For the VBR stream the consumption scheme is given by a value $c(t)$ for all $t \in \mathcal{T}'$, which gives the amount of data that is pulled from the receiving buffer at the end of time unit t. The cost coefficient of the bandwidth is denoted by c_b and the cost coefficient of the receiving buffer size is denoted by c_m.

The decision variables we have to determine are the transmission schedule $x(t), t \in \mathcal{T}'$, the reserved bandwidth b, and the reserved buffer size at the receiver m.

Furthermore, we define for all $t \in \mathcal{T}'$, $C(t) = \sum_{s=1}^{t} c(s)$ as the cumulative consumption scheme and $X(t) = \sum_{s=1}^{t} x(s)$ as the cumulative transmission schedule.

13.2.3   Problem formulation

The algorithms presented in this chapter give an optimal solution for the following problem.

$$
\begin{aligned}
\text{minimize} \quad & c_b b + c_m m \\
\text{subject to} \quad & b \leq B \\
& m \leq M \\
& x(t) \leq b, \ \forall t \in \mathcal{T}' \\
& X(t) - C(t) \geq 0, \ \forall t \in \mathcal{T}' \\
& X(t) - C(t-1) \leq m, \ \forall t \in \mathcal{T}'
\end{aligned}
$$

The bandwidth-buffer trade-off curve gives all feasible solutions that are not dominated by another feasible solution, i.e., the bandwidth of all solutions is minimum given the buffer size, and the buffer size of all solutions is minimum given the bandwidth. The linear cost function then implies that the optimal solution is one of the bend points of the trade-off curve.

We continue this chapter with the explanation of two methods to determine the trade-off curve in Sections 13.3 and 13.4. We compare these methods in Section 13.5.

13.3   Trade-off by increasing buffer size

In this section we describe an algorithm for determining the bandwidth-buffer-size trade-off curve when starting with a solution with minimum buffer requirement. Increasing the buffer size then leads to a decrease in required bandwidth. We will refer to this algorithm as the *buffer-increasing trade-off algorithm* (BIT). For full details of the algorithm we refer to Den Boef et al. [2003a]. The buffer-increasing trade-off algorithm uses methods that minimize either the buffer size (RCBS) or the bandwidth (MVBA). For short descriptions of RCBS and MVBA we refer to Den Boef et al. [2003b] and Feng & Rexford [1999].

The buffer-increasing trade-off algorithm starts with an initial MVBA-schedule. An MVBA-schedule is a piecewise constant bit-rate schedule, with rate changes whenever we have a full or empty buffer, i.e., when $X(t)$ touches either $C(t)$ or $C(t) + m$. The time points $t \in \mathcal{T}$ where the rate in the schedule changes are referred to as *critical points*.

Definition 13.1. Let $[x(1), \ldots, x(T)]$ be an MVBA schedule. A time point $t \in \mathcal{T} \setminus \{0, T\}$ is said to be a critical point if for its adjacent time units t and $t + 1$,

$x(t) \neq x(t+1)$ holds. A critical point t is said to be convex when $x(t) < x(t+1)$, and concave when $x(t) > x(t+1)$. The time points 0 and T are defined as concave critical points.   □

The initial MVBA-schedule is determined as follows. First, the buffer size is minimized using RCBS, with available bandwidth set to the maximum B. Then, using this resulting buffer size, MVBA is used to construct an MVBA-schedule. After this starting solution has been determined, the buffer-increasing trade-off algorithm performs a trade-off between the reserved bandwidth b and the buffer size m by iteratively trying to increase the buffer size m and determining what effect it has on the smallest possible choice of b, i.e., on $\max_t x(t)$. This consists of a trade-off initialization and a trade-off loop as given in the algorithm in Figure 13.1.

The algorithm in Figure 13.1 starts with an initialization of the trade-off. It partitions the time horizon into several distinct intervals T_i, where the intervals are separated from each other by the concave critical points of the MVBA-schedule, as is shown in Figure 13.2. Interval T_i lies between critical points c_i and c_{i+1}.

Next, the algorithm in Figure 13.1 determines the following parameters of each interval T_i; see Figure 13.2. The maximum transmission rate during T_i is denoted by $b_i^{\max}$ and occurs at the end of the interval. The minimum is denoted by $b_i^{\min}$ and occurs at the beginning of the interval. If $b_i^{\max} > b_i^{\min}$, then the algorithm also determines the best achievable maximum transmission rate, b_i^{best}, on T_i, which is equal to the slope of the straight line between $C(c_i)$ and $C(c_{i+1})$. Furthermore, it determines the second highest transmission rate, denoted by $b_i^{\max-1}$, and the second lowest transmission rate, denoted by $b_i^{\min+1}$. Finally, it determines how many time units $b_i^{\max}$ and $b_i^{\min}$ are maintained during T_i, denoted by $y_i^{\max}$ and $y_i^{\min}$, respectively.

When the buffer m is increased, the upper bound $C(t) + m$ on the cumulative transmission scheme increases (the upper grey area in Figure 13.2 moves upwards), which affects the minimum and maximum transmission rates at the intervals for which $b_i^{\max} > b_i^{\text{best}} > b_i^{\min}$. Any other transmission rate during T_i between $b_i^{\min}$ and $b_i^{\max}$ is not affected. The maximum transmission rate decreases for each unit of buffer increase with a rate given by $r_i^{\max} = 1/y_i^{\max}$. This rate is valid for only a limited amount of buffer increase, $\triangle_i m^{\max}$, which gives the buffer increase until either $b_i^{\max} = b_i^{\max-1}$ or $b_i^{\max} = b_i^{\text{best}}$, whichever comes first. Analogously, the rate at which $b_i^{\min}$ increases for each unit of buffer increase is given by $r_i^{\min} = 1/y_i^{\min}$, and the maximum amount that m may increase for $r_i^{\min}$ to remain valid is given by $\triangle_i m^{\min}$. For each interval T_i for which $b_i^{\max} = b_i^{\text{best}} = b_i^{\min}$, we set $r_i^{\max} = r_i^{\min} = 0$, since $b_i^{\max}$ does not change in this case, and $\triangle_i m^{\max} = \triangle_i m^{\min} = M - m$.

Initialization

  determine the set of concave critical points $C = \{c_1, c_2, \ldots, c_k\} \subseteq \mathcal{T}$.

  $T_i = (c_i, c_{i+1}], i \in I = \{1, \ldots, k-1\}$

  for all $i \in I$ *determine*

    $b_i^{\max} = \max_{t \in T_i} x(t) = x(c_{i+1}); \quad b_i^{\min} = \min_{t \in T_i} x(t) = x(c_i + 1);$

    if $b_i^{\max} > b_i^{\min}$, *then determine*

      $b_i^{\text{best}} = (C(c_{i+1}) - C(c_i))/(c_{i+1} - c_i);$

      $b_i^{\max-1} = \max_{t \in T_i, x(t) \neq b_i^{\max}} x(t); \quad b_i^{\min+1} = \min_{t \in T_i, x(t) \neq b_i^{\min}} x(t);$

      $y_i^{\max} = |\{t \in T_i | x(t) = b_i^{\max}\}|; \quad r_i^{\max} = 1/y_i^{\max}$

      $y_i^{\min} = |\{t \in T_i | x(t) = b_i^{\min}\}|; \quad r_i^{\min} = 1/y_i^{\min}$

      $\triangle_i m^{\max} = \begin{cases} y_i^{\max}(b_i^{\max} - b_i^{\max-1}) & \text{if } b_i^{\max-1} \geq b_i^{\text{best}} \\ y_i^{\max}(b_i^{\max} - b_i^{\text{best}}) & \text{otherwise.} \end{cases}$

      $\triangle_i m^{\min} = \begin{cases} y_i^{\min}(b_i^{\min+1} - b_i^{\min}) & \text{if } b_i^{\min+1} \leq b_i^{\text{best}} \\ y_i^{\min}(b_i^{\text{best}} - b_i^{\min}) & \text{otherwise.} \end{cases}$

    fi

    if $b_i^{\max} = b_i^{\min}$ *then*

      $r_i^{\max} = 0; \quad r_i^{\min} = 0; \quad \triangle_i m^{\max} = M - m; \quad \triangle_i m^{\min} = M - m;$

    fi

  endfor

  $I^1 = \{i \in I | b_i^{\max} \geq b_j^{\max}, \forall j \in I\}$

  $I^2 = \{i \in I^1 | r_i^{\max} \leq r_j^{\max}, \forall j \in I^1\}$

  pick $i^* \in I^2$

  for all T_i

    if $r_{i^*}^{\max} > r_i^{\max}$ *then* $\gamma_i = \frac{b_{i^*}^{\max} - b_i^{\max}}{r_{i^*}^{\max} - r_i^{\max}}$

    if $r_i^{\max} + r_{i+1}^{\min} > 0$ *then* $\varepsilon_i = \frac{b_i^{\max} - b_{i+1}^{\min}}{r_i^{\max} + r_{i+1}^{\min}}$

  endfor

Trade-off loop

  while $c_r - c_b r_{i^*}^{\max} < 0$ *do*

    $\triangle m = \min_i \{\gamma_i, \triangle_i m^{\min}, \triangle_i m^{\max}, \varepsilon_i\};$

    $m := m + \triangle m;$ decrease all $\gamma_i, \triangle_i m^{\min}, \triangle_i m^{\max}, \varepsilon_i$ with $\triangle m;$

    adjust transmission rates of all intervals;

    if b shifts to interval T_i *then*

      reset $i^*;$

      redetermine γ_j for each interval $T_j;$

    od

    if the number of convex critical points in interval T_i changes *then*

      if $b_i^{\max} = b_i^{\text{best}} = b_i^{\min}$ *then*

        $r_i^{\max} = r_i^{\min} = 0;$ redetermine $\gamma_i, \varepsilon_{i-1},$ and $\varepsilon_i;$

      fi

      if $b_i^{\max} = b_i^{\max-1}$ *then*

        redetermine $y_i^{\max}, r_i^{\max}, b_i^{\max-1}, \triangle_i m^{\max}, \gamma_i,$ and $\varepsilon_i;$

        if $i = i^*$ *then*

          redetermine γ_j for each interval $T_j;$

        fi

      fi

      if $b_i^{\min} = b_i^{\min+1}$ *then*

        redetermine $y_i^{\min}, r_i^{\min}, b_i^{\min+1}, \triangle_i m^{\min},$ and $\varepsilon_{i-1};$

      fi

    od

    if the number of concave critical points decreases, i.e., T_i merges with T_{i+1} *then*

      adjust boundary of T_i and delete $T_{i+1};$

      determine all parameter values of new $T_i;$

      if $i = i^*$ *then*

        redetermine γ_j for each interval $T_j;$

      fi

      renumber all intervals after $T_i;$

    od

  od

Figure 13.1. Buffer-increasing trade-off algorithm.

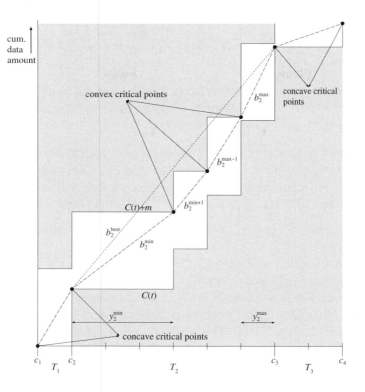

Figure 13.2. Parameters of an MVBA-schedule for the buffer-increasing trade-off algorithm.

Now, we know for each interval T_i that when we increase m by a small amount $\triangle m$ its maximum transmission rate $b_i^{\max}$ decreases by $r_i^{\max}\triangle m$. As $b = \max_i b_i^{\max}$, the algorithm next selects the interval that has the highest transmission rate and the lowest $r_i^{\max}$, i.e., it chooses i^* that lexicographically maximizes $(b_i^{\max}, -r_i^{\max})$. Then b decreases by $r_{i^*}^{\max}\triangle m$, and thus the costs change by an amount $c_m\triangle m - c_b r_{i^*}^{\max}\triangle m = (c_m - c_b r_{i^*}^{\max})\triangle m$. Therefore, if $c_m < c_b r_{i^*}^{\max}$ then the total cost decreases if m is increased by a small amount $\triangle m$.

Before the algorithm can start with the trade-off we first determine the values of parameters γ_i and ε_i as indicated in the algorithm. These parameters give the amount that the buffer size m can be increased before an event takes place that directly or indirectly influences the rate at which the highest transmission rate decreases. Below, we describe all these events, and how large the increase $\triangle m$ is for them to happen.

- The highest transmission rate b can shift from T_{i^*} to another interval T_i. This can happen for T_i with $r_i^{\max} < r_{i^*}^{\max}$ as then $b_i^{\max}$ decreases slower than $b = b_{i^*}^{\max}$, when the buffer is increased with γ_i, i.e., the amount that

m has to be increased such that $b_i^{\max}$ becomes equal to $b_{i^*}^{\max}$. For this, $b_{i^*}^{\max} - r_{i^*}^{\max}\gamma_i = b_i^{\max} - r_i^{\max}\gamma_i$, so $\gamma_i = \frac{b_{i^*}^{\max}-b_i^{\max}}{r_{i^*}^{\max}-r_i^{\max}}$. For i with $r_i^{\max} \geq r_{i^*}^{\max}$, we set $\gamma_i = M - m$.

- A convex critical point may no longer be a critical point, which may affect $r_i^{\max}$ or $r_i^{\min}$. This happens when the buffer is increased with $\triangle_i m^{\max}$ or $\triangle_i m^{\min}$.

- A concave critical point may no longer be a critical point, which means that two intervals T_i and T_{i+1} merge into one. This happens when the buffer is increased with ε_i, i.e., the amount that m has to be increased such that $b_i^{\max}$ becomes equal to $b_{i+1}^{\min}$. For this, $b_i^{\max} - r_i^{\max}\varepsilon_i = b_{i+1}^{\min} + r_{i+1}^{\min}\varepsilon_i$, so $\varepsilon_i = \frac{b_i^{\max}-b_{i+1}^{\min}}{r_i^{\max}+r_{i+1}^{\min}}$. For i with $r_i^{\max} + r_i^{\min} = 0$, we set $\varepsilon_i = M - m$.

Now, the algorithm in Figure 13.1 iteratively increases the buffer size m as long as the rate at which the bandwidth decreases per unit of buffer increase is high enough for an increase in the buffer to be cost efficient, i.e., as long as $c_r - c_b r_{i^*}^{\max} < 0$. The algorithm chooses the increase in buffer size m equal to $\min_i\{\gamma_i, \triangle_i m^{\max}, \triangle_i m^{\min}, \varepsilon_i\}$. This leads to one of the described events, after which some actions are taken to adjust all the parameters for the newly obtained transmission schedule. These actions are merely book-keeping of all the parameter values. Besides adjusting the transmission rates of each interval T_i for the new buffer size, some of the interval parameters have to be redetermined.

The algorithm continues with increasing the receiving buffer as long as $c_r - c_b r_{i^*}^{\max} < 0$. When $c_r - c_b r_{i^*}^{\max} \geq 0$, the total costs increase again with $(c_r - c_b r_{i^*}^{\max})\triangle m$ for a small buffer increase $\triangle m$. Furthermore, due to the convexity of the problem, the costs of the solutions on the trade-off curve with a higher buffer size value are higher. To determine the complete bandwidth-buffer trade-off curve, the algorithm should be continued until the maximum buffer size is obtained; in case of an unlimited buffer size the cumulative consumption at time point T can be taken as the maximum buffer size.

13.4   Trade-off by increasing bandwidth

In this section we describe the *rate-increasing trade-off algorithm* (RIT). For more details on this algorithm we refer to Chang et al. [1998]. This algorithm is based on ON-OFF transmission schedules which we shortly describe in Section 13.4.1. In Section 13.4.2 we describe the rate-increasing trade-off algorithm.

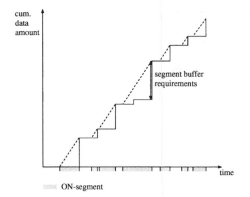
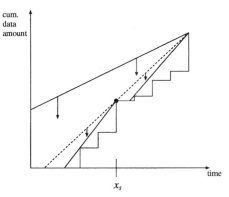

Figure 13.3. Example of an ON-OFF transmission schedule. The maximum buffer requirement during an ON-segment takes place just before a time point, i.e. just before an increase in the cumulative consumption scheme.

Figure 13.4. When the rate increases the transmission schedule touches the cumulative consumption scheme at x_s and the segment is split into two new segments.

13.4.1 ON-OFF bandwidth smoothing algorithm

In the model presented in Section 13.2 the amount of data transmitted during a time unit t is represented by a variable $x(t)$, which is bounded by the reserved bandwidth b. In graphical representations this is shown by a transmission evenly distributed over the time unit. However, the transmission can also be represented by the fraction of time data is transmitted at the reserved bandwidth, leading to so-called ON-OFF schedules as shown in Figure 13.3. Times when transmission takes places are referred to as "ON-times" or "ON-segments", and times when transmission equals zero are referred to as "OFF-times". If $o(t)$ denotes the fraction of time unit t that is part of an ON-segment, then $x(t) = b \cdot o(t)$ holds.

Chang et al. consider an ON-OFF bandwidth smoothing algorithm that for a given bandwidth minimizes the required buffer size. The resulting schedule for a given bandwidth is obtained by working backwards and letting an ON-segment end at an outer-corner of the cumulative consumption scheme as is shown in Figure 13.3. Then the ON-segment starts at the point of the cumulative consumption scheme from which continuous transmission at the maximum bandwidth exactly finishes at the segment end point. The maximum buffer requirement during an ON-segment takes place just before an increase in the cumulative consumption scheme. This can be at the end of the ON-segment, but also at a time point during the ON-segment.

13.4.2   Rate-increasing trade-off algorithm

The idea of the trade-off algorithm described by Chang et al. [1998] is to start with a bandwidth equal to (almost) zero and a buffer size equal to the total amount of data, and then increasing the bandwidth while monitoring the effect on the required buffer size; see Figure 13.4. To determine this effect, the transmission schedule is split up into its different ON-segments or *segments* for short, beginning with one segment for the schedule with transmission rate zero. For each segment the point with largest buffer requirements, denoted as the *largest buffer point*, is determined. The required buffer size is then given by the maximum of the buffer requirements at the largest buffer points. Now, the effect of a transmission rate increase on the buffer requirement at a largest buffer point is as follows. Let e_s denote the end point and f_s the largest buffer point of segment s. As the end point of a segment does not change when the rate is increased, the number of time units between f_s and e_s determine the amount with which the buffer requirements at f_s decrease. So if $\triangle b$ denotes the increase in transmission rate, then the decrease in buffer requirements at f_s is given by $\triangle b(e_s - f_s)$, where the *buffer decreasing slope* of segment s is given by $e_s - f_s$.

Let s^* be the segment with the largest buffer requirements. Then the required buffer size is equal to the buffer requirements at f_{s^*}, and for a small rate increase $\triangle b$ the buffer decrease is given by the buffer decreasing slope of s^* times $\triangle b$. However, when increasing the rate the following events can happen, which may influence the speed at which the buffer decreases.

- A segment s can split into two new segments. When the rate increases, the transmission line of a segment may touch an outer corner of the cumulative consumption scheme at a point x_s; see Figure 13.4. Two new segments are then formed, one ending at the previous end point and one ending at point x_s. A rate at which a segment splits into two new segments is called a *separating rate*, and point x_s is referred to as the *separating point* of segment s.

- The largest buffer point of a segment moves to another point. Since the change in buffer requirements at a point depends positively on the distance between that point and the end of the segment, the decrease in buffer requirements is lower at points closer to the segment end point. So when the rate increases, the largest buffer point of a segment may shift to a point closer to the end point. A rate at which the largest buffer point of a segment shifts is called an *intra-segment equal-buffer rate*.

- The segment with the highest buffer requirement can change. As the change in buffer requirements is generally not equal for each segment, the maximum buffer requirement can change to a segment with a lower decrease in buffer requirements. A rate at which the segment with highest buffer requirement changes is called an *inter-segment equal-buffer rate*.

We continue with describing how the separating rates and equal-buffer rates can be determined.

Separating rates. Consider a segment consisting of at least two time units with end point e. When the rate is increased, the cumulative transmission schedule will decrease at each time point of the segment before e, until it is equal to an outer corner at one of the time points. This time point is the separating point of the segment, and the segment is split into two new segments. Denoting the outer corner of the cumulative consumption scheme at time point t by c_t^{out}, the separating rate of a segment s equals the slope of the line between $c_{x_s}^{out}$ and $c_{e_s}^{out}$. When the rate has increased to a value higher than the maximum consumption during any time unit, the number of segments is equal to the number of time units. Therefore, when increasing the rate every outer corner of the cumulative consumption scheme splits a segment into two new segments, and the total number of separating rates is equal to the total number of outer corners. The separating rates can be determined by working backwards. For each time point t the convex upper envelope of the cumulative consumption scheme between t and T is constructed using the envelope between $t+1$ and T. Figure 13.5 givens an example of the construction of the convex upper envelope. First, in Figure 13.5(a) the line between c_t^{out} and c_{t+1}^{out} is added to the convex upper envelope between $t+1$ and T. Since it does not lead to a convex upper envelope between t and T, the end point of the line piece that is added, is shifted along the upper envelope between $t+1$ and T until the convex upper envelope between t and T has been obtained; see Figures 13.5(b) and (c).

As a separating rate splits a segment into two new intervals, all separating rates can be stored in a binary tree. In the root node the separating rate of the segment comprising the whole time horizon is stored, and in the left and right child of a node the separating rates are stored of the new segment ending at separating point x and the new segment beginning at x, respectively. Figure 13.6 gives an example of the separating rates and the corresponding binary tree.

Intra-segment equal-buffer rates. Consider a segment s. The buffer requirement at a given time t in segment s is given by the difference between the cumulative transmission schedule and the cumulative consumption scheme at time t. Let c_t^{in} denote the inner corner of the cumulative consumption scheme at time point t. As the maximum buffer requirement of a segment takes place just before a time point t, it equals the difference between the cumulative transmission schedule at t and c_t^{in}. Beginning with the transmission rate almost equal to

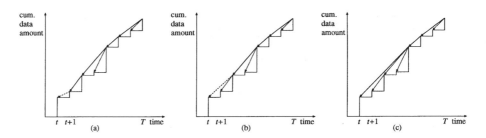

Figure 13.5.   Example of the construction of the convex upper envelope between t and T. The solid arcs in (a) represent the convex upper envelope between $t+1$ and T. The dotted arcs are line pieces of previously constructed envelopes. The dashed arcs in (a) and (b) are the lines which are checked whether they extend (a part of) the convex envelope between $t+1$ and T to a convex upper envelope between t and T. The final convex upper envelope between t and T is given in (c) by the solid arcs.

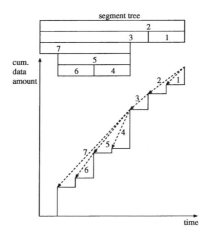

Figure 13.6.   All separating rates and the binary tree comprising all segments. Segment 2 is the main segment and has segments 1 and 3 as right and left child, respectively. Segment 3 has only segment 7 as left child and no right child. Similarly, segment 7 has only segment 5 as right child and no left child. Segment 5 has segments 4 and 6 as right and left child, respectively. The numbering of the segments corresponds to the sequence in which the separating rates and convex upper envelopes are determined.

zero, the largest buffer point of s will be the first time point of s, i.e., at the end of the first time unit of s. Now, when the rate increases the largest buffer point of s may shift closer to the end point of s since the cumulative transmission schedule decreases more at the beginning of s than at the end. Let f be the old largest buffer point of s and f' the new. When the rate equals the equal-buffer rate at which the largest buffer point changes from f to f', the buffer requirements at both points are the same. So the slope of the line between

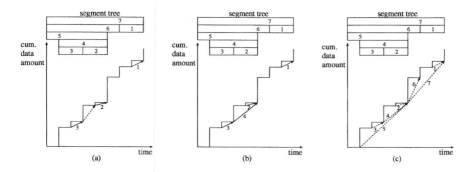

Figure 13.7. Example of the convex lower envelope for a segment. Figures (a) and (b) show how the convex lower envelope of segment 4 is determined using the convex lower envelopes of the two child segments 2 and 3. First, the envelopes of the child segments are connected by a line piece in (a). Since this does not result in a convex lower envelope because the slope of the begin of the envelope of the right child is smaller than the slope of the added line piece, the end point of the added line piece is shifted along the envelope of the right child until the convex lower envelope has been obtained in (b). Figure (c) shows all line pieces determined for the convex lower envelopes of all segments. The equal-buffer rates are given by the slopes of the line pieces. The numbers in the nodes of the segment tree denote the sequence in which the line pieces for the convex lower envelopes are determined, where the envelope of the right child of a segment is determined before the envelope of the left child. The numbers near the line pieces correspond with the segment with the same number in the tree.

c_f^{in} and $c_{f'}^{in}$ must be equal to the equal-buffer rate. Now consider the convex lower envelope of a segment s. It starts at the inner corner of the first time point of s, the initial largest buffer point of s, and ends at the inner corner of the end point of s. Since the envelope is convex, the subsequent line pieces of the envelope have an increasing slope. The shifts of the largest buffer point of s during the increase of the transmission rate follow exactly the convex lower envelope of the cumulative consumption scheme on the time points of s, i.e., when the transmission rate is equal to the slope of a line piece of the convex lower envelope, the largest buffer point shifts from the begin point of the line piece to the end point of the line piece.

Let s be a segment on a leaf of the segment tree. Then, s consists of two time units and its convex lower envelope is given by the line piece between $c_{x_s}^{in}$ and $c_{e_s}^{in}$, e.g., line pieces 1, 2, and 3 in Figure 13.7 for the three segments on the leaves of the segment tree. Now let s be a segment consisting of more than two time units, e.g., segment 4 in the segment tree in Figure 13.7(c). Then its convex lower envelope may contain line pieces of the convex lower envelopes of its child segments in the segment tree. The convex lower envelope of s is then determined by starting with the line piece between its separating point x_s and $x_s + 1$; see Figure 13.7(a). The slope of this line is compared with the slope of the neighboring lines of the convex lower envelopes of the left and right child segment of s. If necessary, the begin point of the added line is shifted along the convex lower envelope of the left child segment, and the end point along the convex lower envelope of the right child segment in order to obtain the correct convex lower envelope of segment s; cf. Figures 13.7(a) and (b). Figure 13.7(c) gives an example of all line pieces of the convex lower envelopes, with the equal-buffer rates given by the slopes of the line pieces.

Inter-segment equal-buffer rates.   With the separating rates and intra-segment equal-buffer rates we can determine for each transmission rate the buffer requirement of a segment. This leads for each segment to a segment trade-off curve which depicts the buffer requirements of a segment for all relevant transmission rates. To determine the bandwidth-buffer trade-off curve we also need to know when the maximum buffer requirement shifts from one segment to another, i.e., at which rate the buffer requirements at two segments are equal. These inter-segment equal-buffer rates can be determined by plotting all segment trade-off curves in the buffer-bandwidth plane. The inter-segment equal-buffer rates are given by the intersections of two segment trade-off curves. However, the full bandwidth-buffer trade-off curve is given by the maximum of the segment trade-off curves at each rate. Therefore, only the intersections at the maximum buffer requirement for a rate need to be considered.

Bandwidth-buffer trade-off curve.   The bandwidth-buffer trade-off curve now can be determined as follows; see also Figure 13.8 for an example of the trade-off curve. First, determine all separating rates and the corresponding segment tree. Then, determine all intra-segment equal-buffer rates by determining for each segment its convex lower envelope. Now, sort all separating rates and intra-segment equal-buffer rates in increasing order. Starting with a rate of zero, draw a first trade-off curve starting from the point with rate 0 and buffer requirement equal to the total data amount. The slope of the curve is equal to the initial buffer decreasing slope of the segment in the root of the tree. All rates are now processed increasingly. When a separating rate is processed, the segment trade-off curves of the two new segments are determined, and it is checked whether they have an intersection with the maximum of the already determined segment trade-off curves. If so, the bandwidth-buffer trade-off curve given by this maximum, is adjusted. When an intra-segment equal-buffer rate is processed, the largest buffer point is adjusted of all segments which are affected, i.e., all segments for which the line piece depicting the equal-buffer rate is a part of the convex lower envelope of the segment. Again it is checked whether the maximum trade-off curve is affected and it is adjusted if neces-

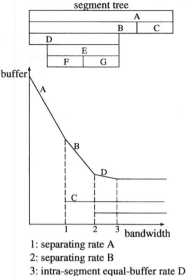

1: separating rate A
2: separating rate B
3: intra-segment equal-buffer rate D

Figure 13.8. Example of the construction of the trade-off curve for the example used in the previous figures. The trade-off curve starts with the segment trade-off curve of segment A. At the separating rate of segment A, the segment trade-off curve of A splits into two new segment trade-off curves of segments B and C. Then, at the separating rate of segment B, the segment trade-off curve of B splits into the flat curve of a one-time-unit segment and the segment trade-off curve of segment D. This latter segment trade-off curve is altered at the intra-segment equal-buffer rate of D. The largest buffer point of D shifts to its last time point, leading to a flat segment trade off-curve. As the segment trade-off curve of D is the maximum of all segment trade-off curves at that rate, the complete trade-off curve now has been obtained. It is given by the uppermost lines, i.e., the segment trade-off curves of segments A, B, and D.

sary. The complete bandwidth-buffer trade-off curve is determined when all rates are processed.

13.5   Comparison of the trade-off algorithms

In this section we compare the buffer-increasing trade-off algorithm and the rate-increasing trade-off algorithm. In Section 13.5.1 we compare the structure of both algorithms. In Section 13.5.2 we discuss the time and space complexity of both algorithms.

13.5.1   Structure of the algorithms

In this section we show that the two algorithms have a remarkable similarity. For this we present a more general structure and show that it underlies the structures of both algorithms.

The problem described in Section 13.2 requires the balancing of two variables for which cost coefficients are given. A solution can be found by changing the value of one of these variables and determining the effect on the optimal value of the other variable, just as both algorithms do. Now consider the following structure for this solution method.

- Determine a starting solution with the minimum value for one variable, *variable 1*, and a value for the other variable, *variable 2*.

- Increase the value of variable 1 and determine how it affects the value of variable 2, i.e., determine the slope of the trade-off curve starting from the point representing the starting solution.

- Determine everything which may affect the slope of the trade-off curve:

    1. The place in the transmission schedule where variable 2 takes its maximum value can change.

    2. The effect on variable 2 may alter due to a change within specified boundaries of the place where it takes its maximum value.

    3. The effect on variable 2 may alter due to a change to the boundaries of the place where it takes its maximum value.

This structure forms a basis for both the buffer-increasing trade-off algorithm and the rate-increasing trade-off algorithm. Taking for variable 1 the buffer size and for variable 2 the bandwidth gives the buffer-increasing trade-off algorithm. The corresponding slope-affecting events are:

1. The highest rate b shifts to another interval.

2. A convex critical point disappears, which changes r^{max} or r^{min}.

3. A concave critical point disappears, causing two intervals to merge into one.

Taking for variable 1 the bandwidth and for variable 2 the buffer size gives the rate-increasing trade-off algorithm. The slope-affecting events then correspond to:

1. The inter-segment equal-buffer rate.

2. The intra-segment equal-buffer rate.

3. The separating rate.

13.5.2   Complexity

We first discuss the time complexity of the buffer-increasing trade-off algorithm. The construction of the starting solution and the initialization have a time complexity $O(T)$. The time complexity of the trade-off loop depends on the amount of events that take place and the actions to be taken to adjust the schedule after an event. The highest transmission rate b can only shift to another interval with a lower $r_i^{\max}$, and it can only shift back to an interval when its $r_i^{\max}$ has changed, which can happen only when a convex critical point disappears or emerges. Denoting the initial number of intervals with K, this means that the former event can take place at most $K + T$ times. At each time unit at most one convex critical point may emerge or disappear, thus the second event can happen at most T times. Finally, since there are K intervals, at most $K - 1$ times two intervals may merge. Since the actions to adjust the parameters after an event have time complexity $O(K)$, the time complexity of the trade-off loop thus becomes $O(KT)$. So, the time complexity of the buffer-increasing trade-off algorithm is $O(KT)$.

Chang et al. [1998] give the following time complexity for the rate-increasing trade-off algorithm. The time complexity of the computation of the separating rates and intra-segment equal-buffer rates is $O(T)$. It takes $O(T \log T)$ time to sort all these rates. Processing all rates again has time complexity $O(T)$, and adjusting the trade-off curve while processing a rate has time complexity $O(\log T)$. The time complexity of the rate-increasing trade-off algorithm therefore is $O(T \log T)$.

If we compare the time complexity of both algorithms, we notice one difference. Where the buffer-increasing trade-off algorithm has a factor K in its time complexity, the rate-increasing trade-off algorithm has a factor $\log T$. Since these are incomparable, theoretically neither one is faster than the other. Therefore, we compare both algorithms' run times by testing them on fifteen instances. Table 13.1 shows the results.

The first column of the table describes the type of video trace, the second column gives the number of frames of the trace. Then results are shown when a buffer at the receiving side has to be minimized, starting with the number of intervals of the starting MVBA schedule, followed by the run time of the buffer-increasing trade-off algorithm to determine the complete trade-off curve, and then the run time of the rate-increasing trade-off algorithm. The following three columns give these results for the problem setting in which a buffer at the sending side has to be minimized. The last two columns give the memory requirements for both algorithms for the setting that minimizes the receiving buffer.

The results clearly show the dependency of the run time of the buffer-increasing trade-off algorithm on the number of intervals. For all traces the

Table 13.1. Run times in seconds and memory requirements in KB for the buffer-increasing trade-off algorithm (BIT) and the rate-increasing trade-off algorithm (RIT), tested on fifteen video traces. "Receiving" gives the results when the buffer at the receiving side is minimized, "sending" when the buffer at the sending side is minimized. For each trace also the number of frames (T) is given, and the number of intervals (K) for the buffer-increasing trade-off algorithm. The tests were performed on a PIII-550.

type	T	K	*receiving* BIT	*receiving* RIT	K	*sending* BIT	*sending* RIT	*memory req.* BIT	*memory req.* RIT
documentary	36,875	646	0.060	0.138	455	0.055	0.135	1,176	2,860
comedy	38,215	787	0.077	0.138	664	0.073	0.136	1,272	2,944
comedy	74,931	1,309	0.164	0.318	1,045	0.140	0.326	2,344	5,676
documentary	75,100	1,598	0.216	0.316	1,060	0.157	0.314	2,448	5,676
documentary	76,750	1,175	0.159	0.317	954	0.141	0.326	2,340	5,828
pop concert	99,785	2,165	0.414	0.449	1,609	0.292	0.459	3,268	7,524
thriller	141,800	2,580	0.478	0.746	1,888	0.364	0.758	4,416	10,628
action	151,132	3,185	0.765	0.774	2,386	0.567	0.803	4,876	11,312
comedy	161,082	1,522	0.282	0.844	1,232	0.252	0.931	4,448	12,052
comedy	164,199	3,585	0.892	0.907	2,542	0.576	0.972	5,324	12,280
action	165,141	1,732	0.414	0.923	1,278	0.310	0.961	4,620	12,356
pop concert	166,765	1,867	0.406	0.940	1,686	0.383	0.968	4,728	12,452
action	184,371	3,816	0.946	0.939	3,425	0.850	0.961	5,944	13,800
scifi	196,160	2,808	0.656	1.148	2,127	0.501	1.124	5,784	14,656
fantasy	256,559	4,589	1.770	1.591	3,681	1.257	1.555	7,924	19,140
average	132,591	2,224	0.513	0.699	1,735	0.395	0.715	4,061	9,946

number of intervals for the sending buffer setting happens to be lower than for the receiving buffer setting, and as a result the corresponding run time of the buffer-increasing trade-off algorithm is less for the sending buffer setting than for the receiving buffer setting. However, for the rate-increasing trade-off algorithm run times for both settings are about the same, as can be expected, since it only depends on the length of a trace. Overall comparison of the run times between both algorithms is slightly in favor of the buffer-increasing trade-off algorithm.

We end with comparing the memory requirements of both algorithms. The memory requirements of the buffer-increasing trade-off algorithm mainly depend on the consumption scheme, an initial transmission schedule, and the interval parameters of the transmission schedule. The memory requirements of the rate-increasing trade-off algorithm depend also on the consumption scheme. Furthermore, memory is required to store at least the separating rates, the structure of the segment-tree, the intra-segment equal-buffer rates, and the largest buffer points. Comparing the memory requirements of both algorithms as given in Table 13.1 shows that in our experiments the rate-increasing trade-off algorithm required more than twice the amount of memory than the buffer-increasing trade-off algorithm.

Overall, the buffer-increasing trade-off algorithm performs better than the rate-increasing trade-off algorithm as it constructs the trade-off line for most traces slightly faster with half the memory requirements.

13.6   Conclusions

Ambient intelligent environments often contain an embedded network connecting devices and resources in the environment. The network and resources are shared by the different applications in the environment. Two of these resources are the available bandwidth and buffer size in the network. In this chapter we have considered the problem of making an optimal trade-off between required bandwidth and required buffer size when transmitting a VBR stream. We presented two algorithms to solve this problem, the buffer-increasing trade-off algorithm which increases the buffer size to decrease the required bandwidth, and the rate-increasing trade-off algorithm which increases the bandwidth to decrease the required buffer size. A comparison of the two algorithms shows that they have a similar structure, but that their time complexity and memory requirements differ. The buffer-increasing trade-off algorithm has a time complexity which depends on the length of the time horizon but also on the number of so-called intervals of the starting MVBA-schedule. The time complexity of the rate-increasing trade-off algorithm however, only depends on the time horizon. This leads to different results when testing both algorithms. The buffer-increasing trade-off algorithm has a better performance since it has slightly faster run times for most traces than the rate-increasing trade-off algorithm and it requires only half the amount of memory.

References

Boef, E. den, W.F.J. Verhaegh, and J. Korst [2003a]. An optimal trade-off between bus and buffer usage for a VBR stream. To be submitted to IEEE/ACM Transactions on Networking.

Boef, E. den, W.F.J. Verhaegh, and J. Korst [2003b]. Smoothing streams in an in-home digital network: Optimization of bus and buffer usage. Accepted for publication in *Telecommunication Systems, special issue on Multimedia Home Telecommunication Systems.*

Chang, R.I., M.C. Chen, M.T. Ko, and J.M. Ho [1998]. Characterize the minimum required resources for admission control of pre-recorded VBR video transmission by an $O(n\log n)$ algorithm. In *Proceedings IEEE 7th International Conference on Computer Communications and Networks*, pages 674–681.

Chang, R.I., M.C. Chen, M.T. Ko, and J.M. Ho [1999]. Optimal bandwidth-buffer trade-off for VBR media transmission over multiple relay-servers. In *Proceedings IEEE Multimedia Systems (ICMCS)*, vol. 2, pages 31–35.

Feng, W. [1997]. Rate-constrained bandwidth smoothing for the delivery of stored video. In *Proceedings SPIE Multimedia Networking and Computing*, pages 316–327.

Feng, W., and J. Rexford [1999]. Performance evaluation of smoothing algorithms for transmitting prerecorded variable-bit-rate video. *IEEE Transactions on Multimedia*, 1(3):302–313.

Salehi, J.D., Z.L. Zhang, J. Kurose, and D. Towsley. Supporting stored video: Reducing rate variability and end-to-end resource requirements through optimal smoothing. *IEEE/ACM Transactions on Networking*, 6(4):397–410.

Chapter 14

DYNAMIC CONTROL OF SCALABLE MEDIA PROCESSING APPLICATIONS

Clemens C. Wüst and Wim F.J. Verhaegh

Abstract   Media processing in software is characterized by highly fluctuating, content-dependent processing times, as well as strict real-time requirements. These real-time requirements can be met by means of a worst-case resource allocation, but this is often not cost-effective. To assign resources closer to the average-case load situation, scalable media processing may be applied. A scalable media processing application allows a trade-off between the resource usage and the output quality, by varying the quality level at which processing is done. We consider the problem of controlling the quality level of a scalable media processing application during run time. The objective is to maximize the quality of the output as perceived by the user, by simultaneously maximizing the quality level and minimizing the number of artifacts that result from both deadline misses and quality-level changes.

First we model the problem as a finite Markov decision process. We use this to determine on-line quality-level control strategies. These strategies enable us to cope with temporal load fluctuations. Next, to handle structural load fluctuations, we present a method called *scaled budget control*. The scaled budget control strategy works well, as we show by several simulation experiments using a scalable MPEG-2 decoder, where its performance comes close to an off-line computed upper bound.

Keywords   Media processing, real-time systems, load fluctuations, scalability, quality-level control, Markov decision process.

14.1   Introduction

Consumer terminals, such as set-top boxes and digital TV-sets, currently apply dedicated hardware components to process media data. In the foreseeable future, programmable hardware with media processing in software is expected to take over. Media processing, such as MPEG decoding, is carried out in software by so-called media processing applications (MPAs). MPAs have two important properties. First, they show resource demands that may vary signif-

W. Verhaegh et al. (eds.), Algorithms in Ambient Intelligence, 259-276.
© 2004 *Kluwer Academic Publishers. Printed in the Netherlands.*

icantly over time [Baiceanu et al., 1996]. This is due to the varying size and complexity of the media data they process. Second, MPAs have severe real-time requirements to guarantee correct output. For instance, decoding a 25 fps (frames per second) video requires strictly periodically a newly decoded picture every 40 ms. One way to meet the deadlines is by assigning an MPA a resource budget based on its worst-case demands. However, to be cost-effective, resources should often be assigned closer to the average-case demand [Bril et al., 2001a; Bril et al., 2001b]. Without countermeasures, this however can lead to the violation of deadlines.

The combination of varying demands and real-time requirements can be handled more effectively by making use of scalable MPAs. A scalable MPA can run at different quality levels, with correspondingly different resource demands [Hentschel et al., 2001; Lan et al., 2001; Peng, 2001]. Hence, real-time requirements can be met by controlling the quality level during processing. The problem we consider in this chapter is how to control the quality level of a scalable MPA which has been assigned a fixed processing-time budget. The objective is to maximize the quality of the output as perceived by the user. This is done by simultaneously maximizing the quality level and minimizing the number of artifacts that result from both deadline misses and quality-level changes. The work described in this chapter is an extension of our earlier work [Wüst & Verhaegh, 2001], in the sense that we introduce a way to compensate for structural load fluctuations.

14.1.1 Related work

In recent years several publications in the area of Quality of Service (QoS) resource management have appeared. Particularly interesting in relation to our work is the work of Lee [1999] and Lee et al. [1999], who present a QoS framework and algorithms to distribute resources over tasks in a resource-constrained environment. In their setup, tasks are scalable with respect to one or more resources, but the resource needs of a task are assumed to be fixed for each chosen quality level. The objective is to maximize the quality of the output of all tasks as perceived by the user, which is modeled by means of utility functions. Whereas this approach addresses the distribution of the resources over the various tasks, we consider the problem of how each single task makes optimal use of its assigned resources, taking care of the variabilities in the task's workload. In that sense, the two approaches complement each other.

Lan et al. [2001] describe a method to regulate the varying computation load of an MPEG decoder. Before decoding an MPEG frame, the required computational resources are estimated, and next the decoding is scaled such that it will not exceed a target computation constraint. In contradiction to our approach, this approach optimizes the quality of the individual frames, and not the overall perceived output quality over a sequence of frames.

Our work is embedded in a larger effort, which defines and builds a framework for QoS resource management for high-quality video. The framework is aimed at robustness and cost-effectiveness. Robustness is achieved by assigning a resource budget to each individual task that is both guaranteed and enforced. In this chapter we consider the problem of how a task can make optimal use of its assigned budget.

14.1.2 Organization

This chapter is organized as follows. In Section 14.2 we give a more detailed description of the problem. Next, in Section 14.3 we model the problem as a finite Markov decision process. Solving this Markov decision process results in an optimal Markov policy, which we use at run time to control the quality level. Next, in Section 14.4 we discuss structural load fluctuations and introduce a method to cope with them, called scaled budget control. In Section 14.5 we evaluate the control strategies in simulation experiments, by comparing the on-line performance to an off-line computed upper bound. Finally, in Section 14.6 we conclude the chapter.

14.2 Problem description

We consider a single scalable media processing application, hereafter referred to as the application. Its task is to continuously fetch a unit of work from an input buffer, next to process the unit of work, and finally to write the processed unit of work into an output buffer. Units of work are processed independently of each other in one of the quality levels supported by the application. The time required to process a unit of work depends on the chosen quality level, and is stochastic due to content dependencies.

The moment at which the processing of a unit of work is finished, is called a milestone. For each milestone there is a deadline, and deadlines are assumed to be strictly periodic in time with a given period P. A deadline corresponds to a moment at which some external process tries to extract a processed unit of work from the output buffer. Units of work are numbered $1, 2, \ldots$. The milestone corresponding to a unit of work i is denoted by m_i, and the corresponding deadline is denoted by d_i. Ideally, $m_i \leq d_i$, otherwise the deadline is missed. For convenience, we consider the moment at which the processing of the first unit of work starts also to be a milestone, numbered 0, although it has no corresponding deadline.

In each deadline period P, the application is guaranteed a fixed processing-time budget b. We define *relative progress* ρ_i at a milestone m_i as the (possibly negative) amount of budget left until deadline d_i, divided by b. Relative progress may become negative, when deadlines have been missed. If the relative progress ρ_i drops below zero, while ρ_{i-1} was still non-negative, then the application has encountered $\lceil -\rho_i \rceil$ deadline misses. To deal with deadline misses, we consider two approaches. One approach is to immediately use the output that is created at milestone m_i. In other words, deadline d_i is postponed until milestone m_i. This results in an adapted relative progress $\rho_i := 0$. All next deadlines $d_{i+1}, d_{i+2}, \ldots$ are also postponed by the same amount as d_i. We refer to this deadline-miss approach as the *conservative approach*. Another approach is to use the output at the first next deadline. This results in an adapted relative progress $\rho_i := \rho_i + \lceil -\rho_i \rceil \geq 0$. The deadlines $d_i, d_{i+1}, \ldots$ are all postponed by $\lceil -\rho_i \rceil$ periods. We refer to this deadline-miss approach as the *skipping approach*. Note that the conservative approach gives the worst-case adaptation that the skipping approach can give.

Figure 14.1 illustrates the skipping approach by means of an example timeline showing milestones and deadlines, in which we assume $b = P$. The relative progress at milestones m_1 to m_3 is given by $\rho_1 = 0.25$, $\rho_2 = 0.5$, and $\rho_3 = -0.5$, respectively. The relative progress at m_3 has dropped below zero, so $\lceil -\rho_3 \rceil = 1$ deadline has been missed, viz. d_3. Applying the skipping approach, the deadlines from d_3 onwards are all postponed by one period. Consequently, ρ_3 is adapted to 0.5, and continuing we find $\rho_4 = 1$ and $\rho_5 = 0.5$.

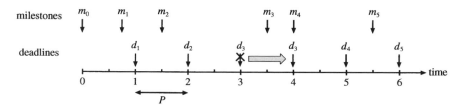

Figure 14.1. Example timeline showing milestones and deadlines, applying the skipping approach.

Since both deadline-miss approaches enforce a non-negative relative progress at each milestone, we have a lower bound on relative progress of zero. Furthermore, due to limited buffer sizes we also have an upper bound on relative progress. The reason for this is that the application is stalled if its output buffer is full, or if its input buffer is empty. We assume therefore an upper bound $\rho^{\max}$ on the relative progress, which is a measure for the number of periods that the application can work ahead. A final remark is that in case of deadline misses we skip the processing of one or more upcoming units of work, to avoid a pile-up in the input buffer.

At each milestone, we can choose the quality level at which the upcoming unit of work is processed. The problem we consider is to choose this quality level at milestones in such a way that the following three objectives are met. First, the quality level at which units of work are processed should be as high as possible. Second, because deadline misses and the skipping of unprocessed units of work both result in severe artifacts in the output, the number of deadline misses should be as low as possible. Third, we also want to keep the number of quality-level changes as low as possible, because quality-level changes result in perceivable artifacts too. A final remark is that a quality-level control strategy runs on the same processor as the application, and therefore should use little computational resources.

14.3 A Markov decision process

The problem described in the previous section is a stochastic decision problem. A common way to handle such a problem is by modeling it as a Markov decision process (MDP) [Van der Wal, 1980]. In this section we apply this technique.

14.3.1 MDP model

We now sketch how we model the problem as a finite MDP. For details, the reader is referred to [Wüst & Verhaegh, 2001]. A finite MDP has a finite set of states, a finite set of decisions for each state, probabilities for state transitions that depend on the decision taken in a state, and revenues for taking a decision in a state. The goal of the MDP is to find a decision strategy that maximizes the average revenue over all state transitions.

States. At each milestone we consider the state of the application. This state is naturally given by the amount of relative progress at the milestone. Because a finite set of states is required, we discretize relative progress into a finite set of equal-sized progress intervals between zero and ρ^{max}. Next, as we want to take quality-level changes into account in the revenues, we also include the quality level at which the previous unit of work was processed.

Decisions. At each milestone a quality level has to be chosen at which the upcoming unit of work is to be processed. Therefore, the set of decisions that can be taken in a state corresponds to the set of quality levels at which the application can run.

Transition probabilities. At milestones m_i we have probabilities p_{xy}^q for making a transition from a state x at milestone m_i to a state y at the next milestone m_{i+1}, if decision q is taken in state x, i.e., if quality level q is chosen at milestone m_i to process the upcoming unit of work. Let random variable X_q denote the time required to process one unit of work in quality level q (the distribution functions for X_q can be derived experimentally). To compute the probabilities p_{xy}^q, we express ρ_{i+1} in ρ_i by

$$\rho_{i+1} = \left(\rho_i + 1 - \frac{X_q}{b}\right)\Bigg|_{[0,\rho^{\max}]} \tag{14.1}$$

where we use the notation

$$\lambda|_{[0,\rho^{\max}]} = \begin{cases} 0 & \text{if } \lambda < 0 \text{ using the conservative approach} \\ \lambda + \lceil -\lambda \rceil & \text{if } \lambda < 0 \text{ using the skipping approach} \\ \lambda & \text{if } 0 \le \lambda \le \rho^{\max} \\ \rho^{\max} & \text{if } \lambda > \rho^{\max} . \end{cases}$$

Unfortunately, not ρ_i, but only the progress interval corresponding to ρ_i is known, as this is kept for state x. Therefore we approximate ρ_i in (14.1) by the lower bound of the corresponding progress interval, which is a worst-case approximation. Clearly, the higher the number of progress intervals, the better the modeling of the transition probabilities becomes, as the approximated values for ρ_i move closer to their real values.

Revenues. At milestones m_i we have revenues r_x^q for taking a decision q in a state x. We use revenues to implement the three problem objectives. First, the quality level at which units of work are processed should be as high as possible. To this end, we introduce a *utility function* $u(q)$, which returns a positive reward for taking decision q. This reward should be directly related to the perceived output quality of the application, running at quality level q. Second, the number of deadline misses should be as low as possible. Given ρ_i, the expected number of deadline misses before reaching milestone m_{i+1} is given by

$$\sum_{k=1}^{\infty} k \Pr\left(-k \le \rho_i + 1 - \frac{X_q}{b} < -k+1\right) .$$

We introduce a *deadline-miss function* $d(x,q)$, which returns this expected number of deadline misses multiplied by a (high) positive deadline-miss penalty. Finally, the number of quality-level changes should be as low as possible. This is achieved by introducing a *quality-level change function* $c(x,q)$, which returns a non-negative penalty for moving from the previously used quality level, which is part of state x, to quality level q. The total revenues are given by $r_x^q = u(q) - d(x,q) - c(x,q)$.

14.3.2   MDP instances

By varying the parameters in the MDP model, we can define different MDP instances. First, we have to choose the relative progress upper bound $\rho^{\max}$, which is usually given by the context of the application, and the number of progress intervals. As mentioned, the higher the number of progress intervals, the better the modeling of the MDP becomes. Second, we have to define the utility function, the deadline-miss function, and the quality-level change function. These revenue functions are the place to incorporate user perception knowledge. Third, to compute transition probabilities and revenues, we need the probability distributions for the random variables X_q. To derive these distributions, we use traces. A trace is a file that contains — for a specific application and for a specific sequence of units of work — per unit of work the processing time required for each of the quality levels at which the application can run. For the experiments described in Section 14.5, we derived traces by measuring actual processing times on a TriMedia platform [Slavenburg et al., 1996]. Finally, we also need to choose the budget b and the applied deadline-miss approach.

The MDP instances can be solved by a variety of dynamic programming related algorithms, such as *successive approximation, value iteration,* and *policy iteration* [Puterman, 1994; Sutton & Barto, 1998; Van der Wal, 1980]. Solving an MDP instance results in an optimal Markov policy (in short: policy), which maps states at milestones to quality-level decisions, independent of the number of the milestone. We solve MDP instances off-line, and our goal is to find a policy that results in the highest average revenue that is gained per state transition, i.e., that maximizes the average quality of the output as perceived by the user. In general, we find so-called *monotonic* policies, i.e., for each previously used quality level it holds that a higher relative progress results in an equal or higher quality-level decision. In the rare situation that a policy happens to be non-monotonic, we approximate it by a suitable monotonic one. We do not expect this to influence the quality of the policy significantly. For storing a monotonic policy, for each previously used quality level only the relative progress bounds at which the policy changes from a particular quality level to the next one have to be stored. A policy then has a space complexity of $O(|Q|^2)$, in which Q denotes the set of quality levels at which the application can run.

We solve MDP instances for varying values of the budget b. At run time, if budget b is used for processing, then a policy derived for b can be applied as follows to control the quality level. At each milestone, we can measure the relative progress of the application. Because the previously used quality level is also known at the milestone, the state of the application is known. Next, in the policy we look up the quality level to be chosen at the milestone. We refer to this control strategy as *static Markov control*. Clearly, this control strategy requires little run-time overhead.

14.4   Scaled budget control

In [Wüst & Verhaegh, 2001], we show by means of a simulation experiment that static Markov control performs well if the processing times of successive units of work are not related. However, in practice these processing times usually are related, due to content dependencies. For example, Figure 14.2 shows the processing times for decoding a sequence of MPEG-2 frames (units of work) in one quality level. In this figure, we identify short-term load fluctuations as, for instance, within the subsequence consisting of frames 1–100 (in short denoted by subsequence [1,100]) and the subsequence [101,310]. We refer to this kind of load fluctuations as *temporal load fluctuations*. If we compare both subsequences with each other then we also observe a long-term load fluctuation. We refer to this kind of load fluctuations as *structural load fluctuations*. Structural load fluctuations are, amongst others, caused by the varying complexity of video scenes. Whereas static Markov control handles temporal load fluctuations well, it fails in handling the structural load fluctuations. Therefore we propose in this section a control strategy that takes structural load fluctuations into account, named *scaled budget control*.

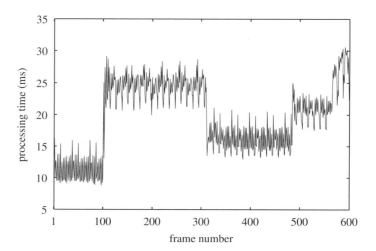

Figure 14.2.   The load for decoding a sequence of MPEG-2 frames in one quality level, showing both temporal and structural fluctuations.

14.4.1   Load complication

In Figure 14.2, the average processing time per frame over sequence [1,600] is about 19.4 ms. For subsequence [1,100], however, the average processing time per frame is about 11.1 ms, and for the subsequence [101,310] it is about 24.4 ms. If the sequence [1,600] is processed using a budget $b = 20$ ms, then applying a policy derived for $b = 20$ ms to control the quality level would result in sub-optimal quality-level decisions. In subsequence [1,100], the policy would be too pessimistic, choosing lower than necessary quality levels. In subsequence [101,310], the policy would be too optimistic, leading to more than expected deadline misses.

To deal with this problem, we take the structural load of the application into account. One way to do this is by bringing the structural load into the state space of the MDP. We define *load complication* as the ratio between the structural load and the expected load for a given quality level. In Figure 14.2, the expected load is given by the average load over the entire sequence, viz. 19.4 ms. A prerequisite for our approach is that the load complication is more or less independent of the quality level used. We need this condition because at run time we can measure the processing time of a unit of work for only one quality level (the one that has been chosen for processing the unit of work), which may be different for the successive units of work. According to measurements for a scalable MPEG-2 decoder, the condition seems fair. In Figure 14.2, the load complication for subsequence [1,100] is about $11.1/19.4 \approx 0.57$, and for subsequence [101,310] it is about $24.4/19.4 \approx 1.26$.

To be included in the state space, load complication should be discretized, just like relative progress. However, a problem is that by extending the state space with load complication, the MDP starts to suffer from the so-called *curse of dimensionality* [Bellman, 1957; Sutton & Barto, 1998]. This means that the number of states grows exponentially with the number of state variables. The state space would become too large for the MDP instances to be solvable in reasonable time. Another drawback is that a lot more measured data would be required to derive reliable statistics for the problem. So, this approach to take the structural load into account is undesirable.

14.4.2 Budget scaling

A better approach to take the structural load into account is *budget scaling*. Assume that the sequence of frames of Figure 14.2 is processed using a budget $b = 20$ ms. In subsequence [101,310], the load complication is about 1.26. Clearly, processing at a load complication of 1.26 using budget b is like processing at a load complication of 1, but using a budget that is 1.26 times smaller than its actual value. So, instead of applying a policy derived for $b = 20$ ms, we apply a policy derived for the scaled budget of 20 ms / 1.26 $\approx$ 15.9 ms. Similarly, in subsequence [1,100] we apply a policy derived for the scaled budget of 20 ms / 0.57 $\approx$ 35.1 ms. We call this approach to control the quality level *scaled budget control*. Note that we do not change the application's budget for processing, but only the budget for which we look up the policy.

Clearly, it is not feasible to pre-compute a policy for each possible (scaled) budget. Therefore, in practice we only derive policies for a small number of budgets, and we apply linear interpolation to approximate a policy for a scaled budget. For example, Figure 14.3 shows a space of policies for a certain previously used quality level, resulting from 21 MDP instances with budgets 20 ms, 21 ms, ..., 40 ms. If the relative progress at a milestone is 0.5, if the previously used quality level corresponds with the one used for the figure, and if we have a scaled budget of 27.5 ms at the milestone, then according to the figure we should choose quality level q_2. This is indicated by the '+' in the figure.

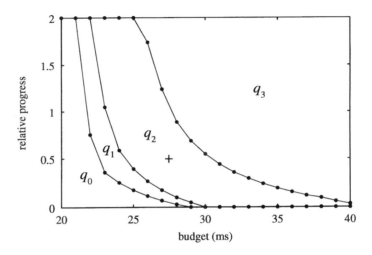

Figure 14.3.   A space of policies for a certain previously used quality level, resulting from 21 MDP instances with budgets 20 ms, 21 ms, ..., 40 ms.

14.4.3   Running complication factor

To compute the load complication during run time, for units of work $i = 1, 2, \ldots$ we introduce a *complication factor* cf_i. If unit of work i, processed at quality level $q(i)$, yields processing time $pt_i(q(i))$, then the complication factor cf_i is defined by

$$cf_i = \frac{pt_i(q(i))}{ept(q(i))},\tag{14.2}$$

where $ept(q(i))$ denotes the expected processing time for quality level $q(i)$. Clearly, the complication factor varies per unit of work and follows both the temporal and the structural load fluctuations. To make it follow only the structural load fluctuations, we filter out the temporal load fluctuations by computing a running average over the complication factors, in short called the *running complication factor.* To compute the running average we use a technique called *exponential recency weighted average* [Sutton & Barto, 1998]. Using an initial estimate $rcf_0 = 1$, the running complication factor for unit of work i is given by

$$rcf_i = rcf_{i-1} + \alpha * (cf_i - rcf_{i-1}), \qquad (14.3)$$

where α $(0 < \alpha \leq 1)$ is a constant step-size parameter. In this equation, each complication factor cf_j, $j = 1, \ldots, i$, has weight factor $\alpha(1 - \alpha)^{i-j}$, and rcf_0 has weight factor $(1 - \alpha)^i$. The weight factors decrease exponentially as i increases, and for a given i they add up to 1. The closer α is to zero, the more farsighted the running complication factor becomes. In case $\alpha = 1$, only the last encountered complication factor contributes to the running complication factor. By carefully choosing step-size parameter α, we can make the running complication factor reflect the structural load.

14.4.4 Trace normalization

As a final step we have to revisit the statistics that we use to compute the transition probabilities and revenues for MDP instances. Because we already take care of structural load fluctuations by means of budget scaling, we want to derive policies only using statistics of temporal load fluctuations. To this end, we first normalize the trace that we use to model MDP instances. Basically, we mimic the run-time effect of scaling and compensate for that in the statistics.

From a trace we create a normalized trace as follows. For each quality level q we first compute the average processing time over all units of work, denoted by $avg(q)$. The resulting values for $avg(q)$ are also used in (14.2) for the values of the expected processing times. Next, by running through the trace, for each quality level q we compute a running complication factor $rcf_i(q)$ over the processing times of all i units of work encountered so far. In (14.3), the running complication factor was based on the varying quality levels used on run time for the successive units of work. This was necessary, because at run time we can only measure the processing time for one quality level, which may vary for the successive units of work. Clearly, in case of a trace we do not have this problem, as a trace contains the processing times of each unit of work for *all* quality levels. Using initial estimates $rcf_0(q) = 1$, the running complication factor for quality level q is hence given by

$$rcf_i(q) = rcf_{i-1}(q) + \alpha * \left(\frac{pt_i(q)}{avg(q)} - rcf_{i-1}(q) \right), \qquad (14.4)$$

using the same step-size parameter α as we use in (14.3). We now create a normalized trace by dividing each processing time of the original trace by the running complication factor over all preceding units of work. To be more precise, the normalized processing time of the i-th unit of work for quality level

q is given by

$$npt_i(q) = \frac{pt_i(q)}{rcf_{i-1}(q)}. \tag{14.5}$$

Note that we use denominator $rcf_{i-1}(q)$ instead of $rcf_i(q)$, to match the run-time situation where at milestone i we only have statistics over the preceding $i-1$ units of work.

14.5 Simulation experiments

To assess the performance of scaled budget control, we have run simulation experiments. These experiments are based on processing-time measurements from a scalable MPEG-2 decoder running on a TriMedia platform [Slaven-burg et al., 1996]. Given an MPEG-2 coded video stream as input, the decoder sequentially decodes the frames of which the stream is made up. We let frames correspond with units of work. Frames can be decoded independently of each other in four different quality levels, in increasing quality order named $q_0, \ldots, q_3$. Using the decoder, we created traces for five MPEG-2 coded video streams: two movies (traces 'mov1', 141,573 frames, and 'mov2', 164,043 frames), a series of television fragments ('tv', 160,885 frames), a documentary ('doc', 74,997 frames), and a pop concert ('pop', 99,619 frames).

14.5.1 Parameters

We set the upper bound on relative progress ρ^{max} to 2, which presumes that the decoder can work ahead by at most two deadline periods. We choose 300 progress intervals, which is a good compromise between the solution quality and the computational complexity of the MDP instances; see [Wüst & Verhaegh, 2001]. Based on discussions with experts in the video domain, we define the revenue functions as follows. The utility function $u(q)$ is defined by $u(q_0) = 4$, $u(q_1) = 6$, $u(q_2) = 8$, and $u(q_3) = 10$. The deadline-miss penalty is set to 10,000, which roughly means that we allow at most one deadline miss per 1000 frames. The quality-level change function is defined by a penalty of zero for not changing the quality level at a milestone, penalties of 10, 100, and 1000 for increasing the quality by 1, 2, or 3 levels, respectively, and penalties of 50, 500, and 5000 for decreasing the quality by 1, 2, or 3 levels, respectively. For tractability reasons, we use the conservative approach to compute the transition probabilities. The evaluation of the strategies is nevertheless done by using the skipping approach in the simulations, which is more realistic for MPEG decoding. Recall that the conservative approach gives the worst-case relative progress adaptation that the skipping approach can give.

14.5.2 An off-line computed upper bound

Given a trace for a sequence of n units of work, we can off-line compute the optimal quality-level decisions that should be taken at run time to obtain a maximum average revenue, by means of dynamic programming [Bellman, 1957]. Using states as defined in Section 14.3, by running back to front through the trace for milestones $i = n - 1, \ldots, 0$ we compute for each possible state at the milestone the optimal quality-level decision to be taken in the state, taking into account the total revenue that is gained from also taking optimal quality-level decisions at successor states. Consequently, given the state of the application at milestone zero, we can compute the resulting average revenue. This average revenue is an upper bound on what we can attain, i.e., there is no control strategy that can result in a higher average revenue during run time for the given sequence of units of work. We use this optimal average revenue to evaluate the performance of on-line control strategies.

14.5.3 The experiments

In this section, we perform two experiments:

- an experiment to determine the best value for the step-size parameter α, and

- an experiment where we compare scaled budget control with other strategies.

To refer to the different control strategies, we introduce the following notation.

- $F(q)$ denotes the simple strategy of choosing the fixed quality level q at each milestone.

- $SMC(\tau)$ denotes static Markov control derived using the statistics of trace τ.

- $SBC(\tau,\alpha)$ denotes scaled budget control derived using the statistics of trace τ and step-size parameter α. We interpolate between policies computed for the budgets 5 ms, 6 ms, ..., 40 ms; see Section 14.4.2.

- UB denotes the upper bound on the average revenue that can be attained, as discussed in Section 14.5.2.

To get a feeling for the experiments, we first discuss strategy SBC(mov1, 0.4) applied in simulations on 'mov1'. Figure 14.4 shows the average revenue that we measured in the simulations for budgets 5 ms, 6 ms, ..., 40 ms. For small budgets, the average revenue is strongly negative, which is due to unavoidable deadline misses. The more budget is given to the application, the

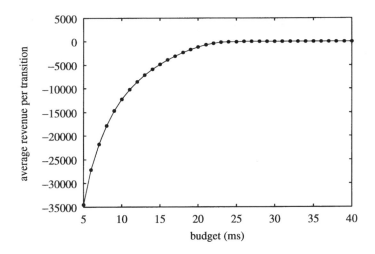

Figure 14.4.   Average revenue for SBC(mov1, 0.4) in simulations on 'mov1', as function of the budget.

better it is capable to meet deadlines and to process at higher quality levels. As the budget increases, the average revenue therefore converges to the maximum value of 10, which is due to the reward of 10 for choosing quality level q_3 at milestones, and the vanishing of both deadline misses and quality-level changes. Clearly, to obtain a positive average revenue, the budget should be chosen high enough.

Experiment 1: Choosing step-size parameter α.   To find a good range for step-size parameter α, we derived a strategy SBC(τ,α) for each trace τ and each α from the set $\{0.001, 0.01, 0.05, 0.1, 0.15, \ldots, 1\}$. Next, we applied each strategy SBC(τ,α) in simulations on the same trace τ for budgets 5 ms, 6 ms,..., 40 ms. Figure 14.5 shows the average revenue that we measured for the different strategies SBC(mov1,α) applied in simulations on 'mov1', for the budgets 28 ms, 29 ms, and 30 ms. The value of α that results in the highest average revenue depends on both the applied trace and the applied budget. Taking the simulations for all five traces into account, we find that the best value for α roughly lies between 0.05 and 0.15.

Experiment 2: Scaled budget control vs. other strategies.   To measure the performance of scaled budget control, we applied the four different strategies F(q), the five different strategies SMC(τ), and the 15 different strategies SBC(τ,0.05), SBC(τ,0.1), and SBC(τ,0.15) in simulations on each of the five traces. Figure 14.6 shows the average revenue that we measured for the strategies F(q_0), F(q_3), SMC(mov1), and SBC(mov1, 0.05) in simulations on

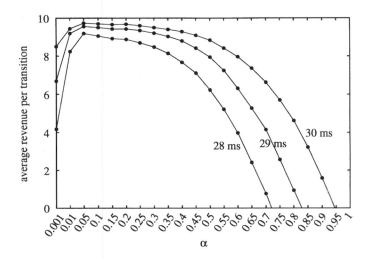

Figure 14.5. Average revenue for 22 strategies SBC(mov1,α) in simulations on 'mov1', for $b = 28\,\text{ms}$, $b = 29\,\text{ms}$, and $b = 30\,\text{ms}$.

'mov1', together with the off-line computed upper bound UB that can be attained on 'mov1'. As the budget increases, the average revenue for $F(q_0)$ converges to 4, which is caused by the reward of 4 for choosing quality level q_0 at milestones, the vanishing of deadline misses for increasing budgets, and the absence of quality-level changes. Similarly, the average revenue for strategy $F(q_3)$ converges to 10, but later, as a higher budget is needed to eliminate deadline misses. A partially better performance is obtained by static Markov control, and a much better performance is obtained by scaled budget control. Static Markov control still performs sub-optimal, which is due to not handling structural load fluctuations well. As aimed for, scaled budget control performs much better, and even reasonably close to the off-line computed optimum. For example, to achieve an average revenue of 9, in the optimum we need a processing budget of 26.9 ms. If we apply scaled budget control we need a slightly higher budget of 27.7 ms, but in case of static Markov control we need a much higher budget of 31.3 ms.

The results of all experiments are given in Table 14.1. Because we are interested in both a positive average revenue and a resource allocation that is lower than worst-case, for each trace we first identified a 'sensible' budget range. We define this sensible budget range as the range for which UB lies between 0 and 9.9. Each entry of Table 14.1 contains the average revenue over the given sensible budget range.

We observe that the fixed quality-level strategies perform poorly, as well as the static Markov control strategies. In case of static Markov control it may even be better to apply a strategy that is derived using the statistics of a dif-

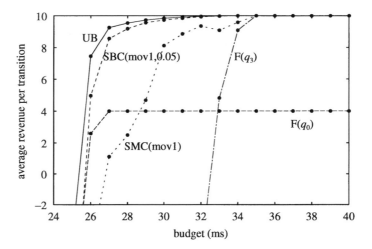

Figure 14.6.   Average revenue for different control strategies applied in simulations on 'mov1', compared to the upper bound UB.

ferent trace. For example, SMC(doc) outperforms SMC(mov2) in simulations on 'mov2'. A possible explanation for this is that a policy derived using the statistics of a different (processing demanding) trace may be more conservative, and therefore results in fewer deadline misses in structurally hard scenes. For the three different values of α we observe that scaled budget control performs close to the off-line computed upper bound. We furthermore see only small differences in the performance of scaled budget control if the statistics used to derive the policies are based on different source traces. This is a favorable result, as in practice the control strategy will be applied to video sequences that have not been observed when deriving it. In conclusion, we can state that scaled budget control performs very well.

14.6   Conclusion

In this chapter we presented the problem of controlling the quality level of a fixed-budget scalable media processing application during run time, in order to maximize the quality of the output as perceived by the user. This is achieved by simultaneously maximizing the quality level and minimizing the number of artifacts that result from both deadline misses and quality-level changes. We first modeled this problem as a finite Markov decision process. Next, based on this model, we introduced a dynamic quality-level control strategy named scaled budget control. The idea is to compensate for structural load fluctuations by computing a scaled budget and applying the corresponding policy. Policies are derived for varying budgets using statistics that only comprise temporal load

Table 14.1. The average revenue measured for different control strategies in simulations on the five traces over a sensible budget range.

simulation trace: *sensible budget range:*	mov1 26–30 ms	mov2 26–30 ms	tv 26–31 ms	doc 27–32 ms	pop 26–33 ms
UB	9.15	9.41	8.22	9.30	8.04
$F(q_0)$	3.72	3.90	3.17	3.84	3.11
$F(q_1)$	3.13	3.82	-1.43	3.62	0.98
$F(q_2)$	−10.31	−13.95	−47.75	−19.54	−30.41
$F(q_3)$	−265.20	−210.41	−416.29	−222.78	−779.23
SMC(mov1)	2.28	1.70	−12.00	−16.92	−20.51
SMC(mov2)	1.66	0.73	−13.95	−18.61	−29.24
SMC(tv)	6.83	7.19	2.51	0.65	−0.79
SMC(doc)	6.94	7.28	3.39	1.77	−1.49
SMC(pop)	6.46	6.95	3.86	3.65	2.80
SBC(mov1, 0.05)	8.40	8.41	7.24	7.03	6.28
SBC(mov2, 0.05)	8.46	8.57	7.38	7.35	6.18
SBC(tv, 0.05)	8.45	8.49	7.44	7.18	6.29
SBC(doc, 0.05)	8.47	8.69	7.44	8.02	6.07
SBC(pop, 0.05)	8.32	8.39	7.26	6.27	6.81
SBC(mov1, 0.1)	8.42	8.67	7.17	7.99	6.04
SBC(mov2, 0.1)	8.45	8.69	7.24	8.28	5.79
SBC(tv, 0.1)	8.49	8.75	7.45	8.23	6.12
SBC(doc, 0.1)	8.38	8.64	7.15	8.35	5.60
SBC(pop, 0.1)	8.46	8.73	7.38	8.14	6.88
SBC(mov1, 0.15)	8.35	8.58	6.86	8.23	5.47
SBC(mov2, 0.15)	8.33	8.60	7.00	8.34	5.24
SBC(tv, 0.15)	8.46	8.73	7.28	8.45	5.67
SBC(doc, 0.15)	8.21	8.50	6.78	8.19	5.09
SBC(pop, 0.15)	8.52	8.74	7.29	8.36	6.74

fluctuations. We interpolate between the derived policies to obtain a policy for a scaled budget.

In simulation experiments based on statistics of a scalable MPEG-2 decoder running on a TriMedia platform we found scaled budget control to perform well for step-size parameters α in the range 0.05–0.15. Using step-size parameters in this range, we found scaled budget control to perform close to off-line computed optima, standing out against static Markov control. More importantly, we observed no significant difference in the performance of scaled budget control if the statistics used to derive the policies are based on different source traces.

References

Baiceanu, V., C. Cowan, D. McNamee, C. Pu, and J. Walpole [1996]. Multimedia applications require adaptive CPU scheduling. In *Proc. IEEE RTSS Workshop on Resource Allocation Problems in Multimedia Systems*, Washington, DC.

Bellman, R.E. [1957]. *Dynamic Programming*. Princeton University Press, Princeton, NJ.

Bril, R.J., M. Gabrani, C. Hentschel, G.C. van Loo, and E.F.M. Steffens [2001a]. QoS for consumer terminals and its support for product families. In *Proc. International Conference on Media Futures (ICMF)*, Florence, Italy, pages 299–302.

Bril, R.J., C. Hentschel, E.F.M. Steffens, M. Gabrani, G.C. van Loo, and J.H.A. Gelissen [2001b]. Multimedia QoS in consumer terminals. In *Proc. IEEE Workshop on Signal Processing Systems (SIPS)*, Antwerp, Belgium, pages 332–343.

Gelissen, J.H.A. [2001]. The ITEA project EUROPA, a software platform for digital CE appliances. In *Proc. International Conference on Media Futures (ICMF)*, Florence, Italy, pages 157–160.

Hentschel, C., R. Bril, M. Gabrani, L. Steffens, K. van Zon, and S. van Loo [2001]. Scalable video algorithms and dynamic resource management for consumer terminals. In *Proc. International Conference on Media Futures (ICMF)*, Florence, Italy, pages 193–196.

Lan, T., Y. Chen, and Z. Zhong [2001]. MPEG2 decoding complexity regulation for a media processor. In *Proc. Fourth IEEE Workshop on Multimedia Signal Processing (MMSP)*, Cannes, France, pages 193–198.

Lee, C. [1999]. *On Quality of Service Management*. Ph.D. thesis, Carnegie Mellon University, Pittsburgh, PA.

Lee, C., J. Lehoczky, R. Rajkumar, and D. Siewiorek [1999]. On Quality of Service optimization with discrete QoS options. In *Proc. Fifth IEEE Real-Time Technology and Applications Symposium (RTAS)*, Vancouver, Canada, pages 276–286.

Peng, S. [2001]. Complexity scalable video decoding via IDCT data pruning. In *Digest of Technical Papers IEEE International Conference on Consumer Electronics (ICCE)*, Los Angeles, CA, pages 74–75.

Puterman, M.L. [1994]. *Markov Decision Processes: Discrete Stochastic Dynamic Programming*. Wiley Series in Probability and Mathematical Statistics. Wiley-Interscience, New York.

Slavenburg, G., S. Rathnam, and H. Dijkstra [1996]. The TriMedia TM-1 PCI VLIW mediaprocessor. In *Eigth Symposium on High-Performance Chips, Hot Chips 8*, Stanford, CA, pages 171–177.

Sutton, R.S., and A.G. Barto [1998]. *Reinforcement Learning: An Introduction*. MIT Press, Cambridge, MA.

Wal, J. van der [1980]. *Stochastic Dynamic Programming*. Ph.D. thesis, Mathematisch Centrum, Amsterdam, The Netherlands.

Wüst, C.C., and W.F.J. Verhaegh [2001]. Quality control for scalable media processing applications. Accepted for publication in *Journal of Scheduling, Special Issue of Selected Papers for the 2001 Philips Workshop on Scheduling and Resource Management*. http://www.extra.research.philips.com/publ/nl-ms/r-21.339.pdf.

Chapter 15

SAVING ENERGY
IN PORTABLE MULTIMEDIA STORAGE

Jan Korst, Joep van Gassel, and Ruud Wijnands

Abstract   We consider a number of strategies for saving energy in portable multimedia disk-based storage devices, including adaptive strategies for putting a disk in standby mode and allocation strategies that aim at storing frequently used files in the outer zones of a disk. In addition, we examine how best-effort requests can be interleaved with real-time requests, in such a way that they interfere as little as possible with the energy saving strategies.

   We provide computational results to give an indication of the energy savings that can be expected from these strategies.

Keywords   Mobile storage, disk spin-down policies, power usage, energy management.

15.1   Introduction

In ambient intelligent environments portable storage devices will play an important role in storing multimedia as well as personal profile data. They offer consistent, easy access to personal multimedia content whether at home or on the move. They will dynamically link to ad-hoc networks, for easy information exchange.

Portable storage devices that only contain solid-state memory are severely restricted in storage capacity and are relatively expensive in terms of cost per Mbyte. Disk-based storage remains an interesting alternative, especially for the storage of video data, as even 1 Gbyte of memory is not enough to store half an hour of 6 Mbit/s video. Magnetic and optical disks offer a large storage capacity at a low cost per Mbyte.

For mobile storage devices, low power consumption is of utmost importance, since battery life is one of the key differentiating features of such products. Magnetic and optical disks may account for a substantial part of the total energy usage. Consequently, it is important to use a disk intelligently by saving energy whenever possible. A well-known strategy that is often used in current

W. Verhaegh et al. (eds.), Algorithms in Ambient Intelligence, 277-290.
© 2004 *Kluwer Academic Publishers. Printed in the Netherlands.*

MP3-players is to repeatedly buffer enough data in solid-state memory to be able to put the disk in standby mode, i.e., the mode where it stops spinning, for several minutes. We will discuss how this basic standby strategy can be adapted to cases where the disk is used for handling multiple variable-bit-rate streams. In addition, for magnetic disks and optical disks that have a constant angular velocity, reading a file from the outside of the disk will cost only 50% to 70% of the energy required to read the file from the inside of the disk. Hence, energy-aware allocation strategies lead to additional energy savings.

Whereas strategies for saving energy are well-studied for portable devices in general, the case of multimedia storage seems to have received little attention in the literature thus far. Adaptive power management has been considered extensively for magnetic disks in notebook computers, see e.g. Douglish & Marsh [1993], Douglish et al. [1994, 1995], and Li et al. [1994]. But the solutions proposed in that area seem less suited for real-time multimedia applications, because they are not geared to the special character of streaming media. For a more recent overview of energy management strategies, we refer to Lorch & Smith [1998].

The aim of this paper is to give an overview of the possible strategies for using disks in an energy-efficient way. The remainder of this paper is organized as follows. In Section 15.2 we first consider how we can model streams and disks. Next, in Section 15.3 we discuss different standby strategies. In Section 15.4 we consider how best-effort requests can be integrated in such a way that they interfere as little as possible with the standby strategy. In Section 15.5 we describe different strategies for allocating data on disk in order to save energy. In Section 15.6 we provide a number of computational results to give an indication of how much energy can be saved. Finally, in Section 15.7 we end with conclusions.

15.2 Modeling streams and disks

In this section, we consider how streams and disks can be modeled. In particular, we consider both constant-bit-rate and variable-bit-rate streams.

Streams. An audio/video stream is stored on disk in a digital, compressed form and often has a variable bit rate. A stream i is characterized by a play-out rate $r_i(t)$, for $t \in [0, l_i]$, where l_i gives the duration of the corresponding audio/video content. In this paper, we consider two types of streams, constant-bit-rate (CBR) and variable-bit-rate (VBR) streams. For CBR streams we have $r_i(t) = r_i$ for all $t \in [0, l_i]$. For VBR streams we do not assume complete knowledge on $r_i(t)$. Instead, we only assume an upper bound $r_i^{\max}$ to be known with $r_i^{\max} \geq r_i(t)$ for all $t \in [0, l_i]$.

Disks. The focus in this paper is on magnetic disks. Similar standby strategies can be derived for optical disks. For a general introduction to the working of magnetic disks, we refer to Ruemmler & Wilkes [1994]. The rate at which data is read from or written to disk is given by r_{disk}. Except in Sections 15.5 and 15.6, this rate will be assumed constant, irrespective of the location where the data is read or written.

With respect to its power use, a magnetic disk can be in several modes, which can be subdivided into two global states: active or inactive. When active, the disk reads, writes, performs seeks, or encounters rotational delays. When inactive, the disk can be either in idle or in standby mode. When idle, the disk is spinning and waiting for access requests to arrive. With respect to energy usage, one sometimes distinguishes multiple idle modes. These modes differ in whether the disk heads are loaded or unloaded, and whether some parts of the electronics are powered on or off. In order not to complicate our analysis, we assume that there is only one idle mode. When the disk is in standby mode, the disk is not spinning. In our analysis, the time for spinning down and spinning up the disk is considered part of the time that the disk is in standby mode.

In addition, we make the following simplifications. We assume that all streams are playback streams and that seek times and rotational delays are zero. In practice, they do take time, obviously, but compared to the standby times that typically amount to at least a minute, they are negligibly small. Furthermore, we assume that the power usage of memory required for buffering is small compared to the power usage of the disk [Lorch & Smith, 1998].

15.3 Standby strategies

In this section we first discuss how the basic standby strategy can be adapted to the case where a disk has to handle multiple data streams, assuming that the refilling of single buffers is not preempted. The global objective in applying these standby strategies is to maximize the average energy saved per time unit. Throughout this paper, we assume that each stream is given a separate buffer.

In Section 15.3.1, we first handle the case where streams have a constant bit rate. In Section 15.3.2 the standby strategy is adapted to variable-bit-rate streams. In that case, the strategy repeatedly tries to postpone the time at which the disk has to spin up again, based on updated information on the buffer fillings. In Section 15.3.3, we examine how energy saving can be further improved if refilling is carried out preemptively.

15.3.1 Standby strategies for CBR streams

Suppose we have n constant-bit-rate streams, numbered $1, 2, \ldots, n$. The buffers of the streams are repeatedly refilled in a round-robin fashion, i.e., in a fixed order, say, first stream 1, then stream 2, etc. After refilling the buffers, the disk is put in standby mode. Figure 15.1 gives the buffer filling as a function of time for two streams 1 and 2 with $r_2 = 2r_1$.

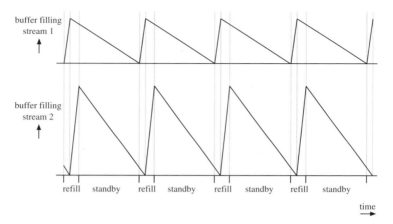

Figure 15.1. The buffer filling of two CBR streams as a function of time. After refilling both buffers, the disk goes into standby mode.

For stream i, the buffer filling increases at a rate $r_{\text{disk}} - r_i$ during refilling, and it decreases at a rate r_i otherwise. Let the size of the buffer for stream i be given by b_i, then the time that is required to refill the buffer of stream i is given by $b_i/(r_{\text{disk}} - r_i)$ and the time that it takes to empty the buffer again is given by b_i/r_i. To optimally use the memory that is available for buffering, we must have for each pair i, j of streams that

$$\frac{b_i}{r_{\text{disk}} - r_i} + \frac{b_i}{r_i} = \frac{b_j}{r_{\text{disk}} - r_j} + \frac{b_j}{r_j}. \tag{15.1}$$

Otherwise, some buffers will have to be refilled before they are empty, if underflow for others is to be avoided. Note that (15.1) implies that the buffer sizes are *not* proportional to the respective bit rates; cf. Korst et al. [1998]. For a stream i with rate $r_i > r_{\text{disk}}/2$, we even observe that the required buffer size b_i decreases when r_i increases; see Figure 15.2.

Now, let us first determine whether or not we actually save energy by repeatedly putting the disk in standby mode. If we put the disk in standby mode, then extra energy will be needed to spin down the disk at the start of a standby interval and extra energy will be needed to spin up the disk again at the end of the standby interval. Energy will only be saved if this extra energy is offset by the energy that is saved during the time that the disk is in standby mode. Otherwise, the disk should preferably remain in idle mode.

Let P_{idle} and P_{standby} be the power usage of the disk in idle and standby modes, respectively, where clearly $P_{\text{standby}} < P_{\text{idle}}$. The energy that is saved per time unit if the disk is in standby mode instead of in idle mode is given by

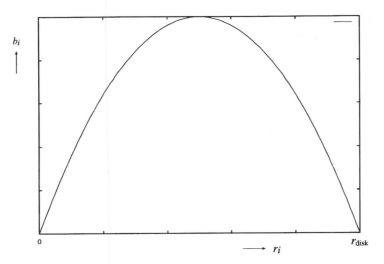

Figure 15.2. For a fixed duration of the refill-standby cycle, the required buffer size b_i as a function of the bit rate r_i is shown.

$\Delta P = P_{\text{idle}} - P_{\text{standby}}$. Furthermore, let E be the extra energy that is required for spinning the disk down and up once, and let p be the duration of a complete refill-standby cycle. The amount of data that is read for stream i in each cycle is given by $p \cdot r_i$. Hence, the total amount of data read in a cycle is given by $p \cdot \sum_j r_j$. Reading this amount of data requires $p \cdot \sum_j r_j / r_{\text{disk}}$ time. The time that remains for standby per cycle is thus given by $p - p \cdot \sum_j r_j / r_{\text{disk}} = p \cdot (1 - \sum_j r_j / r_{\text{disk}})$. Hence, the total amount of energy saved when in standby mode for one cycle is thus given by $p \cdot (1 - \sum_j r_j / r_{\text{disk}}) \cdot \Delta P$ and the break-even point is obtained if this amount equals E. We can now prove the following theorem.

Theorem 15.1. *Let m be the amount of memory that is available for buffering, which is optimally divided over the streams, then putting the disk in standby mode saves energy if and only if*

$$m > \frac{\sum_j r_j \cdot (r_{\text{disk}} - r_j)}{r_{\text{disk}} - \sum_j r_j} \cdot \frac{E}{\Delta P}. \tag{15.2}$$

Proof. Since the amount m of memory is optimally divided over the streams, we have $p = b_i / r_i + b_i / (r_{\text{disk}} - r_i)$ for each stream i. In other words, $p = b_i \cdot \alpha_i$ for each stream i, where $\alpha_i = r_{\text{disk}} / (r_i \cdot r_{\text{disk}} - r_i^2)$. As $m = \sum_j b_j$, we have $m = p \cdot \sum_j \alpha_j^{-1}$. Hence, the time that remains for the disk to be in standby mode can be rewritten as $m / \sum_j \alpha_j^{-1} \cdot (1 - \sum_j r_j / r_{\text{disk}})$. During this time we save ΔP per time unit. Hence, energy is saved if and only if $\Delta P \cdot m / \sum_j \alpha_j^{-1} \cdot (1 - \sum_j r_j / r_{\text{disk}}) > E$. Rewriting the above gives (15.2). $\qquad\square$

Note that we did not assume anything about the time that is required to spin down the disk and the time to spin up the disk. Clearly, the disk has to spin up in time, to be able to start refilling at the appropriate time. We assume that the break-even point is large enough to include the spin-down and spin-up times.

15.3.2   Standby strategy for VBR streams

We next consider the case in which we have n VBR streams, where for each stream i we only know an upper bound $r_i^{\max}$, with $r_i^{\max} \geq r_i(t)$ for all $t \in [0, l_i]$. The buffer sizes can be chosen in a similar fashion as explained in the previous section, where in the calculations we use the upper bound $r_i^{\max}$, instead of the constant rate r_i.

On average, the bit rate of a stream i will be smaller than $r_i^{\max}$. It therefore makes sense not to stick to a fixed duration of the standby time but, instead, check the buffer fillings again just before spinning up is originally scheduled. Based on these buffer fillings we update the latest possible refill intervals. In this way, the standby time can usually be extended. Analyzing the buffer fillings at a time t, we determine a new point in time at which refilling should start as follows. Given the buffer filling $f_i(t)$ of stream i at time t, the *latest possible refill interval* for stream i at time t is defined as

$$\left[t + \frac{f_i(t)}{r_i^{\max}}, \quad t + \frac{f_i(t)}{r_i^{\max}} + \frac{b_i}{r_{\text{disk}} - r_i^{\max}} \right),$$

assuming that the rate of stream i will be equal to $r_i^{\max}$ before and during this interval. Note that the latest possible refill intervals for the different streams may overlap in time and gaps may occur in between them, due to the variability of the bit rates.

To avoid overlap or to remove gaps, some of the refill intervals will have to be advanced, i.e., scheduled earlier in time. By advancing a refill interval, less data will have to be read, and consequently, the length of the refill interval decreases. The following theorem explains how the length of a refill interval is affected.

Theorem 15.2. *If a given refill interval $[s_i, e_i)$ is advanced by decreasing its end time e_i by δ, then the duration of the refill interval will decrease with an amount*

$$\delta \cdot \frac{r_i^{\max}}{r_{\text{disk}}}.$$

Alternatively, if the refill interval is advanced by decreasing its start time s by δ, then the duration of the refill interval will decrease with an amount

$$\delta \cdot \frac{r_i^{\max}}{r_{\text{disk}} - r_i^{\max}}.$$

Proof. Let us first prove the last result. If s_i is advanced by δ time units, then an amount of $\delta \cdot r_i^{\max}$ is in the buffer when refilling starts. Consequently, the refill time will decrease with an amount $\delta \cdot r_i^{\max}/(r_{\text{disk}} - r_i^{\max})$.

Alternatively, if e_i is advanced by δ time units, then the decrease in the refill interval can be proved by a simple geometric argument. The time t at which refilling starts will be in between $s_i - \delta$ and s_i, more precisely t is the point at which the line starting at $(s_i - \delta, 0)$ with slope $r_{\text{disk}} - r_i^{\max}$ crosses the line that ends at $(s_i, 0)$ with slope $-r_i^{\max}$. Consequently, t is given by $s_i - \delta \cdot (r_{\text{disk}} - r_i^{\max})/r_{\text{disk}}$, and the decrease in the refill interval can be expressed as $t - (s_i - \delta)$ which is given by $\delta \cdot r_i^{\max}/r_{\text{disk}}$. $\qquad\qquad\qquad\qquad\qquad\qquad\square$

Note that for avoiding overlap the end time of a refill interval has to be decreased by a given amount, while for removing gaps the start time of a refill interval has to be decreased by a given amount. Figure 15.3 gives an example of an advanced refill interval. Figure 15.4 gives an example where in the top part the latest possible refill intervals are given for streams 1, 2, 3, and 4.

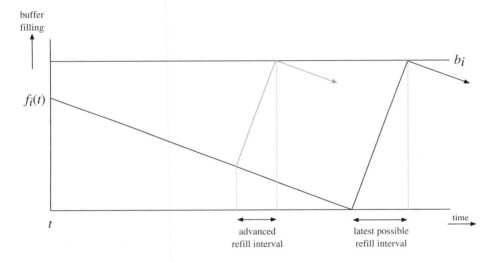

Figure 15.3. The latest possible refill interval, and an advanced alternative are shown, based on the buffer filling at time t, and assuming that stream i is played back at a rate $r_i^{\max}$.

The objective in ordering the refill intervals is to extend the current standby time as long as possible, i.e., to order the refills such that the first refill is started as late as possible. This gives the following problem statement.

Definition 15.1 (Refill ordering problem). *Given are a disk with rate r_{disk} and a set n of streams, where for each stream i the maximum bit rate is given by $r_i^{\max}$, and the latest possible refill interval is given by $[s_i, e_i)$, find an ordering of the refill intervals, such that refilling is started as late as possible.* $\qquad\square$

It can be shown that the refill ordering problem is NP-hard in the strong sense. This can be shown by a reduction from the problem of non-preemptively scheduling tasks with release dates and deteriorating processing times; see Cheng & Ding [1998] and Alidaee & Womer [1999]. The analogy is straight-forward if you realize that an arbitrary instance of the refill ordering problem can be transformed into an instance of the above scheduling problem, by sim-ply reversing time. Consequently, no algorithm with a computation time poly-nomial in n exists that solves the refill ordering problem to optimality, unless P = NP. In practice, for mobile storage devices, the number of streams will be quite small, and consequently an exhaustive search to solve the problem is usually acceptable. To quickly determine a reasonable lower bound on the time that refilling will have to start, we next propose the following heuristic algorithm, called Back-Front-Back (BFB), to schedule the refills for the var-ious streams. The primary objective is to start refilling the buffers as late as possible, while guaranteeing that buffer underflow is avoided.

The BFB algorithm proceeds in two steps.

1. In the first step, the latest possible refill intervals are examined from back to front, i.e., in order of non-increasing end time. In the example of Figure 15.4, first stream 4, then stream 3, etc. If a refill interval $[s_i, e_i)$ starts earlier than the end of a preceding refill interval $[s_j, e_j)$, i.e., if $e_j > s_i$, then this preceding refill interval is advanced over a time $e_j - s_i$. By starting a refill earlier, less data will have to be read, so this will decrease the length of the refill interval, as discussed above. The result is shown in the middle part of Figure 15.4.

2. In the second step, the resulting refill intervals are again examined but now from front to back to remove any remaining gaps. These gaps have an adverse effect on the possible standby time, and they may grow in successive cycles if they are not deleted. So, we move all refill intervals behind a gap forward in time, again resulting in shorter refill intervals.

The result of this second step is shown in the bottom part of Figure 15.4.

Note that by removing gaps we have at the end of a refill batch, i.e., at the time that the disk is spinned down again, that buffers will be at least as full, since the time between ending the refill for a stream and spinning down the disk will not have increased and possibly decreased. Thus, removing gaps will generally increase the duration of the next standby interval.

The BFB algorithm can be repeatedly applied in a single refill-standby cy-cle. Based on updated information on the buffer fillings, the standby time can be repeatedly extended, until the expected remaining standby time approaches the time that is required for spinning up the disk. Each time the standby time is extended by the BFB algorithm, one can additionally try to further extend it with an exhaustive search.

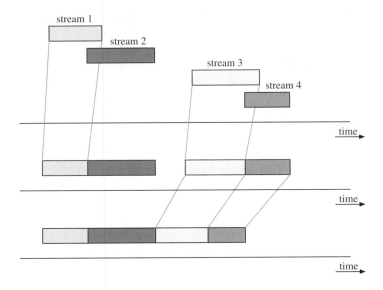

Figure 15.4. The successive steps in the ordering algorithm BFB.

15.3.3 Preemptive refilling

In the preceding Sections 15.3.1 and 15.3.2 we assumed that the buffers for the various streams are refilled one after the other. In addition, we assumed that refilling for one stream was continued until the buffer is completely filled. A disadvantage of this approach is that some of the buffers will not be completely filled at the start of a standby interval.

In this section, we examine what can be gained if we allow preemptive refilling. Assuming that seek times and rotational delays are zero, we can refill all buffers in parallel by adding small quantities to each of the buffers in a round-robin fashion. For convenience, we focus on CBR streams, but preemptions can be applied to VBR streams also.

Let us assume that the buffers are filled in such a way that they are completely filled at (approximately) the same time. In addition, we choose the buffer sizes in such a way that completely emptying the buffers requires the same time for all streams. Consequently, we choose $b_i = m \cdot r_i / \sum_j r_j$. The time that the disk can be in standby mode is thus given by $b_i/r_i = m/\sum_j r_j$.

At the end of the standby interval all buffers will be empty, and refilling for all streams is assumed to start simultaneously. To obtain that all buffers are filled again at the same time, the refill time must also be equal for all streams. Let β_i be the fraction of the disk rate r_{disk} that is spent on refilling the buffer for stream i, with $\sum_j \beta_j = 1$. To obtain that all buffers are refilled at the same time, we have $\beta_i = r_i/\sum_j r_j$. Consequently, the refill time is given by $m/(r_{\text{disk}} - \sum_j r_j)$.

Theorem 15.3. *For a given set of n streams, let f be the fraction of time that has to be spent on refilling, i.e., $f = \sum_j r_j/r_{\text{disk}}$. Then, by using preemptive refilling instead of non-preemptive refilling, the standby time can maximally increase by a factor*

$$\frac{1 - f/n}{1 - f}.$$

Proof.   The standby time for non-preemptive refilling is given by $m \cdot (r_{\text{disk}} - \sum_j r_j)/(\sum_j r_j(r_{\text{disk}} - r_j))$. Dividing $m/\sum_j r_j$ by this expression gives the fraction $\sum_j r_j(r_{\text{disk}} - r_j)/\sum_j r_j \cdot (r_{\text{disk}} - \sum_j r_j)$. This fraction is maximal if we have n identical streams, i.e., $r_j = f \cdot r_{\text{disk}}/n$ for each stream j. In that case, we get the required result.   □

Table 15.1 gives an indication of the increase that can be maximally obtained for $n = 2$ and $n \to \infty$.

Table 15.1.   The maximum attainable increase of a standby interval if we use preemptive refilling instead of non-preemptive refilling, for $n = 2$ and $n \to \infty$, for different values of f.

n	*maximum attainable increase of a standby interval (%)*								
	$f{=}0.1$	$f{=}0.2$	$f{=}0.3$	$f{=}0.4$	$f{=}0.5$	$f{=}0.6$	$f{=}0.7$	$f{=}0.8$	$f{=}0.9$	$f{\to}1$
2	5.6	12.5	21.4	33.3	50.0	75.0	116.7	200.0	450.0	∞
∞	11.1	25.0	42.8	66.7	100.0	150.0	233.3	400.0	900.0	∞

In practice, seek times and rotational delays are not zero. Consequently, the refill time will grow with a fraction that is (slightly) larger than that of the standby time. This may partly nullify the advantage of preemptive refilling.

15.4   Interleaving best-effort requests

The disk in the portable storage device will also be used for storing other types of data than audio/video files. Storing and retrieving these non-real-time types of data results in additional so-called best-effort requests to the disk. These best-effort requests have to be interleaved with the real-time requests that relate to record and playback of audio/video files. If individual best-effort requests are too large to be interleaved with the real-time requests, then obviously they have to be split up in smaller requests to guarantee uninterrupted record and playback of the streams.

If best-effort requests are sufficiently small, then they can be scheduled at times that the disk would otherwise be in standby mode. One straightforward approach to handle best-effort requests, is to postpone them until the end of a refill batch. Then, after completing the best-effort requests one can determine whether there is still enough time left before the next refill batch has to be started for putting the disk in standby mode. Alternatively, when the disk is in standby mode, they may be scheduled just before a refill batch.

Although best-effort requests do not impose strict deadlines on their completion, unnecessarily delaying them may in some cases adversely affect the responsiveness of the portable device as observed by the user. Whether this is the case depends on the exact type of request. For that reason, it makes sense to assign different priorities to the different types of best-effort requests. In that case, high-priority requests may immediately interrupt a standby interval, while low-priority may be postponed until just before or after a refill batch.

If the disk is spinned up to handle a high-priority best-effort request, then after completing the request, it usually makes sense to immediately start refilling the buffers again. Whether this is always the best strategy depends on the arrival distribution of best-effort requests and requires further study.

In addition, high-priority as wells as low-priority may be interleaved in a refill batch, provided that buffer underflow is guaranteed not to occur.

15.5 Energy-efficient allocation strategies

Experiments indicate that power usage when reading or writing does not depend on the location where data is read or written. But, since the transfer rate at the outermost zone may be 50% to 100% larger than at the innermost zone, we obtain that the energy used for reading or writing a file at the outermost zone may be 50% to 70% smaller than when read or written at the innermost zone. This offers an interesting additional source of energy saving.

Files that are frequently used when on the move should preferably be stored on the outer zones. Files that are used less frequently when on the move should be stored in the inner zones. Files that are frequently used but only when connected to the power supply, need not be stored on the outer zones.

In addition, files that are recorded when on the move, can first be stored on the outermost zones, to save energy. Later, when connected to a power supply, these files can possibly be moved to the inner zones, when they are accessed less often when on the move.

15.6 Computational results

To give an impression of the possible energy savings, we consider a number of settings and show how much energy can be saved in each of them. We restrict ourselves to non-preemptive refilling. Preemptive refilling would require a more detailed analysis, taking into account actual seek times and rotational delays.

We assume that we use a Toshiba MK1003GAL 1.8 inch disk drive, which has the following characteristics. The sustainable disk rate $r_{disk} = 72$ Mbit/s, i.e., the sustainable rate at the innermost zone of the disk. The sustainable rate at the outermost zone is 120 Mbit/s. The power consumption of writing, reading, idle and standby modes are given by $P_{write} = 1.4$ J/s, $P_{read} = 1.4$ J/s, $P_{idle} = 0.6$ J/s, and $P_{standby} = 0.2$ J/s. The energy for spinning down and spinning up is given by $E = 3.65$ J. The time required for spinning down and spinning up the disk is given by 0.6 s and 2.5 s, respectively. Hence, $\Delta P = 0.4$ J/s, and the break-even point is approximately 9 s.

Let us first assume that we want to play back a single CBR stream of 6 Mbit/s. If we only have one stream, then clearly for this stream we have $b_i = m$. For different values of m, we give in Table 15.2 lower and upper bounds on the energy saving that is realized by repeatedly putting the disk in standby mode, as a fraction of the energy usage when no standby is used. The lower bound is attained if the data is always read from the innermost zone; the upper bound is attained if the data is always read from the outermost zone. The duration of a refill-standby cycle scales linearly with m, and ranges from 11.6 s for $m = 8$ Mbyte to approximately 25 minutes for $m = 1$ Gbyte.

Table 15.2. For a single playback stream the fraction of energy that can be saved as a function of the available memory for buffering, both for reading from the innermost zone and reading from the outermost zone of the disk.

m (Mbyte)	energy reduction (%) (innermost zone)	energy reduction (%) (outermost zone)
8	8.0	8.6
16	31.5	34.0
32	43.2	46.7
64	49.1	53.0
128	52.1	56.2
256	53.5	57.8
512	54.3	58.6
1024	54.6	59.0
∞	55.0	59.4

Note that for $m \rightarrow \infty$, the energy reduction converges to

$$\frac{(1-f) \cdot (P_{idle} - P_{standby})}{(1-f) \cdot P_{idle} + f \cdot P_{read}},$$

where $f = \sum_j r_j / r_{\mathrm{disk}}$. If we have a VBR stream with $r_i^{\max} = 6$ Mbit/s, then the energy savings for a given memory size m are at least as high as given for a CBR stream, since the standby intervals will generally by larger. The actual savings greatly depend on the difference between $r_i^{\max}$ and the average bit rate.

Let us next see how much energy is saved if we have multiple streams. We assume that we have n CBR streams, each of 6 Mbit/s. Since we assume identical bit rates, the buffer for each stream will be given by m/n. Hence, the duration p of a refill-standby cycle is given by $m/(n \cdot r_{\mathrm{disk}} - n \cdot r_i) + m/(n \cdot r_i)$. Consequently, for a fixed amount m of memory, the cycle time p will be inversely proportional to n. Table 15.3 gives lower and upper bounds on the energy reduction for one up to five streams, for different memory sizes.

Table 15.3. For one up to five streams lower and upper bounds on the energy reduction as a function of the available memory for buffering are given, assuming that reading is only from the innermost or outermost zone of the disk, respectively.

m (Mbyte)	lower and upper bounds on energy reduction (%)				
	$n=1$	$n=2$	$n=3$	$n=4$	$n=5$
8	8.0–8.6	-	-	-	-
16	31.5–34.0	2.7–5.2	-	-	-
32	43.2–46.7	24.1–29.1	8.1–13.4	-	-
64	49.1–53.0	34.8–41.0	22.8–30.3	12.7–20.7	0.4–12.1
128	52.1–56.2	40.1–47.0	30.2–38.8	21.7–31.4	14.5–24.8
256	53.5–57.8	42.8–50.0	33.8–43.0	26.2–36.8	19.8–31.2
512	54.3–58.6	44.1–51.4	35.7–45.1	28.5–39.4	22.4–34.3
1024	54.6–59.0	44.8–52.2	36.6–46.2	29.6–40.8	23.7–35.9
∞	55.0–59.4	45.5–52.9	37.5–47.2	30.8–42.1	25.0–37.5

The standard firmware of the Toshiba disk drive switches from idle mode to low-power idle mode when no requests have been issued to the disk during 15 seconds. For the disk the power usage for low-power idle mode is 0.4 J/s. Comparing repeatedly going into standby mode with repeatedly going into low-power idle mode after 15 seconds, the lower and upper bounds on the energy reduction for $m \to \infty$ are 37.9–42.2%, 29.4–36.0%, 23.1–30.9%, 18.2–26.7%, and 14.3–23.1% for one up to five streams.

15.7 Conclusions

We have considered a number of strategies for saving energy in portable disk-based storage devices. Examples indicate that the savings can be substantial. The energy that can be saved depends on a number of parameters, of which the amount of memory that is available for buffering is an important one. In designing portable disk-based storage devices, it can be worthwhile to be generous in the amount of solid-state memory, since large memories will lead to more energy saving and longer battery lives. Further research is required, however, to trade these benefits against the additional cost and energy requirements of a large solid-state memory.

References

Alidaee, B., and N.K. Womer [1999]. Scheduling with time dependent processing times: Review and extensions. *Journal of the Operational Research Society*, 50:711–720.

Cheng, T.C.E., and Q. Ding [1998]. The complexity of scheduling starting time dependent tasks with release times. *Information Processing Letters*, 65:75–79.

Douglish, F., P. Krishnan, and B. Bershad [1995]. Adaptive disk spindown policies for mobile computers. *Proceedings 2nd USENIX Symposium on Mobile and Location Dependent Computers*, pages 121–137.

Douglish, F., P. Krishnan, and B. Marsh [1994]. Thwarting the power hungry disk. *Proceedings Winter 1994 USENIX Conference*, pages 293–306.

Douglish F., and B. Marsh [1993]. *Low Power Disk Management for Mobile Computers*. Technical Report MITL-TR-53-93, Matshushita Information Technology Laboratory.

IBM Corporation [1999]. Adaptive power management for mobile hard drives. Storage Systems Division, San Jose.

Korst, J., V. Pronk, P. Coumans, G. van Doren, and E. Aarts [1998]. Comparing disk scheduling algorithms for VBR data streams. *Computer Communication*, 21:1328–1343.

Lorch, J.R., and A.J. Smith [1998]. Software strategies for portable computer energy management. *IEEE Personal Communications*, June 1998, 60–73.

Ruemmler, C., and J. Wilkes [1994]. An introduction to disk drive modeling. *IEEE Computer*, 27:17–28.

Toshiba Corporation. 1.8 inch disk drives, MK1003GAL/MK2003GAH Product Specification.

Chapter 16

STORAGE OF VBR VIDEO CONTENT ON A MULTI-ZONE RECORDING DISK BASED ON RESOURCE USAGE

Verus Pronk

Abstract   We compare two disk storage algorithms for storing variable-bit-rate video content on a single, multi-zone recording disk, one based on track pairing (TP) and one based on resource usage. TP is a storage strategy that exploits the average transfer rate of the disk to serve playout processes, whereas resource-usage-based storage (RUBS) exploits the bit rate, playout time, size, and popularity of individual programs to store them at appropriate places on disk to realize high transfer rates.

Including a popularity measure into the problem context builds upon recent trends in ambient-intelligence. Emerging recommender systems aim to rank content according to popularity, so that actual popularity data becomes readily available.

We show that the problem of storing video programs for achieving an optimal RUBS strategy is NP-hard in the strong sense, which implies that polynomial time-bounded solutions are not likely to be found. We propose an $O(n \cdot \log n)$ heuristic algorithm with a remarkably good performance in practice. We then show that RUBS can outperform TP in terms of the maximum number of simultaneously sustainable playout processes.

Keywords   MZR disk, multi-zone recording, constant density, DVD, variable bit rate, video content, resource usage, popularity, ambient intelligence, NP-hard.

16.1   Introduction

The magnetic disk is considered an appropriate mass storage device for use in video-on-demand (VoD) servers to store and efficiently retrieve multiple video programs simultaneously by a number of clients. The storage capacity of a single disk suffices to store tens of digitized and high-quality MPEG-

W. Verhaegh et al. (eds.), Algorithms in Ambient Intelligence
© 2004 *Kluwer Academic Publishers. Printed in the Netherlands.*

encoded variable-bit-rate (VBR) programs, and the rate at which data can be read from disk enables tens of clients to view these programs simultaneously and independently.

When a client decides to view a program, a playout process is started that repeatedly has a data block from this program transferred from disk to a solid-state memory buffer. The speed at which this should happen and the size of the data blocks depend amongst others on the program and on specific settings of the server. This speed should be sustainable to allow uninterrupted playout for the duration of the program by preventing the buffer from under- and over-flowing. The buffer is emptied at a corresponding speed and the data is sent onward to the client, possibly via an access and in-home network. This speed is typically in the order of 5-7 Mbit/s. Besides linear viewing, pausing, and jumping to another scene or part of the movie, trick modes are supported such as reverse viewing, slow motion in either direction and fast reverse/forward at several speeds. Depending on the popularity of a specific program, more than one client may want to see the same program at more or less the same time. This results in a corresponding number of independent playout processes.

Multi-zone recording (MZR) disks are characterized by a transfer rate that depends on the position of the disk head. Data stored near the inner edge of the disk surface are read at a lower rate than data stored near the outer edge. This can be exploited by appropriately storing programs on disk to achieve high transfer rates on average. This chapter presents a storage strategy that aims to realize this. After providing more background on the storage problem, we give an outline of the remainder of this chapter.

16.2   Background

The physical properties of a state-of-the-art disk result in a variable transfer rate at which data is read from (or written to[1]) disk, depending on where the disk head is reading on the disk surface. This results from the constant angular velocity at which a disk rotates and the fact that tracks near the inner edge contain less data than tracks near the outer edge. Typical values are 200 Mbit/s near the inner edge to 400 Mbit/s near the outer edge. Existing disks usually employ multiple zones, in each of which the transfer rate is constant. A zone is a set of contiguous tracks. These multi-zone recording (MZR) disks aim to approximate the ideal situation of a constant-density disk, which is characterized in that the transfer rate decreases linearly as a function of the track number from the outer to the inner edge of the disk surface. See Ruemmler & Wilkes [1994] for an extensive treatment of magnetic-disk modeling.

---

[1] We will discard the difference between reading and writing because of their similarities.

The disk can be considered as a resource that is to be shared among a number of playout processes. Simultaneously sustaining a number of playout processes requires an admission control and a disk scheduling algorithm to guarantee the quality of service required by each of the admitted processes. See Korst et al. [1998] for an overview of disk scheduling algorithms.

Often, the so-called minimum sustainable transfer rate (mSTR), is used to perform admission control with deterministic quality guarantees of new playout processes. The mSTR corresponds to reading data near the inner edge of the disk. Reading at the mSTR can at all times be guaranteed. As an example, a disk with an mSTR of 200 Mbit/s can simultaneously sustain $\lfloor 200/6 \rfloor = 33$ playout processes of 6 Mbit/s each. For reference, the maximum sustainable transfer rate is denoted by MSTR and is attained when reading data near the outer edge of the disk.

To improve the efficiency of reading data from disk, Birk [1995] introduced a storage strategy called *track pairing* (TP). TP is a strategy whereby each data block is split into two sub-blocks. One sub-block is stored closer to the outer edge of the disk, whereas the other is stored closer to the inner edge. The sizes of the sub-blocks and their positions on disk are such that they require an equal reading time and reading two pairing sub-blocks results in a constant and significantly larger transfer rate than the mSTR[2]. This rate is called the average sustainable transfer rate (ASTR) and can also be used to provide deterministic quality guarantees.

Besides transferring data, the disk also performs switch operations to move the disk head from one data block on disk to the next. During these switch operations, data cannot be read, and thus this is overhead. Although this switching overhead can be made arbitrarily small by reading sufficiently large data blocks and need not significantly influence the admission control algorithm, in practical situations, it is taken into account to keep buffer sizes and corresponding response times at an acceptable level. As a result, practical admission control algorithms take the transfer rate as well as the switching overhead characteristics into account.

In this chapter, we introduce an alternative storage strategy, called resource-usage-based storage (RUBS) and show that finding an optimal RUBS strategy is NP-hard in the strong sense. RUBS makes use of several parameters associated with each program, i.e. its bit rate, duration, size, and popularity, to store a set of programs on disk. Where the bit rate and size of a program are often available or can be easily calculated or imposed during compression, the expected duration and in particular the popularity may be obtainable from complementary systems. In an ambient-intelligence environment, it is conceivable

---

[2]For MZR disks, TP is in general slightly more complicated than for constant-density disks, but we do not consider this any further.

that recommender functionality is available that tracks client watching behavior. These recommender systems could provide the necessary additional input, and could even collaborate with a program storage system to make intelligent decisions on which programs to store and which not. These issues, however, are considered outside the scope of this chapter.

We assume that linear and reverse viewing, pausing, and jumping are the predominant modes of operation, and that the remaining trick modes are used sporadically, as is typically the case in a VoD context. We show that, under several simplifying assumptions, RUBS can significantly outperform TP in terms of the maximum number of simultaneously sustainable playout processes.

The remainder of this chapter is organized as follows. In Section 16.3, we formalize the problem of finding an optimal RUBS strategy and investigate its complexity. Section 16.4 discusses related work. We provide a heuristic algorithm in Section 16.5 and assess its performance by simulation. In Section 16.6, we step away from the general case and we compare TP with RUBS with respect to the maximum number of simultaneously sustainable playout processes under a number of assumptions, most notably concerning the popularity of individual programs. In that same section, we also consider the issue of response times. Then, in Section 16.7, we present simulation results, adding the statistical nature of client requests. Finally, in Sections 16.8 and 16.9, we make some concluding remarks and provide directions for future research.

16.3   Problem definition

Informally, the problem we consider is how to store a number n of programs on disk such that disk resource usage is optimized. To this end, each program $i = 1, 2, \ldots, n$, is assumed to be characterized by its bit rate r_i, duration d_i, popularity γ_i, and size s_i. The bit rate r_i corresponds to the sustainable playout speed and is typically based on the maximum average frame size, computed over any k successive frames, whereby k is relatively small. See Dengler, Bernhardt & Biersack [1996]. It may alternatively be based on bit-rate smoothing algorithms, see Feng & Rexford [1999]. Bit-rate smoothing algorithms are used to achieve efficient transmission of VBR data across a network. As such, the bit rate of a program is generally much smaller than its peak rate, determined by a maximum-size frame, but also generally larger than its average rate. The bit rate can be used to provide deterministic quality guarantees.

The duration d_i typically expresses the linear playout time of the entire program, but could alternatively describe the average playout time of an associated playout process in case, e.g., jumping and replaying is performed often. The popularity γ_i is given as the fraction of the total number of client requests per unit time for this program, and the size s_i gives the number of bits of the file in which the program is stored. Note that for VBR program i it generally holds that $r_i > s_i/d_i$, although this is not used in the remainder of this chapter.

When a program i has been stored on disk, a transfer rate R_i can be associated to this program that expresses the minimum rate at which a data block from this program is retrieved from disk. It corresponds to the transfer rate that is attained when reading data from this program that is stored closest to the inner edge of the disk. Note that, when a number of programs are to be stored on disk, the transfer rate R_i of program i depends on the overall allocation of storage space to the individual programs.

For a playout process, the actual transfer rate that is guaranteed may increase during the lifetime of the process, such as when the program is viewed linearly and reading the program from disk is performed from its innermost location outwards. Furthermore, in such a situation, the bit rate may likewise decrease as the program is being viewed. We do not take these complicating issues further into account, but instead allow increased flexibility in viewing a program.

When a playout process is started for program i, the disk has to allocate to this process at least a fraction r_i/R_i of its time available for reading for (an average of) d_i time units. The value r_i/R_i can be considered as the momentary disk load for this process. Allocating less than r_i/R_i may eventually lead to a buffer underflow, as the playout process may consume data at a rate of r_i for an indefinite amount of time. Assuming a minimal, worst-case allocation, this leads to an allocation of a total of $(r_i \cdot d_i)/R_i$ of disk resource to this process. When an arbitrary playout process is started, the expected amount of disk resource to be allocated is thus given by

$$\sum_{i=1}^{n} \frac{r_i \cdot d_i}{R_i} \cdot \gamma_i. \tag{16.1}$$

It stands to reason that minimizing this value leads to an optimal use of the disk resource. The problem we thus consider is to find a storage strategy, such that (16.1) is minimized. It is easily seen that we only have to consider storage strategies where each program is stored contiguously on disk, as interleaving programs cannot reduce the individual transfer rates, and that storing all programs may start from the outer edge of the disk inwards and be contiguous.

(16.1) allows for an alternative interpretation as well. Consider an arbitrary moment in time, and assume that admission control ensures that the popularity of individual programs is reflected in the distribution of the playout processes over the programs[3]. For a randomly chosen playout process at that moment, the probability that it is associated to program i is proportional to $d_i \cdot \gamma_i$, and

---

[3] This need not be the case if certain programs are favored over others for, e.g., economical reasons.

r_i/R_i gives its momentary disk load, given that it is associated to this program. (16.1) thus gives the expected, momentary disk load for a randomly chosen playout process at an arbitrary moment in time. As a result, minimizing the value of (16.1) also implies that the expected number of simultaneous playout processes is maximized.

To simplify the appearance of (16.1), we introduce a weight $w_i = r_i \cdot d_i \cdot \gamma_i$ that is associated to program i. We are now ready to formally state our problem.

Definition 16.1 (The resource-usage-based storage problem (opt-RUBS)).
INSTANCE: A disk of size $S > 0$ with a non-increasing transfer rate function $R > 0$ and n programs numbered $1, 2, \ldots, n$, each program i being characterized by a weight $w_i > 0$ and size $s_i > 0$, with $\sum_{i=1}^{n} s_i = S$.
QUESTION: Find an ordering π of these programs on disk, such that the cost $C_I(\pi)$ is minimal, where I denotes the problem instance above, and $C_I(\pi)$ is defined as

$$C_I(\pi) = \sum_{i=1}^{n} \frac{w_{\pi(i)}}{R(\sum_{j=1}^{i} s_{\pi(j)})}. \qquad (16.2)$$

$\square$

Note that the function R is sufficiently general to cover MZR disks. The ordering π lists the order in which the programs are stored on disk: program $\pi(1)$ is stored first, starting at the outer edge, followed by program $\pi(2)$, et cetera. The transfer rate associated to program $\pi(i)$ is the transfer rate at the position on disk where the last bit of program $\pi(i)$ is stored, which is given by $R(\sum_{j=1}^{i} s_{\pi(j)})$.

We next prove that opt-RUBS is NP-hard in the strong sense. NP-hardness implies that no polynomial-time algorithm for solving the problem exists unless P=NP. We refer to Garey & Johnson [1979] for the extension 'in the strong sense' and for more background on the theory of computational complexity.

Theorem 16.1. *Opt-RUBS is NP-hard in the strong sense.*
Proof. An optimization problem is NP-hard (in the strong sense) if its decision variant is NP-complete (in the strong sense). We only show the NP-hardness. The decision variant K-RUBS of opt-RUBS is defined as follows. Given an instance I and a cost K, is there an ordering π such that $C_I(\pi) \leq K$?

K-RUBS is clearly in NP: given an instance I, a cost K, and an ordering π, it can be checked in polynomial time whether $C_I(\pi) \leq K$. We next present a reduction from PARTITION, a well-known NP-complete problem, see again Garey & Johnson [1979]. PARTITION is defined as follows. Given a set $U = \{1, 2, \ldots, n\}$ of n items, each item i being characterized by positive size a_i, is there a subset V of U such that $\sum_{i \in V} a_i = \sum_{i \in U \setminus V} a_i$?

Let $a_1, a_2, \ldots, a_n$ be an arbitrary instance of PARTITION, and let $U = \{1, 2, \ldots, n\}$. We assume a disk of size $S = \sum_{i=1}^{n} a_i$, containing two equally sized zones of size $S/2$ with transfer rates R_1 and R_2, with $R_1 > R_2$. We consider n programs, each program i being characterized by $w_i = s_i = a_i$, and we define $K = S/(2 \cdot R_1) + S/(2 \cdot R_2)$. We next prove that we have a yes-answer to the instance of PARTITION if and only if we have a yes-answer to this instance I of K-RUBS.

Assume that there is a $V \subseteq U$ such that $\sum_{i \in V} a_i = \sum_{i \in U \setminus V} a_i = S/2$. Then storing the programs in V in the outermost zone and the others in the innermost zone results in a cost equal to $\sum_{i \in V} a_i/R_1 + \sum_{i \in U \setminus V} a_i/R_2 = S/(2 \cdot R_1) + S/(2 \cdot R_2) = K$, so that this instance of opt-RUBS has a yes answer. Conversely, assume that there is an ordering π such that $C_I(\pi) \leq K$, i.e.

$$\sum_{i \in U} \frac{a_{\pi(i)}}{R(\sum_{j=1}^{i} a_{\pi(j)})} \leq \frac{S}{2 \cdot R_1} + \frac{S}{2 \cdot R_2}. \qquad (16.3)$$

Note that the left-hand side of this equation can be written as $\sum_{i \in V} a_i/R_1 + \sum_{i \in U \setminus V} a_i/R_2$, with $\sum_{i \in V} a_i \leq S/2$ for some $V \subseteq U$. This is because there are only two zones with transfer rates R_1 and R_2, respectively, and the total size of all programs with associated transfer rate R_1 is at most the size of the corresponding zone, which is $S/2$. Elementary calculus now shows that, as $R_1 > R_2$, (16.3) can only hold if $\sum_{i \in V} a_i \geq S/2$, so that $\sum_{i \in V} a_i = S/2$. In other words, the instance of PARTITION has a yes answer. Therefore, K-RUBS is NP-complete and hence opt-RUBS is NP-hard.

To show that opt-RUBS is NP-hard in the strong sense, a similar reduction from 3-PARTITION can be applied. The latter problem is known to be NP-hard in the strong sense, see again Garey & Johnson [1979]. □

In the case that all programs have equal size s, the problem becomes much simpler, i.e. it is in P, as is easily seen as follows. In this case, (16.2) simplifies to

$$C_I(\pi) = \sum_{i=1}^{n} \frac{w_{\pi(i)}}{R(i \cdot s)}.$$

In this equation, the two sets of numerators and denominators are fixed. Suppose we have two numerators w_1 and w_2 and two denominators R_1 and R_2, with $R_1 \geq R_2$. It readily follows that if $w_1 \geq w_2$, then $\frac{w_1}{R_1} + \frac{w_2}{R_2} \leq \frac{w_2}{R_1} + \frac{w_1}{R_2}$, so that storing the programs in order of non-increasing weight from the outer to the inner edge of the disk indeed yields an optimal ordering.

16.4 Related work

This section discusses some of the relevant literature on the problem of storing programs on one or more MZR disks to attain high transfer rates.

Ghandeharizadeh et al. [1996] also consider the problem of storing programs on a single MZR disk. The cost function they minimize is the expected time to read an entire program from disk, taking into account that a program may cross zone boundaries. They store programs contiguously from the outer to the inner edge of the disk in order of non-increasing popularity and prove that this is indeed optimal for this cost function.

For each program, they thus consider the total amount of resource, i.e. disk reading time, used by a playout process when it reads the entire program once. In a practical context, this measure is not necessarily representative of the amount of resource required or reserved to provide real-time guarantees to individual playout processes, although it can be used as a lower bound. Actually attaining or approaching this lower bound generally leads to complex admission control, (on-line) renegotiation, and disk scheduling algorithms, as resource requirements may vary over time. This holds in particular for VBR programs, but also for CBR programs that cross a zone boundary.

By allocating an explicit bit rate to a playout process for its entire lifetime to provide real-time guarantees greatly simplifies these tasks, but results in the cost function as given by (16.2).

Kang & Yeom [1999] propose a storage strategy called nearly constant transfer time (NCTT) whereby, for each program, a nearly constant transfer time is realized for each data block stored. They employ a constant time-length (CTL) approach for defining data block sizes, i.e. the size of each data block corresponds to a constant playout time. As part of their storage strategy, they use the popularity of the individual programs.

Kang & Yeom [2000] include multi-rate smoothing of VBR video with prefetching for storing programs on a single disk. They consider the popularity of programs and, in addition to the disk resource, they consider the memory resource restrictions.

Several papers consider generalizations to multiple disks, such as Kim, Lho & Chung [1997], Kim, Lim, Kim & Chung [1997] and Lho & Chung [1998], thereby considering bit rates and/or popularity for sorting and storing programs. Finally, Park, Kim & Chung [1999] consider the heterogeneous case where the MZR disks need not be identical to each other.

16.5   A heuristic algorithm

As opt-RUBS is NP-hard, it is useful to consider heuristic algorithms that produce good, not necessarily optimal results. Surprisingly enough, applying a simple sorting algorithm on the n programs, which takes $O(n \cdot \log n)$ time, yields for practical cases remarkably good results. By storing programs in order of non-increasing weight-size ratio on disk, close to optimal results are generally obtained.

It is noted that, if programs are read at a constant bit rate and only once from beginning to end, then for each program i, it holds that $s_i = r_i \cdot d_i$, and, consequently, $w_i/s_i = \gamma_i$. The ordering suggested above then boils down to storing programs in order of non-increasing popularity, corresponding exactly to the approach by Ghandeharizadeh et al. [1996]. Conversely, by defining $\tilde{\gamma}_i = w_i/s_i$, an alternative popularity value is generated that encompasses, besides the original popularity, also the bit rate, duration, and size of program i.

We next illustrate why this algorithm performs so well and substantiate this further by simulation results.

Performance assessment. To illustrate why the sorting algorithm works so well, we split each program i into s_i sub-programs of unit size, each sub-program j, $j = 1, 2, \ldots, s_i$, of i being characterized by a weight $w_{ij} = w_i/s_i$.

The splitting operation results in a total of $\sum_{i=1}^n s_i$ sub-programs of unit size, whereby all sub-programs of one program have equal weight. As already argued in Section 16.3, storing these sub-programs in order of non-increasing weight from the outer to the inner edge of the disk yields an optimal ordering. In particular, as all sub-programs of one program have the same weight, these sub-programs may be stored contiguously without violating the property of optimality. As such, (16.2) is minimized for this collection of sub-programs.

Now, let us only look at contiguous orderings of the sub-programs whereby all those associated to a single program are stored contiguously. For each such ordering of sub-programs, each sub-program j of program i has a transfer rate R_{ij}, based on its location on disk, and the cost of this ordering is given by

$$\sum_{i=1}^n \sum_{j=1}^{s_i} \frac{w_{ij}}{R_{ij}} = \sum_{i=1}^n \frac{w_i}{s_i} \cdot \sum_{j=1}^{s_i} \frac{1}{R_{ij}}. \tag{16.4}$$

Now, observe that $(\sum_{j=1}^{s_i} 1/R_{ij})/s_i$ denotes the average of the reciprocal values of the bit rates associated to the sub-programs of program i. In case s_i is not too large and the transfer rate function descends relatively smoothly, the individual bit rates in this average will be relatively close to each other, as all sub-programs of program i are stored contiguously, so that replacing this average by $\max_{j=1}^{s_i} 1/R_{ij}$ will result in a cost function that only differs marginally from (16.4). Optimizing (16.4) then also yields a good ordering for this approximating cost function. But then, as this maximum denotes the reciprocal value of the bit rate associated to the bit of program i that is stored closest to the inner edge of the disk surface, it also denotes the reciprocal value of the bit rate associated to the entire program in the original problem, so that this approximating cost function is the cost function of the original problem.

Recapitulating, storing programs in order of non-increasing ratio of their weights and sizes from the outer to the inner edge of the disk may lead to close to optimal orderings, especially when the individual program sizes are not too large and the transfer rate function descends relatively smoothly.

Simulations. To support these findings, we have conducted a set of simulations on 1000 instances using a single, constant-density disk with an mSTR of 200 Mbit/s, and MSTR of 400 Mbit/s and a disk size of 271 Gbit. For each instance, we chose the number of programs randomly in the range $\{5, 6, \ldots, 10\}$, each program being characterized by a randomly chosen weight in the range $[0,1)$ and a randomly chosen integer size in the range $[0, m)$, where m is twice the disk size divided by the number of programs. For the generation of each instance, the file sizes were computed repeatedly until the total size of all files was at most the disk size.

The results are as follows. In approximately 75% of the instances, an optimal ordering was found. For the remaining 25%, the cost of each ordering was at most 1% off the cost of an optimal ordering, and in only 5% of the instances the cost exceeded 0.1%. To give an indication of the relevance of finding good or optimal orderings, we note that the worst orderings were, on average, 26% off the optimal cost. The worst-case worst ordering was 63% off.

We have conducted the same simulations as described above, but instead of using a constant-density disk, we used an MZR disk with 10 zones, each zone containing an equal number of tracks. The constant transfer rate in each zone was chosen equal to the transfer rate on the constant-density disk at the position of the innermost bit of the zone.

The results are as follows. In approximately 25% of the instances, an optimal ordering was found. For the remaining 75%, the cost of each ordering was at most 3.4% off the cost of an optimal ordering. In 10% of the instances the cost exceeded 1% and in only 0.5% of the instances the cost exceeded 2%. For these simulations, the worst orderings were, on average, 28% off the optimal cost, the worst-case worst ordering was 69% off.

Although the results above suggest that the sorting algorithm yields good results, this is not true in the general case. Using transfer rate functions that are less smooth than the ones used in the simulations may have a detrimental effect on the performance of the algorithm. An ordering found by the sorting algorithm can, of course, be used as an initial ordering by other algorithms that attempt to improve upon this ordering. For instance, by scanning an ordering found once from the beginning to the end to see if switching the positions of any two adjacent programs results in an improvement improves upon the results for the MZR disk in the sense that in 66% instead of 25% of all cases an optimal ordering was found.

In the end, obtaining a worst-case performance ratio for the sorting algorithm, possibly extended with additional algorithms, is important to assess its performance for instances with a larger number of programs. This is considered a subject for further research.

16.6 Analysis of a special case: RUBS versus TP

In this and the next section, we consider a special case of the general problem and study it in more detail. In particular, we compare RUBS with TP. We start with an analytical comparison of the maximum number of playout processes that can be sustained simultaneously, under various simplifying assumptions, most notably that the programs only differ in their popularity. We initially ignore the issue of response times, but include this in a second analysis. Section 16.7 provides simulation results, supporting the results of this section while relaxing some of the assumptions.

We consider n programs, numbered $1, 2, \ldots, n$ of equal duration d, equal size s, and equal bit rate r, each program i being characterized by its popularity γ_i, with $\sum_{j=1}^{n} \gamma_j = 1$ and $\gamma_j \geq \gamma_{j+1}$ for $j < n$. The programs are thus numbered in order of non-increasing popularity. We use a single, constant-density disk with an mSTR of R^m and an MSTR of R^M. We assume that the disk is exactly large enough to contain all programs, i.e. its size S equals $n \cdot s$. As all programs are of equal size s and the programs are already sorted appropriately, they should be stored in order of increasing program number from the outer to the inner edge of the disk to minimize the cost.

The bits on the disk are numbered from 1 onwards, starting at the outer edge. Program i thus occupies bits $(i-1) \cdot s + 1, (i-1) \cdot s + 2, \ldots, i \cdot s$. It can be shown that at bit position $i \cdot s$, the transfer rate is accurately described by

$$\tilde{R}(i) = R^M \cdot \sqrt{1 - (1 - \rho^2) \cdot \frac{i}{n}}, \tag{16.5}$$

where $\rho = R^m / R^M$. This rate is based on the assumption that the successive bits on disk are organized as a spiral, rather than a number of concentric circles. The deviation, however, is neglected here.

For program i, the minimum rate used to read data from disk is thus given by $\tilde{R}(i)$. The ASTR is given by $R^A = \frac{R^m + R^M}{2}$, as is shown as follows. When neglecting switching overhead, reading all data blocks using TP, each at rate R^A, results in the same average rate as reading all data blocks in radial direction, which clearly results in an average rate of $\frac{R^m + R^M}{2}$.

Now, assume that a large number m of playout processes simultaneously exist, and that a fraction $\gamma_i \cdot m$ of them is associated to program i. For simplicity, we ignore the fact that these fractions need not be integer-valued. Each of the $\gamma_i \cdot m$ playout processes associated to program i only uses at most a fraction $r/\tilde{R}(i)$ of the time available for reading, the latter of which can be arbitrarily close to 1 per unit time. So, it should hold that

$$\sum_{i=1}^{n} \gamma_i \cdot m \cdot \frac{r}{\tilde{R}(i)} < 1,$$

or, equivalently,

$$m < \frac{1}{r \cdot \sum_{i=1}^{n} \frac{\gamma_i}{\bar{R}(i)}}.$$

(16.6)

Note that the right-hand side of this inequality is maximized if the sum in the denominator is minimized. This illustrates the relevance of opt-RUBS.

To substantiate this result further, we assume that the popularity of programs is given by Zipf's law, see Breslau et al. [1999], which states that, for each program i,

$$\gamma_i = \frac{\frac{1}{i}}{\sum_{j=1}^{n} \frac{1}{j}}.$$

(16.7)

Note that the denominator is just a normalization constant. Substituting (16.5) and (16.7) in (16.6) expresses m as a function of the known parameters.

Numerical results. We use $n = 10$ programs with bit rate $r = 6$ Mbit/s and size $s = 32.4$ Gbit, $R^m = 200$ Mbit/s, and $R^M = 400$ Mbit/s, so that $\rho = \frac{1}{2}$ and $R^A = 300$ Mbit/s.

When using TP, a maximum of 49 ($= \lfloor (300 - \varepsilon)/6 \rfloor$, for some small $\varepsilon > 0$) playout processes can be sustained simultaneously. Using RUBS and assuming Zipf's law, numerical evaluation of Equation 16.6 yields a maximum of 55 simultaneous playout processes, an increase of a little over 12% when compared to TP.

If, instead of Zipf's law, we assume that $\gamma_i \sim \frac{1}{i^2}$, calling it Zipf^2's law, RUBS allows 60 simultaneous playout processes, an increase of a little over 22% when compared to TP. The additional skew in Zipf^2's law can also be considered as an additional skew in the bit rates of the individual programs, as the r in Equation 16.6 can be shifted into the summation.

For completeness, when using the mSTR of 200 Mbit/s, only 33 playout processes can be sustained simultaneously, and the absolute maximum number of simultaneously active playout processes is given by $\lfloor R^M/r \rfloor = 66$. The latter is possible if all processes only read data at the outer edge of the disk.

16.6.1   Dealing with response times

In practice, the disk transfer rate is not fully exploited, in order to keep the response times and buffer requirements at an acceptable level. In this section, we investigate how this influences the maximum number of simultaneously sustainable playout processes, for TP and RUBS.

We assume that the m playout processes are served using the well-known triple-buffering algorithm, see Korst et al. [1998]. When using RUBS, this algorithm works as follows. The time axis is divided into successive periods of length p. Each playout process has an associated buffer of size $3 \cdot b$, where

$b = p \cdot r$ is the data block size, which is the amount of data each playout process maximally consumes during a single period. During each period, those playout processes that can already receive an additional data block of size b in their buffers at the start of this period obtain one new data block of this size. A playout process may start consuming data from its buffer at the end of the period during which its first data block has been fetched from disk.

When using TP, the division of a data block into two sub-blocks slightly complicates the scheduling algorithm. In order not to require two accesses per period to fetch a single data block of size b, we use TP such that each data block of size $2 \cdot b$ is divided into two sub-blocks, a larger one and a smaller one. The time to read any sub-block is constant, i.e. $\frac{b}{R^A}$. In this way, it suffices to fetch at most one sub-block per playout process from disk in each period. By always fetching the larger of two pairing sub-blocks before the smaller, data is effectively read ahead of time during the first of the two transfers, and this is compensated during the second transfer[4]. With some additional modifications in the scheduler and an appropriate increase in the buffer size of each playout process to cater for this read ahead, buffer over- and underflow can be prevented.

To efficiently use the disk, reading a number of data blocks from disk during a period is done by performing a single sweep of the reading head across the disk surface from the inner to the outer edge or vice versa, thereby reading the data blocks on its way. The switching overhead incurred when performing m disk accesses in a single sweep can be bounded from above by $s(m)$, defined as

$$s(m) = \alpha + \beta \cdot m \qquad (16.8)$$

for some constants α and β. This is based on results by Oyang [1995]. As a result of performing sweeps, a data block may arrive already at the beginning of a period, or not until the end of the period.

The worst-case response time for a new playout process is $2 \cdot p$. If a request for a new playout process arrives just after the start of a period, the first data block for this new process arrives during the next period, after which it may start consuming this data. This results in a delay of $2 \cdot p$. The average case response time is $\frac{3}{2} \cdot p$, since on average, a request arrives half way during a period. It is noted that the average response time can be lowered significantly by starting a new sweep immediately upon completion of the previous sweep. For further details, see again Korst et al. [1998].

Clearly, the period length should be large enough to read one data block from disk for each of the m playout processes. For TP, reading a single large or small sub-block results in a transfer time of $\frac{p \cdot r}{R^A}$, whereas the switching over-

---

[4]This in effect complicates implementing trick modes in reverse direction, but we will ignore this fact here.

head is $s(m)$, so that it should hold that

$$p \geq s(m) + m \cdot \frac{p \cdot r}{R^A}.$$

Using (16.8), this can be rewritten as

$$m \leq \frac{p - \alpha}{\beta + \frac{p \cdot r}{R^A}}. \tag{16.9}$$

For RUBS, each of the $\gamma_i \cdot m$ playout processes associated with program i requires a read time of at most $p \cdot r / \tilde{R}(i)$ for each data block. Consequently, for RUBS, it should hold that

$$p \geq s(m) + \sum_{i=1}^{n} \gamma_i \cdot m \cdot \frac{p \cdot r}{\tilde{R}(i)},$$

which can likewise be rewritten as

$$m \leq \frac{p - \alpha}{\beta + p \cdot r \cdot \sum_{i=1}^{n} \frac{\gamma_i}{\tilde{R}(i)}}. \tag{16.10}$$

Numerical results. We next compare (16.9) and (16.10) for several values of p and assuming Zipf's and Zipf^2's law, respectively. For the parameters of the switching overhead, see (16.8), we use the representative values $\alpha = 1/15$ s and $\beta = 1/72$ s. The other parameters are as before. The results are shown in Table 16.1. For each value of p, it lists the maximum values of m satisfying (16.9) and (16.10). Figure 16.1 shows the comparison graphically.

As α and β vanish in (16.10) for growing values of p, the equation becomes nearly identical to Equation 16.6, so that the three curves approach 49, 55, and 60, respectively, as p becomes sufficiently large.

When assuming Zipf's law, RUBS outperforms TP and even more when assuming Zipf^2's law, the absolute differences generally becoming more pronounced as the period length increases. Conversely, to be able to simultaneously sustain, say, 43 playout processes, TP leads to a worst-case response time of 9.5 s, whereas for RUBS assuming Zipf's law, this is only 6.5 s and assuming Zipf^2's law only 5 s. To achieve the for TP maximum number of 49 playout processes (not shown in the table), TP leads to a worst-case response time of 75 s, whereas for the other two, this is only 13.5 and 8 s, respectively. Note that to achieve this using TP, prohibitively large data block sizes (of 225 Mbit) and buffers are necessary, since these scale linearly with the worst-case response times.

Table 16.1. Comparison of TP with RUBS assuming Zipf's and Zipf^2's law, respectively, for the maximum number of simultaneously sustainable playout processes.

p	TP	Zipf	Zipf^2	p	TP	Zipf	Zipf^2
0.25	9	9	10	2.75	38	42	45
0.50	18	18	19	3.00	39	42	46
0.75	23	24	26	3.25	40	43	47
1.00	27	29	30	3.50	40	44	48
1.25	30	32	34	3.75	41	45	48
1.50	32	34	37	4.00	41	45	49
1.75	34	36	39	4.25	42	46	50
2.00	35	38	41	4.50	42	46	50
2.25	37	39	42	4.75	43	46	50
2.50	38	41	44	5.00	43	47	51

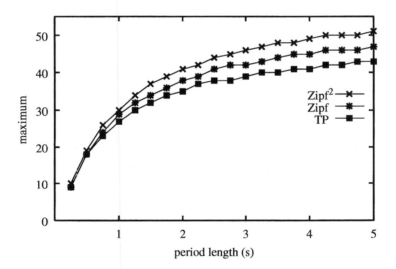

Figure 16.1. Graphical comparison of TP with RUBS for the maximum number of simultaneously sustainable playout processes.

16.7 Simulations

The results in Section 16.6.1 are obtained while assuming an ideal division of the playout processes among the programs, i.e., program i has $\gamma_i \cdot m$ associated playout processes. In practice, deviations will generally exist, most notably because $\gamma_i \cdot m$ need not be integer, but also because Zipf's law is only followed statistically.

To obtain insight into the actual number of simultaneously sustainable play-out processes using RUBS and assuming Zipf's law, we have conducted two sets of 10^6 independent simulation runs for each of the worst-case response times of 2, 5, and 10 s, corresponding to period lengths of 1, 2.5, and 5 s, respectively. The parameters are as before. For each worst-case response time, the two sets differ in their admission control. In the first set, called G for *greedy*, we start each run with zero playout processes, successively generate additional playout processes assuming Zipf's law, and stop just before the disk would become overloaded by adding another playout process. The second set, called F for *fair*, differs from G in that we stop adding playout processes just before the disk would become overloaded by adding a playout process with largest disk resource requirements, in this case with minimal transfer rate.

The major difference between F and G is best explained by considering an interactive setting, where playout processes are created and terminated in the course of time. For ease of exposition, the admission control criteria for sets F and G are also called F and G, respectively. F is fair in the sense that, over time, the popularity distribution of the programs is reflected in the distribution of playout processes as it does not discriminate between programs: a playout process is either admitted or not, irrespective of the program requested.

G, on the other hand, is greedy in the sense that it uses a milder admission control criterion and potentially admits more playout processes. However, G favors programs with small disk resource requirements: in a near-overload situation, a playout process with small disk resource requirements may be admitted, whereas a playout process with too large disk resource requirements is not admitted. When such near-overload situation persists for a long time, the result will be that, after some time, the majority of playout processes running will be associated with programs with small disk resource requirements. This situation generally does not reflect the popularity distribution of the programs, the desirability of which is at least questionable. Only if near-overload situations are of short duration, this mismatch is only marginal. Note that the simulations pertain to this latter case.

Figure 16.2 illustrates the six normalized frequency histograms of the maximum number of simultaneously sustainable playout processes found during each run for the three values of the response time and for both F and G. The vertical, dashed lines directly to the left of each histogram indicate the corresponding values for TP. It shows that TP is outperformed by RUBS, using either F or G, with high probability for each of the three cases. As expected, G yields better results than F, but the difference is marginal.

We did the same comparison assuming Zipf^2's law. The results are shown in Figure 16.3, which shows even more pronounced results between RUBS and TP.

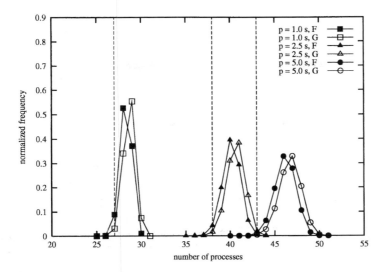

Figure 16.2. Normalized frequency histograms for period lengths 1, 2.5, and 5 s and for both F and G, assuming Zipf's law. For further explanation, see the running text.

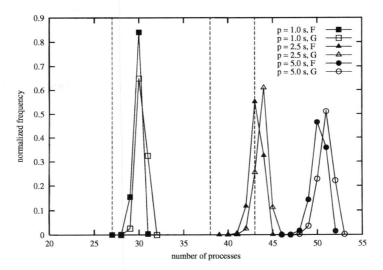

Figure 16.3. Normalized frequency histograms for period lengths 1, 2.5, and 5 s and for both F and G, assuming $Zipf^2$'s law. For further explanation, see the running text.

16.8 Concluding remarks

We have addressed the problem of resource-usage-based storage (RUBS) of video programs on a single disk and showed that finding an optimal RUBS strategy is NP-hard in the strong sense. For the general case, we provided a heuristic algorithm based on sorting the programs, using a number of program-specific parameters, with a close to optimal performance in practice.

For the special case that individual programs only differ in their popularity, we provided analytical as well as simulation results on the effects of using RUBS on the maximum number of simultaneously sustainable playout processes. For the popularity, we assumed Zipf's law, an often used distribution in the literature. We compared it with an alternative storage strategy called track pairing (TP), which is independent of usage patterns such as popularity. The results indicate that RUBS can outperform TP.

We concentrated on the differing popularity of programs only, but the results can be extended to incorporate bit rates or durations of individual programs, leading to a possibly much more skewed distribution than Zipf's law. We therefore also used a more skewed distribution than Zipf's law to illustrate the possible gains with respect to TP when using RUBS.

Embedding a program storage system using RUBS in an ambient intelligence environment for recording programs can enhance performance, while RUBS itself can benefit from the availability of client information, such as the popularity of programs, generated by a recommender system. The latter information could even be used to recommend which programs to store and which not.

16.9   Future research

Although linear and reverse viewing, pausing, and slow motion in either direction is inherently supported by VBR disk scheduling algorithms, providing fast forward/reverse modes requires additional provisions. A few possibilities are the following.

- Some disk scheduling algorithms are robust against increases in the actual rate at which a playout process consumes data from its buffer in the sense that the quality of service of playout processes in linear viewing mode, slow motion, or pause is not compromised when other processes are in fast-reverse/forward mode. This results in a kind of best-effort fast reverse/forward mode.
- Some disk bandwidth is reserved to provide support for these modes for a limited number, much smaller than n, of playout processes.
- Several separate fast-forward and -reverse versions of each program are created and stored on disk. For this, the disk size should be sufficient. These versions could be considered as separate programs with possibly low popularity or average duration.

To apply the results of this chapter in an on-line setting where new programs must be stored and old ones deleted, consider the following approach. We discern a number of program classes, and assign a *class ratio* and a *size* to each class. The sizes sum up to the disk space used for storing video programs. The classes are assigned their portion of the disk space in order of decreasing class ratio from the outer to the inner edge of the disk. Recording a new program is done in the disk space allocated to the class whose class ratio corresponds best to the weight-size ratio of the program. Once stored, the program obtains its own transfer rate, depending on its location on disk. If there is not enough space available in the chosen class, one or more programs from this class, the oldest, for instance, are removed from this class, or migrated to another appropriate class. The class ratios and sizes can be obtained, based on experience, for instance, on collected client profiles.

Problems for further investigation from a theoretical viewpoint include the worst-case performance ratio of the heuristic algorithm and an in-depth comparison, in a more general setting, of RUBS with the various alternative storage approaches proposed in the literature. From a more practical perspective, assessing the performance of RUBS in a practical context, such as storing, say, the last 24 hours of video content from a broadcast channel, thereby also providing fast-forward/reverse functionality, would be worthwhile.

DVDs (digital versatile or video discs) store data at a constant density. Current DVD players also rotate a DVD at a constant angular velocity, as opposed to the constant linear velocity used in older players to attain a constant transfer rate, so that storing video programs on a DVD can also benefit from RUBS. Recording programs on a DVD, however, is performed at a constant angular velocity that depends on the location on the DVD where the data is stored. Integrating recording and playing on a DVD thus results in a more complex model for resource usage. Further investigation may reveal the actual benefits of using RUBS in this context.

Acknowledgment

Thanks are due to Jan Korst for his fruitful comments and providing the NP-hardness proof of opt-RUBS.

References

Birk, Y. [1995]. Track pairing: A novel data layout for VoD servers with multi-zone recording disks, *Proceedings of the IEEE International Conference on Multimedia Computing and Systems*, IEEE ICMCS'95, Washington, CO, May 15–18, pages 248–255.

Breslau, L., P. Cao, L. Fan, G. Philips, and S. Shenker [1999]. Web caching and Zipf-like distributions: evidence and implications, *Proceedings of the IEEE Conference on Computer Communications*, INFOCOM'99, New York, NY, March 21–25, pages 126–134.

Dengler, J., C. Bernhardt, and E. Biersack [1996]. Deterministic admission control strategies in video servers with variable bit rate streams, *Proceedings of the 3rd International Workshop on Interactive Distributed Multimedia Systems and Services*, IDMS'96, Berlin, March 4–6, pages 245–264.

Feng, W., and J. Rexford [1999]. Performance evaluation of smoothing algorithms for transmitting prerecorded variable-bit-rate video, *IEEE Transactions on Multimedia*, 1(3):302–313.

Garey, M.R., and D.S. Johnson [1979]. *Computers and Intractability: A Guide to the Theory of NP-Completeness*, W.H. Freeman and Company, New York.

Ghandeharizadeh, S., D.J. Ierardi, D. Kim, and R. Zimmermann [1996]. Placement of data in multi-zone disk drives, *Proceedings of the 2nd International Baltic Workshop on Databases and Information Systems*, BalticDB'96, Tallin, Estonia.

Kang, J., and H.Y. Yeom [1999]. Placement of VBR video data on MZR disks, *Proceedings of the 9th International Workshop on Network and Operating System Support for Digital Audio and Video*, NOSSDAV'99, Basking Ridge, NJ, June 23–25, pages 231–236.

Kang, S., and H.Y. Yeom [2000]. Placement of multi-rate smoothed VBR video objects to MZR disks. *Proceedings of the IEEE International Conference on Multimedia and Expo*, ICME'00, New York, NY, July 30–August 2, pages 1739–1742.

Kim, J.-W., Y.-U Lho, and K.-D. Chung [1997]. An effective video block placement scheme on VOD server based on multi-zone recording disks, *Proceedings of the 4th IEEE International Conference on Multimedia Computing and Systems*, ICMCS'97, Ottawa, Ontario, June 3–6, pages 29–36.

Kim, J.-W., H.-R. Lim, Y.-J. Kim, and K.-D. Chung [1997]. A data placement strategy on MZR for VoD servers, *Proceedings of the International Conference on Parallel and Distributed Systems*, ICPADS'97, Seoul, South Korea, December 11–13, pages 506–513.

Korst, J., V. Pronk, P. Coumans, G. van Doren, and E. Aarts [1998]. Comparing disk scheduling algorithms for VBR data streams, *Computer Communications*, 21:1328–1343.

Lho, Y.-U., and K.-D. Chung [1998]. Performance analysis and evaluation of allocating sub-banded video data blocks on MZR disk arrays, *Proceedings of the Advanced Simulation Technologies Conference*, ASTC'98, Boston, MA, April 5–9, pages 335–340.

Oyang, Y.-J. [1995]. A tight upper bound of the lumped disk seek time for the scan disk scheduling policy, *Information Processing Letters*, 54(6):355-358.

Park, Y.-S., J.-W. Kim, and K.-D. Chung [1999]. A continuous media placement using B-ZBSR on heterogeneous MZR disk array, in: D. Panda and M. Takizawa (Eds.), *International Workshops on Parallel Processing*, ICPP Workshops'99, Wakamatsu, Japan, September 21–24, pages 482–487.

Ruemmler, C., and J. Wilkes [1994]. An introduction to disk drive modeling, *IEEE Computer*, 27(3):17–29.

Chapter 17

TEST RESOURCE MANAGEMENT AND SCHEDULING FOR MODULAR MANUFACTURING TEST OF SOCS

Sandeep Kumar Goel and Erik Jan Marinissen

Abstract   This chapter deals with the design of on-chip architectures for testing large system chips (SOCs) for manufacturing defects in a modular fashion. These architectures consist of wrappers and test access mechanisms (TAMs). For an SOC, with specified parameters of modules and their tests, we design an architecture which minimizes the required tester vector memory depth and test application time. In this chapter, we formulate the problem of test architecture design. Subsequently, we derive a formulation of an architecture-independent lower bound for the SOC test time. We present a heuristic algorithm that effectively optimizes the test architecture for a given SOC. The algorithm efficiently determines the number of TAMs and their widths, the assignment of modules to TAMs, and the wrapper design per module. Experimental results for the *ITC'02 SOC Test Benchmarks* show that, compared to manual best-effort engineering approaches used in Philips, we can save up to 75% in test times, while compared to previously published algorithms, we obtain comparable or better test times at negligible compute time.

Keywords   SOC test, TAM and wrapper design, lower bound, test scheduling, idle bits.

17.1   Introduction

The realization of the 'ambient intelligence' vision requires the omnipresence of powerful integrated circuits to execute a multitude of computation tasks. Modern semiconductor design methods and manufacturing technologies enable the creation of a complete system on one single die, the so-called *system-on-chip* or SOC. Such SOCs typically are very large integrated circuits, consisting of millions of transistors, and containing a variety of hardware modules. In order to design these large and complex system chips in a timely manner and leverage external design expertise, increasingly reusable cores are

W. Verhaegh et al. (eds.), Algorithms in Ambient Intelligence, 311-336.
© 2004 *Kluwer Academic Publishers. Printed in the Netherlands.*

utilized. *Cores* are pre-designed and pre-verified design modules, meant to be reused in multiple SOC designs [Gupta & Zorian, 1997]. Examples of cores are CPUs, DSPs, media co-processors, communication modules, memories, and mixed-signal modules.

Due to imperfections in their manufacturing process, all integrated circuits need to be individually tested for manufacturing defects. System chips are no exception to that rule. Modular test development is increasingly used for SOCs. Non-logic modules, such as embedded analog circuitry and memories require stand-alone testing due to their 'abnormal' circuit structure. Black-boxed third-party cores, such as *hard* (layout) cores and encrypted cores, for which no implementation details are known, need to be tested by the tests as supplied by their provider, and therefore also require stand-alone testing. But even for logic modules of which the implementation details are known, modular test development is an attractive alternative. Here, a modular 'divide-and-conquer' test development approach helps to reduce the test generation compute time and associated data volume. Finally, a modular test approach enables test reuse, which especially pays off if a core or module is used in multiple SOC designs.

In order to enable modular test development, an embedded module should be isolated from its surrounding circuitry and electrical test access needs to be provided. Zorian et al. [1998] introduced a generic conceptual test access architecture enabling modular testing of SOCs, consisting of three elements per module-under-test: (1) a test pattern source and sink, (2) a test access mechanism (TAM), and (3) a wrapper. The wrapper can isolate the module from its surroundings and provides switching functionality between functional access to the module and test access through the TAM. The test architecture has a large impact both on the required vector memory depth per tester channel, as well as on the test application time of the SOC, two key parameters in the overall test cost of the SOC. In the remainder of this chapter, we loosely refer to these two parameters as 'test time'.

This chapter addresses the issue of effective and efficient design of test access architectures consisting of wrappers and TAMs. The sequel of this chapter is organized as follows. Section 17.2 reviews prior work in this domain. Section 17.3 defines the problem of test architecture optimization with respect to required tester vector memory depth and test application time, assuming the relevant parameters of modules and a maximal SOC TAM width are specified. In Section 17.4, we derive an improved lower bound for the test time of a given SOC. Section 17.5 classifies and analyzes the three types of idle bits that increase the test time beyond the theoretical lower bound value. Section 17.6 presents our architecture-independent heuristic optimization algorithm named TR-ARCHITECT. Section 17.7 contains experimental results for four of the *ITC'02 SOC Test Benchmarks* [Marinissen et al., 2002b]. We compare test time results of TR-ARCHITECT and those obtained by other methods to the theoretical lower bound. At negligible compute cost, TR-ARCHITECT, outperforms manual best-effort engineering results, and, on average, also outperforms other test architecture optimization algorithms. Section 17.8 concludes this chapter.

17.2 Prior work

17.2.1 Test architecture design

Various test architectures have been described in literature. Aerts & Marinissen [1998] described three basic scan-based test architectures, depicted in Figure 17.1: (a) the *Multiplexing* Architecture, (b) the *Daisychain* Architecture, and (c) the *Distribution* Architecture.

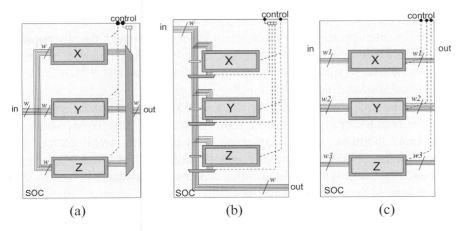

Figure 17.1. (a) Multiplexing, (b) Daisychain (b), and (c) Distribution Architectures [Aerts & Marinissen, 1998].

In the Multiplexing and Daisychain Architectures, all modules get access to the full available TAM width. In the Multiplexing Architecture, only one wrapper can be accessed at a time. This implies that the total test time is the sum of the individual module test times, but, more importantly, module-external testing (i.e., testing the circuitry and wiring in between the modules) which requires simultaneous access to two or more wrappers is cumbersome or even impossible.

The Daisychain Architecture allows access to one or more wrappers at the same time and hence better supports module-external testing. In the Distribution Architecture, the total available TAM width is distributed over the modules. This allows modules to be tested concurrently, and hence the total SOC test time is the maximum of the individual module test times. In a Distribution Architecture, the width of an individual TAM should be proportional to the amount of test data that needs to be transported to and from a module connected to the TAM in order to minimize the SOC test time.

In test architecture design, we distinguish two issues: (1) the TAM type, and (2) the architecture type.

Two different *TAM types* have been proposed in the literature: the test bus and the TestRail. The *test bus* [Varma & Bhatia, 1998], is in essence the same as what is described by the Multiplexing Architecture: modules connected to the same test bus can only be tested sequentially. The mutual exclusion for test bus access between multiple modules can be implemented by means of multiplexers, tri-state elements, or otherwise. Modules connected to a common test bus suffers from the same drawback as in the Multiplexing Architecture, viz. module-external testing is difficult or impossible.

The *TestRail* [Marinissen et al., 1998], is in essence the same as what is described by the Daisychain Architecture: modules connected to the same Test-Rail can be tested simultaneously, as well as sequentially. The TestRail can be implemented by simply concatenating the scan chains of the various modules and their wrappers. The advantage of a TestRail over a test bus is that it allows access to multiple or all wrappers simultaneously, which facilitates module-external testing.

From literature, we can distinguish at least three different *architecture types*. The first architecture type is one in which there is only one TAM, which connects to all modules. The Multiplexing and Daisychain Architectures [Aerts & Marinissen, 1998] are examples of such architectures. The Multiplexing Architecture has only one TAM of type test bus, while the Daisychain Architecture has only one TAM of type TestRail.

The second architecture type is one in which every module has its own private TAM. This architecture corresponds to the Distribution Architecture [Aerts & Marinissen, 1998]. As there is only one module per TAM, the TAM type is actually irrelevant in this type of test architecture. As each TAM needs to consist of at least one wire, this architecture requires that there are at least as many TAM wires as modules. When designing this architecture, the partitioning of the total number of available TAM wires over the various modules has a large impact on the resulting test time.

The third architecture type is the hybrid combination [Goel & Marinissen, 2002b] of types one and two. In this architecture, there are one or more TAMs, which each connect to one or more modules. This architecture is in fact a generalization, of which Multiplexing, Daisychain, and Distribution Architectures are special cases.

Test architectures based on TAM-type test bus only support *serial* test schedules; the modules connected to a common test bus are tested in an arbitrary, but sequential order [Goel & Marinissen, 2002b]. Parallelism only exists in case of multiple test buses, which may operate in parallel. Test architectures based on TAM-type TestRail support both *serial* and *parallel* test schedules. In a parallel test schedule, we start to test all modules connected to a common TestRail in parallel. This continues until one of them runs out of test patterns. We then turn on the bypass for this module, while the testing of the remaining modules continues. This process is repeated until all modules on the TestRail have been completely tested. Figure 17.2(a) shows an example of a hybrid TestRail architecture. Figure 17.2(b) shows a possible corresponding serial test schedule, while Figure 17.2(c) shows a possible corresponding parallel test schedule.

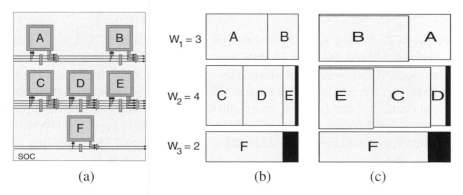

(a)   (b)   (c)

Figure 17.2. (a) Example hybrid TestRail architecture and (b) possible corresponding serial and (c) parallel test schedules.

17.2.2   Test architecture optimization

Most test time minimization algorithms published so far have concentrated on hybrid test bus architectures. Chakrabarty [2000] described an architecture optimization approach that minimizes test time through Integer Linear Programming (ILP) and then extended the optimization criteria with place-and-route and power constraints [Chakrabarty, 2000a]. Ebadi & Ivanov [2001] replaced ILP by a genetic algorithm. Huang et al. [2001] mapped test architecture design to the well-known problem of two-dimensional bin packing and used a Best Fit Decreasing algorithm to solve it. Iyengar et al. [2002c] were the first to formulate the problem definition of integrated TAM/wrapper design. Despite its NP-hard character, they solved it using ILP and exhaustive enumeration. Iyengar et al. [2002a] presented efficient heuristics for the same problem. A heuristic optimization algorithm based on rectangle packing for a test bus architecture with one single test bus that is allowed to fork and merge was presented by Iyengar et al. [2002b] Iyengar et al. [2002d] extended this work by including precedence, preemption, concurrency, and power constraints.

Goel & Marinissen [2002a] described two heuristic algorithms for co-optimization of wrappers and TAMs for hybrid TestRail architectures. The algorithms of Goel & Marinissen [2002a] have a limitation that the total TAM width should be greater than or equal to the number of modules inside the SOC. Therefore the approach presented by Goel & Marinissen [2002a] is not suitable for small TAM widths.

17.3   Problem definition

To design a test architecture for a given set of modules and a given number of test pins, an SOC integrator has to select TAM and architecture types and then determine (1) the number of TAMs, (2) the widths of these TAMs, (3) the assignment of modules to TAMs, and (4) the wrapper design for each module.

Definition 17.1 (Test architecture design problem (TADP)). Given is a set of modules M, and for each Module $m \in M$ the number of test patterns p_m, the number of functional input terminals i_m, the number of functional output terminals o_m, the number of functional bidirectional terminals b_m, the number of scan chains s_m, and for each scan chain k, the length of the scan chain in flip flops $l_{m,k}$. Furthermore are given TAM type, architecture type and a number $w_{\max}$ that represents the maximum number of SOC-level TAM wires that can be used. Determine a test architecture and a wrapper design for each module such that the overall SOC-level test time T (in clock cycles) is minimized and $w_{\max}$ is not exceeded.   □

TADP is NP-hard, as was shown by Iyengar et al. [2002c]. TADP assumes *hard* modules, i.e., modules for which the number of scan chains and their lengths are fixed. A variant of TADP is the one that assumes *soft* modules, i.e., in which the module-internal scan chains are not designed yet. In that case, the number of scan chains s_m and the length of these scan chains $l_{m,k}$ are not given. Instead, for each Module m the number of scan flip flops f_m is given, and s_m and $l_{m,k}$ need to be determined such that $f_m = \sum_{k=1}^{s_m} l_{m,k}$. Many real life SOCs contain a mix of hard and soft modules.

Even though the problem formulation requires data for the module-internal scan chains, this does not mean that the problem is limited to scan-testable modules only. The problem definition is equally well applicable to logic modules with full scan (where f_m equals the flip flop count of the module in question), partial scan (where f_m equals the *scan* flip flop count of the module in question), and no scan (where $f_m = 0$). The latter case is also applicable to non-logic modules, such as embedded memories, that per definition have no module-internal scan chains.

17.4   Lower bound on test time

Chakrabarty [2001] presented the following architecture-independent lower bound on the SOC test time.

$$LB_T^1 = \max_{m \in M} \min_{1 \le w \le w_{\max}} t(m, w),$$

where $t(m, w)$ denotes the test time for Module m with TAM width w. The idea behind this lower bound is that every Module $m \in M$ requires a test time of at least $\min_{1 \leq w \leq w_{\max}} t(m, w)$, and hence the overall SOC test time cannot be smaller than the maximum of these minimum module test times.

LB_T^1 is a tight lower bound only in those cases where the SOC test time is determined by one 'bottleneck' module with a large test time. We call a module a bottleneck if it dominates the overall SOC test time and increasing its TAM width does not further reduce its test time. In many cases, multiple modules are connected to one TAM and together determine the overall SOC test time. In such cases, LB_T^1 is not a tight lower bound. In this section we improve the lower bound.

We start with a lower bound on the test time of a module. Per test pattern, test stimuli need to be loaded into the wrapper input cells of the module-under-test, as well as into the module-internal scan chains. Similarly, test responses need to be unloaded from the module-internal scan chains, as well as from the wrapper output cells of the module-under-test. For Module m, this requires per test pattern ts_m test stimuli bits and tr_m test response bits, with

$$ts_m = i_m + b_m + f_m \quad \text{and} \quad tr_m = o_m + b_m + f_m.$$

The unload of the responses of one test pattern can be overlapped in time with the load of the stimuli of the next test pattern. Therefore, a lower bound on the test time of Module m is

$$LB_m = \left\lceil \frac{\max(ts_m, tr_m) \cdot p_m + \min(ts_m, tr_m)}{w_{\max}} \right\rceil + p_m. \qquad (17.1)$$

The second term of (17.1) represents the time needed to apply/capture the test patterns; this depends only on the number of test patterns and is independent from TAM width $w_{\max}$.

An architecture-independent lower bound on the test time of the entire SOC is in principle the sum of the lower bounds for all individual modules. However, in case of multiple TAMs, it can be that the TAM with the largest test time contains only the module with the smallest number of test patterns. Hence the second term of (17.1) is taken out of the summation in (17.2) and replaced by the minimum of the test pattern counts for all modules in the SOC. Also, the unload of the responses of the last pattern for a module can be overlapped with the load of stimuli of the first pattern for the another module. Therefore, with the assumption $ts_{|M|+1} = 0$, a lower bound LB_T^2 on the test time of a SOC can be written as

$$LB_T^2 = \left\lceil \sum_{m=1}^{|M|} \frac{\max(ts_m, tr_m) \cdot p_m + \min(ts_m, tr_m) - \min(tr_m, ts_{m+1})}{w_{\max}} \right\rceil + \min_{m=1}^{|M|} p_m.$$

(17.2)

Lower bounds LB_T^1 and LB_T^2 lead to an improved lower bound LB_T:

$$LB_T = \max(LB_T^1, LB_T^2).$$

Note that this lower bound does *not* take into account the test time required for the interconnect tests of the top-level SOC itself and assumes that all SOC modules are at the same level of design hierarchy.

LB_T^1 was originally defined by Chakrabarty [2001] for the problem with *hard* modules only. The same formula can also be used to calculate a lower bound for the problem variant with *soft* modules. However, the value of LB_T^1 in the case of soft modules is limited, as LB_T^2 usually exceeds LB_T^1.

For SOC p22810 [Marinissen et al., 2002b], Figures 17.3(a) and (b) graphically display the values of LB_T^1 and LB_T^2 for TADP with *hard* and *soft* modules respectively.

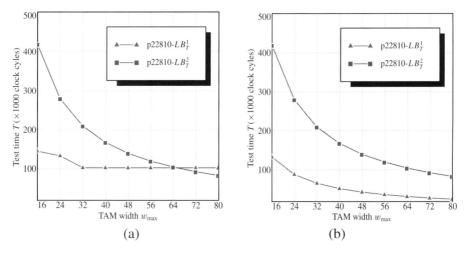

(a)   (b)

Figure 17.3. For SOC p22810 architecture-independent lower bounds on test time for TADP with (a) hard and (b) soft modules.

From Figure 17.3(a), we can see that for TADP with hard modules, the values of LB_T^1 stop decreasing for $w_{\max} \geq 32$. This is due to the fact that there is at least one module that forms the bottleneck in T and for which increasing its w does not decrease T any more. This phenomenon does not occur for LB_T^2, which continues to decrease for increasing w. Hence, for large enough $w_{\max}$, LB_T^1 becomes the dominant lower bound. For the case shown in Figure 17.3(a), LB_T^1 starts dominating for $w_{\max} \geq 66$. For TADP with soft modules, LB_T^1 usually exceeds LB_T^1 as shown in Figure 17.3(b). From the figures, we can also see that LB_T^1 yields different values for hard and soft modules, whereas LB_T^2 is independent of the problem at hand.

17.5 Idle bits analysis

Ideally, all available TAM width should be used without any under-utilization for subsequent testing of all modules of the SOC. In practice, this is often not achievable. This implies that one or more TAM wires are used to feed *idle bits* into and out of the SOC. In this section, we analyze these idle bits.

We distinguish three different types of idle bits.

17.5.1 Type-1 idle bits

In general, scheduling can be defined as the allocation of limited resources to tasks over time [Pinedo, 1995]. In our case, the tasks are the tests of the various modules, and the limited resources are the TAMs, or, defined at a finer grain, the individual TAM wires. The overall SOC-level test time T is defined by the completion time of the last module test on any TAM. In a concrete schedule, one TAM might complete its tasks before other TAMs do. Between the completion time of an individual TAM and the overall completion time, the TAM in question is not utilized. We refer to the bits that cause this type of under-utilization as *Type-1 idle bits*. In general, it is the objective of scheduling approaches to minimize this type of idle time.

17.5.2 Type-2 idle bits

Pareto-optimal width.
Wrapper design for a module involves the partitioning of the set of scan elements of the module over the TAM wires assigned to the module. The set of scan elements of a module consists of the wrapper input cells, the wrapper output cells, and the module-internal scan chains [Marinissen et al., 2000]. For increasing TAM width w, the scan elements get redistributed over the TAM wires, resulting in another partitioning. However, the scan time per test pattern (and hence the test time for the module) only decreases if the increase in TAM width is sufficient to reduce the length of the longest scan chain.

Consider the example depicted in Figure 17.4. A module has four fixed-length internal scan chains of length 100 flip flops each. If assigned two TAM wires ($w = 2$), the scan time per test pattern is 200 clock cycles, as shown in Figure 17.4(a). If the number of TAM wires is increased to three ($w = 3$), the test time does *not* decrease, as shown in Figure 17.4(b). Instead, the number

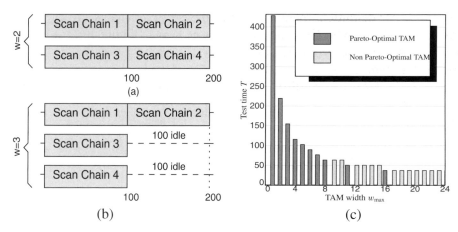

Figure 17.4.   Example showing increasing TAM width *w* does not always lead to reduced test time *T*.

of idle bits transported over the TAM wires is increased with 200 bits per test pattern.

This phenomenon leads to a 'staircase' behavior in case we plot the test time of a module as function of its TAM width *w* [Iyengar et al., 2002c]. Figure 17.4(c) shows the test time as function of TAM width for Module 1 of SOC d695. In this figure, the staircase behavior can clearly be recognized. For example: increasing the TAM width from 11 to 15 does not reduce the test time, as the next improvement in test time is only obtained for $w = 16$.

For a Module *m*, a TAM width *w* for which holds that $T_m(w-1) > T_m(w)$ (assume $T_m(0) = \infty$) is known as a *Pareto-optimal* TAM width of Module *m* [Iyengar et al., 2002c]. In Figure 17.4(c), the Pareto-optimal TAM widths are represented by the dark bars. If a module is assigned to a TAM with a non Pareto-optimal TAM width, we refer to the (redundant) bits transported along the excess TAM wires as Type-2 idle bits. Note that Type-2 idle bits only are a serious problem for hard modules, i.e., modules with fixed-length scan chains.

17.5.3   Type-3 idle bits

Even if we only consider wrappers with Pareto-optimal TAM widths, there might be still under-utilization of the available TAM width due to imbalanced scan lengths of the TAM wires. Idle bits due to imbalanced wrapper scan chains after wrapper design, are called Type-3 idle bits.

The phenomenon is explained by means of an example, depicted in Figure 17.5(a). Consider a module with three internal scan chains of lengths 100, 100, and 70 respectively. In Figure 17.5(a), we consider the cases $w = 1$, $w = 2$, and $w = 3$, which are all three Pareto-optimal. Figure 17.5(a)(i) shows the situation of $w = 1$. All module-internal scan chains are assigned to this one TAM wire, and, per definition, there are no imbalanced scan chains. Hence, there are no Type-3 idle bits. However, for the cases $w = 2$ (Figure 17.5(a)(ii)) and $w = 3$ (Figure 17.5(a)(iii)) there are respectively 70 and 30 bits of Type-3 idle bits per test pattern, due to the imbalanced scan chain lengths.

Figure 17.5(c) shows that Module 2 of SOC p34392 [Marinissen et al., 2002b] has the following set of Pareto-optimal TAM widths: $\{1, 2, 3, 4, 5, 6, 7, 8, 9, 13, 14, 15, 16\}$. Figure 17.5(b) then shows the total amount of Type-3 idle bits for these Pareto-optimal TAM widths, which amounts to $> 3 \cdot 10^6$ bits for some cases.

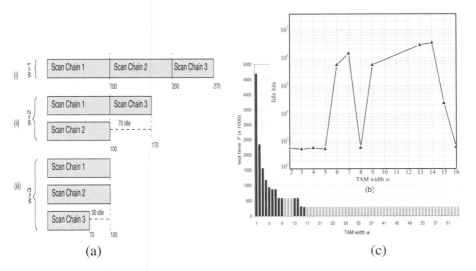

(a)   (c)

Figure 17.5. (a) Example showing the cause of Type-3 idle bits, (b) amounts of Type-3 idle bits for Module 2 in SOC p34392, and (c) Pareto-optimal TAM widths for Module 2 in SOC p34392.

Typically, TAM wires get assigned a mix of wrapper input cells, module-internal scan chains, and wrapper output cells [Marinissen et al., 2000]. The Type-3 idle bits due to imbalanced scan chains are caused by fixed-length module-internal scan chains. For soft modules, the scan chains can be designed such that Type-3 idle bits are limited to at most one bit per TAM wire. The wrapper input and output cells, which are treated as scan chains of length 1, can be used to reduce the amount of idle bits, both for hard and soft modules.

17.6 Test architecture design algorithm

In this section we present an effective and efficient algorithm called TR-ARCHITECT for designing a test architecture for an SOC. The algorithm optimizes a test architecture for a given SOC with respect to test time. It uses the input parameters as described in TADP in Section 17.3.

In our algorithm, a TAM r is represented as a set of modules, which are connected to r. Our algorithm determines a test architecture, which consists of the following.

- The set of TAMs R, such that $M = \bigcup_{r \in R} r$ and $\forall_{r_1, r_2 \in R} (r_1 \cap r_2 = \emptyset)$, i.e., every module is assigned to exactly one TAM.

- The width $w(r)$ of every TAM $r \in R$, such that $\sum_{r \in R} w(r) \leq w_{max}$, i.e., the summed width of the TAMs does not exceed w_{max}.

- The wrapper design for each module $m \in M$.

The algorithm TR-ARCHITECT has four main steps, as shown in Figure 17.6. Each of these steps is explained in more detail in the sequel of this section.

TR-Architect
1. CreateStartSolution;
2. Optimize-BottomUp;
3. Optimize-TopDown;
4. Reshuffle

Figure 17.6.   Algorithm TR-ARCHITECT.

17.6.1   Wrapper design and test time calculation

Procedure WRAPPERDESIGN(m, w) designs a wrapper for Module m and TAM width w. It yields the resulting maximum scan-in time si_m and maximum scan-out time so_m of any of the chains through wrapper cells and module-internal scan chains. si_m and so_m can be defined as follows.

$$si_m = \min_{\mathcal{P} \in \text{part}_w(S_i) \,\wedge\, \mathcal{P}=\{P_1,P_2,\dots,P_w\}} \left(\max_{1 \leq i \leq w} \left(\sum_{p \in P_i} l(p) \right) \right) \tag{17.3}$$

$$so_m = \min_{\mathcal{P} \in \text{part}_w(S_o) \,\wedge\, \mathcal{P}=\{P_1,P_2,\dots,P_w\}} \left(\max_{1 \leq i \leq w} \left(\sum_{p \in P_i} l(p) \right) \right) \tag{17.4}$$

where S_i is the set of input wrapper cells and module-internal scan chains, S_o is the set of module-internal scan chains and output wrapper cells, $\text{part}_w(S)$ defines the set of all partitions of set S into w parts, and $l(p)$ defines the scan length (in clock cycles) of p.

For TADP with *hard* modules, calculating si_m and so_m actually constitutes an optimization problem that was shown to be equivalent to the well-known

NP-hard problems of Bin Design and Multi-Processor Scheduling [Marinissen et al., 2000]. Heuristics that solve this problem in an effective yet efficient way are LPT [Marinissen et al., 2000], COMBINE [Marinissen et al., 2000], and DESIGN_WRAPPER [Iyengar et al., 2002c]. Our procedure WRAPPERDESIGN uses the COMBINE algorithm. For TADP variant with *soft* modules, calculating si_m and so_m equals bin-design with all items of size 1 and hence reduces to a simple balanced division of the scan flip flops and wrapper cells over w TAM wires.

Figure 17.7 shows an example wrapper. Example Module A has 8 inputs, 11 outputs, and 9 internal scan chains of lengths 120, 60, 80, 60, 60, 120, 60, 80, and 80 flip flops respectively. The wrapper in Figure 17.7 is designed to connect to a three-bit wide TAM, with its terminals WPI[0:2] and WPO[0:2]. The wrapper is designed to be compliant with the standard-under-development IEEE P1500 SECT [Marinissen et al., 2002a; P1500 Web].

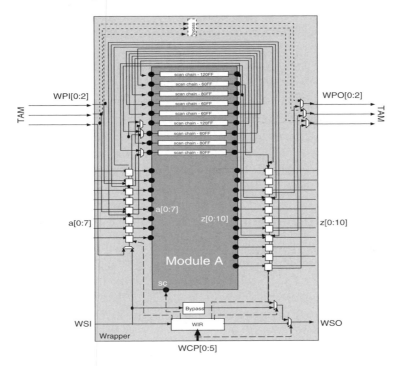

Figure 17.7. Example of a wrapper design, connecting to a three-bit wide TAM.

Procedure TESTTIME(r, w) computes the test time $t(r)$ for a TAM r with width w. It uses procedure WRAPPERDESIGN(m, w) as a subroutine for all modules $m \in r$. Depending on the TAM type (test bus or TestRail), a different version of the procedure TESTTIME is selected by TR-ARCHITECT. For a test bus TAM, we assume that the test bus functionality is implemented by means of multiplexers or tri-statable drivers, and hence the test access to individual modules does not require additional clock cycles. In this case, procedure TESTTIME(r, w) simply sums the test times of the individual modules $m \in r$. The implementation of TESTTIME for TestRail TAMs is slightly more complex [Marinissen & Goel, 2002]. The total test time T for a test architecture is the maximum of the test times of the individual TAMs.

17.6.2 Creating a start solution

The procedure CREATESTARTSOLUTION, as outlined in Figure 17.8, is meant to create an initial test architecture, which will be further optimized by the procedures to follow. It consists of a short initialization, followed by three main steps.

In Step 1 (Lines 3–8), we assign modules to one-bit wide TAMs. If $w_{max} \geq |M|$, each module gets assigned; if $w_{max} < |M|$, only the largest w_{max} modules get assigned. 'Large' is here defined by the test data volume for each module, according to which the modules have been sorted in Line 1. In case $w_{max} = |M|$, the procedure is now finished.

In case $w_{max} < |M|$, we still have unassigned modules left. In Step 2 (Lines 9–16), these modules are added iteratively to the one-bit wide TAM with the shortest test time. This procedure is based on the Largest Processing Time (LPT) algorithm [Graham, 1969] for Multi-Processor Scheduling.

In case $w_{max} > |M|$, we still have TAM wires left. In Step 3 (Lines 17–24), these wires are added iteratively to the TAM with the longest test time. This procedure is based on the algorithm for the Scan Chain Distribution Problem (SCDP) [Aerts & Marinissen, 1998].

17.6.3 Optimize bottom up

The procedure OPTIMIZE-BOTTOMUP tries to optimize the test time of a given test architecture. It does so by trying to merge the TAM with the shortest test time with another TAM, such that the wires that are freed up in this process can be used for an overall test time reduction. Figure 17.9 lists the pseudo-code for procedure OPTIMIZE-BOTTOMUP. It is an iterative procedure, of which every iteration consists of two steps.

In Step 1 (Lines 3–13), the procedure finds a TAM r_{min} with minimum test time, i.e., $t(r_{min}) = \min_{r \in R} t(r)$. The modules in TAM r_{min} and the modules in one of the other TAMs, say r, are merged into a new TAM, say r^*, with width $\max(w(r_{min}), w(r))$. TAM r is selected from $R \backslash \{r_{min}\}$ such that $t(r^*)$ is minimum and $t(r^*)$ does not exceed the current overall test time T.

In Step 2 (Lines 14–24), the merge is effected and R is updated. As the new TAM r^* only uses $\max(w(r_{min}), w(r))$ wires, $\min(w(r_{min}), w(r))$ wires are now freed up. The freed-up wires are distributed over all TAMs, in order to reduce

CreateStartSolution

1. *sort M* such that $\text{TESTTIME}(\{1\}, 1) \geq$
   $\text{TESTTIME}(\{2\}, 1) \geq \ldots \geq \text{TESTTIME}(\{|M|\}, 1)$;
2. $R := \emptyset$;
3. /* Step 1: Assign modules to one-bit TAMs */
4. *for* $i := 1$ *to* $\min(w_{max}, |M|)$ {
5. $r_i := \{i\}; R := R \cup \{r_i\}$;
6. $w(r_i) := 1$;
7. $t(r_i) := \text{TESTTIME}(r_i, w(r_i))$;
8. };
9. /* Step 2: Add modules to least-filled TAMs */
10. *if* $w_{max} < |M|$ {
11.   *for* $i := w_{max} + 1$ *to* $|M|$ {
12.   find r^* for which $t(r^*) = \min_{r \in R} t(r)$;
13. $r^* := r^* \cup \{i\}$;
14. $t(r^*) := \text{TESTTIME}(r^*, w(r^*))$;
15.   };
16. };
17. /* Step 3: Add wires to most-filled TAMs */
18. *if* $w_{max} > |M|$ {
19.   *for* $i := |M| + 1$ *to* w_{max} {
20.   find r^* for which $t(r^*) = \max_{r \in R} t(r))$;
21. $w(r^*) := w(r^*) + 1$;
22. $t(r^*) := \text{TESTTIME}(r^*, w(r^*))$;
23.   };
24. };

Figure 17.8. Algorithm CREATESTARTSOLUTION.

the overall test time T; for this we use a procedure based on the algorithm for the Scan Chain Distribution Problem (SCDP) [Aerts & Marinissen, 1998], which also formed the basis for Step 3 in Figure 17.8. The procedure ends if all TAMs have been merged into one single TAM, or when no TAM r can be found such that $t(r^*)$ does not exceed the current overall test time T.

The operation of one iteration of procedure OPTIMIZE-BOTTOMUP is illustrated by means of an example, depicted in Figure 17.10. Figure 17.10(a) shows a test architecture instance. TAM 3, containing Modules A and D, has the shortest test time and hence r_{min} is TAM 3.

Optimize-BottomUp

1. *improve := true*;
2. *while* $|R| > 1 \wedge$ *improve* {
3.   /* Step 1: Find merge candidate */
4.   find $r_{\min}$ for which $t(r_{\min}) = \min_{r \in R} t(r)$;
5. $T := \max_{r \in R} t(r)$; $t(r^*) := \infty$;
6.   *for all* $r \in R \backslash \{r_{\min}\}$ {
7. $r_{\text{temp}} := r_{\min} \cup r$;
8. $w(r_{\text{temp}}) := \max(w(r_{\min}), w(r))$;
9. $t(r_{\text{temp}}) := \text{TESTTIME}(r_{\text{temp}}, w(r_{\text{temp}}))$;
10.   *if* $(t(r_{\text{temp}}) < T) \wedge (t(r_{\text{temp}}) < t(r^*))$ {
11. $r^* := r_{\text{temp}}$; $r_{\text{del}} := r$;
12.   };
13.   };
14.   /* Step 2: Merge and Distribute freed-up wires */
15.   *if* $t(r^*) < T$ {
16. $w_{\text{free}} := \min(w(r_{\min}), w(r_{\text{del}}))$;
17. $R := R \backslash \{r_{\text{del}}, r_{\min}\} \cup \{r^*\}$;
18.   *for* $i := 1$ *to* w_{free} {
19.   find r^* for which $t(r^*) = \max_{r \in R} t(r)$;
20. $w(r^*) := w(r^*) + 1$;
21. $t(r^*) := \text{TESTTIME}(r^*, w(r^*))$;
22.   };
23.   };
24.   *else* { *improve := false* };
25. };

Figure 17.9.   Algorithm OPTIMIZE-BOTTOMUP.

Subsequently, the procedure looks for another TAM with which TAM 3 can be merged. TAM 1, containing Module C, does not qualify, as it already determines the overall SOC test time T, and adding the modules of TAM 3 to it, would only increase that test time. However, TAM 2 does qualify, and hence a new TAM is created containing Modules A, B, and D (Figure 17.10(b)). The w_3 wires of TAM 3 are now freed up, and in Step 2, they are distributed over the two remaining TAMs. Figure 17.10(c) shows that this leads to a decrease in test time of both TAMs, and hence decreases the overall test time T.

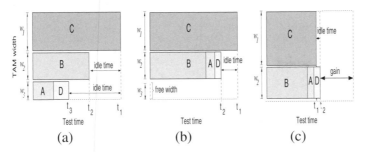

Figure 17.10. Two subsequent steps of an iteration of procedure OPTIMIZE-BOTTOMUP.

17.6.4 Optimize top down

The procedure OPTIMIZE-TOPDOWN tries to optimize the test time of a given test architecture in two subsequent steps. In Step 1, the algorithm iteratively tries to merge the TAM with the longest test time with another TAM, such that the overall test time is reduced. In case Step 1 does not yield test time improvement any more, we move to Step 2. In this step, the algorithm iteratively tries to free up wires by merging two TAMs that do not have the longest test time, under the condition that the test time of the resulting TAM does not exceed the overall test time. The wires that are freed up can be used for an overall test time reduction. Figure 17.11 lists the pseudo-code for procedure OPTIMIZE-TOPDOWN.

In Step 1 (Lines 1–18), the procedure iteratively does the following. It finds a TAM r_{max} with the longest test time. Subsequently, the procedure tries to find a TAM $r \in R\backslash\{r_{max}\}$, which could be merged with TAM r_{max} into a new TAM r^* with $w(r^*) = w(r_{max}) + w(r)$, such that $t(r^*)$ is minimum and $t(r^*)$ does not exceed the current overall test time T. If such a TAM r is found, then the merge is effected and R is updated (Line 13); else, we put TAM r_{max} into R_{skip} and move to Step 2.

Step 2 (Lines 19–51) is quite similar to Step 1, apart from the following two differences: (1) As merge candidates, it only considers the TAMs in $R\backslash R_{skip}$; (2) The width of the merged TAM $w(r^*)$ is determined by linear search between the lower limit $w_L = \max(w(r_{max}), w(r))$ and the upper limit $w_U = w(r_{max}) + w(r)$, such that $w(r^*)$ is minimum. In this way the freed-up TAM width, denoted as w_{fmax}, is maximized. If the search is successful, the freed-up wires w_{fmax} are distributed over the TAMs to minimize the test time of the architecture. If the search was not successful, then TAM r_{max} is added to set R_{skip}.

Optimize-TopDown
1.   /* Step 1: Assign sum of wires */
2.   *improve* := false;
3.   *while* $|R| > 1 \wedge improve$ {
4. $T := \max_{r \in R} t(r); t(r^*) := \infty;$
5.   find r_{max} for which $t(r_{max}) = \max_{r \in R} t(r);$
6.   *for all* $r \in R \backslash \{r_{max}\}$ {
7. $r_{temp} := r_{max} \cup r;$
8. $w(r_{temp}) := w(r_{max}) + w(r);$
9. $t(r_{temp}) := \text{TESTTIME}(r_{temp}, w(r_{temp}));$
10.   *if* $(t(r_{temp}) < T) \wedge (t(r_{temp}) < t(r^*))$ {
11. $r^* := r_{temp}; r_{del} := r;$
12.   };
13.   };
14.   *if* $t(r^*) < T$ {
15. $R := R \backslash \{r_{del}, r_{max}\} \cup \{r^*\};$
16.   };
17.   *else* {*improve*:= *false*; $R_{skip} := \{r_{max}\}$ }
18. };
19. /* Step 2: Assign #wires by Linear Search */
20. *while* $R_{skip} \neq R$ {
21. $T := \max_{r \in R} t(r); t(r^*) := \infty;$
22.   find r_{max} for which $t(r_{max}) = \max_{r \in R \backslash R_{skip}} t(r);$
23.   *for all* $r \in R \backslash (R_{skip} \cup \{r_{max}\})$ {
24. $r_{temp} := r_{max} \cup r;$
25. $w_U := w(r_{max}) + w(r);$
26. $w_L := \max(w(r_{max}), w(r));$
27.   *found* := *false*; $w(r_{temp}) := w_L;$
28.   *while* $\neg found \wedge (w(r_{temp}) \leq w_U)$ {
29. $t(r_{temp}) := \text{TESTTIME}(r_{temp}, w(r_{temp}));$
30.   *if* $t(r_{temp}) < T$ {
31.   *found* := *true*;
32. $w_{free} := w_U - w(r_{temp});$
33.   *if* $w_{free} \geq w_{fmax}$ {
34. $w_{fmax} := w_{free};$
35. $r^* := r_{temp}; r_{del} := r;$
36.   };
37.   };
38. $w(r_{temp}) := w(r_{temp}) + 1;$
39.   };
40.   };
41.   *if* $t(r^*) < T$ {
42. $R := R \backslash \{r_{del}, r_{max}\} \cup \{r^*\};$
43.   /* Distribute freed-up wires */
44.   *for* $i := 1$ *to* w_{fmax} {
45.   find r^* for which $t(r^*) = \max_{r \in R} t(r);$
46. $w(r^*) := w(r^*) + 1;$
47. $t(r^*) := \text{TESTTIME}(r^*, w(r^*));$
48.   };
49.   };
50.   *else* { $R_{skip} := R_{skip} \cup \{r_{max}\}$ };
51. }

Figure 17.11.   Algorithm OPTIMIZE-TOPDOWN.

17.6.5   Reshuffle

The procedure RESHUFFLE tries to minimize the test time of a given test architecture by placing one of the modules assigned to a TAM with the longest test time to another TAM, provided that this reduces the overall test time. Figure 17.12 lists the pseudo-code for procedure RESHUFFLE.

Reshuffle

1. *improve := true*;
2. *while improve* {
3.   find r_{max} for which $t(r_{max}) = \max_{r \in R} t(r)$;
4.   *if* $|r_{max}| = 1$ { *improve := false* };
5.   *else* { /* number of modules more than one */
6.   find module j^* for which
    $$t(j^*) := \min_{j \in r_{max}} t(j);$$
7.   *TAMFound := false*; $T := \max_{r \in R} t(r)$;
8.   *while* $r \in R \backslash \{r_{max}\} \wedge \neg \, TAMFound$ {
9. $r^* := r \cup \{j^*\}$; $w(r^*) := w(r)$;
10. $t(r^*) :=$ TESTTIME $(r^*, w(r^*))$;
11.   *if* $t(r^*) \le T$ {
12.   *TAMFound := true*;
13. $r_{max} := r_{max} \backslash \{j^*\}$
14. $R := R \backslash \{r\} \cup \{r^*\}$;
15.   };
16.   };
17.   *if* $\neg TAMFound$ { *improve := false* };
18.   };
19. }

Figure 17.12.   Algorithm RESHUFFLE.

In Line 3, the procedure identifies a TAM r_{max} with the longest test time. If r_{max} contains multiple modules, we identify the Module j^* with the smallest test time. The procedure searches through the other TAMs, to see if there is one of them to which j^* can be added without exceeding the overall test time T. If that is the case, Module j^* is indeed moved from the TAM with the longest test time to this other TAM (Lines 13–14). This procedure is repeated until the TAM with the longest test time contains only one module, or when no beneficial module re-assignment can be found.

17.7   Experimental results

In this section, we present experimental results for TR-ARCHITECT. As benchmarks, we used the set of *ITC'02 SOC Test Benchmarks* [Marinissen et al., 2002c; Marinissen et al., 2002b]. In our experiments, we have assumed that an SOC only contains two levels of hierarchy, viz. (1) the SOC itself and (2) all its embedded modules, even though some of these SOCs originally contain multiple levels of design hierarchy. Also, we have only considered the module-internal tests of the SOCs, i.e., we have not taken into account the interconnect tests for the top-level SOC itself.

First we compare the test time results of TR-ARCHITECT to the manual best-effort engineering approaches that were used on three of the *ITC'02 SOC Test Benchmarks*. These SOCs are p22810, p34392, and p93791. A Daisy-chain Architecture was implemented on SOC p93791, while Distribution Architectures were used for SOCs p22810 and p34392.

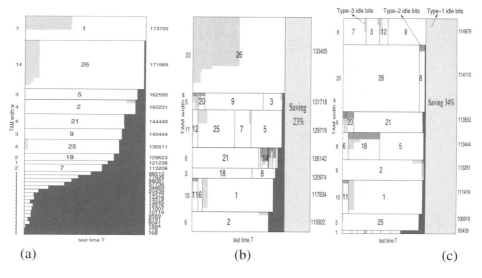

Figure 17.13.   (a) Distribution Architecture schedule, (b) hybrid Test Bus Architecture schedule, and (c) hybrid Test Bus Architecture schedule with one soft module for SOC p22810 and $w_{\max} = 64$.

Figure 17.13(a) shows the test schedule for an optimal Distribution Architecture for SOC p22810 with $w_{\max} = 64$. The horizontal axis of the schedule represents test time, while the left vertical axis represents the widths assigned to the various TAMs. The total test time for this schedule is determined by Module 1 and is equal to 173,705 clock cycles. From Figure 17.13(a), we can see that this schedule contains a large amount of Type-1 idle bits. This is due to the fact that all modules in a Distribution Architecture have separate TAMs and irrespective of the test data requirements of modules, every module gets at least one TAM wire. This results in less TAM wires available for the modules with a large test data volume. The schedule contains $3,404,593$ Type-1 idle bits ($= 31\%$), 0 Type-2 idle bits ($= 0\%$), and $599,951$ Type-3 idle bits ($= 6\%$).

Figure 17.13(b) shows the test schedule for a hybrid test bus architecture as computed by TR-ARCHITECT for SOC p22810 with $w_{max} = 64$. The total test time for this schedule is $133,405$ clock cycles, which is a saving of 23%. The amount of Type-1 idle bits has been reduced to $420,460$, due to the fact that a hybrid architecture allows more than one module to connect to the same TAM. This schedule contains $420,460$ Type-1 idle bits ($= 5\%$), $94,866$ Type-2 idle bits ($= 2\%$), and $1,178,495$ Type-3 idle bits ($= 14\%$).

It is important to note here, that different types of idle bits shown in Figure 17.13(a) and (b) not only represent the wasted test access bandwidth in the schedules, but also give insight in the SOC design itself. For example, in Figure 17.13(b), we can see that the test of Module 26 contains a large amount of Type-3 idle bits and that represents $> 55\%$ of the total idle bits present in the schedule. This is due to the imbalanced scan chains inside the module. If we are allowed to modify the internal scan chains of this module only, we can reduce the overall test time further by 11% as shown in Figure 17.13(c). From Figure 17.13(c), we can also see that there are few idle bits in the schedule; this schedule contains $145,964$ Type-1 idle bits ($= 2\%$), $141,797$ Type-2 idle bits ($= 2\%$), and $207,901$ Type-3 idle bits ($= 3\%$).

Figure 17.14 shows the hybrid test bus architecture that corresponds to the test schedule shown in Figure 17.13(c). This architecture consists of eight TAMs with the following width distribution: $8 + 20 + 6 + 8 + 6 + 10 + 5 + 1 = 64$. The module assignment vector for this architecture is $(6,5,1,8,4,4,1,2,1,8,6,1,8,8,8,8,5,4,3,3,3,8,3,8,7,2,8,8)$.

For a range of w_{max} values, Table 17.1 presents a comparison between the test time results obtained from TR-ARCHITECT and the manual best-effort engineering approaches i.e., the Daisychain and Distribution Architectures. TR-ARCHITECT works for both test bus and TestRail TAMs and for both serial and parallel schedules. For comparison we present results for hybrid test bus and hybrid TestRail architectures with serial schedules.

The header of the table indicates which architecture was used (where 'TB' stands for hybrid test bus architecture, and 'TR' denotes hybrid TestRail architecture). A '–' entry denotes that the approach could not yield an architecture for the corresponding w_{max}. The column ΔT shows the percentage difference between the best of the TR-ARCHITECT solutions and the best of the manual best-effort engineering approaches. All test time numbers in Table 17.1 are based on all hard modules.

From the table, we can see that TR-ARCHITECT outperforms the manual engineering approaches and can lead to more than 75% reduction in required tester vector memory and test time.

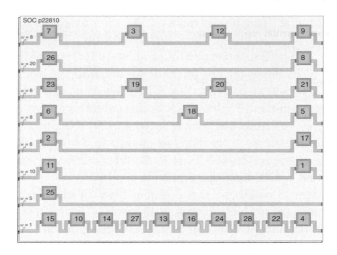

Figure 17.14. Hybrid test bus architecture with one soft module (Module 26) for SOC p22810 and $w_{max} = 64$.

Next, we compare the test time results of TR-ARCHITECT to the improved lower bound presented in this chapter and to three previously published approaches. The three approaches are: (1) the hybrid test bus architecture optimization method based on ILP and exhaustive enumeration in [Iyengar et al., 2002c], (2) the heuristic *Par_eval* in [Iyengar et al., 2002a] for hybrid test bus architecture optimization, and (3) the generalized rectangle-packing-based optimization (GRP) in [Iyengar et al., 2002b]. Table 17.2 presents the test time comparison for a range of w_{max} values for four benchmark SOCs. These four SOCs are selected, as they are the only ones for which [Iyengar et al., 2002c] [Iyengar et al., 2002a][Iyengar et al., 2002b] reported results. Note that p22810 and p34392 are referred to as p21241 and p33108 respectively in [Iyengar et al., 2002a], but these constitute the same SOCs.

In the terminology used throughout this chapter, ILP/Enum [Iyengar et al., 2002c], *Par_eval* [Iyengar et al., 2002a], and GRP [Iyengar et al., 2002b] use a hybrid test bus architecture in conjunction with a serial schedule. TR-ARCHITECT works for hybrid test bus and hybrid TestRail architectures and for serial as well as parallel schedules. For comparison, we present results for hybrid test bus architectures with serial schedules only. Per line of the table, the bold-font entries denote the lowest test time over all methods.

The ILP/enumeration method [Iyengar et al., 2002c] requires compute times in the range of minutes to hours, depending on the complexity of the SOC and the total available TAM width. The *Par_eval* method [Iyengar et al., 2002a] requires up to 288 seconds compute time. For all other methods, including our TR-ARCHITECT, compute time is less than 10 seconds for all SOCs and all TAM widths, and hence negligible.

Table 17.1. Experimental results for hard modules for test times of manual best-effort engineering approaches and TR-ARCHITECT.

Input SOC	w_{max}	Manual best-effort eng. Daisychain	Distribution	TR-Architect TB	TR	ΔT (%)
p22810	16	1338667	–	458068	476301	−65.8
	24	1282005	–	299718	310249	−76.6
	32	1218012	591585	222471	226640	−62.4
	40	1211583	353619	190995	190995	−46.0
	48	1196626	258602	160221	160221	−38.0
	56	1196626	206023	145417	145417	−29.4
	64	1196402	173705	133405	133405	−23.2
p34392	16	2694767	–	1010821	1032049	−62.5
	24	2636922	1693419	680411	721244	−59.9
	32	2612246	875499	551778	552746	−37.0
	40	2602957	587609	544579	544579	−7.3
	48	2592799	544579	544579	544579	0.0
	56	2592799	544579	544579	544579	0.0
	64	2568127	544579	544579	544579	0.0
p93791	16	2584315	–	1791638	1853402	−30.7
	24	1985588	–	1185434	1240305	−40.3
	32	1936078	5317007	912233	940745	−52.9
	40	1845070	1813502	718005	786608	−60.4
	48	1384343	1108358	601450	628977	−45.7
	56	1371382	918576	528925	530059	−42.4
	64	1371379	716679	455738	461128	−36.4

From the table, we can see that LB_T^2 is usually higher than LB_T^1 and hence determines the lower bound. This shows that the lower bound presented in this chapter is indeed an improvement over the lower bound [Chakrabarty, 2001], i.e., LB_T^1.

TR-ARCHITECT proves very effective in optimizing the SOC test time. For hybrid Test Bus Architectures, its main competitor is the ILP/Enumeration approach [Iyengar et al., 2002c], which takes orders of compute time more.

For SOC p34392, for large w_{max}, the test time for this SOC does not decrease beyond 544, 579 clock cycles. This is an example where LB_T^1 is actually achieved. This is due to Module 18 of this SOC, which becomes a bottleneck module for large enough TAM widths. Module 18 reaches its minimum test time value when assigned to a TAM of width 10, and increasing the TAM width does not further reduce its test time. All algorithms find this minimum test time. GRP [Iyengar et al., 2002b] reaches a test time of 544, 579 clock cycles for $w_{max} = 32$. TR-ARCHITECT reaches this lower bound for $w_{max} = 33$ (not shown in Table 17.2) for the hybrid test bus architecture. The total TAM width

Table 17.2. Experimental results for hard modules for lower bound, test times of TR-ARCHITECT and three others algorithms.

Input SOC	w_{max}	Lower bound LB_T^1	Lower bound LB_T^2	ILP TB Serial	Par_eval TB Serial	GRP TB Serial	TR-Arch. TB Serial
d695	16	12192	40951	**42568**	42644	44545	44307
	24	9989	27305	**28292**	30032	31569	28576
	32	9869	20482	21566	22268	23306	**21518**
	40	9869	16388	17901	18448	18837	**17617**
	48	9869	13659	16975	15300	16984	**14608**
	56	9869	11709	13207	12941	14974	**12462**
	64	9869	10247	12941	12941	11984	**11033**
p22810	16	145417	419466	462210	468011	489192	**458068**
	24	133405	279644	361571	313607	330016	**299718**
	32	102965	209734	312659	246332	245718	**222471**
	40	102965	167787	278359	232049	199558	**190995**
	48	102965	139823	278359	232049	173705	**160221**
	56	102965	119848	268472	153990	157159	**145417**
	64	102965	104868	260638	153990	142342	**133405**
p34392	16	544579	932790	**998733**	1033210	1053491	1010821
	24	544579	621903	720858	882182	759427	**680411**
	32	544579	466459	591027	663193	**544579**	551778
	40	544579	373193	**544579**	**544579**	**544579**	**544579**
	48	544579	311016	**544579**	**544579**	**544579**	**544579**
	56	544579	266603	**544579**	**544579**	**544579**	**544579**
	64	544579	233294	**544579**	**544579**	**544579**	**544579**
p93791	16	341858	1746657	**1771720**	1786200	1932331	1791638
	24	227978	1164442	1187990	1209420	1310841	**1185434**
	32	227978	873334	**887751**	894342	988039	912233
	40	223598	698670	**698883**	741965	794027	718005
	48	114317	582227	**599373**	**599373**	669196	601450
	56	114317	499053	**514688**	**514688**	568436	528925
	64	114317	436673	460328	473997	517958	**455738**

is partitioned over four test buses of widths $1, 6, 16$, and 10. The module assignment vector for this architecture is $(1,3,1,2,2,2,2,2,2,3,2,2,2,2,2,2,2,4,2)$. The overall SOC test time is determined by test bus 4, which contains Module 18 only.

17.8 Conclusion

In this chapter, we presented the test architecture design problem for SOCs. We derived an improved architecture-independent lower bound on testing time, based on the amount of test data to be transported into and out of the SOC and the total available TAM width. We also presented a classification of the three types of idle bits that occur in practical schedules, and that might prevent us from obtaining the theoretical lower bound.

We presented a novel heuristic algorithm named TR-ARCHITECT. It optimizes test architectures with respect to required ATE vector memory depth and test application time. TR-ARCHITECT optimizes wrapper and TAM design in conjunction. TR-ARCHITECT works for test bus and TestRail TAM types.

For four *ITC'02 SOC Test Benchmarks*, we compared test time results of TR-ARCHITECT with two manual best-effort engineering approaches being used in Philips, as well as to three other automated optimization approaches. Compared to manual best-effort engineering approaches, TR-ARCHITECT can reduce the required tester vector memory and test time up to 75%. This emphasizes the need for an automated optimization approach for designing SOC test architectures. Our test time results are comparable or better than the three other automated optimization approaches. TR-ARCHITECT requires a negligible amount of compute time and therefore is also suitable for large w_{max} values; this is especially an improvement over the CPU-intensive ILP/enumeration-based method in [Iyengar et al., 2002c].

As future work, we are including TAM wire length minimization into our approach by means of a layout-driven version of TR-ARCHITECT. Also are we investigating the possibilities of including the tests of intra-module circuitry and design hierarchy constraints into our approach.

Acknowledgments

We thank our colleagues Bart Vermeulen and Harald Vranken for their useful comments on an earlier draft version of this chapter.

References

Aerts, J., and E.J. Marinissen [1998]. Scan chain design for test time reduction in core-based ICs. In *Proceedings IEEE International Test Conference (ITC)*, pages 448–457.

Chakrabarty, K. [2001]. Optimal test access architectures for system-on-a-chip. *ACM Transactions on Design Automation of Electronic Systems*, 6(1):26–49.

Chakrabarty, K. [2000]. Design of system-on-a-chip test access architectures using integer linear programming. In *Proceedings IEEE VLSI Test Symposium (VTS)*, pages 127–134.

Chakrabarty, K. [2000a]. Design of system-on-a-chip test access architectures under place-and-route and power constraints. In *Proceedings ACM/IEEE Design Automation Conference (DAC)*, pages 432–437.

Ebadi, Z.S., and A. Ivanov [2001]. Design of an optimal test access architecture using a genetic algorithm. In *Proceedings IEEE Asian Test Symposium (ATS)*, pages 205–210.

Goel, S.K., and E.J. Marinissen [2002a]. Cluster-based test architecture design for system-on-chip. In *Proceedings IEEE VLSI Test Symposium (VTS)*, pages 259–264.

Goel, S.K., and E.J. Marinissen [2002b]. Effective and efficient test architecture design for SOCs. In *Proceedings IEEE International Test Conference (ITC)*, pages 529–538.

Gupta, R.K., and Y. Zorian [1997]. Introducing core-based system design. *IEEE Design & Test of Computers*, 14(4):15–25.

Graham, R.L. [1969]. Bounds on multiprocessing anomalies. *SIAM Journal of Applied Mathematics*, 17:416–429.

Huang, Yu et al. [2001]. Resource allocation and test scheduling for concurrent test of core-based SOC design. In *Proceedings IEEE Asian Test Symposium (ATS)*, pages 265–270.

Iyengar, V., K. Chakrabarty, and E.J. Marinissen [2002a]. Efficient wrapper/TAM co-optimization for large SOCs. In *Proceedings Design, Automation, and Test in Europe (DATE)*, pages 491–498.

Iyengar, V., K. Chakrabarty, and E.J. Marinissen [2002b]. On using rectangle packing for SOC wrapper/TAM co-optimization. In *Proceedings IEEE VLSI Test Symposium (VTS)*, pages 253–258.

Iyengar, V., K. Chakrabarty, and E.J. Marinissen [2002c]. Co-optimization of test wrapper and test access architecture for embedded cores. *Journal of Electronic Testing: Theory and Applications*, 18(2):213–230.

Iyengar, V., K. Chakrabarty, and E.J. Marinissen [2002d]. Integrated wrapper/TAM co-optimization, constraint-driven test scheduling, and tester data volume reduction for SOCs. In *Proceedings ACM/IEEE Design Automation Conference (DAC)*, pages 685–690.

Marinissen, E.J., et al. [1998]. A structured and scalable mechanism for test access to embedded reusable cores. In *Proceedings IEEE International Test Conference (ITC)*, pages 284–293.

Marinissen, E.J., S.K. Goel, and M. Lousberg [2000]. Wrapper design for embedded core test. In *Proceedings IEEE International Test Conference (ITC)*, pages 911–920.

Marinissen, E.J., and S.K. Goel [2002]. Analysis of test bandwidth utilization in test bus and TestRail architectures for SOCs. In *Proceedings IEEE Design and Diagnostics of Electronic Circuits and Systems Workshop (DDECS)*, pages 52–60.

Marinissen, E.J., et al [2002a]. On IEEE P1500's standard for embedded core test. *Journal of Electronic Testing: Theory and Applications*, 18(4/5):365–383.

Marinissen, E.J., V. Iyengar, and K. Chakrabarty [2002b]. A set of benchmarks for modular testing of SOCs. In *Proceedings IEEE International Test Conference (ITC)*, pages 519–528.

Marinissen, E.J., V. Iyengar, and K. Chakrabarty [2002c]. *ITC'02 SOC Test Benchmarks*. http://www.extra.research.philips.com/itc02socbenchm/.

IEEE P1500 Web Site. http://grouper.ieee.org/groups/1500/.

Pinedo, M. [1995]. *Scheduling - Theory, Algorithms, and Systems*. Prentice Hall, Englewood Cliffs, New Jersey.

Varma, P., and S. Bhatia [1998]. A structured test re-use methodology for core-based system chips. In *Proceedings IEEE International Test Conference (ITC)*, pages 294–302.

Zorian, Y., E.J. Marinissen, and S. Dey [1998]. Testing embedded-core based system chips. In *Proceedings IEEE International Test Conference (ITC)*, pages 130–143.

Index